FRIENDSHIP,
FLATTERY AND FRANKNESS
OF SPEECH

SUPPLEMENTS TO
NOVUM TESTAMENTUM

VOLUME LXXXII

FRIENDSHIP, FLATTERY, AND FRANKNESS OF SPEECH

Studies on Friendship in the New Testament World

EDITED BY

JOHN T. FITZGERALD

E.J. BRILL

LEIDEN · NEW YORK · KÖLN

1996

The paper in this book meets the guidelines for permanence and durability of the Committee on Production Guidelines for Book Longevity of the Council on Library Resources.

Library of Congress Cataloging-in-Publication Data

BS
2545
.F75
F75
1996

Friendship, flattery, and frankness of speech / by John T. Fitzgerald (ed.).
    p.   cm. — (Supplements to Novum Testamentum, ISSN 0187-9732 ; v. 82)
Includes bibliographical references (p.) and indexes.
ISBN 9004104542
1. Friendship—Biblical teaching.. 2. Friendship—Rome.
3. Flattery—Biblical teaching. 4. Flattery—Rome. 5. Parrhēsia
(The Greek word). 6. Bible. N.T.—Criticism, interpretation, etc.
7. Ethics, Ancient. 8. Rome—Religion. I. Fitzgerald, John T.,
1946- . II. Series.
BS2545.F75F75   1995
225.8'.1776—dc20

95-25110
CIP

Die Deutsche Bibliothek - CIP-Einheitsaufnahme

Friendship, flattery, and frankness of speech / by John T.
Fitzgerald (ed.). – Leiden ; New York ; Köln : Brill, 1996
  (Supplements to Novum testamentum ; Vol. 82)
  ISBN 90–04–10454–2
NE: Fitzgerald, John T. [Hrsg.]

ISSN 0167-9732
ISBN 90 04 10454 2

PRINTED IN THE NETHERLANDS

CONTENTS

PART THREE
ΠΑΡΡΗΣΙΑ IN THE NEW TESTAMENT

PREFACE

This volume is a collection of essays dealing with the topics of friend-ship (φιλία), flattery (κολακεία), and frankness of speech (παρρησία) in the Greco-Roman world. These three topics were often related during this period, with candor or frank criticism viewed as the trait that distinguished the true friend from the flatterer.

The book's eleven essays are divided into three parts. Part One introduces the volume and discusses the three topics in the thought of Philodemus and Plutarch. Part Two deals with Paul's use of friend-ship language in his correspondence with the Philippian church. Part Three examines the concept of παρρησία in Paul, Acts, Hebrews, and the Johannine corpus.

The contributors to the volume are members of the Society of Biblical Literature's Hellenistic Moral Philosophy and Early Chris-tianity Group, an interdisciplinary group of scholars who are diverse in their training and presuppositions but united by their interest in Christian origins. Because the volume treats the topics of friendship, flattery, and frankness in both Christian and non-Christian texts, it is intended for New Testament and patristic scholars, classical philolo-gists, specialists in ancient philosophy, social historians, and modern theologians and ethicists who are interested in the theory and prac-tice of friendship.

John T. Fitzgerald

LIST OF CONTRIBUTORS

Ken L. Berry
Translation Consultant
World Bible Translation Center
Fort Worth, Texas

Troels Engberg-Pedersen
Associate Professor of New Testament
University of Copenhagen
Copenhagen, Denmark

John T. Fitzgerald
Associate Professor of New Testament
University of Miami
Coral Gables, Florida

David E. Fredrickson
Associate Professor of New Testament
Luther Theological Seminary
St. Paul, Minnesota

Clarence E. Glad
Research Fellow
The Icelandic Research Council &
The Institute of Theology at the
   University of Iceland
Reykjavík, Iceland

William Klassen
Visiting Research Professor
École Biblique
Jerusalem, Israel

David Konstan
Professor of Classics
Brown University
Providence, Rhode Island

Abraham J. Malherbe
Buckingham Professor Emeritus of New
    Testament Criticism and Interpretation
Yale Divinity School
New Haven, Connecticut

Alan C. Mitchell, S.J.
Associate Professor of Biblical Studies
Department of Theology
Georgetown University
Washington, DC

John Reumann
Ministerium of Pennsylvania Professor
    (Retired) of New Testament and Greek
Lutheran Theological Seminary
Philadelphia, Pennsylvania

Sara C. Winter
Director of Religious Studies
Eugene Lang College
New School for Social Research
New York, New York

ABBREVIATIONS

The abbreviations used for the titles of modern books, periodicals, translations, and series follow, where possible, the guidelines of the Society of Biblical Literature as published in the *Journal of Biblical Literature* 107 (1988) 579–96. Other abbreviations are either self-evident or are derived from *L'Année philologique* (Paris: Société d'Édition Les Belles Lettres).

AB	Anchor Bible
ABD	D. N. Freedman (ed.), *Anchor Bible Dictionary*
ACW	Ancient Christian Writers
AGPh	*Archiv für Geschichte der Philosophie*
AJP	*American Journal of Philology*
ALGHJ	Arbeiten zur Literatur und Geschichte des hellenistischen Judentums
AnBib	Analecta biblica
ANRW	*Aufstieg und Niedergang der römischen Welt*
APOT	R. H. Charles (ed.), *Apocrypha and Pseudepigrapha of the Old Testament*
ARW	*Archiv für Religionswissenschaft*
AUU	Acta Universitatis Upsaliensis
BAGD	W. Bauer, W. F. Arndt, F. W. Gingrich, and F. W. Danker, *Greek-English Lexicon of the New Testament*
BDF	F. Blass, A. Debrunner, and R. W. Funk, *A Greek Grammar of the New Testament*
BETL	Bibliotheca ephemeridum theologicarum lovaniensium
BHT	Beiträge zur historischen Theologie
Bib	*Biblica*
BJRL	*Bulletin of the John Rylands University Library of Manchester*
BJS	Brown Judaic Studies
BU	Biblische Untersuchungen
BVC	*Bible et vie chrétienne*
BWANT	Beiträge zur Wissenschaft vom Alten und Neuen Testament
BZNW	Beihefte zur Zeitschrift für die neutestamentliche Wissenschaft
CAH	*Cambridge Ancient History*

CBQ	*Catholic Biblical Quarterly*
CErc	*Cronache Ercolanesi*
CP	*Classical Philology*
CQ	*Classical Quarterly*
CR	*Corpus Reformatorum*
DAC	James Hastings (ed.), *Dictionary of the Apostolic Church*
DB	James Hastings (ed.), *Dictionary of the Bible*
Ebib	Études bibliques
ERE	James Hastings (ed.), *Encyclopedia of Religion and Ethics*
EvT	*Evangelische Theologie*
EWNT	H. Balz and G. Schneider (eds.), *Exegetisches Wörterbuch zum Neuen Testament*
ExpT	*Expository Times*
FB	Forschung zur Bibel
FC	Fathers of the Church
FFNT	Foundations and Facets: New Testament
GCS	Die griechischen christlichen Schriftsteller der ersten drei Jahrhunderte
GRBS	*Greek, Roman, and Byzantine Studies*
GTA	Göttinger theologische Arbeiten
HNT	Handbuch zum Neuen Testament
HNTC	Harper's New Testament Commentaries
HTKNT	Herders theologischer Kommentar zum Neuen Testament
HTR	*Harvard Theological Review*
HUCA	*Hebrew Union College Annual*
ICC	International Critical Commentary
IDB	G. A. Buttrick (ed.), *Interpreter's Dictionary of the Bible*
IDBSup	Supplementary volume to the *IDB*
Int	*Interpretation*
JAC	Jahrbuch für Antike und Christentum
JB	Jerusalem Bible
JBL	*Journal of Biblical Literature*
JECS	*Journal of Early Christian Studies*
JHS	*Journal of Hellenic Studies*
JR	*Journal of Religion*
JRS	*Journal of Roman Studies*
JSHRZ	Jüdische Schriften aus hellenistisch-römischer Zeit
JSNT	*Journal for the Study of the New Testament*
JSNTSup	Journal for the Study of the New Testament Supplement Series

KzNT	Kommentar zum Neuen Testament
LCL	Loeb Classical Library
LEC	Library of Early Christianity
LS	C. T. Lewis and C. Short, *A New Latin Dictionary*
LS	*Louvain Studies*
LSJ	Liddell-Scott-Jones, *Greek-English Lexicon*
LTK	*Lexikon für Theologie und Kirche*
MeyerK	H. A. W. Meyer, Kritisch-exegetischer Kommentar über das Neue Testament
MH	*Museum Helveticum*
MM	J. H. Moulton and G. Milligan, *The Vocabulary of the Greek Testament*
MNTC	Moffatt New Testament Commentary
MThSt	Marburger theologische Studien
MTZ	*Münchener theologische Zeitschrift*
MüThSt	Münchener theologische Studien
NCB	New Century Bible
NEB	New English Bible
NedTTs	*Nederlands theologisch tijdschrift*
Neot	*Neotestamentica*
NIGTC	The New International Greek Testament Commentary
NIV	New International Version
NovT	*Novum Testamentum*
NovTSup	Supplements to Novum Testamentum
NPNF	Nicene and Post-Nicene Fathers
NRSV	New Revised Standard Version
NTS	*New Testament Studies*
OJRS	*Ohio Journal of Religious Studies*
OLD	P. G. W. Glare (ed.), *Oxford Latin Dictionary*
OTP	J. H. Charlesworth (ed.), *The Old Testament Pseudepigrapha*
PCPhS	*Proceedings of the Cambridge Philological Society*
PG	J. Migne, *Patrologia graeca*
PGL	G. W. H. Lampe (ed.), *A Patristic Greek Lexicon*
PL	J. Migne, *Patrologia latina*
PLG	T. Bergk (ed.), *Poetae Lyrici Graeci*
PW	Pauly-Wissowa, *Real-Encyclopädie der classischen Altertumswissenschaft*
RAC	*Reallexikon für Antike und Christentum*
RB	*Revue biblique*
RhM	*Rheinisches Museum*
RIGI	*Revista Indo-Greco-Italica di filologia lingua antichità*

RSR	*Recherches de science religieuse*
SBB	Stuttgarter biblische Beiträge
SBLDS	Society of Biblical Literature Dissertation Series
SBLRBS	Society of Biblical Literature Resources for Biblical Study
SBLSBS	Society of Biblical Literature Sources for Biblical Study
SBLSP	Society of Biblical Literature Seminar Papers
SBLTT	Society of Biblical Literature Texts and Translations
SBT	Studies in Biblical Theology
SCHNT	Studia ad Corpus Hellenisticum Novi Testamenti
SNTSMS	Society for New Testament Studies Monograph Series
SP	*Studia Pastrica*
SR	*Studies in Religion / Sciences religieuses*
ST	*Studia theologica*
Str-B	H. Strack and P. Billerbeck, *Kommentar zum Neuen Testament*
TANZ	Texte und Arbeiten zum neutestamentlichen Zeitalter
TAPA	*Transactions of the American Philological Association*
TDNT	G. Kittel and G. Friedrich (eds.), *Theological Dictionary of the New Testament*
THKNT	Theologischer Handkommentar zum Neuen Testament
TLNT	C. Spicq, *Theological Lexicon of the New Testament*
TRE	*Theologische Realenzyklopädie*
TToday	*Theology Today*
TU	Texte und Untersuchungen
TWNT	G. Kittel and G. Friedrich (eds.), *Theologisches Wörterbuch zum Neuen Testament*
TynBul	*Tyndale Bulletin*
TZ	*Theologische Zeitschrift*
UTB	Uni-Taschenbücher
WBC	Word Biblical Commentary
WUNT	Wissenschaftliche Untersuchungen zum Neuen Testament
YCS	*Yale Classical Studies*
ZKG	*Zeitschrift für Kirchengeschichte*
ZNW	*Zeitschrift für die neutestamentliche Wissenschaft*
ZST	*Zeitschrift für systematische Theologie*
ZPE	*Zeitschrift für Papyrologie und Epigraphik*
ZTK	*Zeitschrift für Theologie und Kirche*

INTRODUCTION

The essays contained in this volume reflect the work of the Hellenistic Moral Philosophy and Early Christianity Group, a program unit of the Society of Biblical Literature. The group, which is composed primarily of New Testament scholars and classical philologists, has been active since the beginning of the decade. The first official session was held at the 1990 SBL Annual Meeting in New Orleans, where Professor Abraham J. Malherbe delivered an address on "Hellenistic Moral Philosophy and the New Testament."[1] In that address Professor Malherbe not only provided a retrospective analysis of approximately 100 years of research but also suggested various subjects that merit more detailed investigation as we approach a new century of biblical scholarship.[2] Foremost among the subjects that he mentioned was friendship, a topic that recently has been of great interest to modern scholars.

Adopting Professor Malherbe's proposal, the group devoted both sessions at the 1991 SBL Annual Meeting in Kansas City to the topic of friendship in the Greco-Roman world. Five papers were presented on friendship in the philosophical tradition (Aristotle, Cicero, Plutarch, the Neopythagoreans, Philo of Alexandria), and another five were devoted to friendship language in a variety of Greek authors and documents (Dionysius of Halicarnassus, Chariton, Lucian, the documentary papyri, and the New Testament). Revised versions of these papers are scheduled for publication in the SBL's Resources for Biblical Study Series.[3]

---

[1] Portions of this address were incorporated into Professor Malherbe's "Hellenistic Moralists and the New Testament," *ANRW* 2.26.1 (1992) 267–333.

[2] The SBL Program Committee highlighted Professor Malherbe's address by making it part of the Society's series on "Biblical Scholarship in the 21st Century."

[3] John T. Fitzgerald (ed.), *Greco-Roman Perspectives on Friendship* (SBLRBS; Atlanta: Scholars Press, forthcoming). Essays in this companion volume include the following: John T. Fitzgerald, "Friendship in the Greek World Prior to Aristotle"; Frederic M. Schroeder, "Friendship in Aristotle and Some Peripatetic Philosophers"; Benjamin Fiore, "The Theory and Practice of Friendship in Cicero"; Edward N. O'Neil, "Plutarch on Friendship"; Johan C. Thom, "'Harmonious Equality': The *Topos* of Friendship in Neopythagorean Writings"; Gregory E. Sterling, "The Bond of Humanity: Friendship in Philo of Alexandria"; David L. Balch, "Political Friendship in the Historian Dionysius of Halicarnassus, *Roman Antiquities*"; Ronald F. Hock, "An Extraordinary Friend in Chariton's *Callirhoe*: The Importance of Friendship in the

Following the 1991 meeting, the group decided to proceed simultaneously in two different directions. First, we wanted to explore further the nexus of friendship, flattery, and frankness of speech that emerged during the Greco-Roman period. Second, we wanted to examine the use of friendship language in an early Christian text. In order to do so, we devoted one session at the 1992 Annual Meeting in San Francisco to the relationship of friendship, frankness, and flattery in the hellenistic moralists, and we focused our attention at the other session on Paul's use of friendship language in his correspondence with the church at Philippi.

With one exception, the essays contained in Parts One and Two of this volume are revised versions of papers presented at the 1992 meeting.[4] The first of the three essays in Part One is intended as an introduction to the volume as a whole. In that essay (Chapter One) David Konstan discusses the emergence of the friendship-frankness-flattery triad in hellenistic discourse and traces its subsequent history up to Themistius in the fourth century CE. Chapters Two (by Clarence E. Glad) and Three (by Troels Engberg-Pedersen) contain examinations of this conceptual complex in two hellenistic philosophers, Philodemus of Gadara in Syria and Plutarch of Chaeronea in central Greece. The former was an Epicurean philosopher who was active in Italy during the first century BCE (ca. 110/100–ca. 40/35 BCE). A student of Zeno of Sidon, he not only was concerned with friendship but also wrote works on both flattery (κολακεία) and frankness of speech (παρρησία).[5] The latter was a Middle Platonist who addressed one of his works to Prince Philopappus on the subject of "How To Tell a Flatterer from a Friend" (*Quomodo adulator ab amico internoscatur*). Significantly, Plutarch identified frank speech as one of the distinctive traits of the genuine friend.

Greek Romances"; Richard I. Pervo, "With Lucian: Who Needs Friends? Friendship in the *Toxaris*"; Katherine G. Evans, "Friendship in Greek Documentary Papyri and Inscriptions: A Survey"; Alan C. Mitchell, "'Greet the Friends by Name': New Testament Evidence for the Greco-Roman *Topos* on Friendship."

[4] Professor Malherbe's paper was not presented in Washington but at the 1992 International SBL Meeting in Melbourne, Australia.

[5] A draft translation of Philodemus' work on frankness (Περὶ παρρησίας, *De libertate dicendi*, ed. A. Olivieri [Leipzig: Teubner, 1914]) was presented by two dozen members of the Hellenistic Moral Philosophy and Early Christianity Group at the 1993 SBL Annual Meeting in Washington. Five members of the group—Diskin Clay, Clarence E. Glad, David Konstan, Johan C. Thom, and James Ware—are currently revising this translation for publication. Once completed, it will be published in the SBL's Texts and Translations (Greco-Roman) Series.

The four essays in Part Two (Chapters Four–Seven) deal in various ways with Paul's use in Philippians of language that was traditionally associated with friendship. The presence of such language has led various scholars, including the editor of this volume, to characterize Philippians as a "letter of friendship." That characterization of Philippians is relatively recent in the history of scholarship and constitutes one of the current debates about the letter. John Reumann provides in Chapter Four a history of this designation of Philippians and an assessment of its adequacy and accuracy. The other three contributors to this part of the book draw on the discussion of friendship in the ancient world in order to interpret Philippians. In Chapter Five, Ken L. Berry identifies the vocabulary of friendship in Phil 4:10–20 and offers suggestions about its function. One of the terms that Paul uses in that section of the letter is the adjectival form of αὐτάρκεια, which is the standard Greek term for self-sufficiency. In Chapter Six, Abraham J. Malherbe argues that Paul's claim to self-sufficiency in Phil 4:11 is to be interpreted in light of his use of friendship language in the letter. Instances of friendship terminology elsewhere in Philippians, especially in 4:1–9, are noted in Chapter Seven, which contains the editor's argument that Paul is seeking to correct the Philippians' understanding of friendship and place it on a higher ethical plane. In doing so, the apostle occasionally makes use of παρρησία (frankness of speech), which is the general topic of the essays in Part Three.

Three of the four essays in this final section of the book are revisions of papers presented at the 1993 SBL Annual Meeting in Washington, DC.[6] In taking up the topic of παρρησία, we saw ourselves in part as extending our study of friendship by exploring a topic that was intimately connected with it in the Greco-Roman world. That connection also appears in the NT. 1 Thessalonians, for example, is a friendly paraenetic letter in which Paul reminds the recipients that he did not flatter them when he was in Thessalonica (1 Thess 2:5) but rather addressed them with παρρησία (1 Thess 2:2). Yet the authors of the NT also use the term παρρησία in contexts where friendship and flattery do not appear. Thus our examination of παρρησία also led us partially in a new direction of research, with attention focused on the various ways in which early Christian authors utilized one of ancient Greece's most evocative words.

---

[6] The exception is the contribution by Alan C. Mitchell, S.J., who prepared his essay at the request of the editor.

In Chapter Eight, David E. Fredrickson argues that Paul uses the term παρρησία to describe the boldness of his speech, not the confidence which served as the psychological basis of that verbal boldness. In so arguing, he challenges a long-standing tradition of interpreting Paul's references to his παρρησία. In Chapter Nine, Sara C. Winter argues that Acts uses παρρησία in a variety of ways—both classical and hellenistic—and that the term plays a key role in the author's depiction of the Jews. Alan C. Mitchell, S.J., focuses on παρρησία in Hebrews, reviewing the history of its interpretation by modern scholars and arguing that the author's use of the term is psychagogic and intended to help persuade recently converted Jewish Christians not to return to the synagogue (Chapter Ten). Finally, in Chapter Eleven William Klassen examines the use of the term παρρησία in Cynic and Stoic materials, the Septuagint and the Pseudepigrapha, and the Johannine corpus of writings. He concludes his treatment by comparing Johannine usage to that of the Cynics and by relating his findings to recent depictions of Jesus as a Jewish Cynic.

Unless otherwise indicated, contributors have provided their own translations of ancient Greek and Latin authors or used those of the Loeb Classical Library (LCL).

The contributors to this volume are grateful to the editors of Supplements to Novum Testamentum for accepting this collection of essays in E. J. Brill's distinguished series. As editor, I wish to thank my fellow contributors for their participation in the work of the Hellenistic Moral Philosophy and Early Christianity Group. I also express my gratitude to the editors at E. J. Brill for their patience and assistance in guiding this volume through the process of publication. Finally, for help in compiling the indexes, I extend thanks to Lisa C. Nasser, Edward Perez, Ilona Walters, and especially W. T. Dickens, whose assistance was as valuable as it was timely.

John T. Fitzgerald

PART ONE

FRIENDS, FLATTERERS, AND FRANK SPEECH IN THE GRECO-ROMAN WORLD

FRIENDSHIP, FRANKNESS AND FLATTERY

David Konstan

Plutarch and Maximus of Tyre (according to the title inscribed in the margin to *Oration* 14) devoted essays to the question of how one may distinguish a true friend from a flatterer (cf. also Cicero, *Amic.* 88–100). In the latter portion of his treatise, Plutarch discusses in detail the topic of frank speech or παρρησία; the reason is that frankness is the primary indicator of the openness and honesty characteristic of the friend as opposed to the dissimulation that marks the toady. Thus, the three concepts—friendship, flattery, and frankness—are closely connected: candor is the sign of the genuine friend, while the pretender gives himself away by a self-interested adulation that is exploitative rather than altruistic.

While the association between the three terms may appear to be natural, it is in fact the product of a specific cultural moment. Friends were not at all periods of Greek history implicitly contrasted with flatterers or parasites, nor was forthrightness inevitably and in all contexts treated as the hallmark of the true comrade. In this introductory chapter, I attempt briefly to indicate how the conceptual complex consisting of friendship, flattery, and frankness emerged in Hellenistic discourse, and to trace very generally the subsequent history of the several terms it embraces.

It is not clear that there is a specific vocabulary of friendship in the earliest Greek texts, that is, the *Iliad* and *Odyssey* of Homer. The term φίλος, which in the classical period of the fifth and fourth centuries comes to signify more or less what "friend" does in English, still functions in epic language chiefly as an adjective meaning "dear" or "loving," and thus has a quite general application, including family, countrymen, country itself, and even precious parts of the body, such as the heart or knees when they are felt to be vulnerable in the hazards of war.[1] The word ἑταῖρος refers to comrades in arms or shipmates, and does not necessarily single out those bound

---

[1] See David Robinson, "Homeric φίλος: Love of Life and Limbs, and Friendship with One's θυμός," *Owls to Athens: Essays on Classical Scholarship Presented to Sir Kenneth Dover* (ed. E. M. Craik; Oxford: Clarendon, 1990) 97–108.

by amicable feelings.[2] The combination φίλος ἑταῖρος or "dear comrade" comes closest to identifying a beloved person who is unconnected by kinship and is more or less of one's own age and status; this phrase, among others, is used, for example, of Patroclus' relationship to Achilles. As a social category, however, friendship seems only loosely defined: φίλος picks out members of various classes, whether kin or squire (θεράπων) or fellow warrior, who are objects of a special affection.

In the classical period, the noun φίλος, which may be marked by the presence of the definite article (not a feature of Homeric syntax), is generally restricted to intimate associates who are not closely related by blood or marriage, although there remain a few instances, confined to high poetry such as tragedy, of the broader Homeric usage in the sense of "dear ones." There was reason for the specification of friends as a distinct group, one may suppose, in the development of the city-state and its institutions. On the one hand, a sharp sense of citizen identity, expressed by terms such as πολίτης, marked off fellow-citizens both from foreigners and from those belonging to a more intimate circle of acquaintances. On the other hand, the codification at law of the status of the individual family or household (οἶκος) as the fundamental unit of proprietorship in the city rendered necessary a clear differentiation between immediate kin, who stood as heirs, and those outside the family, however close the personal bond might be. Terms related to φίλος might still refer to a wide variety of affectionate bonds: thus, as an adjective φίλος continues to mean "dear," and the verb φιλεῖν ("to love") as well as the abstract noun φιλία (misleadingly translated as "friendship") cover relationships between parents and children, comrades in arms, and other formal connections. But for friends in the modern sense, Greek now had available a particular and generally unambiguous expression.[3]

But the idea of friendship in the classical period of the democratic city-state, and in particular at Athens, from which the bulk of the evidence derives, was further determined by the ideology of equality and freedom from dependency that was central to the Athenian civic ideal. Friends were to be relied upon for assistance in times of crisis, but the assumption was that friends were more or less of equal sta-

---

[2] Christoph Ulf, *Die homerische Gesellschaft: Materialen zur analytischen Beschreibung und historischen Lokalisierung* (Munich: C.H. Beck, 1990) 127–38.

[3] I discuss this development in detail in "Greek Friendship," forthcoming in *AJP*.

tion, and that the obligations that friendship might impose were in principle mutual and symmetrical. Frankness or liberty of speech was thus taken for granted as a principle obtaining among friends, as indeed it obtained among fellow-citizens in general, all of whom were equally entitled to express themselves openly and without fear of neighbors or of those in power. This right of free speech was what the Athenians of the classical period meant when they employed the term παρρησία.

Arnaldo Momigliano, in a survey of freedom of speech in the ancient world, writes of the Assembly in Athens: "In the second part of the fifth century and during the greater part of the fourth century every Athenian citizen had the right to speak unless he disqualified himself by certain specified crimes. . . . We need hardly add that this extraordinary amount of freedom of speech in the assemblies was accompanied by an exceptional amount of freedom of speech in the theater and generally speaking in ordinary life." Momigliano continues: "we shall not be surprised if the notion of freedom of speech turns out to be an Athenian fifth-century idea."[4] The term of art that was appropriated to express this right at Athens was, as Momigliano observes, παρρησία: "*Parrhesia* represented democracy from the point of view of equality of rights" (259). It has, we may add, no particular association with the idea of friendship.

After the defeat of the Athenian democracy by Philip of Macedon and the consequent dependency of Athens upon foreign powers, there was a shift in the political discourse of free speech. As Momigliano puts it, "Menander replaced Aristophanes, and *parrhesia* as a private virtue replaced *parrhesia* as a political right" (260). As a private virtue, παρρησία denoted that personal candor which was prized between true friends as opposed to the liberty to declare openly one's opinions in the civic space or assembly. But the discourse of friendship too, in this period, underwent a change. The emphasis on equality that was characteristic of the popular democracy gave way, in treatises of the period, to a concern with relations between people of unequal station and power. Instead of attending to the bond between independent and, at least in principle, autarkic individuals who might on occasion find themselves in reduced circumstances and thus

---

[4] Arnaldo Momigliano, "Freedom of Speech in Antiquity," *Dictionary of the History of Ideas: Studies of Selected Pivotal Ideas* (ed. P. P. Wiener; 5 vols.; New York: Charles Scribner's Sons, 1973–74) 2.258.

in need of help from reliable associates, writers in the Hellenistic epoch tended to focus rather on monarchs or wealthy men and their retinues, who were conceived of as bound to their patron by amicable ties. Thus, just as the egalitarian assumptions behind the universal right to self-expression gave way to an ideology centered on rank and authority, it became necessary to recommend and insist on παρρησία as a duty rather than to prize it as a universal mark of citizen status.

Where there are inequalities in status and wealth between friends, there is room for exploitation. In the classical discourse of the democratic city-state, the perversion of friendship was in general manifested, as I have said, as a failure to come to the assistance of another in times of crisis: the central problem is that of the fair-weather friend. Friends were imagined as constituting a network of mutual assistance, not so much because subsistence agriculture required such a practice—after all, in this respect not all that much changed in the Hellenistic age—but rather as a reflex of the democratic ideology, according to which all citizens were presumed to be more or less equal and economically autonomous.[5]

In the altered ideological environment of the Hellenistic period, in which friendship between the powerful and their dependents was the focus of attention, the chief worry concerning the perversion of friendship was the possibility that a person motivated by narrow self-interest would insinuate himself into the coterie of a superior and, by a pretense of friendship, achieve his own gain at the expense of his master. Simultaneously, it was imagined that the flatterer would seek to corrupt the honorable character and social conscience of his benefactor, in order to profit from expenditure on private entertainments as opposed to public service. Thus, the character of the flatterer was doubly determined as selfish for gain and inclined to the baser pleasures. The philosophers of friendship were, accordingly, concerned to discriminate the type of the flatterer or adulator from that of the true friend, and the surest sign of the difference was candor and honesty—the παρρησία characteristic of the true friend as opposed to the deceitfulness that marked the parasite.

In the classical period, the figure of the flatterer was not a key subject of ideological attention, no doubt because to represent a citi-

---

[5] See my paper, "Reciprocity and Friendship," *Reciprocity in Ancient Greece* (ed. C. Gill, N. Postlethwaite and R. Seaford; Oxford: Oxford University Press, forthcoming).

zen in an adulatory posture was compromising to the ideal of civic freedom and autonomy. As Paul Millett writes: "It seems a plausible hypothesis that the democratic ideology, with its emphasis on political equality, was hostile to the idea of personal patronage, which depended on the exploitation of inequalities in wealth and status."[6] Aristotle, to be sure, mentions the vice of flattery: "Of those who try to give pleasure, he who does this with no ulterior motive aims at being pleasant and is anxious to please; but he who does so in order that some advantage may fall to him in respect of money, or anything else that money procures, is a *kolax* [flatterer]."[7] Theophrastus, in turn, devotes the second of his series of character sketches to the type of the flatterer. But the flatterer is plainly a debased type, and neither Theophrastus nor Aristotle sees in this figure a threat to genuine friendship among free and equal citizens. One place in which Aristotle does associate the terms κόλαξ and φίλος indicates the distance between the two ideas: a man who has greatness of soul "must be unable to make his life revolve around another, unless it be a friend (φίλος); for that is slavish, and for this reason all flatterers are hirelings and those lacking in self-respect are flatterers."[8] In his central treatment of φιλία in Books 8 and 9 of the *Nicomachean Ethics*, Aristotle all but wholly ignores the issue of flattery.[9] The only arena in which the flatterer is perceived as posing a threat is politics, where those who fawn upon the populace or δῆμος may be criticized for misleading the people for their own private benefit (Aristophanes' *Knights* is a memorable caricature of the demagogue as toady). But the sovereign δῆμος was the unique entity toward which a citizen was expected, under the democracy, to show deference; in regard to a fellow citizen, such inequality signified a loss of freedom.

The figure of the κόλαξ or flatterer came into its own in the Hellenistic period. Middle and New Comedy exploited the stereotyped image of the parasite (παράσιτος) who seeks admission to the tables of the rich, though in general there is no confusion in the plays between such servile types and true friends and equals.[10] Phormio in

---

[6] Paul Millett, "Patronage and its Avoidance in Classical Athens," *Patronage in Ancient Society* (ed. A. Wallace-Hadrill; London: Routledge, 1989) 17.

[7] *Eth. Nic.* 4.6.1127a7, quoted after Millett, "Patronage," 32.

[8] *Eth. Nic.* 4.3.1124b30–1125a2, quoted after Millett, "Patronage," 32; cf. also 2.7.1108a26–30.

[9] Note however 8.8.1159a14–15: "the flatterer is a friend who is inferior."

[10] See, however, Diphilus, frg. 23.1–2 Kassel-Austin: "For the flatterer overturns a general and prince and friends and cities with his evil speech, giving pleasure for

Terence's play of that name (based on a Menandrean original) comes closest to blurring the lines, but this is by virtue of his honest commitment to the young protagonist: genuine friends never sink to the practice of fawning.[11] But the stage was set for flattery, now seen as a corrupt form of participation in the entourage of grandees, to emerge as the antithesis of the personal integrity and sincerity expected of loyal associates. This was to become especially relevant in the political sphere, where kings in Syria, Egypt and elsewhere recruited privy councils that were known formally as The Friends.[12] Here, the personal allegiance and principled behavior of subordinates were crucial to governance. In turn, intimate associates in the houses of wealthy patrons aspired to the status of friends rather than mere dependents.[13] In this context, παρρησία or candor came to be seen as a touchstone for discriminating the true friend from the self-serving toady.

Παρρησία also entered into the vocabulary of the Hellenistic philosophical schools. Here the concern was with frank criticism in relation to instruction. Disciples require honest and constructive correction: the problem is to administer just criticism in a temperate way, avoiding both the excessive harshness that may discourage the moral improvement of the disciple and a lenient indulgence of the aspirant's lax ways. The Cynics went in for stinging reproaches. Consider, for example, the picturesque expression attributed to the Cynic Diogenes by the compiler John Stobaeus, in the section devoted to frankness (*Peri parrhēsias*, 3.13.44): "Diogenes said: Other dogs bite their enemies, I [bite] my friends—so that I may save them."

The issue was addressed in subtler terms both by Stoics and Epicureans. There survives an especially valuable witness to the Epicurean approach, the treatise by Philodemus entitled *Peri parrhēsias* or *On Frank Criticism*, which was preserved among the charred papyri in the house of the Piso family in Herculaneum. Philodemus makes

---

a short time"; cf. Heinz-Günther Nesselrath, *Lukians Parasitendialog: Untersuchungen und Kommentar* (Berlin: Walter de Gruyter, 1985) 99–111; P. G. Mc. C. Brown, "Menander, Fragments 745 and 746 K-T, Menander's *Kolax*, and Parasites and Flatterers in Greek Comedy," *ZPE* 92 (1992) 98–103. Pollux, *Onom.* 6.123, says that in the playwrights of New Comedy the flatterer was called a parasite.

[11] Cf. Friedrich Zucker, *Freundschaftsbewährung in der neuen attischen Komödie: Ein Kapitel hellenistischer Ethik und Humanität* (Berlin: Akademie-Verlag, 1950) 33–34.

[12] See F. W. Walbank, "Monarchies and Monarchic Ideas," *CAH* 7.1 (1984) 62–100.

[13] The practice is satirized in Lucian's essay *On Those who Associate for a Fee* (*De Mercede conductis*); cf. Hor. *Epist.* 1.18, Juv. *Sat.* 5, and my "Patrons and Friends," forthcoming in *CP*.

it clear, as I understand the text, that only the sage will have the proper awareness to criticize others in a balanced way, attuned to their natures and therefore neither too harsh nor too indulgent (see columns IV–VII). It is worth noting that Philodemus' treatment of frankness differs from that of Plutarch and Maximus of Tyre in their treatises on flattery and friendship insofar as Philodemus is concerned primarily with the candor that the superior party—the teacher—exhibits in relation to a student under his authority. While philosophers, like other writers, might laud a courageous forthrightness in the presence of power,[14] in their teaching they promoted a nurturing or therapeutic use of παρρησία. Philodemus also recognizes, however, that differences in social status complicate the task of the teacher: a humble Greek instructing a powerful Roman aristocrat may pose ticklish problems in a hierarchical society. Whereas Lucian wrote an entire essay (*On Those who Associate for a Fee*) on the humiliation suffered by Greek professors in the homes of Roman noblemen, Philodemus contents himself with offering some practical advice on how to treat students of high station (columns IVb, Xa, and especially XIVa).

Frankness was not just a pedagogical strategy on the part of the teacher, however. Openness and the revelation of personal faults were also required on the part of the disciple as a condition of moral development. Philodemus indicates that the teacher himself may stand in need of criticism on occasion (column VIII). Thus frankness ranges from the practice of balanced criticism undertaken by the sage to the disclosure of private sentiments for the purpose of correction. Contrariwise, flattery was represented as the vice opposed to the virtue of friendship, as in Philodemus' essay *On Flattery*.[15]

Seneca, in his *Moral Epistles* addressed to Lucilius (3.2–3), puts particular emphasis on the importance of frank expression among friends. With regard to a friend, he counsels:

> tam audaciter cum illo loquere quam tecum . . . cum amico omnes curas, omnes cogitationes tuas misce. . . . Quid est, quare ego ulla verba coram amico meo retraham? Quid est, quare me coram illo non putem solum?

---

[14] Cf. Momigliano, "Freedom of Speech," 261; Shadi Bartsch, *Actors in the Audience* (Cambridge, MA: Harvard University Press, 1995) 148–87.

[15] Discussion in Francesca Longo Auricchio, "Sulla concezione filodemea dell'-adulazione," *CErc* 16 (1986) 79–91.

> Speak as boldly with him as with yourself... share with your friend
> all your worries, all your thoughts.... Why should I hold back any
> words in the presence of my friend?

Seneca's letters to Lucilius are designed to educate an aspirant in
Stoic philosophy. Stoics and Epicureans had adopted the idea of
friendship as a figure for the relationship among members of the
school, and the frankness that was encouraged between their followers was thus associated here too with the language of friendship.

A further development of the practices of the philosophical schools
is perhaps to be detected in the attitudes concerning self-revelation
encouraged by Saint Ambrose in the final chapters of his treatise
addressed to novice priests, the *De officiis ministrorum*. This work is based,
as the title indicates, on the *De officiis* of Cicero and draws also, in
the last section, upon Cicero's essay *De amicitia*. Ambrose repeatedly
insists on the need to disclose all to one's friends, e.g. (3.22.135):

> Dedit [sc. Deus] formam amicitiae quam sequamur, ut faciamus amici
> voluntatem, ut aperiamus secreta nostra amico quaecumque in pectore
> habemus, et illius arcana non ignoremus. Ostendamus illi nos pectus
> nostrum, et ille nobis aperiat suum. *Ideo*, inquit, *vos dixi amicos quia omnia
> quaecumque audivi a Patre meo, nota feci vobis* [John 15:14]. Nihil ergo occultat
> amicus, si verus est: effundit animum suum, sicut effundebat mysteria
> Patris Dominus Jesus.

> [God] gave the form of friendship we follow, that we may perform the
> wishes of a friend, that we may open our secrets, whichever we have
> in our bosom, to a friend, and that we may not be ignorant of his
> hidden things. Let us reveal our bosom to him, and let him reveal his
> to us. *Therefore*, he said, *I have called you friends, because all that I have heard
> from my Father, I have made known to you*. Therefore a friend hides noth-
> ing, if he is true: he pours forth his mind, just as Lord Jesus poured
> forth the mysteries of his Father.

The conditions of monastic or collective life that obtained among monks
and priests put a premium on practices designed to minimize dissension and personal squabbling. An emphasis on general candor was
especially useful in advancing solidarity and collaboration in moral
development. In both respects, perhaps, Ambrose's advice and concerns are analogous to those of the Stoics and Epicureans, to the
extent the latter can be recovered.[16]

---

[16] For discussion, see my paper, "Problems in the History of Christian Friendship," forthcoming in *JECS*.

We may note that such a requirement of frankness is quite a different matter from the idea that one may confide in close friends during times of crisis. Cicero, in his treatise on friendship, observes that openness is possible only among true friends, in whom one can trust and to whom one may safely reveal even dangerous opinions concerning public affairs (*Amic.* 22). In tense political times such as the political upheavals and civil wars of the late Roman republic, reliability among friends was particularly desirable. One may communicate only to the most loyal friends opinions that might incur the wrath of those in power. But the idea that one *may* reveal secrets to friends is quite a separate proposition from the idea that one *should* or even *must* reveal such secrets as a condition of friendship.

One particular modulation of the ideal of frankness or παρρησία is the Christian ideal of perfect openness before God. Indeed, while παρρησία is rendered into Latin during the republic and early empire as *libertas* or *licentia*, in Latin versions of the Bible it is commonly translated as *fiducia*, *fidentia*, or *constantia*.[17] Even in this context, the idea of candor is not entirely detached from that of the proper relations among friends. For the possibility of friendship with God was plainly indicated both in the Septuagint version of the Old Testament and in Jesus' words in the New Testament. In the Septuagint, Moses is unambiguously identified as a "friend of God."[18] From such texts, as well as from Luke 12:4 and especially John 15:14 (ὑμεῖς φίλοι μού ἐστε, ἐὰν ποιῆτε ἃ ἐγὼ ἐντέλλομαι ὑμῖν; "you are my friends if you do what I bid you"), the theme of friendship with God entered into Jewish (Philo) and Christian exegesis.[19]

The classical Greek writers in general treated the attraction between friends as a function of virtue, at least insofar as the highest form of friendship was concerned; Aristotle admitted that pleasure and utility too might be the basis of a friendly relationship, but denied that such bonds could be as enduring or profound as those based on the character of the friend. Cicero and other authors, both Greek and Roman, tended in the main to follow Aristotle's view on

---

[17] See Giuseppe Scarpat, *Parrhesia: Storia del termine e delle sue traduzioni in latino* (Brescia: Paideia, 1964) 109, 117–43.

[18] Exod 33:11 LXX. For Abraham as the friend of God, see Jas 2:23 and the Vulgate's rendering of 2 Chr 20:7 and Isa 41:8. See also Wis 7:27, and, for discussion, Erik Peterson, "Der Gottesfreund: Beiträge zur Geschichte eines religiösen Terminus," *ZKG* 42 (1923) 172–73, 177.

[19] Amply documented by Peterson, "Gottesfreund," 172ff.

this point. It has sometimes been supposed that the Romans placed a greater emphasis on the practical aspects of *amicitia*, reducing the relationship to one of *quid pro quo* reciprocity and all but evacuating it of sentimental or emotional content. While it is true that the Romans, like the Greeks, recognized that favors entailed debts or obligations and paid scrupulous attention to the duties and forms attaching to the exchange of informal courtesies, such regulated interactions did not pertain essentially to the domain of friendship as such. The seven books of Seneca's *De beneficiis*, which meticulously define the protocols of benefactions and gratitude, have virtually nothing to say about *amicitia*. Cicero and Sallust are conscious of the forms of reciprocity, but again, they do not situate their comments in the context of friendship; thus, for example, Cicero, in his letters of recommendation, speaks of the clients who petition favors from him as acquaintances or familiars, but seems careful to reserve the term *amicus* for people bound to him by true amity. Such affection was understood to be altruistic and looked to the good of the friend rather than to one's own advantage. It was earned by the virtuous disposition of the other.

The connection between virtue and friendship seems to have been problematic to certain Christian writers. The reason is not so much, in my view, the injunction to universal love, which might come into conflict with the partial or particular affection represented by friendship. Both the Old Testament and the New indicated the possibility, as we have seen, of friendship with God or with Jesus; the Bible thus provided warrant for individual attachments, and the Christian writers appealed to its authority in this regard. Rather, classical friendship, and the ideals of equality and mutual virtue that it suggested, may have appeared incompatible with Christian humility and the sense of sin. Thus, writers such as Saint Basil in Greek and Paulinus of Nola in Latin forsook the vocabulary of friendship—*amicitia* or φιλία—and substituted for it terms such as ἀγάπη or its Latin equivalent, *caritas*, that were associated with grace and overabundant love.[20]

In his 22nd oration entitled "On Friendship" (*Peri philias*), the fourth-century A.D. rhetorician Themistius observes: "For a friend [φίλος] is nowhere near a flatterer [κόλαξ], and is furthest removed in this, that the one praises everything, while the other would not go along

---

[20] For full discussion, see my forthcoming paper cited in note 16 above.

with you when you are erring; for the former is set on making a profit or stuffing his belly by his efforts, and is not impressed with you, but with your money or your power [δυναστεία]" (276c). Here Themistius reproduces the conventional Hellenistic contrast between friendship and adulation. But Themistius also remarks that the pursuit of friendship is endangered above all by "that which is called hypocrisy [ὑπόκρισις] by people in our time" (267b). Themistius ends his discourse with a version of the tale of Heracles' choice, related first by Prodicus in Xenophon's *Memorabilia* (2.1.21–34). In Xenophon's version, the two allegorical female figures between whom Heracles is invited to choose are identified as Virtue ('Αρετή) and Vice (Κακία), who describes herself as Happiness (Εὐδαιμονία, 26). Maximus of Tyre opens his oration on friendship with a brief adaptation of Prodicus' fable, in which the two routes are labeled Virtue and Pleasure ('Ηδονή, 14.1). Themistius retains Xenophon's personae, but gives each a companion: Friendship (Φιλία) for Virtue, Hypocrisy ('Υπόκρισις) for Vice (280b). In contrasting friendship with hypocrisy, Themistius is varying the traditional opposition between the friend and the flatterer; indeed, Themistius locates Flattery (Κολακεία) on approach to Hypocrisy's mountain, in the role of forerunner.

Flattery is a form of self-interested deception. Hypocrisy in Themistius is evidently a deeper kind of pretense, a kind of inauthenticity that displays itself as friendship but does not have friendship's unfeignedness. "Hypocrisy had a painted face, not a genuine beauty; instead of a peaceful smile she had a deceitful grin. In order to appear desirable, she pretended to feel desire for those who came to her. Since no one would come any distance to her on his own, she would run out and submit herself to people, go meet them herself and take them back with her" (282a).[21] This Hypocrisy seems a forlorn and desperate sort rather than a calculating cheat, such as flattery is conceived to be. No motive is offered for her self-prostitution; she is simply a fake version of friendship.

I suggest that in Themistius' discourse the opposite to friendship is not so much betrayal or the exploitation of an intimate relationship, as the earlier tradition had represented it, but rather a failure of sincerity that presents a false image to the admirer. Hypocrisy in this sense is almost devoid of practical content: it is revealed not in action

---

[21] I am grateful to Robert Penella for allowing me to see the manuscript of his translation of this oration; my version is adapted from his.

or motive so much as in a fundamental bad faith with oneself.

There are some signs in Themistius' discourse that the classical priority of virtue as the basis of friendship has begun to give way, albeit partially, to a conception of friendship founded on personal attraction. Themistius follows Xenophon's lead (*Mem.* 2.6) in identifying the qualities of a potential friend as a sense of gratitude, ability to endure physical hardships, generosity, an absence of spite and arrogance (268c–69b), but he then introduces a new point that is perhaps of his own invention: given that it is difficult to achieve moral perfection, one ought at least to seek as a friend someone whose vices are the opposite of one's own (270c–71b); similarly, Themistius later advises that one may avoid invidious competition by selecting friends whose occupations are different from one's own (275d). After first recommending that one make oneself as virtuous as possible in order to attract the other (271d; cf. Xen. *Mem.* 2.6.14, 35), Themistius goes on to suggest a method that begins to resemble Ovid's *Art of Love* more than Plato's or Xenophon's prescriptions on securing worthy friends, viz., that one should cast winning glances, trace out the haunts of one's prey, offer praise, and ingratiate oneself with the other's relatives (272a–73b). In this part of the discourse, the question of the character of the friend recedes to the point of indifference. What one is tracking is simply the object of desire. The very image of hunting down a friend, inspired by Plato's *Lysis* (218C) and Xenophon (*Mem.* 2.6.8) but blown up into a conceit by Themistius, involves just the skills that are emblematic of Friendship's antitype, Hypocrisy, and her entourage of Deception ('Ἀπάτη), Plotting ('Ἐπιβουλή), and Trickery (Δόλος, 282b).

A flatterer could simulate frankness, of course; techniques and policies were devised to detect such impostors to true παρρησία. But in general the discourse of candor did not seek to address the more hidden places in the self or to create a metaphysic of sincerity and authenticity. Rather, the strategies proffered for discriminating friends from flatterers remained on the level of rhetoric and overt behavior. The κόλαξ, however subtle, was betrayed by an excessive compliance with his companion's desires, without regard to the demands of virtue or honor: his was a failure of forthrightness.

Seen as the opposite term to hypocrisy, however, παρρησία may have undergone a new inflection, from frankness to a kind of personal sincerity. Today, intimate self-revelation is closely associated with the idea of friendship: "The bond of trust between deep friends is cemented by the equal self-disclosure of intimate information."[22] Steve Duck affirms: "The main feature that stabilizes, establishes and develops relationships of all types is proper and dexterous control of *self-disclosure*; that is, the revelation of personal layers of one's self, personal thoughts, or even one's body."[23] Acquaintanceship falls short of friendship precisely because it "is not a relationship of intimacy or exchange of confidences," even though "a great amount of information may be passed between those who are acquaintances."[24]

There is a deep gulf between ancient conceptions of the self and modern notions of authenticity and inwardness.[25] However, the complex of friendship, sincerity, and hypocrisy in Themistius may at least adumbrate a distinct inflection of the triad of friendship, frankness, and flattery that bears a certain resemblance to twentieth-century conceptions of intimacy.

---

[22] Laurence Thomas, "Friendship," *Synthese* 72 (1987) 223; bibliography at 235 n. 9.
[23] Steve Duck, *Friends, for Life: The Psychology of Close Relationships* (New York: St. Martin's Press, 1983) 67.
[24] Robert R. Bell, *Worlds of Friendship* (Beverly Hills: Sage Publications, 1981) 22.
[25] Cf. Christopher Gill, "Peace of Mind and Being Yourself: Panaetius to Plutarch," *ANRW* II.36.7 (1994) 4599–4640.

FRANK SPEECH, FLATTERY, AND FRIENDSHIP IN PHILODEMUS

Clarence E. Glad

Philodemus: Life and Works

By the middle of the first century BCE a flourishing Epicurean community existed at Naples under the leadership of the Greek teacher Siro. At nearby Herculaneum the Syrian Epicurean, Philodemus of Gadara, the house-philosopher of the influential patron Calpurnius Piso, father-in-law of Julius Caesar, was attracting a wide circle of students. Epicureanism also had its contemporary exponents in Latin—Catius Insuber, Rabirius, C. Amafinius, whose prose tracts enjoyed popularity in Rome and in various Italian towns, and the poet Lucretius. The relationship among the Epicurean groups in Italy is not clear but apparently Siro's group in Naples and that of Philodemus at Herculaneum had an open exchange of views.[1] Both Philodemus and Siro were former pupils of Zeno of Sidon, the scholarch of the Epicurean school in Athens, and one would expect a certain co-ordination in their efforts in promoting Epicurean views in southern Italy. Both groups cultivated interest in literary and philosophical study, thus escaping the charge traditionally levelled at Epicureans that they maintained a deliberate disregard for general learning; Cicero, for example, refers to both Siro and Philodemus as the "excellent and learned friends" of Torquatus.[2]

Philodemus' scholarly interest is evident from the number of papyrus rolls recovered from Piso's suburban villa at Herculaneum.

---

[1] We know that the poets of Siro's group, L. Varius Rufus and Quintilius Varus, and possibly Virgil and Plotius Tucca, associated with Philodemus as well, and that the discussion between Philodemus and his fellow Epicureans at Naples extended also to philosophical matters (PHerc. 312). See A. Körte, "Augusteer bei Philodem.," *RhM* 45 (1890) 172–77, H. M. Howe, "Amafinius, Lucretius, and Cicero," *AJP* 77 (1951) 57–62; D. P. Fowler, "Lucretius and Politics," *Philosophia Togata: Essays on Philosophy and Roman Society* (ed. M. Griffin and J. Barnes; Oxford: Clarendon, 1989) 120–50; and H. Jones, *The Epicurean Tradition* (London and New York: Routledge, 1989) 65–69. Cf. Cic. *Fam.* 15.16.1; 19.2; *Acad.* 1.5; *Tusc.* 4.7.

[2] Torquatus is the Epicurean spokesman in Cicero's *On Ends* (*De finibus*). See *Fin.* 2.119.

These include both Philodemus' transcripts of the lecture notes he took at Zeno's classes in Athens—for example, his book *On Frank Criticism*, which I shall discuss below—and Philodemus' own compositions, which include his writings on historical matters, on scientific method, on rhetoric, music, and poetry, on theology, including *On Piety* and *On the Gods*, and, finally, on ethics.[3] The ethical writings include an introduction to ethics, a work in several books *On Death*, and a work in ten books *On Vices and the Opposing Virtues*, which includes one book *On Household Management*, one book *On Arrogance*, and probably three books *On Flattery*.[4] Finally, Philodemus wrote an *Epitome on Conduct and Character, from the Lectures of Zeno*, which includes a work *On Anger* and the above mentioned *On Frank Criticism*.[5]

In his fragmentary works on flattery we can gain insight into Philodemus' views on flattery, particularly as it relates to frank speech, friendship and patronage. Philodemus contrasts flattery with friendship as he defensively justifies his relationship with his patron Piso. Interestingly, not only do traditional characteristics of flattery appear in these works but also a dispute over the use of obsequiousness in friendship. This problem of obsequiousness as well as that of harshness in the frank correction of faults can also be seen in Philodemus' *On Frank Criticism*, which reveals a dispute among Epicureans over methods of correcting disciples within the Epicurean school.[6]

---

[3] See E. Asmis, "Philodemus' Epicureanism," *ANRW* 2.36.4 (1990) 2369–2406. Historical works: PHerc. 1018, *Index Stoicorum*; PHerc. 164 and 1021, *Index Academicorum*; PHerc. 155 and 339, *On the Stoics*; PHerc. 1232 and 1289, *On Epicurus*; PHerc. 1418 and 310, *Works on the Records of Epicurus and Some Others*; PHerc. 1005, *To Friends of the School*. On scientific method: PHerc. 1065, *On Phenomena and Inferences*; see P. H. De Lacy and E. A. De Lacy, *Philodemus: On Methods of Inference* (2d ed.; Naples: Bibliopolis, 1978). Works on rhetoric, music, and poetry: *On Rhetoric* and *On Poems* are preserved in numerous papyri; PHerc. 1497, *On Music*; PHerc. 1507, *On the Good King according to Homer*. Theological writings: PHerc. 1428, *On Piety*; PHerc. 26, *On the Gods*; PHerc. 152 and 157, *On the Way of Life of the Gods*.

[4] The untitled introduction to ethics (PHerc. 1251) is known as the *Comparetti Ethics* in honor of its first editor; PHerc. 1050, *On Death*; PHerc. 1424, *On Household Management*; PHerc. 1008, *On Arrogance*; PHerc. 222, 223, 1082, 1089, 1457, and 1675, *On Flattery*. See also PHerc. 346, edited by M. Capasso, *Trattato etico epicureo* (Naples: Universita degli Studi di Napoli/Giannini, 1982).

[5] PHerc. 182, *On Anger*; PHerc. 1471, *On Frank Criticism*. Philodemus' work *On Anger* was edited by C. Wilke, *Philodemi de ira liber* (Leipzig: Teubner, 1914) and has been re-edited, with a translation and commentary, by G. Indelli, *Filodemo, L'ira* (La Scuola di Epicuro 5; Naples: Bibliopolis, 1988).

[6] For a more detailed discussion of some of the issues raised in this article, see chapters three and four of my *Paul and Philodemus: Adaptability in Epicurean and Early Christian Psychagogy* (NovTSup 81; Leiden: E. J. Brill, 1995).

Flattery and Patronage in Philodemus

At the end of his work *On Household Management*, Philodemus discusses sources of income for the philosopher, concluding that the best way to make money is to share philosophical discourses with receptive men; the next is to be a gentleman farmer; and the third is to manage a reputable business.[7] These occupations are worthwhile because they allow, as Philodemus explains, the "leisurely retreat with friends" to enjoy the Epicurean way of life. This hierarchy of occupations undoubtedly reflects Philodemus' own position and that of his patron Piso. As house-philosopher or "friend" of a wealthy patron, Philodemus had the leisure not only to indulge his scholarly interests but also to participate in the instruction of recruits who attached themselves to the Epicurean group at Herculaneum. Philodemus has correctly been described as "a typical teacher of Epicureanism, spreading his school's gospel at the intersection of the Greek and Roman worlds."[8]

What is left of Philodemus' works on flattery is important because, except for the treatises of Plutarch and Maximus of Tyre, there are few extant texts on this subject subsequent to Theophrastus' depiction of the flatterer in his *Characters*.[9] Six Herculanean papyri have been attributed to Philodemus' work *On Flattery*.[10] Content and paleographical evidence confirm the existence of (at least) three books on flattery (PHerc. 222, 1457, and 1675), belonging to Philodemus' large work *On Vices and the Opposing Virtues* (Περὶ κακιῶν καὶ τῶν ἀντικειμένων ἀρετῶν).[11] *On Flattery* is influenced by Aristotle's classification of virtue

---

[7] *Oec.* col. 23.22–36; on this see Asmis, "Philodemus' Epicureanism," 2388.

[8] D. Sedley, "Philosophical Allegiance in the Greco-Roman World," *Philosophia Togata: Essays on Philosophy and Roman Society* (ed. M. Griffin and J. Barnes; Oxford: Clarendon, 1989) 103.

[9] Theophr. *Char.* 2. O. Ribbeck in his fundamental study on flattery (*Kolax: Eine ethologische Studie* [Abhandlungen der philologisch-historischen Klasse der Königlich Sächsischen Gesellschaft der Wissenschaften 9.1; Leipzig: S. Hirzel, 1884] 1–114) did not consider the Herculanean papyri, both because his interest lay in literary texts of Greek and Latin comedy, and because at the time of writing Philodemus' texts on flattery had not yet been published in critical editions. Note F. Longo Auricchio, "Sulla concezione filodemea dell'adulazione," *CErc* 16 (1986) 79, 82, and 91.

[10] The following papyri probably belonged to Philodemus' *On Flattery*: PHerc. 222, 223, 1082, 1089, 1457 and 1675.

[11] *Pace* Longo Auricchio, "Adulazione," 79–82. The subscriptio of PHerc. 222 confirms that it was the seventh book of *On Vices*. Longo Auricchio conjectures that PHerc. 1457 could be the eighth book; T. Gargiulo suggests that PHerc. 1675 was

as a medium between two vices where friendship is viewed as the mean between flattery and enmity.[12]

The first book on flattery (PHerc. 1675) examines both the flatterer's view and disposition towards the flattered ones and the relationship between Alexander and the persons next to him. Philodemus is critical of the flattered one, his servants and relatives.[13] Philodemus' second book on flattery (PHerc. 222) contrasts flattery and friendship, and offers a new Epicurean evaluation of love of fame and glory. Two other papyri, viz. PHerc. 1082 and 1089, also contrast flattery and friendship; PHerc. 1089, in addition, gives a dispositional analysis of the flatterer and the friend.[14] Finally, the third book on flattery (PHerc. 1457) concentrates on obsequiousness after a classificatory excursus on vices akin to flattery. Here Philodemus quotes in its entirety the fifth *Character* of Theophrastus and gives evidence for the tradition that combined the definitions of the obsequious person and the flatterer.[15]

The importance of the issue of flattery among Epicureans has been explained variously. Firstly, one should not forget the importance of flattery in ancient ethics; from the fifth century onwards flatterers, just like slaves, were a recognized component of society and the vice they personified assumed an elevated importance in subsequent ethical and rhetorical treatises. Secondly, given the importance of friendship in Epicureanism, its opposite vice was bound to have been worthy of consideration.[16] Thirdly, Philodemus' works on flattery probably aimed at correcting the behavior of the Epicurean wise man, who, like Horace a generation later, was charged with servility towards the rich and powerful.[17] Consequently, a discussion of this subject

the sixth book ("PHerc. 222: Filodemo sull'adulazione," *CErc* 11 [1981] 103). Besides the seventh book (*On Flattery*), only book 9 (*On Household Management*, PHerc. 1424) and book 10 (*On Arrogance*, PHerc. 1008) can be securely placed.

[12] See, for example, PHerc. 1082, col. 2.3–4, φιλία, ἧς ἀντ[ί]παλός ἐστιν ἡ κολακεία. See Gargiulo, "PHerc. 222," 104–05, and Longo Auricchio, "Adulazione," 82.

[13] V. De Falco, "Appunti sul ΠΕΡΙ ΚΟΛΑΚΕΙΑΣ di Filodemo: Pap. erc. 1675," *RIGI* 10 (1926) 15–26; Longo Auricchio, "Adulazione," 81.

[14] E. Acosta Méndez, "PHerc. 1089: Filodemo 'Sobre la adulación,'" *CErc* 13 (1983) 121–38.

[15] E. Kondo, "I 'Caratteri' di Teofrasto nei papiri ercolanesi," *CErc* 1 (1971) 73–87; idem, "Per l'interpretazione del pensiero filodemeo sulla adulazione nel PHerc. 1457," *CErc* 4 (1974) 43–56.

[16] Gargiulo, "PHerc. 222," 103.

[17] M. Gigante, "La biblioteca di Filodemo," *CErc* 15 (1985) 24; idem, *Ricerche filodemee* (2d ed.; Naples: Gaetano Macchiaroli, 1983) 32–40; Longo Auricchio, "Adulazione," 82; W. Allen, Jr. and P. H. De Lacy, "The Patrons of Philodemus," *CP* 34 (1939) 59–65.

was incumbent on Philodemus, not only in view of his relationship with Piso but also because flattery was part of the charge of servility in anti-Epicurean polemic. Epicurus was said to have flattered Mithras and Idomeneus for his own pleasure, and Epicurus' symposia were seen as assemblies of flatterers, excessively praising each other. Finally, Cicero's unflattering account of Piso's and Philodemus' relationship was well known.[18]

The topic of adaptability and servility to the great, connected with the issue of personal independence as illustrated in the relationship of a patron and a client, was debated under the late Republic and the early Empire; this is seen in both Philodemus and Horace,[19] and later in Dio Chrysostom, Plutarch, Lucian, and Maximus of Tyre.[20] Although the contrast between flatterers and friends was not new,[21]

---

[18] Cic. *Pis.* 28.70–29.71. Cicero calls Philodemus a "flatterer" (*assentator*, 70). See also Ath. 5.182a; 7.279f.; Diog. Laert. 10.4–5. Gargiulo ("PHerc. 222," 105) suggests that the apologetic tone of PHerc. 222 (where the behavior of the wise man is contrasted to that of the flatterer) should be interpreted in light of Cicero's invective.

[19] The issue is debated in two well-known Horatian works, *Epist.* 1.17–18 and *Sat.* 1.4. Horace was probably influenced by Philodemus. See C. Jensen, "Die Bibliothek von Herculaneum," *Bonner Jahrbücher* 135 (1930) 56–59; N. W. De Witt, "Parresiastic Poems of Horace," *CP* 30 (1935) 312–19; idem, "Epicurean Doctrine in Horace," *CP* 34 (1939) 127–34; A. K. Michels, "Παρρησία and the Satire of Horace," *CP* 39 (1944) 173–77; R. L. Hunter, "Horace on Friendship and Free Speech (Epistles 1.18 and Satires 1.4)," *Hermes* 113 (1985) 480–90. Horace defends himself as a sycophant of the great, contrasting the Cyrenaic Aristippus, who could adapt to any circumstance, with the less sensible behavior of Diogenes the Cynic, who courted the common people and knew only how to live amid sordid surroundings. Horace plays on the contrast between friends and faithless parasites, saying to Lollius the "most outspoken of men" that he will shrink from "appearing in the guise of a parasite" when he has "professed the friend." Horace also includes criticism of the "clownish rudeness" which passes for "simple candor" = παρρησία (*Epist.* 18.1–16).

[20] See Dio Chrys. *Or.* 15; Plut. *How to Tell a Flatterer from a Friend* (= *Adulator*); Lucian, *On Salaried Posts in Great Houses*; *Apology for the 'On Salaried Posts in Great Houses'*; *The Parasite*; and Max. Tyr. *Or.* 14 (= *How to Tell a Flatterer from a Friend*).

[21] For the φίλος–κόλαξ antithesis, see Alciphron III 8, 3; 62, 3; Xen. *Mem.* 2.9; and Antiphon's remark: πολλοὶ δ' ἔχοντες φίλους οὐ γιγνώσκουσιν, ἀλλ' ἑταίρους ποιοῦνται θῶπας πλούτου καὶ τύχης κόλακας (Ribbeck, *Kolax*, 32–33 n. 3). In the view of G. Heylbut (*De Theophrasti libris Περὶ φιλίας* [Bonn: C. Georgi, 1876] 28, 33), Theophrastus' work *On Flattery* was part of his *On Friendship* and Plutarch drew on Theophrastus' *Characters* in his *How to Tell a Flatterer from a Friend*. With regard to the text from Xenophon where Archedemus could be called either a flatterer or a friend of Crito, P. Millett says: "This anticipates a common device of Roman patronage: preserving appearances by disguising clients as amici" ("Patronage and its Avoidance in Classical Athens," *Patronage in Ancient Society* [ed. A. Wallace-Hadrill; London: Routledge, 1989] 33). Plutarch's *How to Tell a Flatterer from a Friend* and Maximus of Tyre's work of the same title, as well as Philodemus' works on flattery, focus on this issue.

the fact that independent works appeared dealing with this issue shows its resurgence during late Republican times and under the early Empire.[22] The main contours of the discussion of how to distinguish flatterers from friends had already been set in the fourth century BCE in discussions of the flatterer and related characters, such as the obsequious person and the pretentious one, with the focus on issues of pleasure and pain, the good and the beneficial, personal advantage, and versatility. The flatterer, in the judgment of his critics, has only his personal advantage in view. In an attempt to secure his advantage he consents to everything, speaks in order to please, is charming, affable, and witty. In rendering his services he accommodates himself to those he flatters, and is, like the friend of many and the polyp, cunning in his affable, versatile, and all-adaptable approach. As such, his behavior is seen as "soft" and servile.

Philodemus' work *On Flattery* also spotlights traditionally noted features of flattery. Here Philodemus contrasts flattery with friendship as he attempts to account for the practice of the wise man—presented in the *persona* of Epicurus—whose service to a patron might be compared to that of the flatterer.[23] As such, Philodemus' attempt is comparable to that of Plutarch and Maximus of Tyre, who both wrote works which delineate criteria by which flatterers and friends can be distinguished. Philodemus' concern to secure his status with his literary patron is also comparable to Plutarch's attempt to make clear to prince Philopappus that he can be trusted as a faithful friend and advisor; as such a person, he is not on a par with other so-called "friends" who in reality are flatterers misleading Philopappus by pandering to his baser appetites.

Although one would expect that most of the Epicureans at Herculaneum saw no problem with Philodemus' relationship with Piso, other Epicureans apparently viewed things differently. This is evident from the defensive mode of Philodemus' argument. As Philodemus

---

[22] In late Republican Rome and in the early Empire the matter is complicated because of the overlapping of "patron-client terminology" and that associated with the "institution of amicitia." See R. P. Saller, *Personal Patronage under the Early Empire* (Cambridge: Cambridge University Press, 1982) 11–15; idem, "Patronage and Friendship in Early Imperial Rome: Drawing the Distinction," *Patronage in Ancient Society* (ed. A. Wallace-Hadrill; London: Routledge, 1989) 49–62; P. White, "*Amicitia* and the Profession of Poetry," *JRS* 68 (1978) 80–82; P. A. Brunt, "'Amicitia' in the Late Roman Republic," *PCPhS* n.s. 11 (1965) 1–20.

[23] Gargiulo, "PHerc. 222," 103–127; Longo Auricchio, "Adulazione," 80; Acosta Méndez, "PHerc. 1089," 121–138.

argues for the right of the wise man to associate with a patron, other issues emerge which are more pertinent to my present concerns. Philodemus recognizes that the wise man shares traits commonly associated with flattery, and he, furthermore, encourages his philosophical friends not to shun such features but to recognize their attendant dangers. What emerges then is a positive evaluation of obsequiousness among friends of the community. Philodemus concedes,

> ... there will be some likenesses. ... But the wise man will never behave in the same way as the flatterer, although some could suspect him of doing so, because he bewitches the mind like the fabulous siren.[24]

Evidently, although Philodemus claims that the wise man is free from the vice of flattery, he defensively recognizes some of the apparent likenesses of flatterers and friends. The wise man thus talks so wonderfully that he fascinates the soul of his audience ("bewitching the mind like the fabulous siren") and has particular prestige among his friends. But in spite of apparent similarities to a flattering discourse, the content of the wise man's speeches is morally formative, not corrupting.[25]

Philodemus warns of the dangers of obsequiousness in the circle of friends, recognizing at the same time that continuous nearness often leads to hypocrisy, bragging, and an attempt to please others.[26] It is possible, however, with the help of philosophy and in the company of friends, to be free from the sly and persuasive vice of obsequiousness.[27] Also, there are many people who like to tell and do pleasant things, never accomplishing an evil or unfair deed, because, as Philodemus explains, we have to treat many people with regard.[28]

---

[24] PHerc. 222, col. 2.1–7. Like Socrates (Pl. *Symp.* 216A), the wise man charms just like the fabulous Sirens. See Diog. Laert. 10.9: "all who knew him, held fast as they were by the siren-charms of his doctrine."

[25] In regard to the formation of character, Philodemus notes that the wise man appears edifying and commends the goods of wisdom, and he says that the sage stands out also in discerning vices (PHerc. 222, cols. 2.1–12, 20–21; 4). The Epicurean Polystratus makes the same charge in his *On Irrational Despite of Popular Opinions*; see PHerc. 336/1150, col. 18.2–4: "Those who for the sake of obsequiousness or deception towards their neighbor generate every kind of chatter in order to get assent and temporary persuasion of people which does not aim at correction or a better life, either for themselves or their listeners." See Longo Auricchio, "Adulazione," 87, and G. Indelli, *Polistrato, Sul disprezzo irrazionale delle opinioni popolari* (La Scuola di Epicuro 2; Naples: Bibliopolis, 1978) 118.

[26] PHerc. 1457, cols. 10.17–19; 8.1–3.

[27] Ibid., col. 11.10–15.

[28] Ibid., col. 11.16–25, οἱ πολλοὶ πεφύκασιν χα[ρί]ζεσθαι ... μηδὲν [αἰ]σχρὸν ἢ ἄδικον ἐπιτηδεύοντας ὑπὲρ οὗ προσδεόμεθα τοὺς πολλοὺς ἀπ[ο]θεραπεύειν.

Philodemus distinguishes here between the verbs ἀνδάνειν and ἀρέσκειν as he criticizes the Epicurean Nicasicrates who saw "delighting your neighbors as a dangerous pleasure."[29] Philodemus also distinguishes here between τὸ τοῖς πέλας ἀνδάνειν and ἀρέσκεια. If we take οἱ πολλοί in col. 11 as a reference to "the multitude," as the common comparison of flatterers and demagogues suggests, we have a contrast here between "neighbors" (οἱ πέλας) and the "multitude," which is, I submit, analogous to Philodemus' contrast elsewhere between "insiders" or "intimate fellows" (οἱ συνήθεις) or "members of the household" (οἱ οἰκεῖοι), namely, fellow Epicureans, and "outsiders" (οἱ ἔξωθεν) or "those outside the intimate fellowship" (οἱ ἔξω τῆς συνηθείας), namely, those who do not belong to the Epicurean group.[30] This contrast suggests that the Epicurean communities were separate entities from society at large, perhaps even "alternative communities."[31]

This understanding of "neighbors" as fellow students and disciples in the Epicurean community is confirmed by a fragment in *On Frank Criticism* where Philodemus speaks of the way in which the teacher admonishes his disciples "in a way not understandable to τοῖς πέλας."[32] Thus pleasing your fellow students (τοῖς πέλας ἀνδάνειν) is not a damaging complaisance, whereas pleasing the multitude is (τοῖς πολλοῖς ἀρέσκειν).[33] Similarly, Philodemus distinguishes the frank

---

[29] Ibid., col. 10.11–13, τὸ τοῖς πέλας ἀνδάνειν ὡς [ζ]η[μ]ιο[ῦσαν] τὴν ἀρέσκειαν.

[30] PHerc. 1232 (*On Epicurus*), frg. 8, col. I, 6–12, "[But Epicurus says] that he invites these very people to join in a feast, just as he invites others—all those who are members of his household (οἱ κατὰ τὴν οἰκίαν) and he asks them to exclude none of the 'outsiders' (οἱ ἔξωθεν) who are well disposed both to him and to his friends" (trans. by D. Clay, "The Cults of Epicurus," *CErc* 16 (1986) 13–14); *Lib.* col. 14a10–11, "For he also despises outsiders"; App. Tab. III F ("difficulties caused by outsiders"). See also *Ir.* 26.24–25 Indelli (οἰκείους τε καὶ τῶν ἔξωθεν ἀνθρώπους); PHerc. 1457, frg. 16.3–5 (τῶν συνηθ[ῶ]ν–τῶν ἔξω τῆς συν[ηθείας; Kondo, "Interpretazione," 48); *Vit.* cols. 2.32–35; 8.28–30 (καὶ τὸ πρὸ[ς τοὺς φίλους ἐν τοῖς ἔξωθεν ἴσον εἶναι τῶν ἄλλων ἐπι[τρ]ε[χ]όντων καὶ τοὺς ἐ[φόδιον ὡσ[εἰ παρὰ [φίλ]ου δεομένο[υς]). See C. Jensen, *Ein neuer Brief Epikurs* (Berlin: Weidmann, 1933) 17, 27, 44.

[31] See B. D. Frischer's description of the Epicurean community as a surrogate family in *The Sculpted Word: Epicureanism and Philosophical Recruitment in Ancient Greece* (Berkeley: University of California Press, 1982) 206–07. Frg. 3.8–10 of *On Frank Criticism* speaks of ill repute in the eyes of the "public" (οἱ πολλοί) and of separation from one's family members. In col. 7a2–3, Philodemus speaks of the teacher in the same breath as a father and an elder, and in frg. 44.7 he says that the teacher feels [family] affection (στέργειν) for his students (cf. also frg. 54.1; col. 8b2; and App. Tab III H).

[32] Phld. *Lib.* frg. 61.

[33] My interpretation of PHerc. 1457 is in line with that of Kondo, "Interpretazione," 54–56. See frg. 187 Usener, where Epicurus is reported as having said, "I never

speech directed towards one's fellow disciples and others and says:

> Let us make it clear to them that the goods of friendship are very durable and that flattery is the antagonist of friendship; let us also consider well the goods that rise from frank speech, both (the frank speech) directed towards one's intimate associates and (the frank speech) directed towards all men, and let us avoid as vain the company of adulators, and still more let us not mix with them but seek cohabitation with those who speak candidly.[34]

Continuing the contrast of flattery and conversation at the beginning of the pericope, Philodemus thus encourages the readers to seek to live with those who talk freely and to avoid flatterers. According to Philodemus, conversations, reasoning together, and mutual contemplation are indispensable among the Epicureans and, for that reason, are central elements of divine friendship.[35] Παρρησία or frank speech is thus a type of ὁμιλία and a *sine qua non* of friendship.[36] Based on the title of the work in which it appears, παρρησία is a behavior or a way of life.[37] Therefore, just as assent, speaking in order to please, praise, and other flattering techniques are characteristics of flattery, so is frank speech of friendship.[38] This contrast between the "frank speaker" who correctly guides his friends and the flatterer who beguiles others also surfaces in *On Frank Criticism*, to which we now turn.[39]

---

tried to please the multitude (τοῖς πολλοῖς ἀρέσκειν) because I do not know what they like and what I know they do not understand." Cf. *SV* 64, 67. Philodemus' *On Rhetoric* contains some disparaging remarks on pleasing the multitude and on different means of persuasion which either please or displease the multitude (Cf. S. Sudhaus [ed.], *Philodemi Volumini Rhetorica* [2 vols. and a supplement; Leipzig: Teubner, 1892–96], v. 1, col. 8, p. 237; col. 94, p. 373; v. 2, frg. 17, p. 157; col. 8, p. 11; col. 23, p. 17; col. 24, pp. 18–19; cols. 15–18, pp. 219–223; col. 93, p. 245; col. 98, pp. 252–53), but I have not yet been able to determine the extent to which these statements reflect Philodemus' views or those of his Epicurean critics at Rhodes and Cos.

[34] PHerc. 1082, col. 2.1–14. For the Greek text, see Gargiulo, "PHerc. 222," 104–05.

[35] Phld. *D.* 3, frg. 84, col. 13,36–39,36 Diels. For συζητητικὸς τρόπος as a pedagogical technique, see *Ir.* 19.25–26 Indelli, *Lib.* frg. 53.2, and *SV* 74.

[36] On PHerc. 873, Περὶ ὁμιλίας, see F. Amoroso, "Filodemo sulla conversazione," *CErc* 5 (1975) 63–76.

[37] And not, as maintained by R. Philippson ("Philodemos," PW 19.2 (1938), cols. 2460, 2467–74), a virtue opposed to the vice of κολακεία. So Gigante, *Ricerche filodemee*, 59–62.

[38] Cf. Acosta Méndez, "PHerc. 1089," 122–24.

[39] On "frank speakers" (οἱ παρρησιαζόμενοι), see PHerc. 1457, frgs. 2.1–3; 12.5–6; and col. 1.23–24.

Philodemus on Friendship and Frank Speech

Philodemus' handbook *On Frank Criticism* (Περὶ παρρησίας),[40] which contains the lecture notes of Zeno,[41] Philodemus' teacher at Athens, is of great importance for the social history of Epicureanism.[42] The work, which appears together with *On Anger* in a larger work *On Conduct and Character*, describes the education of Epicurean friends, not only in Zeno's school at Athens, but also in Philodemus' circle at Herculaneum and in Siro's group at nearby Naples, and presumably in other Epicurean centers around the Mediterranean basin. These lecture notes contain questions and answers on the appropriate form of moral guidance, focusing on character formation, on the right and wrong form of obsequiousness, and the appropriate mode of persuasion; the discussion reveals a dispute over methods of correcting disciples within the Epicurean school. Emphasis falls on the correction of error and participation in mutual psychagogy. This emphasis on reciprocal correction in friendship is congruent with the ideal of friendship of many and runs counter to the common saying that one should judge a person's character before friendship is proffered. Also, Philodemus advocates an ideal of openness, which suggests that Epicureans valued friendship both for its attendant benefits as well as in itself.

Although *On Frank Criticism* is not fully extant, we can gain from it a fairly complete picture of late Epicurean psychagogy. This can be achieved by focusing on questions which the handbook itself raises, questions which are faced by any practitioner in the "art of moral guidance."[43] Also, we can better understand the psychagogy exempli-

---

[40] Or, the περὶ παρρησίας λόγος (as cited in *Ir.* col. 36.24–25 Indelli). See the reference to περὶ παρρησίας πραγματεία in PHerc. 1082, col. 1.1–7 (so W. Crönert, *Kolotes und Menedemos* [Leipzig: E. Avenarius, 1906; reprinted, Amsterdam: Hakkert, 1965] 127 n. 534) and τὸ τάγμα τῆς παρρησίας in *Lib.* col. 13b4 and *Rh.* 2.1 Sudhaus. See Gigante, *Ricerche filodemee*, 60. Wilke proposed in his edition (*Philodemi de ira liber*, vii) that *On Anger* belonged to the same epitome of Zeno's work as Περὶ παρρησίας.

[41] *De libertate dicendi*, PHerc. 1471. The only edition is that of A. Olivieri, *Philodemi ΠΕΡΙ ΠΑΡΡΗΣΙΑΣ libellus* (Leipzig: Teubner, 1914). The subscript of PHerc. 1471 is: Φιλοδήμου τῶν κατ' ἐπιτομὴν ἐξειργασμένων περὶ ἠθῶν καὶ βίων ἐκ τῶν Ζήνωνο [ς σχο]λῶν ... ὅ ἐστι περὶ παρρ[η]σίας. We also find a reference to ἐκ τῶν Ζηνῶνος σχολῶν in PHerc. 1389. See Kondo, "Interpretazione," 45.

[42] See Gigante, *Ricerche filodemee*, 55–113; N. W. De Witt, "Organization and Procedure in Epicurean Groups," *CP* 31 (1936) 205–11; idem, "Epicurean Contubernium," *TAPA* 67 (1936) 55–63; and D. Clay, "Individual and Community in the First Generation of the Epicurean School," Συζήτησις: *Studi sull'epicureismo greco e romano offerti a Marcello Gigante* (2 vols.; Naples: Gaetano Macchiaroli, 1983) 1.270.

[43] Cf. De Lacy and De Lacy, *Philodemus, On Methods of Inference*, 201 n. 64. There

fied by focusing on the recurrent analogy of conjectural art and medical practice. Frank speech is presented as a stochastic method used in the art of the therapeutic healing of souls, a method which is comparable to the methods used by physicians in the art of healing. The medical analogy thus spotlights issues of method, form, and procedure for the "moral physician," thereby underscoring the conjectural nature of psychagogy, the need for adaptation to the particular case, the legitimate use of harshness, and the importance of openness for correct diagnosis. Finally, we can better understand the view of moral guidance by focusing on the many hortatory terms used, terms which often reveal the nature of the guidance in question. The many variations of hortatory blame and the frequency of such terms as error and correction are thus significant in a work entitled Περὶ παρρησίας.[44] They show that frank speech is a form of blame or frank criticism of error. The most appropriate translation of Περὶ παρρησίας is thus *On Frank Criticism*.

Philodemus discusses frank speech under the topic of how and when frankly to reprimand your friends' failings. The topic of frank speech is thus a part of the theme of moral education, namely, the correction of faults among friends in the improvement of character, a subject which was discussed earlier by Plato, Aristotle, Xenophon, and Isocrates.[45] It is especially in Isocrates that we find the change in connotation of the word παρρησία, which earlier was used in the political sphere of the right of the free-born Athenian to express his views unhindered. From now on, the word παρρησία is seen as a

---

are series of answers to problems or *topoi* (cf. frg. 81) scattered throughout the treatise, including the following: "Will the wise man candidly refer his own affairs to his friends?" (frg. 81); "Why do people resent frank criticism from those that they recognize as more clever and, indeed, as instructors?" (col. 20.1–15); "Why do women resent frank criticism [more than men]?" (col. 22); "Why do famous people resent it more than others?" (col. 22) "Why are old people more resentful?" (col. 24).

[44] See the index of Olivieri's edition for the use of ἐξ-/ ἁμαρτάνω, ἁμάρτ-ημα /ία, ἁμαρτωλός, διαμαρτ-άνω / ία, διά-/παράπτωσις, διαπίπτω, παραλογίζεσθαι, διορθ-εύω/ ωσις and μετάθεσις. Terms of blame and dissuasion include ἀποτρέπω, νουθεσία, νουθέτησις, νουθετέω, ἐπιτίμησις, ὀνειδίζεσθαι, λοιδορία /-εῖν and διασυρτικός.

[45] Pl. *Prt.* 325AB; *Grg.* 525A–C; *Soph.* 229E–230A. Aristotle explains that the young need friends to keep them from error, the old to care for them and support the actions that fail because of weakness, and those in their prime in order to do fine actions (*Eth. Nic.* 1155a12–16; cf. 1171a21–1172a15; 1180a6–14; *Eth. Eud.* 7.10.17–20, 30–35; *Mag. Mor.* 2.17.1–2). Xen. *Mem.*; *Oec.* 13.6–12; 14.8; Isoc. *Demonicus* 1–6, 11–12, 20, 22, 24–26, 29–31, 45–46; *To Nicocles* 2, 28, 42–43, 45–53; *Antidosis* 206–14, 288–90; *Nicocles* (=The Cyprians) 55, 57; *On the Peace* 14–15, 70, 72; *To Antipater* 3–7, 9.

sign of goodwill towards one's friends and close in meaning to ἐλέγχω and νουθετέω.[46] Frank speech is, as Philo of Alexandria was later to remark, "akin to friendship," or, as Plutarch said, the "language of friendship" and the "most potent medicine in friendship."[47] Περὶ παρρησίας is then a περὶ φιλίας τόπος. The pinnacle of this development is seen in the *Pedagogue* of Clement of Alexandria, who discusses the use of twelve different words of hortatory blame in the divine word's use of frank speech in philanthropic psychagogy.[48] Philodemus' *On Frank Criticism* is a valuable example of this tradition.[49]

The frank counselor had, like the flatterer, precise collocations in Greco-Roman society.[50] He was often compared to a physician, just

---

[46] E. Peterson, "Zur Bedeutungsgeschichte von Παρρησία," *Reinhold Seeberg Festschrift* (ed. W. Koepp; 2 vols.; Leipzig: D. W. Scholl, 1929) 1.285–86; G. Bohnenblust, *Beiträge zum Topos ΠΕΡΙ ΦΙΛΙΑΣ* (Diss. Bern; Berlin: Gustav Schade [Otto Francke], 1905) 35–36; G. Scarpat, *Parrhesia: Storia del termine e delle sue traduzioni in latino* (Brescia: Paideia, 1964). Related terms include ἐξουσία, ἐλευθεροστομέω, θαρρέω, and εὐτολμία. The change in meaning of παρρησία is clear in Isocrates' remark that things which contribute to the education of men in private life include a "freedom of speech (παρρησία) and the privilege which is openly granted to friends to rebuke (ἐπιπλῆξαι) and to enemies to attack each other's faults" (*To Nicocles* 3, trans. by G. Norlin in the LCL; cf. *To Philip* 72; *Demonicus* 20–31). Παρρησία is a σημεῖον τῆς εὐνοίας τῆς πρὸς τοὺς φίλους (Isoc., *To Antipater* 4). Isocrates' discourses include a scathing critique of the Athenians (*To Philip* 1.1, 22; *To Nicocles* 48). From a later period, see *Ep. Arist.* 125 for the connection of παρρησία and φιλία in the relationship between "friends" and counselors of kings (*APOT* 2:107).

[47] Philo, *Her.* 5.19, 21, παρρησία δὲ φιλίας συγγενές; Plut. *Adulator* 74D.

[48] See Clem. Al. *Paed.* 76.1–4 on νουθέτησις (GCS 134,13–32 Stählin-Treu; cf. 65.2; 94.2); 77.1–2 on ἐπιτίμησις (GCS 134,33–135, 10); 81.2 on κατανεμέσησις (GCS 137,20–26); 78.1 on ἐπίπληξις (GCS 135,21–28; cf. 66.5; 82.2; 94.2); 79.2 on ἐπισκοπή (GCS 136,20–28); 77.3 on μέμψις (GCS 135,11–20); 78.2–4 on ἔλεγχος (GCS 135, 29–136, 12; cf. 64.1; 72.1; 82.2; 85.4; 88.1); 79.1 on φρένωσις (GCS 136,13–19); 80.1 on λοιδορία (GCS 136,29–32; cf. 66.2); 80.2 on ἔγκλησις (GCS 137,1–7); 80.3 on μεμψιμοιρία (GCS 137,8–12); and 81.1 on διάσυρσις (GCS 137,13–19). I have rearranged Clement's ordering, grouping together similar terms. Thus ἐπίπληξις and κατανεμέσησις follow ἐπιτίμησις, because they are both said to be a variation of it, and ἐπισκοπή, being a variation of ἐπίπληξις, follows it. See also 65.1 on reproach (ὀνειδισμός; GCS 128,8–10) and 75.1 on threats (GCS 133,29–31).

[49] I have placed St. Paul within this tradition in my *Paul and Philodemus*, arguing that Pauline psychagogy resembles Epicurean psychagogy in the way persons enjoying a superior moral status and spiritual aptitude help to nurture and correct others, guiding their souls in moral and religious (re)formation.

[50] Related to the frank counselor was the simple (ἁπλοῦς), forthright (αὐθέκαστος) or truthful person, commonly contrasted with the self-deprecator, the pretentious and unscrupulous person. Plutarch, *Adulator* 52E; *Comp. Alc. et Cor.* 2.1; Ath. 13.588a; Dio Chrys. *Or.* 77/78.33; Lucian, *Alexander* 25; Arist. *Eth. Nic.* 1127b; Phld., PHerc. 222, col. I, 3–4; *Piet.* 123,17. On Lucian as Παρρησιάδης, "son of Truthful, grandson of Exposure" in *Piscator* 19, see R. B. Branham, *Unruly Eloquence: Lucian and the Comedy of Traditions* (Cambridge, MA: Harvard University Press, 1989) 229, and M. D. Macleod, "Lucian's Activities as a μισαλάζων," *Philologus* 123 (1979) 326–28.

as flatterers were compared to cooks. The diary of Crates, for example, contrasts the "professions" of a cook and a physician, a flatterer and a frank counselor, and a prostitute and a philosopher.[51] A person who would sufficiently test a soul as to rectitude of life should go to work with three things, namely, knowledge, goodwill, and frank speech;[52] a correct kind of caring demands frank speech which dares to expose and censure faults, a caring which might hurt on occasion. Such beneficial pain, however, leads to true pleasure.[53] One must then regard as the most faithful of friends not those who praise everything one does or says but those who criticize one's mistakes. These issues surface in discussions of how to distinguish flatterers from friends and can be seen with clarity in Philodemus' *On Frank Criticism*, where members admonish and censure each other in friendship. The preponderance of terms associated with the ethic of friendship in the extant fragments demands, therefore, that we view these correctional practices as an extension of the ethic of friendship.[54]

As Philodemus debates issues of harshness in moral guidance with other Epicureans, he focuses on the use of harsh exhortation with different types of students. Two types of students or dispositions surface throughout the fragments, namely, the "weak" and obedient ones and the "strong" or disobedient ones.[55] The former are also referred

---

[51] Pl. *Grg.* 464D; 465B; 500B and 501A (culinary art is a form of flattery); 520C–522E; *Resp.* 3.404C–D; Philo, *Ios.* 62; Max. Tyr. *Or.* 14.8g–i (181,3–11 Hobein); Plut. *De tranq. anim.* 472F.

[52] Pl. *Grg.* 487A; Clem. Al. *Paed.* 97.3 (GCS 148,2–10 Stählin-Treu).

[53] Plut. *Adulator* 49EF; 55B–E; Sen. *Ep.* 52.12ff. and 75.5, "Our words should aim not to please but to help" (trans. by R. M. Gummere in the LCL); Epict. *Diss.* 3.23.30, "Man, the lecture-room of the philosopher is a hospital; you ought not to walk out of it in pleasure, but in pain" (trans. by W. A. Oldfather in the LCL). See also Hermog. *Prog.* 7,13–15 (Rabe), "Isocrates said that the root of education is bitter, but the fruit is sweet."

[54] Friendship terms, scattered throughout the fragments, include φιλία, φιλέω, φίλησις, φίλος, φιλικός, ἀγαπάω, ἀγάπη, ἀγάπησις, ἐράω, στέργω, στοργή and φιλοπαρρησιαστής. See *Lib.* tab. V extrem. frg. (App.), βού[λεται μὲν δ]ιὰ φ[ιλίας νουθετεῖν, "for he wants to admonish through friendship." Ἐπιτίμησις, a variation of παρρησία, is united with φιλέω in *Ir.* 35.19 Indelli, διὰ τὸ φ[ιλεῖν] ἐπιτίμησις.

[55] Philodemus refers to the former as ἀπαλοί and the latter as ἰσχυροί (frg. 7.1–5). See frgs. 36.4–9; 45.7–11; 65.9–11; cols. 13a12–13. Cols. 22b and 24a of *On Frank Criticism* combine the theme of strength and weakness with that of contempt. The latter relates weakness to older people as it asks why old people are more resentful of frankness than others. In the former the strong are advised not to look with contempt on the weak. Judged from the question asked, "why do women resent frank speech more than men?" the weak refer to women and the strong to men (col. 24a7–14). However, both women and the old are part of the community and thus among its pupils. Women are also referred to in col. 6a, which lists different types of students.

to as those who are insecure in their new philosophic way of life or have apostatized from philosophy. The latter are referred to as stubborn or recalcitrant pupils, those who find it difficult to stand the frank criticism of others or violently resist frank speech, and the irascible and incurable ones. Each of these types of students needs a unique treatment. Philodemus often refers to these types collectively as the "young" or as "those in preparation." We have here, therefore, a variation of the theme of care of the young (ἐπιμέλεια τῶν νέων). The "young" are recent converts or beginning students of philosophy, irrespective of their age, who constitute not solely a temporal category but also a modal and qualitative one.[56] The different types of students are referred to not only as the young, but also those in (co-) preparation,[57] fellow students,[58] one's neighbors,[59] pupils,[60] laymen,[61] children,[62] intimate fellows[63] and friends.[64] Sometimes, the pupils are simply referred to as "some" (of the friends).[65] The "teachers," besides being called the "wise," "philosophers," or "scholars," are also referred to as friends, albeit sometimes as the "most excellent of friends."[66]

Besides discussing different types of pupils, Philodemus also asks questions concerning the application of frank speech to persons of different professions, gender, and age. Those particularly resentful of frank criticism include politicians,[67] famous people,[68] wom-

---

[56] Lib. frgs. 31.2; 36.5; 52.4; 71.8; 83.8; cols. 6a6; 16a10; Rh. 1.267, col. 30.34ff. Sudhaus. Cf. Pl. Leg. 659E; 951DE; Herm. Vis. 3.5.4, Νέοι εἰσὶν ἐν τῇ πίστει . . .; and 3.13.4. See M. P. Nilsson, Die hellenistische Schule (Munich: Beck, 1955) 34–42, 77.

[57] Or (συν)κατασκευαζόμενοι: Lib. frgs. 2.3; 25.6; 53.4, 7; 55.3; 71.2; 76.3; col. 12b7.

[58] Or οἱ συσχολάζοντες, -οντοι. Cf. Lib. frgs. 75.4–5; 79.2–3.

[59] Or οἱ πέλας. Cf. Lib. frg. 61.2.

[60] Or μαθηταί. Cf. Lib. frg. 87.1–4.

[61] Or ἰδιώτης. Cf. Lib. col. 11b1. See also PHerc. 222, col. iv, 6–7; Oec. col. 9, 14–16; Mort. col. 23.9; 31.12; 35.28; Ind. Sto. col. 17.10, 57; Diog. Oen. frg. 20, II 4–5 Chilton; Pl. Soph. 221C–D; and Arist. Pol. 1266a31. See Gargiulo, "PHerc. 222," 107, 117.

[62] Lib. frg. 18.1; col. 24b10; Vit. col. 8.15, Jensen, Neuer Brief, p. 29.

[63] Or οἱ συνήθεις. Cf. Lib. frgs. 42.2; 52.12; 54.11.

[64] Lib. frgs. 8.10; 41.7; 50.7; 55.7; 70.3; 81.3, 8; 84.2; col. 13a10.

[65] Lib. frgs. 61; 70.8; col. 19a11; 19b10f.; 13a10, ἄλλοι φίλοι.

[66] For "teachers" (καθηγηταί), see frgs. 31.11; 45.5; 80.2; cols. 7a2; and 20a3–4; for the "wise" (σοφοί), see frgs. 35.3; 46.1–3; 62.7–9; 81; cols. 7a5; 8a–b; et al.; for "philosophers" (φιλόσοφοι), see frgs. 1.7; 35.3; cols. 8a8; 10a1; and 10b13; and for "scholars" (φιλόλογοι), see fr. 37; cols. 8a9 and 10a2. For the reference to the "most excellent of friends," see frg. 41.7–8.

[67] Lib. col. 18a–b.

[68] Lib. col. 22b10–13, "Why, all other things being equal, do wealthy and famous people resent frank criticism more than others?" In col. 7a7–10, Philodemus ex-

en,[69] and old people.[70] In the case of politicians, this is so because of their ambition and desire for renown. Reminiscent of Clement of Alexandria two centuries later and his discussion of reasons why salvation is difficult for a rich man, Philodemus remarks that students are "not difficult to save," except if they feel the need to show off before crowds.[71] In the case of women, part of the problem is that there is greater psychological insecurity involved.[72] Famous people and old men, by contrast, are resentful because they think that they are criticized from impure motives and believe that they are wiser than others.[73] As Philodemus focuses on the effect frank speech has on people of different professions, gender, and age, he also asks what effect frank speech has on pupils of different dispositions. Here different types of students emerge, namely, those violently resisting frankness, those who are irascible, those who cannot tolerate frank criticism, and, finally, those of a lesser intellectual ability. The capacity of the young of different dispositions to bear the frank speech of the sage is a major concern of the handbook.[74]

As Philodemus expresses his views on the nature of frank speech, he rejects both sycophantic techniques and the unrelieved use of

---

plains that both those who are superior and the common people must be admonished as the individual case demands.

[69] *Lib.* col. 21b12–14, "Why do women resent frank criticism?" Philodemus emphasizes that as the teachers in the community differ, so do the students: "just as a boy differs from a woman, and at the same time old men will differ from young men" (col. 6a4–8).

[70] *Lib.* col. 24a7–9, "Why are old people more resentful?" Cf. cols. 24b1–12 and 6a4–8; 7a1–2.

[71] *Lib.* frg. 34.3–8. See Clem. Al. *Quis div. salv.* 2.

[72] Women are thus more sensitive than others when frankly criticized, more distressed by disgrace, and more wont to suspect evil motives on the part of those who admonish them. See col. 22a–b.

[73] Famous people think that they are rebuked out of envy and that they see their sins more clearly than the wise (col. 23a–b). Old men think that people criticize them out of disdain and that they are wiser because of their age (col. 24a–b).

[74] Philodemus thus explains that the nature of frank speech will differ depending on whether it is spoken toward a student who has become upset, or toward one who has relapsed, or toward one who is agitated, or toward one who is bashful, or, finally, toward one who is very obstinate (col. 4a1–8). See frgs. 5.4–8, "It is possible to see from what has been said also how one ought to be frank with the one who violently resists frankness"; 31.1–8, some of the young become very irritated when rebuked: "they receive whatever is said in frankness annoyingly"; 67.9–11, "whether he should also speak frankly toward those who cannot endure it and toward an irascible person?"; 70.5–7 "how will he deal with those who become angry with him on account of his frankness?" and col. 20a1–5, "Why do people resent frank speech from those whom they recognize as more clever, and, indeed, as leaders?"

harshness. Philodemus' remarks are in a defensive mode since both obsequiousness and harshness converge with a legitimate aspect of frank speech.[75] Philodemus advocates a versatile approach; whatever hortatory means are available, including harshness, should be used.[76] This was seen as problematic since both the one who reviles and the one who corrects inevitably use the same words. Also, Philodemus' remarks reveal a debate with other Epicureans on the appropriate mode of exhortation in the cure of moral ills.[77] Philodemus is concerned with real and counterfeit frankness, and he uses a dispositional analysis to distinguish the one who correctly wields frank speech from the one who does so incorrectly. The one who pretends to use frankness is an ἀλαζών, and the person of a roguish character is compared to the flatterer.[78] Philodemus rejects their pretentiousness, sycophantic techniques, and reviling, but he applauds the frank speech of a person of refined character—one who is actuated by goodwill, is steadfast in principle,

> immune from any tendency to demagogy, free from envy, saying only what fits the occasion, and is not likely to be carried away so as to revile, abuse, bully, or hurt, by using insolence and sycophantic techniques.[79]

---

[75] PHerc. 1457, col. 10.10ff. contrasts ἀρέσκειν with ἀνδάνειν. Cf. Kondo, "Interpretazione," 54–56. See above, pp. 26–29.

[76] Phld. *Lib.* frgs. 68.1–7; 10.1–2; 58.6–9, and 86.5–7.

[77] Philodemus also contrasts two methods of exhortation, distinguishable by harshness, in *On Anger* (cols. 1.8–27; 19.12–27; 27.19–39; 35.18–39.7; 44.15–27). See esp. cols. 27.19–21 (τῆι ἀνεπιεικεῖ καὶ ἀνημέρωι καὶ τραχείαι διαθέσει), 38.1–3; and 42.30–31 (ἀνήμρος διάθεσις).

[78] *Lib.* col. 1a1–4, "How shall we distinguish between the one whose frank criticism arises from a cultivated disposition, and the one whose frank criticism arises from a boorish disposition" (διάθεσις ἀστείας vs. διάθεσις φαύλης/μοχθηρᾶς). The discussion runs from col. 1 with the statement of the problem to col. 2b. Cf. 3a1–3, "Enough, then, has been said on this topic." Philodemus also uses a dispositional analysis in his *On Anger* in order to distinguish different types of exhortation. The ἀστεῖος person is opposite to the ἄγροικος and ἀηδής, the ill-bred man (Theophr. *Char.* 20; Phld. *Ir.* col. 24.1 Indelli). Philo also contrasts ὁ ἀστεῖος and ὁ φαῦλος in his discussion of παρρησία (*Her.* 5.19; *Abr.* 3.20; 4.22). Pretentiousness among the students is also a concern in the fragments of Philodemus (cf. *Lib.* col. 16b2–9). Frg. 88 asks, "how shall we recognize the one who has borne frank criticism correctly and the one who only pretends to have done so?"

[79] Phld. *Lib.* col. 1b5–13. In frg. 85.7–9, the teacher (ὁ καθηγούμενος) is characterized as being of a "cheerful, loving and gentle disposition" (διάθεσις εὐήμερος καὶ φιλόφιλος καὶ ἤπιος). For the use of κολακευτικαὶ τέχναι in col. 1b13, compare *Rh.* II, XLI 35–XLII 1 Longo Auricchio, φανερὸν γὰ[ρ δ᾽ ὅ]τι καὶ τεχ[ν]ίτην ... κ[αὶ] κόλακα, and PHerc. 1089, col. 7.5f., κολακι]κῶς ὁμιλῆσ[ι; cf. Amoroso, "Filodemo," 63–64.

Such a person is not prone to blame others, nor easily provoked nor bickersome; contrary to the person of a depraved disposition, moreover, he is not harsh or bitter.[80] Different character types thus use different forms of persuasion. Philodemus contrasts two types of persuasion in order to suggest how to use frank speech correctly in psychagogic guidance. Such a contrast also provides a way to detect pretentious people in the community. This contrast between two character types and their respective modes of persuasion reflects a dispute among Epicureans about the nature of moral exhortation.[81] This dispute is also evident in contexts that discuss how to treat the weak, those who have apostatized from philosophy, and the incurable ones. Fragment 59 notes two among many reasons why some abandon philosophy: "For they are either weak or incurable by frankness."[82] Fragment 60.1–7 continues:

> And some maintained that one should apply frank speech towards people like this, but others—as if they (themselves) are reviled even from malevolence—(wished to apply frank speech towards people like this), since bitter frankness has a similarity to abuse.

The following lines speak of charmers who "with their deceitful and manifold pleasantries turn many away by seizing the intensity of the emotions and subduing them by enchantment" (60.8–12). As Philodemus rejects the "psychagogy" of those of an unrefined disposition, so he also rejects that of these charmers because of its detrimental effect on friends of the community. He also rejects the use of bitter frank speech in the form of reviling in the case of the incurable

---

[80] *Lib.* col. 2a1–9.

[81] Phld. *Oec.* col. 23.22–36: Philosophical discourses are non-combative, full of tranquillity, produce peace of mind, and are contrary to the destructive nature of the discourses of sophists, demagogues and sycophants, which destroy the tranquil life. He questions the claim of sophists that only they know how to praise or blame, and he condemns sophistic rhetoric since it has often been "a lying and pernicious discipline" (*Rh.* 1.216–224; 2.256–263 Sudhaus). Epideictic oratory requires insight into the nature of virtue and vice as well as praise and blame (v. 4, col. 30a19–32a6 and xxxiia6ff. Sudhaus). Only philosophers have such knowledge, Philodemus implies, referring to his own non-extant book *On Praise* (v. 1.219, col. 38a.24–25). "If Peithos is rightly thought a goddess," he writes, "this is due to philosophy; unlike rhetorical persuasion, philosophical persuasion does not harm" (v. 1.269, col. 32.2–10; 270, col. 32.32–37 Sudhaus). On this, see Asmis, "Philodemus' Epicureanism," 2388, 2401–02.

[82] Phld. *Lib.* frg. 59.9–11; 59.1–2, "and sometimes he will even abandon philosophy." Recent converts experience dejecting influences which, as the result of weakness, affect them, including the sober advice of friends and bitter criticism of the unfriendly, which "have even made some persons renounce philosophy altogether" (cf. Plut. *De prof. virt.* 78AB; *De aud.* 46E).

and those who are insecure; such frankness would simply destroy
them. When the young are weak, the wise should take them in their
arms and remind and reproach them, but only with moderate censure, just as Epicurus addressed Pythocles.[83] If censure is used at all,
it is counterproductive if not followed by praise; the sting of censure
should be relieved by subsequent praise.[84] Also, one should not reprove the weak in the presence of others.[85]

Throughout the fragments Philodemus advocates a varied and mixed
use of frank speech. The "good method," as he says, is "varied and
mixed with bountiful praises, and exhorts [them] to do those things
which follow the good attributes they possess."[86] The wise man mixes
praise and blame; the pupil will "be regained in that manner, namely,
when the sting of censure is followed by praise."[87] Philodemus thus
rejects an abusive and disparaging approach and advocates a gentle
one.[88] In his work *On Anger*, Philodemus disapproves of the mere
censure of an angry man. The mere censure of the emotions, advocated by Bion and Chrysippus, is ineffectual.[89] One should rather
visualize the illness; when the shameful consequences of such a vice
are put before the eyes of those suffering, they become intent on a
cure.[90] One should not revile or treat the erring one spitefully; rather,

---

[83] *Lib.* frg. 6.7. See also frg. 93.4–6 Herc., Ἐὰν δ[ὲ τὴν ἀσ]θένειαν . . . ἀναλήψε-
ται . . . τ[ὸν νέ]ον ἐπ[ιτιμ]ῶν μετρίαις ὑπ[ο]μνήσεσιν (Gigante, *Ricerche filodemee*, 109–10).
Olivieri did not include in his edition of *On Frank Criticism* six fragments which are
found in the first edition, *Herculanensium Voluminum quae supersunt* (10 vols.; Naples: Ex
Regia typographia, 1793–1855), vol. 5, part 2 (1843), frgs. 77, 79, 84, 87, 91 and
93. See M. Gigante, "Motivi paideutici nell'opera filodemea sulla libertà di parola,"
CErc 4 (1974) 37–42.
[84] *Lib.* Tab. IV I, p. 66f. Olivieri. Frg. 58.5–9 refers to this mixed method, also
advising that one ought to consider whether the student is able to improve when he
has gotten worse over a long period of time. Frg. 59 continues the saga, noting that
when a person falls away from philosophy he will perhaps quickly hate the sage;
some, however, will tolerate his frank speech, whereas others cannot be helped unless
they previously have received some benefit.
[85] The one who does not use frankness correctly "will submit even the weak to
a cross-examination in the presence of many or all" (*Lib.* Tab IIIG). See also Tab.
IV J, "not haughtily ridiculing their weaknesses."
[86] *Lib.* frg. 68.1–10, ποικίλη φιλοτεχνία. See frgs. 10.1–7; 8b.6–7; 38.5; cols. 8b8;
11a1; 14b3.
[87] *Lib.* Tab. IV I, p. 66f. Olivieri.
[88] Therapy should be done with a "moderate discourse" or "moderate censure"
(frg. 6.7–8; 20.1–2). See also frgs. 26.8; 85.9; 38; 52.2; cols. 4b8–9; 8b12 and 16a8,
"rebuke gently and agreeably" (cf. *Ir.* 19.19; 28.39; 44.27 Indelli).
[89] Phld. *Ir.* col. 1.7–20 Indelli, εἰ μὲν οὖν ἐπετίμα τοῖς ψέγουσι μ[ό]νον . . . ὡς Βίων ἐν
τῶι Περί τῆς ὀργῆς καὶ Χρύσιππος ἐν τ[ῶ]ι Πε[ρ]ὶ παθῶν θεραπευ[τι]κῶι, κἂν μετρίως ἵστατο.
See M. Gigante and G. Indelli, "Bione e l'epicureismo," *CErc* 8 (1978) 125–26.
[90] Phld. *Ir.* col. 1.21–27; 3.13; 4.15–16 Indelli. A debate concerning the degree of

"errors should be taken up in sympathy, not ridicule."[91] The "natural weakness" of the erring should rather be pitied and forgiven, not derided or "bespattered with mud."[92]

The teacher should thus not hate the one who commits pardonable mistakes, "remembering that he himself is not perfect and that all men are accustomed to err."[93] If the young are ridiculed or inopportunely reproved, they become downcast and accept criticism badly: "Therefore some of them, mocked, cannot endure to listen to the teacher with goodwill" (31.9–12). The sage should calm his angry students just as Heracles calmed the Stymphacian birds.[94] He should apply frank speech opportunely and cheerfully in order to increase the goodwill between himself and those in preparation (25.3–8). If he fails, the young, because of the chastisement, might become irritated and "hate everyone in the world" (26.2–4).[95] The use of

---

harshness used in the cure of moral ills can be seen in PHerc. 831 (Περὶ μετεωρισμοῦ), which recommends philosophy for curing fickleness. The work, probably a treatise by Demetrius the Laconian, is a paraenesis that admonishes the reader to avoid this evil (R. Philippson, "Papyrus Herculanensis 831," *AJP* 64 (1943) 148–62; reprinted in his *Studien zu Epikur und den Epikureern* [ed. C. J. Classen; Hildesheim: Olms, 1983] 284–98). The author rejects harshness in curing fickleness, "but to rail the aforementioned abnormality is out of place, but it is necessary to cure it" (col. 5.9–11, [ἄτοπον] δὲ λοιδορεῖν τὸ πρ[οειρημέ]νον παράλλαγμα, ἀλλ[ὰ δεῖ θερ]απ[εύειν). The Epicurean author who stood to the addressee in the relation of teacher to pupil follows a common form of arrangement, namely, diagnosis, defining the nature of the moral error, and a prescribed cure (θεραπεία). Chrysippus' method in his work on the emotions was prescriptive and is found in numerous popular treatises on vices and passions; see, for example, Cicero (*Tusc.* 3–4), Seneca (*On Anger*), Plutarch, and Philodemus (*On Anger*). See Philippson, "Papyrus Herculanensis 831," 285; idem, "Das dritte und vierte Buch der Tusculanen," *Hermes* 67 (1932) 245–94; idem, "Philodems Buch über den Zorn," *RhM* 71 (1916) 425–60. Chrysippus' *On the Passions* was in four books, the first three defining the nature of the different passions and the fourth—called τὸ περὶ παθῶν θεραπευτικός—their cure. See *SVF* 3.111.8–12 (§458); 112.1–13 (§460); Diog. Laert. 7.111.

[91] *Lib.* frg. 79.9–12; Tab III G; IV J; frg. 37.5–9, ". . . nor frankly to criticize in a haughty and harsh way, nor to say any insolent and abusive thing, or sarcastic things. . . ."

[92] *Lib.* frgs. 46.5–11; 20.5–6. Cf. col. 22b2–4, μὴ προπηλακίζεσθαι (LSJ, s.v.). See also Tab. IV J ("not haughtily ridiculing their weaknesses") and frg. 23.1–5.

[93] *Lib.* frg. 46.5–11. Occasionally, Philodemus speaks of the wise as "perfect" in contrast to one who fails to understand, is senseless, or ignorant. See frg. 55.8; cols. 8a2–9; 9a7–8, and 10a8–10. Note also frg. 74.5–9, which refers to a person who has "shed some faults" but "does not achieve perfection in everything." The wise is then not perfect in the sense that he is faultless.

[94] *Lib.* frg. 87.1–4, "as Heracles singing and throwing out the opinions of herds of winged students." Cf. frg. 74.1–2, "lifted up by odes."

[95] The young need to be reproved when they are envious or scornful or when they are inconsiderately harsh themselves. The young err in their excessive and intemperate use of παρρησία, characterized as a tumor that needs a drastic operation

inconsiderate frank speech thus severs the social relations among friends of the community.[96]

For some students παρρησία suffices, but others require a more bitter dose, particularly stubborn pupils who, although rebuked and "shouted at," will hardly change.[97] Some of the pupils have become stiff; whatever means available should be used to attempt to change their false thoughts and behaviors. In order to change them the teacher "will use a harsh type of frank speech."[98] One fragment, where we overhear the voice of the student, graphically depicts such harsh measure as a "beating":

> I did not sin then, but now he will deem me deserving of frank criticism if he catches me. . . . For I declare that I did not even sin before, but I fell of my own will into the ignorance of youth; and on account of that he had to give me a beating.[99]

Philodemus explains that the teacher will "often use his varied and excellent art in this fashion," namely, in a mixed manner; "but," Philodemus continues, "he sometimes exercises his frank speech 'simply,' thinking that one must sometimes take a risk if they will not listen otherwise."[100] Such frank speech is, I believe, "simple" rather than mixed because only blame is involved. Philodemus' suggestion here that harshness alone should be used is contrary to the method he regularly advocates, spotlighted both in his description of

---

(col. 17a). The retaliatory nature of the young, reflected in their use of "biting frankness" (δηκτικὸν . . . τῆς παρρησίας), must be corrected (col. 17a; frg. 62.1–4). Philodemus also rejects a retaliatory approach in his work On Anger. Cf. J. Annas, "Epicurean Emotions," GRBS 30 (1989) 155–56.

[96] Right and wrong psychagogy is seen in the contrast between an admonition actuated by the concern for the good of others and an admonition which is altogether biting with moderate irony. See Lib. frg. 26.4–7, κηδεμονικὴ νουθέτησις. See also 42.6; col. 13b12, κηδεμονικ[ὸ]ν ἐπαινέσει. The "cheerful admonishing" (νουθετεῖν ἱλαρῶς), contrasted with νουθετεῖν ἀγνώστως (frg. 61), reverberates with the joyous use of the philotropeic method (frg. 43, εὐφροσύνη). See Plut. Adulator 55B, παρρησία κηδεμονική. Clement was later to define νουθέτησις as "benevolent blame" and recognized also a benevolent use of λοιδορία (Paed. 74.2; 76.1, ψόγος κηδεμονικός).

[97] Lib. frg. 6.1–4; 7.1–11. The stubborn pupils are called οἱ ἰσχυροί. For ἰσχυρός, see frgs. 7.2, 6; 10.9, and col. 22b5; Tab. IIIG.

[98] Lib. frg. 7.9–11, τῶι σκληρῶι χρήσεται τῆς παρρησίας εἴδει. See also frg. 91 Herc. (Gigante, Ricerche filodemee, 108–09); cols. 7b11–13; 11b10–12.

[99] Lib. frg. 83.7–10. Μαστιγόω is probably used here metaphorically for harsh criticism or castigation. Earlier in the fragment the student claims he will not fear the teacher. Fear, however, is paramount for successful correction—at least in the case of slaves: "For confidence breeds carelessness, slackness, disobedience: fear makes men more attentive, more obedient, more amenable to discipline" (Xen. Mem. 3.5.5).

[100] Lib. frg. 10.1–7.

φιλοτεχνία as ποικιλή, and in his reference to the μεικτὸς τρόπος in frg. 58.7–9.[101]

When Philodemus refers to the "simple" use of frank speech in fragment 10, he focuses on the appropriate mode of persuasion for recalcitrant and stubborn pupils.[102] The simple or plain use of frank speech is equivalent to "harsh frankness" and is not mixed with praise or gentler means of persuasion. The mixed or subtle use is employed when the erring one is addressed with both praise and blame. Such an approach yields to a more forthright approach in the case of those who are "exceedingly stubborn"; one must sometimes "take a risk in the case of those who will not listen otherwise."[103] The risk consists in the blunt approach which might become counterproductive. Or, when the passions are at their height, it might be ineffectual.

---

[101] In this I find myself in agreement with De Witt, who sees "ethical correction" as either "simple (ἁπλῆ, 10.4; 35.8), that is straightforward and direct, or mixed (μικτή, 58.7–8), that is, compounded of reproof, generous praise and exhortation (68.3–7)" ("Organization and Procedure," 209). In this I am at variance with Gigante's position in "Philodème: Sur la liberté de parole," *Association Guillaume Budé: Actes du VIII' Congrès* (Paris: Société d'Édition <Les Belles Lettres>, 1969) 208–09. Gigante correctly points out that the other occurrence of ἁπλῶς in frg. 35.8–9 does not support De Witt's position; it occurs in a completely different context and refers to someone who is "simply altogether accused" because of a transgression. In my view, the other three fragments, viz., frgs. 10, 58 and 68, support De Witt's position. In Gigante's view, frg. 58.7–8 (κατὰ μεικτὸν τρόπον διαπτ[ώ]σεως γενομέ[ν]ης) refers to the complexity of ways in which the sage can fail; he translates, "selon le genre mixte de l'erreur qui s'est produite." I, on the other hand, take the whole clause— οὐκ ὀλι<γ>άκις δὲ κατὰ μεικτὸν τρόπον διαπτ[ώ]σεως γενομέ[ν]ης—as dependent on παρρησιάσασθαι (πρὸς αὐτούς) in lines 5–6, and translate, "to speak frankly towards them, not seldom, but in a mixed manner when failure has occurred." I take διαπτ-[ώ]σεως γενομέ[ν]ης, therefore, as a genitive absolute. Such a reading, as well as frgs. 68 and 10, supports the contrast between a mixed and simple method of moral exhortation. Frg. 68 both refers to the varied nature of the good method (ποικίλης τε φ[ιλοτ]-εχνίας οὔσης) and to the fact that it is "mixed with bountiful praises" and exhortation. Frg. 10 refers to the "simple" application of frankness in case of the recalcitrant student. Gigante, however, takes it to refer to the conjectural nature of frankness and translates: "Cependant, il exercera parfois la liberté de parole sans 'art' (ἁ[πλ]ῶς). . . ."

[102] The matter addressed is a continuation of the one sounded in frg. 5.4–8, "It is possible to see from what has been said also how one ought to be frank with the one who violently resists frank speech." This is clear from the contrast in frg. 6.1–4 between frank speech and a more bitter approach, from the reference in 6.7–8 to "moderate censure," from the reference in 7.9–11 to a "harsh form of frank speech," and, finally, from the reference to "simple frankness" in 10.4–5. Col. 2b10–12 similarly notes that it is not necessary always to guide by [simple] frankness. This remark occurs after Philodemus' recognition of the legitimate use of harshness, which in this context is referred to by the analogy of wormwood. The term "simple" is contextually implied.

[103] *Lib.* frg. 10.5–9. The above reading of the "simple method" in frg. 10 is also supported by Philodemus' work *On Gratitude*, col. 15.14, ἁπλῶ λόγω.

But it is needed because of the condition of the recalcitrant students.

Those who violently resist frank speech and become easily irritated when criticized are like the "incurable ones" who are irredeemable because of their hostile attitude.[104] Philodemus, however, has a positive view of the human condition. Such a view is one of the main reasons why moralists advocated a gentle approach. This is also why Philodemus rejects the view of "some" in frg. 60, who maintained that not only those who are difficult to heal with frank speech but also the weak should be addressed with reviling. In Philodemus' view, there are no incurable ones, no faults which cannot be redeemed, although anger and ambition thwart one's progress. "Those making no progress" (ἀπρόβατοι) are unable to advance because "they refrain from participating in the common search of the good."[105] Without the assistance of others, the young remain "unexamined"; until a diagnosis is made which could provide a plausible means of correcting their faults, they remain untreated.[106] Although one might think on the basis of probable signs that a sick person will not be cured, the psychagogue will imitate physicians and exhort on the basis of reasonable, although uncertain, signs (69.4–10); an angry man frowns, a modest one blushes, at least in most cases! Angry persons do not make progress because they are "unable to put up with the teacher or their fellow students who reprove and correct them."[107] The reason why they cannot bear the reproving is explained by a medical analogy: "just as malignant ulcers cannot bear the use of soothing pharmacies."[108] A stronger dose of medicine is required. This is the backdrop against which to view fragments 5–10 of *On Frank Criticism*.

In Philodemus' view harsh censure (ἐπιτίμησις) can be applied when the sickness in question demands it, as in the case of recalcitrant students who violently resist frank criticism, and even then, only in moderation. Benevolent care can then include blame, the severity of which is contingent on the nature of the illness in question. The teachers use harsh remedies as wise doctors do when they correct the inappropriate use of the "biting frankness" of the young. The

---

[104] *Lib.* frg. 5; Plut. *De prof. virt.* 82A.

[105] *Ir.* col. 19.25–27, μήτε [τ]οῦ διὰ συζητήσεως μετέχειν ἀγαθοῦ.

[106] *Lib.* frg. 84.8–14, ἀθεράπευτοι. Cf. Gigante, *Ricerche filodemee*, 72.

[107] *Ir.* col. 19.12–17 Indelli.

[108] *Ir.* col. 19.17–21. For ἤπια φάρμακα, see Hom. *Il.* 4.218; 11.515. Philodemus compares angry people to epileptics (*Ir.* 9.21). See also Plut. *De coh. ira* 453E; 455C; and Sen. *Ir.* 3.10.3). Cf. Gigante, *Ricerche filodemee*, 100–01.

retaliatory nature of the young, therefore, must be harshly corrected.[109] But there is no discrepancy between fragments 59–60, which reject bitter frankness in the form of λοιδορία for the weak or those who might be thought to be "incurable," and fragments 6–10, which allow the use of ἐπιτίμησις, a harsher form of frank speech.[110] In the latter instance, the focus is on the recalcitrant students who violently resist frankness; in the former, on those whose commitments to the philosophic way of life are at risk because they either are weak or have not been able to benefit from the frank criticism of the sage. A bitter frank speech in the form of λοιδορία would simply destroy them.

A certain typology emerges of those critics of Philodemus who wanted to use a more forceful approach in the treatment of the weak and incurable ones. These critics, who are, in fact, the recalcitrant students, are compared to pretentious persons who do not recognize their own faults. With these Philodemus debates issues of harshness in moral exhortation. Interestingly, the description given of these students reveals that they themselves are like the "incurable ones"! Among the erring ones, the incurable have a hostile attitude and show a hot temper towards those who take them to task. They are contrasted with those who "patiently submit to admonition and welcome it" and disclose their depravity and do not "rejoice in hiding their faults or take satisfaction in its not being known, but confess it, and feel the need of somebody to take them in hand and admonish them"; but the one who "does not regret his error is incurable!"[111] They do not submit to or welcome admonition and resist when some of their fellow students or teachers criticize them; furthermore, they are not remorseful or grieved by their error, as they should be, and are not forthcoming with regard to their faults.[112]

The obstinacy of these students and the fact that they do not recognize their own sins obstruct the task of correctional psychagogy in the community. When rebuked, they think that they have not sinned or that their sins will not be detected. These pupils thus hide their sins and are not forthcoming, contrary to the ideal of openness expounded throughout the fragments.[113] When rebuked they are

---

[109] *Lib.* col. 17a. See Gigante, *Ricerche filodemee*, 86 n. 158.

[110] Λοιδορία might even be necessary in some instances. See Phld. *Ir.* col. 35.18–36.6; cf. 35.22–23, πολλάκις δὲ καὶ λοιδορητικὴ ψυχῆς εὐκινησίαι.

[111] Arist. *Eth. Nic.* 1150a23; 1137a29; 1165b18–23; Plut. *De prof. virt.* 82A.

[112] Phld. *Lib.* cols. 15a–21b; cf. 15a8–10; 16a10–12.

[113] *Lib.* cols. 15b7–14; 17a8–13; 18b13–14; 19b8–9. Cf. frgs. 41.4–10; 65.11–13; 66.13–15.

irritated and their sinful disposition and pretentiousness are exposed.[114] However, because of their desire for popularity, they do not benefit from frank criticism (cols. 17b6–9; 18b2–10). Because they think they are perfect, they are more willing to engage in frank criticism of others than to receive it. They even resent being frankly criticized by those whom they recognize as more knowledgeable and as leaders. They thus claim to be wise and mature enough to correct others, since "those who admonish others are called 'more knowledgeable' and 'wise'"!"[115] But those who think they need no correction, Philodemus charges, suffer from self-deception; they are "foolish" and not perfect at all, contrary to what they claim.[116] Harsh means are appropriate for these pretentious and recalcitrant students who do not repent or recognize their need for correction.

Participatory Psychagogy and the Ideal of Openness

Although Philodemus rejects the notion that some people are incurable, he concedes in his work *On Anger* that those who are full of anger and "refrain from participating in the common search of the good" make no progress. Without the assistance of others and until a diagnosis is made, which could provide a plausible explanation of the disease, the young remain untreatable. Anger thwarts the progress of people both because they do "not share in the good of joint inquiry" and because they are "unable to put up with the teacher and their fellow students who reprove and correct them."[117] Reformation of character thus requires an emotional change and the active participation of all. Correction of errors, a requisite for progress in wisdom, is part of character formation, which is achieved through mutual

---

[114] *Lib.* cols. 16b1–2, 6–7; 17a2–3; 18b7–10.

[115] *Lib.* col. 21b5–7. The reason why these students are more willing to engage in frank criticism than to receive it is because "they think that they are wiser than others" and "that the task of frank criticism belongs to them"; they, therefore, "reprove others who are slower" (col. 19a5–8). These students thus resent being frankly criticized even by those whom they acknowledge as more clever because they think that they are far superior in their understanding of what is best for the conduct of life; they concede, however, that the teachers are more clever in putting "questions into words" (col. 20a5–10).

[116] *Lib.* col. 10a6–10, τῶν ἀφρ[όνω]ν καὶ μ[ὴ] τελείων.

[117] *Ir.* col. 19.14–27 Indelli, ἀπροβάτους . . . τῶι μήτε καθηγητὰς ἀνέχεσθαι μήτε συσχολάζοντας, ἂν ἐπιτιμῶσι καὶ διορθῶσιν . . . μήτε [τ]οῦ διὰ συζητησέως μετέχειν ἀγαθοῦ.

correction and encouragement.[118] *On Frank Criticism* reveals a network of social relations in which participation of friends is presupposed in mutual edification, admonition, and correction.

The participatory nature of late Epicurean psychagogy is evident throughout the fragments. Fragment 45.1–6 says: "We will admonish others with great confidence, both now and when we have become prominent, the offshoots of our teachers." The "we," probably leaders in the school, admonish "others" both before and after having gained a visible position in the community. The "others" also emerge in fragment 61:

> [The guide] gives grief to the admonished one in a way unintelligible to his comrades. . . . [the pupil], however, does not feel the pain of [the teacher's] words if admonished by someone in a cheerful way. Sometimes the teacher does not realize that his success is fictitious, while it has often become obvious to the others.[119]

The reference in this fragment to the πέλας, ἄλλοι, and ἔνιοι is significant. These are the fellow students who assist in the teacher's correction.[120] The admonition delivered is no private affair. The presence of others is not only assumed but explicitly stated. The teacher may grieve the admonished one "in a way unintelligible to others near him."[121] These fellow students do not understand the reason for the teacher's admonition. On occasion, Philodemus rejects the harshness of "some" of the students (cols. 7b1; 17ab); here the ἔνιοι, on the other hand, know how to admonish correctly. The admonished one does not suffer counterproductive pain if admonished by someone in a calm and cheerful way. The purpose of the teacher's admonition is to inflict grief which engenders repentance, but he should be careful so that the erring one is not overcome by grief.[122] "Others" who are present alleviate the distress caused by the teacher by

---

[118] Reformation of character is described as "turning the reason around." *Lib.* frg. 13.7–8, τὴν διάνοιαν ἀποστρέφεσθαι; frg. 22; col. 14b9–11.

[119] *Lib.* frg. 61.1–10. I follow here the textual emendation of Gigante for line 4: .α.καὶ μεδ<ἐν> ἂν ἱλαρῶς ἐνίοις. Cf. *Ricerche filodemee*, 81–83.

[120] I.e. οἱ συσχολάζοντες and οἱ συνήθεις. The following lines draw a contrast between the καθηγούμενος and the ἄλλοι, confirming that the ἄλλοι are identical to the πέλας and ἔνιοι. Philodemus refers to the ἔνιοι throughout the treatise: frgs. 26.11; 48.4; 53.10; 70.8; 77.1; 81.4; cols. 7b1; 8b4; 14b8 and 17b13.

[121] Ἀγνώστως τοῖς πέλας. For οἱ πέλας, see *SV* 67 and PHerc. 1457, col. 10.

[122] He who uses frank speech without becoming angry and devotes himself to the erring one with goodwill, gives little pain but heals greatly; *Lib.* frgs. 2.1–7; 53.10–13; 38.1–6; 86.7–8.

attending to and correctly admonishing the one who was inconsiderately admonished. The teacher's success should not be "wrapped in
doubt," but clear and obvious (61.6–12). It is authentic only if it
is obvious to others too; other members are an integral part of the
process.

The teacher is thus not the only one in a position to examine
others who find it difficult to disclose their faults. Some are therapeutically treated, gently and with ease, and without the teacher's
knowledge, by those who have shared their experience.[123] Other
members are sometimes in a better position to discover their fellow
students' mistakes. Then they should either correct them or report
them to the teachers, just like Polyaenus, who reported Apollonides'
status to Epicurus when the student was losing his ardor for his pursuit
of Epicureanism (49.7–10). It is not difficult to imagine that such a
reporting of misdemeanors might be looked on unfavorably by the
erring ones and that students might refrain from engaging in such a
practice: "Most people restrain themselves from accusing, so that they
themselves be not slandered, who criticize others who think badly"
(51.5–10). Because of this reluctance, Philodemus has to explain pre-
emptively (50.3–10):

> For if a person desires his friend to attain correction, he [sc. Epicurus]
> will not consider him a slanderer, when he is not this sort of person,
> but one who loves his friend: for he knows the difference well between
> these two sorts of people.

The fragment continues, noting that one who does not report the
errors of his fellow students is mean to his friend and a lover of evil!
This contrasts sharply with the description of the teacher as cheerful
and gentle, one who loves his friend.[124] But reporting of errors should
not go too far: "And we do not run to the teachers in order to
appear to show them goodwill, by reporting what one said or did
against them, and against one's intimate fellows" (52.6–12). The pupils
should rather behave with loyalty towards their fellow students and
not run to the teachers as adulators and slanderers. The students
refuse to be brutal toward those who do not confess their mistakes,

---

[123] Frg. 8.4–11. The "young" thus assist in the admonitory practices of the confraternity. Col. 17a shows that the young themselves fail in their exhortation. The
young have a tendency to use bitter frankness when they admonish. This needs to
be corrected by a surgical operation.
[124] Frgs. 50.10–12 (κ[ακό]φιλον καὶ φιλόκακον) and 85.7–9 (ὁ [κ]αθηγούμενος
ε[ὐη]μέρωι καὶ φιλοφίλωι [καὶ ἡ]πίωι . . .).

giving "measure for measure" (52.1–3); instead of accusing and being brutal with fellow students, we should rather, Philodemus advises, "become accusers of ourselves, if we err in any respect" (51.2–5).

Philodemus, similar to Diogenes of Oenoanda's description of the purpose of his colonnade two centuries later, speaks in salvific terms of the reciprocal practice of benefiting each other. The students perceive their sins together in order to gain salvation; they "support" and "save each other."[125] They can accomplish this because they have the "strength to bear easily and have as support a grand goodwill" (36.2). Frankness also "strengthens the reciprocal goodwill of those in preparation."[126] One of the means, therefore, of attaining progress, besides self-correction (52.2–5), is reciprocal and consists in benevolent help from both leaders and fellow students: "that he himself may be able to be therapeutically treated, either by us or by another of the fellow students" (79.1–4).

Four dimensions of Epicurean correctional practice are evident. The first involves self-correction; the second is when a correction is administered by "others"; the third is when members report errors to the teachers for them to correct; and the fourth is when the wise correct each other. The question whether the wise will also change each other with frank speech (col. 3a3–5) thus receives an affirmative answer. "If, then, the wise men know each other, they will be reminded gladly by one another in the ways we have described, as [they are reminded] by themselves, and will feel the most gentle sting and will be grateful" (cols. 8b6–13). The wise remind each other when they reason fraudulently because of great weakness or because of the unpleasantness of the toils that have befallen them. The wise

---

[125] See Epicur. frg. 522 Us., on gaining salvation. Phld. *Lib.* frgs. 1; 36.1–2, καὶ τὸ δ[ι' ἀλ]λήλων σώ<ι>ζεσθαι. For other instances of σώζειν, see frgs. 34.3; 78.6; and col. 6b3, which speaks of a person who has been "saved" by frank criticism. For σωτήρ, see frg. 40.8, and for σωτηρία, see frg. 4.9; T. II D2 (App.). See Diog. Oen., frgs. 1 and 2, "I wished by making use of this colonnade to set forth in public the remedies which bring salvation, remedies of which I would say in a word that all kinds have been revealed" (frg. 2, V–VI Chilton, τὰ τῆς σωτηρίας φάρμακα). The preceding translation is that of C. W. Chilton, *Diogenes of Oenoanda: The Fragments* (London and New York: Oxford University Press [for the University of Hull], 1971) 4.

[126] *Lib.* frg. 79.2–4 Herc. See also frg. 25.3–8. Cf. Gigante, *Ricerche filodemee,* 101–02. Philodemus' treatise *On Gratitude* (PHerc. 1414; cf. cols. 10 and 16) reveals that goodwill and gratitude for benevolent help are basic to the Philodemean ideal of mutual psychagogy and friendship. See A. Tepedino Guerra, "Filodemo sulla gratitudine," *CErc* 7 (1977) 96–113.

heighten the awareness they have of each other's presence and progress and increase the cohesiveness of their relationship by mutual correction and confession of faults (col. 9a1–8). The topic itself, "Whether the wise man will candidly refer his own affairs to his friends?" is significant, since it signals, if a negative response is given, a practice contrary to the one advocated. One could sharpen the question by asking, should the mature continue to participate in the communal practice of openness? The answer is yes, and it is important for our conceptualization of the relationships advocated as part of the Epicurean fellowship. Mature members should not disassociate themselves from others less mature. On the contrary, the wise are advised to be forthcoming to those in preparation "for the sake of their restoration" (55.5–6).

Besides the frank and friendly correction of faults among the friends of the community, *On Frank Criticism* reflects an ideal of non-concealment. Participatory psychagogy indeed requires a forthcoming attitude, necessary for successful diagnosis. Through confession, errors are brought out into the open for critique and correction. In such a practice we witness the Epicurean response to Stoic pedagogy which, so the charge went, was indirect instead of plainly speaking the truth. Indirection, instead of disclosing the truth, closed it up even further.[127] Philodemus uses medical imagery to emphasize the importance of openness. The pupil is encouraged to follow the example of medicine and put himself entirely in the power of the doctor. He must "give (himself) over to" and "put (himself) into the hands of the teacher." He must, says Philodemus, "throw (himself), so to speak, into the hand of the leaders and depend on them alone" (frg. 39.2–4).

> The pupil must show him his failings without concealment and tell his defects in the open. For if he considers him the one guide of correct speech and deed, the one whom he calls the only savior and to whom, saying 'with him at my side,' he gives himself over to be therapeuti-

---

[127] See M. T. Riley, "The Epicurean Criticism of Socrates," *Phoenix* 34 (1980) 67–68, on the rejection of Socrates' philosophical style. For Epicurean practice, see P. Rabbow, *Seelenführung: Methodik der Exerzitien in der Antike* (München: Kösel, 1954) 260–79. See also K. Kleve, "Scurra Atticus: The Epicurean View of Socrates," Συζήτησις: *Studi sull'epicureismo greco e romano offerti a Marcello Gigante* (2 vols.; Naples: Gaetano Macchiaroli, 1983) 1.227–53, and A. A. Long, "Socrates in Hellenistic Philosophy," *CQ* n.s. 38 (1988) 150–71. According to Plut. *Adv. Colotem* 1117D, Colotes charged that Socrates' arguments were ἀλαζόνες or charlatans. In his discussion of forcible diction, Demetrius contrasts cross-examination with plain teaching (σαφῶς διδάσκοντι ἔοικε καὶ οὐκ ἐλέγχοντι). See *Eloc.* 5.279.

cally treated, then how could he not show the things in which he requires
therapeutic treatment, and receive his criticism?[128]

In order to gain legitimacy for such a practice, Philodemus focuses
on Heracleides' "confession," which was praised by Epicurus. Heracleides was forthcoming

> because he thought the censures he would receive on account of what
> he revealed were less important than their benefits; and so he disclosed
> his errors to Epicurus.[129]

The student's basic fear was that his openness would evoke an even
sharper critique than if he concealed his faults. In light of the perceived tendency of the age to speak ill of others and expose their
shortcomings, this concern is understandable.[130] How far should one
go in revealing one's secrets? This question is put forward in light of
a basic vulnerability and distrust of others. It was feared that the
information disclosed might prove disgraceful.[131] Some of the setbacks
and a critique of such a forthrightness are detailed in Dio Chrysostom's
discourses *On Trust* and *On Distrust*, in Plutarch's *Concerning Talkative-
ness* and *On Curiosity*, as well as in Epictetus' *That One should Enter
Cautiously into Social Intercourse* and *To Those Who Lightly Talk About Their
Own Affairs*.[132] The issues raised by these authors were particularly

---

[128] *Lib.* frg. 40. Transl. by M. C. Nussbaum, "Therapeutic Arguments: Epicurus
and Aristotle," *The Norms of Nature: Studies in Hellenistic Ethics* (ed. M. Schofield and
G. Striker; Cambridge: Cambridge University Press, 1986) 49. See *Ir.* col. 4.4–23
Indelli. M. Gigante has also recognized the connection between the need for openness and correct diagnosis; see his "'Philosophia medicans' in Filodemo," *CErc* 5
(1975) 52, 57. Note De Witt's remark: "Lastly, the leaders were genuine psychia-
trists, engaged in purifying men of their faults just as the physician purified their
bodies of disease" ("Organization and Procedure," 211).

[129] Phld. *Lib.* frg. 49.2–7. For Heracleides' "confession," Philodemus uses the term
μηνύω, "to reveal" or "disclose what is secret." For Epicurean confessional practice,
see S. Sudhaus, "Epikur als Beichtvater," *ARW* 14 (1911) 647–48, and W. Schmid,
"Contritio und 'ultima linea rerum' in neuen epikureischen Texten," *RhM* N. F.
100 (1957) 301–14, and "Epikur," *RAC* 5 (1962) cols. 741–43.

[130] Cf. Plut. *De cur.* 521E; Ath. 5.220a; Epict. *Diss.* 1.18.10. See also Isoc. *To
Nicocles* 47; *Antidosis* 147–48.

[131] The flatterer successfully uses openness; in an attempt to strengthen "fellow
feeling" he brings out into the open even "innermost secrets" (ἀπόρρητα). If he, for
example, knows that the flattered one is unfortunate in his marriage or suspicious
towards his household, he divulges certain secret faults of his in similar matters.
This makes their fellow-feeling stronger, which leads the flattered one to disclose
some of his own secrets. Then he is afraid to abandon the confidential relation.
Plut. *Adulator* 53F–54A. For ἀπόρρητα, see PHerc. 1089, col. 5.6–7. Cf. Acosta Méndez,
"PHerc. 1089," 134.

[132] Dio Chrys. *Or.* 73 and 74; Plut. *Mor.* 502B–515A and 515B–523B; Epict. *Diss.*
3.16 and 4.13.

pressing in light of Epicurean communal psychagogy, especially so if we are correct in assuming that members were people of unequal power and status. Intimate acquaintanceship, a constitutive part of the Epicurean ideal of fellowship, was the guarantee and basis of their friendly relations and allowed the friends to be forthright with each other in spite of attendant dangers.

The handbook thus encourages the friends, in spite of attendant dangers, not to hold back but to reveal their faults and innermost secrets to others. The benefits of such an openness outweigh any conceivable setback. By bringing errors into the open they no longer remain hidden and can be corrected.[133] Openness is encouraged, concealment discouraged. "To act in secret is doubtless most un-friendly; the one who does not bring everything out into the open will be hiding these from the most excellent of friends."[134] Philodemus relates that "many (most) of the intimate associates will spontane-ously disclose what is secret, without the teacher examining closely with concern and in detail" (frg. 42), subtly bringing home the point that not all are forthcoming. Then the teacher has to investigate or closely examine the one who is reluctant to disclose his errors or be otherwise forthcoming. In such an investigation:

> He will (should) become attached to a person's character. And, if he attaches himself to those of a noble character, why not also to those of a wicked character? (He will dedicate himself to the character of each person), to the noble on account of cheerfulness, and to the wicked because of sympathy, on account of which we receive aid (frg. 43.1–8).

The forthcoming attitude advocated is said to be one of the finest things coming out of friendship:

> while many fine things come out of friendship, none of them is as great as having someone to whom one may discuss what is in one's heart, and to whom one can listen when he does the same. For nature intensely desires to disclose what one thinks to others (frg. 28.1–10).

---

[133] Cf. Epicur. frg. 522 Us., "... initium est salutis notitia peccati." See Sen. Ep. 97.15–16 = frg. 531 Us. See also Plut. De prof. virt. 82AB. The "young" are advised not to hide their errors but to entrust them to the teacher. If they confess their mistakes, the teacher will give them an attentive ear. Phld. Lib. frgs. 28; 51.1 (ἀκ[ού]σει μᾶλλον); 79.9 Herc.

[134] Phld. Lib. frg. 41.2–8. The "most excellent of friends" is the wise teacher. On Epicurus (PHerc. 1232 fr. 9, col. I 8f. ed. Vogliano, p. 72) refers to Epicurus as ἐ]ξοχώτατον λαμβά[νειν τοῦτ]ο τἀνδρός; see F. Longo Auricchio, "La scuola di Epicuro," CErc 8 (1978) 24.

This fragment emphasizes the intimacy of friendship without accentuating the security resulting from it. But such openness is instrumental for correct diagnosis and shows the intricate connection of friendship with its attendant benefits. Friendship is then valued both as a means to an end and for itself, as part of the end.[135]

As Philodemus discusses reputable occupations in his *On Household Management*, he not only advocates occupations which secure the leisure to be in the company of friends and enjoy the Epicurean way of life, but he also underscores the importance of friendship. Sharing one's income with friends is essential to its acquisition and preservation; caring for friends and others is more profitable than caring for one's fields, and friends are "the safest treasures with respect to fortune." People should gratify both themselves and their friends in prosperity, but in times of need people should even put the needs of their friends above their own. In both prosperity and adversity one should consult with one's friends before reaching a decision. Friends are so important that one must make sure that they will be provided for upon one's death, just like one's own children. Epicureans thus form a mutual support and relief group for all members in case of death.[136] Here Philodemus underscores the physical benefits accruing

---

[135] Pl. *Resp.* 2.357. Cf. A. A. Long, "Pleasure and Social Utility—The Virtues of Being Epicurean," *Aspects de la philosophie hellénistique* (ed. H. Flashar and O. Gigon; Entretiens sur l'Antiquité classique 32; Geneva: Foundation Hardt, 1986) 305–06 n. 22. According to Cicero, three views on friendship were in vogue among Epicureans. The first underscores the importance of pleasure in friendship but recognizes also an altruistic element; the second emphasizes pleasure and utility as the original impulse towards friendship, which later grows into intimacy and love for the friend's own sake; and the third holds that men have made a sort of compact to love their friends no less than themselves (*Fin.* 1.66–70, 78–85). The identification of the second view with that held by Siro and Philodemus was made by R. Hirzel, *Untersuchungen zu Cicero's philosophischen Schriften* (3 vols. in 4; Leipzig: S. Hirzel, 1877–83) 1.170ff.; cf. W. Brinckmann, *Der Begriff der Freundschaft in Senecas Briefen* (Diss. Köln; Köln: Gouder und Hansen, 1963) 17. The apparent tension between those sayings of Epicurus which claim that only one's own pleasure is desirable for itself and those which suggest an altruistic concern for others' interests is not evident in Philodemus; we find rather a tension due to the spatial and psychological closeness of friends in mutual psychagogy, manifest in bursts of anger and partiality towards others, countered through a recurrent warning against anger and contempt in *On Frank Criticism*. For the above tension see *SV* 23, Cic. *Fin.* 1.68, and P. Mitsis, *Epicurus' Ethical Theory: The Pleasures of Invulnerability* (Ithaca: Cornell University Press, 1988) 100–01. For a critique, see D. K. O'Connor, "The Invulnerable Pleasures of Epicurean Friendship," *GRBS* 30 (1989) 182–84.

[136] *Oec.* cols. 24.19–25.4; 26.1–14; 26.18–28; 27.6–9; *Mort.* cols. 23.2–15; 35.24–34; 37.23–25, 27–29; 39.1–25. See Asmis, "Philodemus' Epicureanism," 2389–90. The Epicurean fellowship thus was concerned with both spiritual and physical well-being.

from friendship; but Epicurean friends were also concerned with each other's spiritual well-being, as is evident from the intimacy of their friendship and the forthrightness advocated for members in the community.

Some of Epicurus' sayings on friendship and justice can be seen as a precipitating cause for later Epicurean emphasis on openness.[137] These sayings emphasize the negative aspect of concealment, the mutual pledge of not harming, mutual noninterference, compacts of mutual help, as well as the ἀσφάλεια and πίστις of friendship and the attendant mental relief.[138] Although fear of other humans is not encapsulated in "the fourfold remedy" ("God presents no fears, death no worries. And while good is readily attainable, evil is readily endurable"), such fear was, alongside fear of the gods and death, considered a threat against human security and thus needed to be combatted like the other fears.[139] Fear of other humans was attacked by a preemptive strike, so to speak: by maintaining an open attitude designed to deflate any signs of hostility. *On Frank Criticism* is our prime evidence for such an activity. Therefore, frank speech was considered necessary when combating fear of death and the gods as well as fear of other humans.

One should try by any means whatsoever to procure security from threats posed by others. Becoming renowned is a wrong way to obtain such security; a more secure route is a quiet life withdrawn from the multitude in the company of friends.[140] One can never attain such security if one is still alarmed by unexplained natural phenomena.[141] Some of Epicurus' sayings emphasizing the need for a communal pledge not to harm others do accentuate threats of physical damage,

---

Lib. frg. 4.4–10 gives evidence for a physical support system among the Epicureans. For concerns with the spiritual well-being of members, see below.

[137] P. Mitsis (*Epicurus' Ethical Theory*, 109–10 n. 22) speculates that ambiguities of *amicitia* might have facilitated a later conflation of Epicurus' theories of justice and friendship. For the former, see R. Philippson, "Die Rechtsphilosophie der Epikureer," *AGPh* 23 (1910) 433–46.

[138] Epicur. *SV* 7, 23, 34, 61, 66, 70; *RS* 6, 7, 13, 14, 17, 28, 29, 31–35, 39, 40; Lucr. 2.16ff.; 3.37ff.; 5.1020–26; Cic. *Fin.* 1.68.

[139] Phld. *Adv. [soph].* col. 4.10–14 Sbordone; see the discussion by F. Sbordone, "Il quadrifarmaco epicureo," *CErc* 13 (1983) 117–19.

[140] On the company of friends in retreat, see Phld. *Oec.* col. 23.11–18.

[141] See Epicur. *RS* 6, 7, 13, 14 (ἡ ἐκ τῆς ἡσυχίας καὶ ἐκχωρήσεως τῶν πολλῶν ἀσφάλεια); 27, 38, 39, and 40, and *SV* 34 and 61. For ordinary fear, the object of which is clearly apprehended and which represents a real threat to safety, contrasted with "unexplained" fear with respect to something vague, resulting in a sense of alarm, see D. Konstan, *Some Aspects of Epicurean Psychology* (Leiden: Brill, 1973) 16–18.

but it would be a mistake to empty such a security of all psychological significance. The Epicurean fellowship also aims at the alleviation of mental disturbances. *Vatican Sentences* 34 and 61 underscore this psychological security. What really helps us when we are assisted by our friends is not so much our friends' help but rather "the confidence of their help."[142] Help is to be expected from friendship; indeed, all friendship, although "choiceworthy for itself, has its beginning in utility."[143] Epicureans were confident that they could depend on each other for assistance. Trust between members remained an ideal; openness was a virtue, concealment a sin. If a friend did not participate in communal correction, he aroused distrust; and if someone proved unfaithful, the lives of his friends were confounded.[144]

Some of Epicurus' sayings also draw attention to the intimacy of a fellowship. According to *SV* 61, "the most beautiful too is the sight of those near and dear to us, when our original kinship makes us of one mind; for such sight is a great incitement to this end."[145] The closeness between friends required by the practice of openness is then congruent with an ideal voiced by Epicurus. The *Letter to Menoeceus* concludes with an exhortation to study its contents "night and day by yourself and with someone like you"; conversations and mutual contemplation are also central elements of divine friendship according to Philodemus.[146] Such evidence not only confirms a group study approach—also clearly indicated by the communal practices I have documented—but also accentuates the form and content of the friends' likeness. A φιλὸς ὅμοιος is one who participates in shared pursuits;

---

[142] Epicur. *SV* 34, πίστεως τῆς περὶ τῆς χρείας.

[143] *SV* 39 and 23, Πᾶσα φιλία δι᾽ ἑαυτὴν αἱρετή· ἀρχὴν δ᾽ εἴληφεν ἀπὸ τῆς ὠφελείας.

[144] Phld. *Lib.* frg. 1; Epicur. *SV* 56–57. Diogenes Laertius' statement (εἰ δ᾽ ἀπίστων οὐδὲ φίλων), even though noting Epicurus' disagreement with the Pythagorean maxim κοινὰ τὰ φίλων, captures the importance of trust in Epicurean friendship, which required mutual mental support and relief. According to Diogenes, the reason why Epicurus did not think that property should be held in common was that "such practice... implied mistrust" (10.11).

[145] Epicur. *SV* 61 and 18, "Remove sight, association and contact, and the passion of love is at an end."

[146] A. A. Long and D. N. Sedley, *The Hellenistic Philosophers* (2 vols.; Cambridge: Cambridge University Press, 1987–89) 1.144; Phld. *D.* 3, frg. 84, col. 13,36–39,36 Diels. Such sentiments were ascribed by E. Zeller to Epicurus' "effeminacy" and the need for Epicurean friends to ground the truth of their convictions in mutual approval; see his *Die Philosophie der Griechen in ihrer geschichtlichen Entwicklung* (6 vols.; Leipzig: Reisland, 1903–22) 3.1.467, and *The Stoics, Epicureans and Sceptics* (New York: Russell & Russell, 1879) 495. Cf. Mitsis, *Epicurus' Ethical Theory*, 123 n. 49. See Diog. Laert. 10.5, 135.

his "likeness" is not predicated on his character traits but on a shared activity and a common way of life, on "likeness of pursuits" (ὁμοιότης ἐπιτηδευμάτων).

The Friendship of Many in Philodemus

Most of the information in *On Frank Criticism* is practical; we must, however, ask ourselves what possible implications the practice of communal psychagogy has in light of some more systematic discussions of friendship. Perhaps we should allow Cicero's contrasting of Epicurean practice with their tenets to guide our reconstruction. Cicero implies that Epicureans valued the common friendship of the many; he does so both when he contrasts their friendship with that between eulogized pairs of friends and when he lambastes the Epicurean and Cyraenaic friendship based on weakness and need.[147] Cicero's emphasis would seem to be in tune with known Epicurean recruitment practices.[148] The apparent ease with which recruits joined the Epicurean groups of friends has implications for the view of friendship valued. An associational type of friendship is less strict in the screening process than a contractual type, which typically gives more formal expression to the mutual obligations of friendship. Later Epicurean willingness to accept new friends flies in the face of Epicurus' own

---

[147] Cic. *Amic.* 45–47, 51–52. After having referred to legends of pairs of friends, to which he adds Scipio and Laelius, Cicero says: "Yet Epicurus in a single house and that a small one maintained a whole company of friends, united by the closest sympathy and affection; and this still goes on in the Epicurean school" (*Fin.* 1.65, trans. by H. Rackham in the LCL; cf. Sen. *Ep.* 6.6). Later Cicero, again after a reference to eulogized pairs of steadfast friends (Phintias and Damon, and Pylades and Orestes), charges that Epicurean tenets on expediency and pleasure undermine the very foundations of friendship, and to the interlocutor's remarks ("But Epicurus himself had many friends" and "But he won many disciples") he replies that the witness of the crowd does not carry much weight and "the fact that Epicurus himself was a good man and that many Epicureans both have been and today are loyal to their friends ... [serves only to] enforce the value of moral goodness and diminish that of pleasure ... these people's deeds ... seem to be better than their words" (*Fin.* 2.80–81, trans. by H. Rackham in the LCL). The interlocutor's objection is only meaningful if he and those he represents valued the friendship of many. Cicero's reference to the "multitude" and Epicurean practice suggests the same. See Phld. *Rh.* 1.267, col. 30.34ff. Sudhaus, "they assist the young and offer many people many services and have many and noble friends."

[148] B. Frischer, *The Sculpted Word*, has argued for passive Epicurean recruitment. For a critique, see D. D. Obbink, "POxy. 215 and Epicurean Religious θεωρία," *Atti del XVII Congresso internazionale di papirologia* (3 vols.; Naples: Centro internaz. per lo stud. dei papiri. ercol., 1984) 2.607–19. Compare Epict. *Diss.* 3.23.27.

stricture against such a practice.[149] The fault, however, lies in the open-ended nature of the fellowship, which, because its obligations were not primarily to the *polis*, could admit both slaves and women.[150] In my view, we can explicate both the Epicurean willingness to accept friends without a screening process and the correctional aspects of their psychagogy in light of discussions of the friendship of many. No character or nobility test had to be passed before individuals could join the community of friends. Character formation became an intramural affair among the Epicureans.

Such contingencies of life as time, or rather the lack of it, to form friendship on the basis of permanency of character and likeness of virtue, precluded the possibility of having many friends.[151] Both the friend of many and the flatterer display the abhorred features of the versatile, pliant, and readily changeable person, which a period of testing should eradicate.[152] Such "negative" features should be confronted by screening the prospective friend. The importance of testing a person's character before friendship was proffered was a recurring theme among writers on friendship, who often noted the Theophrastean maxim—οὐ φιλοῦντα δεῖ κρίνειν, ἀλλὰ κρίναντα φιλεῖν.[153] A similar maxim was that of Cleitarchus, "Do not be rash to make friends and, when once they are made, do not drop them."[154] A nobility test is emphasized by those who value friendship of

---

[149] Epicur. *SV* 28, "We must not approve either those who are always ready for friendship, or those who hang back, but for friendship's sake we must even run risks." The preceding translation is that of Cyril Bailey, *Epicurus: The Extant Remains* (Oxford: Clarendon, 1926) 111.

[150] A.-J. Festugière, *Epicurus and his Gods* (Oxford: Blackwell, 1955) 29–30; J. M. Rist, "Epicurus on Friendship," *CP* 75 (1980) 127; D. Clay, "The Cults of Epicurus," 24 n. 15.

[151] Ath. 6.255c, flattery is "a short-lived profession"; Max. Tyr. *Or.* 14.6, "Friendship is increased, flattery confuted, by time" (177,19–22 Hobein).

[152] A man of many friends resembles promiscuous women whose friendship has been split up into a multitude of loyalties (Lucian, *Tox.* 37; Plut. *De am. mult.* 93C; *Adulator* 59F). It is no coincidence that the flatterer is introduced after Cicero's discussion of the Theophrastean precept and his treatment of steadfast friendship, or that Plutarch contrasts the polypic character of the friend of many with the reliable friend. See Cicero, *Amic.* 85–86 and 88–95/100, respectively; Plut. *De am. mult.* 96–97.

[153] Theophr. frg. 74, p. 181, ed. Wimmer. Cic. *Amic.* 85; Sen. *Ep.* 3.2; 9.6; *Ben.* 2.2.1; Plut. *De frat. amor.* 482B; *Adulator* 49D; *De am. mult.* 94B; Diog. Laert. 1.60; Max. Tyr. *Or.* 20.3; Them. *Or.* 327D; Stob. *Flor.* 4, p. 659, ed. Hense; Heylbut, *Theophrast.*, 22–24; Bohnenblust, *Beiträge*, 32–34; Brinckmann, *Freundschaft in Senecas Briefen*, 23–24, 34. Cf. Sir 6:7–17.

[154] This is referred to as a saying of Solon in Diog. Laert. 1.60; cf. *Clitarchi sent.* 88f. (ed. Elter), μὴ ταχέως τοὺς φίλους κτῶ. οὓς ἂν κτήσῃ φίλους τήρει.

character. Such "perfect friendship" is based on similarity of character, found among noble and virtuous men.[155] An underlying issue in the friendship of many is the question of association and what criteria should be established as boundary markers of association. What are the criteria adhered to in selecting a friend? Epicureans of late Republican times rejected virtue as a prerequisite for the establishment of friendship. They were instead willing to befriend noble and base, men and women, slaves and free, thus establishing a community of friends which cut across other recognized forms of individual and group boundaries.[156]

The friendship attacked by Cicero places more value on mutual aid and expediency than on intimacy. Those least endowed with firmness of character and strength of body have the greatest longing for such friendship; and "helpless women more than men, seek its shelter, the poor more than the rich, and the unfortunate more than those who are accounted fortunate."[157] Cicero's disgust with this "noble philosophy" is apparent, notwithstanding his defensive remark that virtue is not unfeeling, unwilling to serve, or proudly exclusive.[158] The watered-down friendship of many is clearly less preferable to him than character friendship. We ought, he says, to put the disposition of prospective friends "as we do those of horses, to a preliminary test."[159] One should love one's friend after having appraised him and not appraise him after having begun to love him. Cicero, to be sure, sides with the middle Stoic position that no one has ever become "wise," adapts the word "virtue" to the standards of everyday life, and recognizes that the terms "friend" and "human" can be coextensive;[160] yet his views still fall within the ideal of true friend-

---

[155] Stob. *Flor.* 2.33.7 W., ὅτι ἡ ὁμοιότης τῶν τρόπων φιλίαν ἀπεργάζεται. See Diog. Laert. 7.124, noting Zeno's views.

[156] Plut. *Alc.* 23.4; Phld. *Lib.* frg. 43. This squares well with the view that members of the Epicurean movement were at this time largely recruited from the lower classes of Rome and Italy. Cf. T. Maslowski, "The Chronology of Cicero's Anti-Epicureanism," *Eos* 62 (1974) 75–76; H. Jones, *The Epicurean Tradition*, 69–70.

[157] Cic. *Amic.* 13.46–47; 15.52.

[158] Cic. *Amic.* 5.19; 9.32; 13.48; 14.50–51. Cf. 46–51 and 8–9, 26–32. For the views of Aristippus of Cyrene on friendship, see Diog. Laert. 2.91–93.

[159] Cic. *Amic.* 17.62–63. Cf. also 18.65; 22.85.

[160] Although the term "friendship" can be applied to a relationship among the many, such as that which exists among fellow countrymen or relatives, such relationships are inconstant and not destroyed if goodwill is eliminated from them, something which is unthinkable in true friendship (cf. Sen. *Ep.* 48.1–4; 47.1, 15–19). Although it is true in one sense that the terms "friend" and "human being" are coextensive in Stoicism, the Stoics' actual practice and their emphasis on aristo-

ship among aristocratic males, equal in virtue and aspiration.[161] According to this ideal, self-sufficiency and virtue are requisite for friendship and constitute the point of attraction in the beloved.[162] Affectionate bonds unite two persons only, or, at most, a few good men.

It can be demonstrated, on the one hand, that the Latin-speaking contributors to the spread of Epicureanism in Italy were more successful than their Greek counterparts and that members of the Epicurean movement were at this time largely recruited from the lower classes; Cicero, at any rate, critiques the "unsophisticated" audience of the former.[163] Philodemus' *On Frank Criticism*, on the other hand, reflects the presence of individuals of different social status and power.[164] Philodemus also shows that he, in spite of his relationship with Piso, has faith in common, ordinary people. He emphasizes the commonality of all, recognizing that all humans are subject to the weaknesses of anger and favoritism and that all are accustomed to err and in need of correction; furthermore, he insists that when correcting others, one should without distinction attach oneself to the person's character, be it noble or base.[165] As one might expect, Philodemus also places all humans on the same level in his work *On Death*: all inhabit a city that is unfortified against death; everyone is ephemeral, like vessels of glass and clay that will not remain unbroken. Philodemus also makes clear, although he cites illustrious

---

cratic and moral friendship suggest that they did not—in spite of evidence to the contrary (Diog. Laert. 7.124 = *SVF* 3.161 [§631])—value the friendship of many. For criticism of the practice of having many friends, see esp. Plut. *De am. mult.*

[161] Cf. Cic. *Amic.* 5.18–20; 6.21ff. Although Cicero (or Panaetius) discusses "ordinary or vulgar friendships" (21.76–26.100) and lightens the rigorism of the older Stoics (Brinckmann, *Freundschaft in Senecas Briefen*, 21, 26), the qualification in the text is needed. Women, although influential in Roman society, were classed with the weak and unfortunate (*Amic.* 46).

[162] Cicero loved Africanus "because of a certain admiration for his virtue"; see *Amic.* 8.28; 9.30,32; 13.48; 14.48–51; 17.61. He also uses the traditional motif of "friendship is likeness" (14.50).

[163] Cic. *Acad.* 1.5; *Tusc.* 4.7; *Fam.* 15.19.2.

[164] One of the questions *On Frank Criticism* asks is why eminent persons are more resentful of criticism than others (col. 22b10–24a6). Col. 7a8–10 notes that eminent men and common people must be admonished differently. The "great man who is coming to philosophy" in col. 14a6–10 is probably Piso. Those particularly resentful of frank criticism include politicians, famous people, women, and old people. It is clear from col. 22a–b that women are part of the community and are, in this context, classified with the weak students. Women are also referred to in col. 6a, which lists different types of students. Col. 12a5–6 refers to slaves. Women were also part of the Epicurean community at Athens. See C. J. Castner, "Epicurean Hetairai as Dedicants to Healing Divinities," *GRBS* 23 (1982) 51–57.

[165] Phld. *Ir.* col. 43.14–41; *Lib.* frgs. 46 and 43.

examples in his work *On Death*, that the same values belong to the humble. Some ordinary people also bear the yoke of an unjust condemnation no less courageously than some famous men; even many ordinary people have friends who care about them.[166]

Aristotle said that if it is possible to live with and share the perceptions of many at once, it is desirable that they should be the largest number possible; however, as that is very difficult, active community of perception must of necessity be in a smaller circle.[167] Such community of perception is expanded in Epicurean psychagogy where errors are communally perceived.[168] The friends openly confess and correct each other's shortcomings. Such correction is subsequent to the establishment of friendship, not antecedent as required by the Theophrastean maxim. The reason for this is twofold. First, a non-rigid recruitment criterion is operative. Second, a common and indiscriminate or "vulgar" friendship with the many is valued.[169]

The friendship of many means that individuals of different characters and social statuses could join the Epicurean groups of friends. In general, it holds true for most writers on friendship—Plato's intricacies in his *Lysis* notwithstanding—that the friendship of unlikeness is the kind whose basis is profit. The friendship of likeness is the friendship of the good and morally upright, whereas the friendship of unlikeness is the friendship of the pliant flatterer and the friend of many and of the base. Therefore, although virtue is not unimportant in Epicurean philosophy, the emphasis on advantage as the basis or initial impulse towards friendship and the social realities of the Epicurean movement in the first century BCE, where the friends of different social status benefited each other in their mutual support-group, are more congruous with the friendship of pleasure and utility than with that of character.

Conclusion

In conclusion, perhaps the ideal of frank speech and openness in participatory psychagogy between the Epicurean friends had no revo-

---

[166] *Mort.* cols. 23.2–15; 35.24–34; 37.23–25. See Asmis, "Philodemus' Epicureanism," 2392–93.

[167] Arist. *Eth. Eud.* 7.2.48; 1245b20–26, τὴν ἐνέργειαν τῆς συναισθήσεως.

[168] Phld. *Lib.* frg. 1.2–3, συναισθάνεσθαι τὰς ἁμαρτίας. *Contra* LSJ, which translates συναισθάνεσθαι in frg. 1 as "*to be aware of in oneself,* τὰς ἁμαρτίας" (LSJ, s.v. III).

[169] Cf. Plut. *De am. mult.* 96A, Πολύκοινος καὶ πάνδημος φιλία.

lutionizing consequences in the social realm; perhaps this ideal remained just that and did not cut across existing norms of social rank and dominance. It is difficult to tell. However, this impractical ideal had been voiced, and the problems raised in the handbook *On Frank Criticism* suggest that frank speech and openness between friends of unequal power and status did not remain an ephemeral ideal but became a tension-filled social reality. The authority of the friends in the fellowship is predicated, not on an "office" or an attributed status, but on an acquired status, which derives from their ability to heal and admonish others.[170] The sole authority of the one who admonishes and the admonished one, of the doctor and the patient, is Epicurus. He is "the purifier of every (error)," including the errors of the wise.[171] There is thus a built-in hierarchy within the fellowship, with Epicurus as the sole authority at the top. The authority of others within the confraternity is predicated on their function or ability to heal and admonish others. The fragments clearly reveal the tensions present because of such a diastratic solidarity, which allows even those of an inferior character and social position to admonish others.[172] This would, finally, not be such an anomaly for the Epicurean friends of unequal power and status, since frank speech was associated predominately with the topic of unequal friendship in Greco-Roman antiquity.[173]

---

[170] The one who admonishes is "wise" and "clever" (*Lib.* cols. 20a1–5; 21b4–7); his authority is predicated on a functional capacity, viz., the ability to heal, not on an "office" or attributed status. Frg. 44.6–9 speaks of the one who is pure, who loves, who is morally superior, and knows how to heal.

[171] "The basic and most important [principle] is that we will obey Epicurus, according to whom we have chosen to live" (*Lib.* frg. 45.8–11, trans. by Asmis, "Philodemus' Epicureanism," 2394). For the reference to the "purifier of every (error)" (ὁ παντὸς ἀγνεύων), see frg. 55.10–11.

[172] On tensions present because of diastratic solidarity, or the participation of individuals of different moral character and social status, see frgs. 36.4–9; 43; 44.6–9; 46 and cols. 12b6–9 and 14a. Frg. 36.4–9 says that one should even at times "obey [the admonitions] of those of an inferior disposition" and accept such admonitions in the right spirit. In frg. 75.1–8, "fellow-students" are said to offer themselves to carry out the task of correction in cases where the rebuke is not administered by the teachers. Col. 12b6–9 says that those in preparation frankly criticize others who accept it grudgingly or not at all, and col. 14a3–10 advises that one who exhorts others should "remember who he is and to whom he gives exhortation," be they those who are inferior or "the great man who is coming to philosophy," namely, Piso. See also cols. 7a7–10; 20a8–12; and frgs. 52.4–5; 86.1.

[173] See D. Konstan, "Friendship, Frankness and Flattery," chapter one in this volume. The writing of this article has been made possible by a grant from the Icelandic Research Council.

PLUTARCH TO PRINCE PHILOPAPPUS ON HOW TO TELL A FLATTERER FROM A FRIEND

Troels Engberg-Pedersen

The following analysis of Plutarch's treatise *How to Tell a Flatterer from a Friend* (*Quomodo adulator ab amico internoscatur*, henceforth *Adulator*) has been undertaken with the express purpose of coming to see what (if anything) may be learned from the work concerning the relationship between Hellenistic moral philosophy and early Christianity. I have of course been analysing *Adulator* on its own, trying to understand *that* work. But the questions I have asked have to some extent been shaped by the other concern.

They have also been shaped by a different concern: What were the role and wider cultural functions of the kind of ethical *koine* that had originally been developed and formulated by the great moral philosophers standing at the gateway to the Hellenistic period, but which in its Platonic-Peripatetic-Stoic form had then become a general framework shared, it seems, by non-philosophers at almost all levels of Greco-Roman society (and even in parts of Hellenistic Judaism)? Why was the "moral system" of the philosophers accepted by everybody as the framework within which to think? Why did people think, throughout antiquity, that it paid to be good—even if they did not act on their belief?

There are evidently many components in a full answer to this question. And they all serve to define the overall shape of the Hellenistic and Roman "moral mentality" and hence the moral landscape within which the early Christian were operating. The reading of *Adulator* that I offer will suggest one component in the answer and hence one signpost in that landscape.

The Structure of Adulator

Unlike some of Plutarch's treatises, *Adulator* is very clearly organized. Plutarch is careful to mark the transitions from one topic to the next. The result is the following structure:[1]

---

[1] There are structural markers in chap. 6 (51D), chaps. 8–9 (53BC), chap. 10

Chaps. 1–5	Introduction. Chaps. 1–2: Address to Philopappus. Chaps. 3–5: The theme is the skillful flatterer, who is very close to the friend (chap. 3, 50C; chap. 4, 50EF) and difficult to detect (51A). The aim is to use the (remaining) differences to unwrap him and lay him bare (chap. 5, 51D).
Chaps. 6–11	A number of differences (διαφοραί) that are mixed up with the flatterer's imitations (μιμήσεις, chap. 10, 54B) and attempts to make himself conform with the friend (ἐξομοιώσεις, 54D).
Chaps. 12–16	The flatterer's praise.
Chaps. 17–20	The flatterer's use of frank criticism (blame and admonition).
Chaps. 21–23	The difference between flatterer and friend in the area of services rendered and undertakings.
Chaps. 24–25	Return to introduction.
Chaps. 26–37	Analysis of "the true and friendly παρρησία" (cf. chap. 17, 59E).

There is only one question that requires comment here, viz. the relationship of the final section (chaps. 26–37) to the rest. In these chapters Plutarch provides a thorough, more or less technical analysis of παρρησία or frank criticism. The section has been culled independently of the rest for its detailed material on the ancient understanding of frank criticism, an exercise which is of course wholly legitimate, but is not my concern here.[2] Rather, I wish to consider how frank criticism coheres with friendship and flattery, what the exact logic is of the nexus of friendship, flattery and frank criti-

---

(54B and D), chap. 11 (54D), chap. 17 (59A, D), chap. 19 (60D), chap. 21 (62BC) etc. (On chaps. 25ff. see below.) I have used the edition of *Adulator* in *Plutarch's Moralia*, Vol. I (trans. F. C. Babbitt; LCL; London: Heinemann; Cambridge, MA: Harvard University Press, 1927). I have made extensive use of Babbitt's translation, though with corrections where needed.

[2] Thus it is copiously cited by Abraham J. Malherbe in his chapter on "Methods of Instruction and Moral Nurture" in *Moral Exhortation: A Greco-Roman Sourcebook* (Philadelphia: Westminster, 1986). (Chaps. 31–half of 32 and 36–37 are quoted.) Chaps. 26ff. also provide the topic for a recent comparison of Plutarch and Philodemus on frank criticism by Italo Gallo, "La *parrhesia* epicurea e il trattato *De adulatore et amico* di Plutarco: Qualche riflessione," *Aspetti dello stoicismo e dell'epicureismo in Plutarco* (ed. I. Gallo; Quaderni del Giornale Filologico Ferrarese 9; Ferrara, 1988) 119–28. (I have not had access to the recent annotated edition by I. Gallo and E. Pettine, *Plutarco, Come distinguere l'adulatore dall'amico* [Napoli: D'Auria, 1988].)

cism, according to Plutarch. Some scholars have indeed felt that structurally the section on frank criticism has only a slight connection with the rest, and the recent translator in the Budé series, Jean Sirinelli, has argued a little more extensively that what we have are in fact two separate treatises both addressed to Prince Philopappus and more or less skilfully stitched together in chap. 25.[3] That, I shall argue, is wrong. It is true that Plutarch returns in chaps. 24–25 to a number of themes that he has raised in the introduction to the work and that he also repeats, from its very first sentence, his explicit address to Philopappus. But the final section on παρρησία has also been explicitly anticipated already in chap. 17 (59E).[4] Moreover, it is introduced in a very careful manner (chap. 25, 66DE, see below under First Thesis [6]). And as we shall see, Plutarch even explains in the very last chapter of the work the special function of the whole final section on παρρησία in relation to the rest of the work. Note also how the theme of applying frank criticism in the proper way, that is, as done by the person who is analogous to a doctor, is brought in throughout the treatise: in chap. 11 (54E), chap. 17 (59D, in a section that also refers forward to chaps. 26ff.), chap. 25 (66B), chap. 36 (73D + 74D), and chap. 37 (74D). These are highly revealing passages: Plutarch, as we shall see, understands himself vis-à-vis Philopappus as an ἰατρὸς εὐγνώμων (73D).

In short, we are working with a carefully constructed and unified treatise.[5]

---

[3] *Plutarque, Oeuvres morales*, Tome I, 2e partie (Collection Budé; Paris: Les Belles Lettres, 1989) 66–71. Apparently, Sirinelli wishes to divide the treatise somewhere in the middle of chap. 25, in 65F either before or after the mention of Alexander (p. 70). 66AB is Plutarch's attempt to stitch the two treatises together in a way which is "peut-être habile mais elle sent l'artifice" (p. 71). And when Plutarch mentions Philopappus a second time (in 66C, the first time being at the very beginning of the work, 48E), he does it "en titre de la seconde partie" (p. 70), that is, as introducing the new "treatise." Sirinelli concludes (p. 71): "le traité dans son état actuel procède de la réunion, à un moment qui reste indéterminé et selon des modalités qui peuvent être diversement analysées, de deux textes distincts peut-être déjà destinés séparément à Philopappos, mais dont Plutarque a voulu faire un présent à la mesure du dédicataire." (Italo Gallo would agree with Sirinelli; cf. "La *parrhesia*," 120.)

[4] Sirinelli himself, of course, sees this but thinks that this is just "une annonce dépourvue de précision" (*Plutarque*, 69).

[5] I have not seen Karl Brokate, *De aliquot Plutarchi libellis* (Diss. Göttingen; Gottingae: Typsis Roberti Noske Bornensis, 1913), whose analysis of the structure of the treatise was accepted by Konrat Ziegler in his classic account of Plutarch in the *Real-Encyclopädie*. See "Plutarchos," PW 21.1 (1951) cols. 635–962, esp. col. 802.

Three Theses

The three theses that I wish to argue for are as follows:

[1] *Adulator* is not only addressed, honorifically, to Prince Philopappus but directly aimed at him. Though standing in a long and variegated moral philosophical tradition, *Adulator* is topical and directly concerned with an issue of immediate relevance to its author and addressee. It is not just a general "essay" with the name of an addressee more or less gratuitously tacked on to it. It is a direct appeal clothed in general, philosophical dress.

[2] *Adulator* is about friendship, flattery and frank criticism in a specific social situation among many others in which these phenomena might be found: the relationship between a philosophical adviser (Plutarch) and a political leader (Philopappus). The work is political (not just "ethical") and belongs to a group of political writings within the Plutarchean corpus which also includes, significantly, the treatise *That a Philosopher Ought to Converse Especially with Men in Power* (776A–779C).

[3] *Adulator* appeals throughout centrally to the "moral system." This system had a long history in the professional philosophical tradition (Plato, Aristotle, the Stoics), but it was also a system that was accepted as normative by both Plutarch (as the author of *Adulator*) and his addressee. *Adulator* reveals to us *why*, in particular, why it will have been accepted as normative by its specific addressee, the political leader. Thus *Adulator* shows why the nexus of friendship, flattery and frank criticism was deemed of central importance in the social, moral, and political perception actually had by two men living in that specific time and place (cf. [1]) and standing in that specific social relationship (cf. [2]).

The First Thesis

Throughout the work Plutarch is speaking far more directly to his addressee, Prince Philopappus, than is customarily assumed.[6] He is

---

[6] On Philopappus, see Johannes Kirchner, "Philopappos," PW 20.1 (1941) col. 75. There is a description of Philopappus by Plutarch in *Table-Talk* I.10, 1–2 (628AD). Philopappus is described as a "king" (βασιλεύς) who has presided at a choral contest in a notable manner and with great munificence (ἐνδόξως καί μεγαλοπρεπῶς), and he

exhorting Philopappus that he *should* distinguish flatterers from the true friend, *viz. Plutarch himself*, and he is doing this by elaborating on how to draw the distinction.

Here are some relevant passages:

[1] Chap. 1 contains a warning, stated in a sentence explicitly addressed to Philopappus, against "love of self" (φιλαυτία, 48F) and "ignorance of self" (ἄγνοια ἑαυτοῦ, 49B). Plutarch explicitly returns to this theme in chap. 25 (65E, cf. also his use of "conceit," οἴησις, in 65E and chap. 1, 49A), in which we also find a renewed apostrophe of Philopappus (66C). Furthermore, at the beginning of chap. 25 (65E), Plutarch explicitly refers back to the beginning of the work, saying that just as he had then "exhorted" (whom?), so now he "exhorts" (again whom?) "to eradicate from ourselves self-love and conceit." It seems impossible not to take this as referring directly to Philopappus. Is Plutarch exhorting Philopappus not to give in to self-love by listening to flatterers?

[2] In chap. 2 Plutarch states that he will discuss the form of flattery which attacks "great houses and great affairs, and oftentimes overturns kingdoms and principalities" (49C) by setting to work on "ambitious, honest, and promising characters" (49B). He returns to this theme in chap. 24 (65E). It is difficult not to take this as an almost explicit reference to Philopappus himself and his situation. In addition, there may be some reason why Alexander plays such an important role in chaps. 24–25 (65C,D,F). Is Plutarch not flattering Philopappus at the same time as he is admonishing him? Note also in chap. 35 (73A) the point that a friend may need to engage in giving admonition "when matters of importance and of great concern are at stake."

[3] In chap. 2 Plutarch attacks people who in the name of friendship insist that "all who are socially agreeable at once stand openly convicted of being flatterers" (49E, cf. 50B). Instead, he warmly defends a certain amiability in friendship. This theme, too, is one to which he returns in chap. 25 (66B and 66D), two passages which surround the direct apostrophe of Philopappus. Is not Plutarch here speaking of his own preferred kind of friendship in his relationship with Philopappus and defending himself against critics?

---

is praised for his φιλανθρωπία and φιλομάθεια. Ziegler ("Plutarchos," col. 668) thought it unlikely that Plutarch had any closer relationship with Philopappus (of the kind he undoubtedly had with certain Roman leaders). I shall argue against this.

[4] In chap. 25, just after his reference to love of self and conceit, Plutarch states that "in our own case" (as opposed to that of Alexander, with whom Plutarch would probably never compare himself), "if we are careful to observe many and many a fault of our own, shameful and grievous, both of omission and commission, we shall constantly be detecting our own need, not of a friend to commend and extol us, but of a friend to take us to task, to be frank with us, and indeed to blame us when our conduct is bad. For there are but few among many who have the courage to show frankness rather than favour to their friends. And again, among those few you (εὕροις) cannot easily find men who know how to do this, but rather you shall find men who think that if they abuse and find fault they use frank criticism" (66A). Clearly the "we" primarily stands for Philopappus and the friend who knows how to use frank criticism is Plutarch.

[5] In chap. 24 Plutarch states that "the great difference between flatterer and friend may be perceived not least by his (the flatterer's) attitude towards the other friends" (65A). Is it not probable that Plutarch is thinking of the attitude of certain people around Philopappus towards Plutarch himself?

[6] In chap. 37, the last chapter of the treatise, Plutarch states that "... persons who use admonition with skill do not simply apply its bitterness and sting and then run away; but by further converse and gentle words they mollify and assuage [the recipient of their admonition] ..." (74D). And he concludes the whole work with these words: "... those who employ admonition should ... not take their leave too soon, nor allow anything painful and irritating to their acquaintances to form the final topic of conversation at an interview" (74E). It seems impossible not to understand Plutarch as referring here to what he has himself done in the "conversation and interview" (ὁμιλία and συνουσία) that he has just been having with Philopappus in this very treatise. In that case, Plutarch's own "soothing attempt" will be his whole disquisition on παρρησία in chaps. 26–37, which he introduces like this: "Since it is a shameful thing to fall into flattery in aiming to please, and a shameful thing also, in trying to avoid flattery, to destroy the friendly thoughtfulness for another (τὸ φιλικὸν καὶ κηδεμονικόν, cf. also 66E,F) by immoderate frank criticism, we ought to keep ourselves from both the one and the other extreme, and in frank criticism, as in anything else, achieve the right from the mean. The subject itself requiring, as it does, consequent elaboration, seems to determine that this be the completion (κορωνίς) of our

work" (chap. 25, 66DE). It seems obvious that Plutarch has planned all of this very carefully as part of his direct approach to his addressee.

In addition to these more or less certain indications that Plutarch is speaking of his own relationship with Philopappus, there are other, less certain indications.

[7] There is no room for φιλαυτία in παρρησία (chap. 26, 66E). Thus Plutarch applies to himself as frank critic the admonition he has addressed to Philopappus (against φιλαυτία) and thereby follows a principle of self-application that he explicitly formulates elsewhere in the treatise (chap. 33, 71F).

[8] The reference to the frank critic's use of special occasions (chaps. 30, 31, cf. chap. 36, 74CD) may be topical, too. But we do not know.

[9] Plutarch's disquisition on how παρρησία from a friend should be *accepted* by the target of frank criticism (chap. 34) may have a direct address as well.

[10] The same goes for Plutarch's claim that παρρησία is only appropriate when matters of importance and of great concern are at stake (chap. 35).

[11] Finally, the claim that "a man needs to be supplied with good friends or else with ardent enemies" may be directly relevant to Philopappus' situation, too. Friends will instruct him and enemies will take him to task. "But," says Plutarch, "it is better to guard against errors by following proffered advice [given by one's friends] than to repent of errors because of men's [the enemies'] upbraiding." And "this is the reason why it is necessary to treat frank criticism as a fine art, inasmuch as it is the greatest and most potent medicine in friendship, always needing, however, all care to hit the right occasion, and a tempering with moderation" (chap. 36, 74CD). We are at the end of Plutarch's disquisition on frank criticism. So who has treated frank criticism as a fine art? Evidently Plutarch himself. Conversely, it is Philopappus who is in need of a friend who knows how to use that greatest and most potent medicine in friendship to guard against the other's errors by making him follow proffered advice.[7]

What all this comes to is the following. Plutarch implicitly describes Philopappus as a man who risks falling prey to his own love

---

[7] This, incidentally, points to the following worthwhile line of investigation: try to read chaps. 1–25 as Plutarch's *application* of the rules he formulates in chaps. 26–37.

of self and ignorance of self and thereby becoming an easy target for
flattery. By contrast, Plutarch himself is the true friend (as opposed
to a flatterer) who not only is prepared to take Philopappus to task
(to "exhort" him and criticize him frankly) for Philopappus' sake, that is,
for *his* good, but also is able to do so in the way that is precisely
appropriate to the friend, viz. mildly and caringly. In short, Philopappus is in need of friendly advice and criticism, and Plutarch is
the true friend, who lies in the mean between the flatterer and the
harsh person who decries any kind of friendly attitude. Moreover,
Plutarch's own treatise *is* his piece of frank criticism.

I conclude: "the essay seems to be intended primarily for some
one person's edification or entertainment." This is a quotation from
the Loeb translator writing about a different work in the Plutarchean
Corpus.[8] But it is true of *Adulator* too. The work the Loeb translator
was writing about was that significantly entitled treatise *That a Philosopher Ought to Converse Especially with Men in Power* (776A–779C)! So
in *Adulator*, Plutarch the philosopher is conversing with a man in
power, Prince Philopappus, about how to tell a flatterer from a friend.
But he is doing it with the quite specific aim of *exhorting* Philopappus
that he *should* distinguish flatterers from the true friend, viz. Plutarch
himself. *Adulator* is a piece of exhortation (cf. the use of παρακελεύεσθαι
in 65E).

It is very important to see that the treatise is addressing this quite
concrete situation. For it is the fact that the treatise is addressed to
a particular "man in power" (or political leader) with the aim of
persuading him that forces on us the question I shall pursue of why
the addressee should have been persuaded. *Adulator* is not just a sort
of general essay that converses gently of matters of only mild and
fairly abstract interest. It is just as concrete as, say, a Pauline letter.

The Second Thesis

The political character of *Adulator* follows from the first thesis combined with the actual status of Plutarch (the philosopher) and Philopappus (the political leader). Note then also: *That a Philosopher Ought
to Converse Especially with Men in Power* is addressed to a *philosopher*,

---

[8] H. N. Fowler, *Plutarch's Moralia*, Vol. X (LCL; London: Heinemann; Cambridge,
MA: Harvard University Press, 1936) 27.

arguing its case (that he *should* engage with political leaders) in moral terms. Such terms, then, must have appealed to that kind of addressee (which is not strange). By contrast, *Adulator* is addressed to a political leader, again arguing its case (that he *should* distinguish between flatterers and the true friend) basically in moral terms. Here, too, these terms must have appealed to the addressee. But here there is an important question: *Why?*[9]

The Third Thesis

Why was what I shall call the ancient Greek "moral system" (see below) found to be generally attractive, and also to a political leader? I shall collect material from *Adulator* that suggests an answer. I have organized the material in seven points that should be understood as being progressive in character. In other words, they gradually deepen the picture Plutarch gives his reader of the danger inherent in flattery. It is only towards the end that we shall be able to see the full sense of the attractiveness of the "moral system."

[1] Plutarch repeats throughout the work what he considers to be the main difference between the flatterer and the friend: that the latter is wedded to the "moral system," whereas the former is not.

[1.i] Chap. 9: The true friend (ὁ ἀληθὴς φίλος) imitates and commends only what is good (53C). The flatterer, by contrast, is like the chameleon in that he can make himself like to every color, except white (53D).

[1.ii] Chap. 10: Or if he does imitate any of the good qualities of the person whom he flatters, for strategic reasons he always gives him the upper hand (54BC). In other words, he is not at all concerned about the good qualities themselves.

[1.iii] Chap. 11: The flatterer goes for pleasure in the person he is trying to flatter. That is his τέλος (moral ends of acts). The friend, by contrast, goes for what is noble and profitable for him (54F,

---

[9] The two treatises are even more relevant to each other. Thus it appears that the main problem in *Maxime cum principibus philosopho esse disserendum* is whether a philosopher who converses with a man in power is φιλόδοξος or not, as opposed to being φιλόκαλος, πολιτικός and φιλάνθρωπος. As already noted, it seems likely that Plutarch's implicit "opponents" in *Adulator* (those referred to in 49E, 50B and 66B and D) have similarly criticized *him* for being a little too amiable towards Philopappus—out of φιλοδοξία.

55B,CD). Often he is also pleasant, but he is always profitable (55D).

[1.iv] Chap. 20: One way to avoid the flatterer is to remember the two sides of the soul: "on the one side are truthfulness, love for what is honourable, and power to reason, and on the other side irrationality, love of falsehood, and the emotional element." The friend is always found on the better side, the flatterer on the other side (61D).

[1.v] Chap. 23: In the matter of services rendered (ὑπουργίαι) and undertakings (ἐπαγγελίαι), too, the best distinction between flatterer and friend may be found in the nature of their service, "whether it is honourable or dishonourable, and whether its purpose is to give pleasure or help" (64BC).

[2] By means of these passages we may obtain a sufficiently clear picture of what I have referred to as the "moral system." It is a system made up of a set of specific values (the noble or καλόν, the beneficial or συμφέρον/ὠφέλιμον, the pleasant or ἡδύ) and a concomitant moral psychology (reason versus the senses). This system was common ground in the Hellenistic period. Technically it is Platonic and Aristotelian rather than Stoic. But as is well known, even a Stoic like Posidonius had adopted the Platonic-Aristotelian conceptualization and incorporated it into his Stoicism, and in Cicero's day it was intensely discussed whether there was in fact any "real" difference between the original Stoic conception and the Platonic-Aristotelian tradition. In point of fact, there are fairly clear reminiscences of Aristotle in 52A, 54F and 66C–D and of Stoicism in 73D and 74A.

[3] In the introduction to the work and elsewhere Plutarch states that the flatterer whom he is discussing is closely similar to (though still, of course, different from) the friend and hence to some extent involved with the "moral system."

[3.i] Chap. 3: The theme of the work is the genuine (ἀληθινός!), skilful and technical flatterer (50C, cf. chap. 14, 57F: ὁ τεχνίτης κόλαξ), whom it is difficult to distinguish from the friend.

[3.ii] Chap. 4: He is the one who "acts the part of friend with the gravity of a tragedian" (a τραγικός . . . φιλίας ὑποκριτής, 50E). So again, he is not easy to detect.

[3.iii] Chap. 5: In fact, it is the very aim of the flatterer to be taken for a friend. It is this which makes him hard to detect (δυσφώρατος, 51D).

[3.iv] Chaps. 6ff.: Plutarch's theme is how, by attending to the similarities, one may use the differences to "unwrap" the flatterer and "lay him bare" (chap. 5, 51D; chap. 7, 52A; chap. 9, 53C; chap. 10, 54D; chap. 21, 62C; chap. 24, 65A).

[4] However, as already partly glimpsed, the flatterer is not just similar to the friend. He positively and on purpose *imitates* the friend in order to hide his devious aims.

[4.i] Chap. 5: "That which most especially cements a friendship begun is a likeness of pursuits and characters" (51B). And so the flatterer "adjusts and shapes himself . . . endeavouring to adopt and mould himself to fit those whom he attacks through imitation" (51C). Further, "perceiving that frank criticism, by common report and belief, is the language of friendship (as an animal has its peculiar cry), and, on the other hand, that lack of frank criticism is unfriendly and ignoble, he does not allow even this to escape imitation" (51C).

[4.ii] Chaps. 6–8: Same theme. Friendship starts from a perception of similarity between the friends. The flatterer constantly attempts to bring about, in his own speech and action, the same similarity between himself and the person whom he is flattering.

[4.iii] Chaps. 13–15: The flatterer uses indirect means in order to avoid giving the impression of being a flatterer. Thus, for instance, he will not praise directly the person whom he wants to flatter (57AB). In so doing, he precisely imitates the friend.

[4.iv] Chap. 17: The flatterer "arrays himself to masquerade in the badges and insignia proper to a friend" and even puts his hand on and imitates frank criticism, which he ought to leave alone as the one thing belonging to friendship only (59B).

[5] But, of course, this imitation of the friend is through and through false. Here we must begin to listen more carefully. We must take note of the many connotations of Plutarch's metaphors for describing the flatterer and the social implications of his descriptions of the flatterer, and we must do this with a view to detecting the social and psychological presuppositions that underlie the treatise and reveal (to us) the attractiveness and functions of the "moral system." We should not, therefore, just note in a list how the flatterer is described as a fake. Rather, we should listen to the implications of Plutarch's descriptions. (In fact, we should do in relation to Plutarch's discussion what Plutarch himself tells us to do in relation to the flatterer: φωρᾶν him.)

The flatterer is dangerous.

[a] The flatterer is a fake and therefore dangerous to any individual with whom he is involved.

[5.a.i] Chap. 4: The flatterer is a "hypocritical actor of friendship" (φιλίας ὑποκριτής) and so all the opprobrium that was felt to lie on actors and acting will lie upon him too (50E).

[5.a.ii] Chap. 8: The flatterer is a person who, like a mirror, only catches the images (εἰκόνες) of alien feelings, lives and movements (53A). He is not the real thing.

[5.a.iii] Chap. 23: If you test flattery in arduous and dangerous services, it does not ring clear, but has an ignoble tone jangling with some excuse (64E). Chap. 17: Similarly, the flatterer's use of "counterfeit frank criticism" has "a hollow, false, and unsound bulk" (it is ὕπουλος—LSJ: with festering sores underneath, unsound, hollow, treacherous, false, fallacious, deceitful, concealed, festering within) and is inflated and swollen (59D).

[5.a.iv] Chap. 24: The flatterer is false, spurious, and debased, inasmuch as he fully understands that he is committing a crime against friendship, which in his hands becomes a counterfeit coin as it were (65B; for similar language see 49D and 50A). Whenever, then, the flatterer, who is but a light and deceptive plated-ware, is examined and closely compared with genuine and solid-wrought friendship, he does not stand the test (65BC).

In all this Plutarch is clearly appealing to a risk one runs by becoming involved with a flatterer. The flatterer is dangerous.

[b] But the flatterer is also dangerous to the moral system as such. For he *perverts* it.

[5.b.i] Chap. 2: Flattery must be thoroughly exposed (περίφωρος) in order to prevent it from injuring friendship or (in fact) making it (altogether) spurious (διαβάλλειν, 49C).

[5.b.ii] Chap. 12: The flatterer takes hold of ambitious men's ears, and once settled there, he is hard to dislodge (55E). In fact, with their praise flatterers pierce to the man's character, and indeed even touch his habit of mind with their flattery, and so they pervert (διαστρέφειν) the very first principle and fountainhead of living (this being the disposition and character from which a man's actions spring), inasmuch as they are investing vice with the names that belong to virtue (56B). (For other comparable versions of the same motif of perverting the virtues, see chap. 14, 57CD, and chap. 19, 60D–61B.).

[5.b.iii] Chap. 15: Flatterers, we remember, especially fawn upon persons of power, wealth or repute. But they do it in the particularly pernicious way of proclaiming that these people are not only prosperous and blessed, but also rank first in understanding, technical skill and every form of virtue (58D,E). Thereby they almost pervert language.

[5.b.iv] Chap. 18: One highly unscrupulous thing about flatterers is that they employ frank criticism and reprehension in order to give pleasure (60B). That in itself is a perversion. But even worse, they may even explicitly invoke frank criticism for their own devious purposes, for instance, when they get up saying that "as free men they ought to use frank criticism and not to dissemble or refrain from discussing anything that might be for the general good" (60C). Similarly, the unscrupulous, while being well aware that frank criticism is a great remedy for flattery, may themselves "flatter by means of frank criticism itself" (61C).

[5.b.v] Chap. 21: The result of all this is that the flatterer brings about "a great confusion and uncertainty in regard to the difference between himself and the friend" (62BC). But as I am urging, this is not just an uncertainty as to whether in a given case one is confronted with a friend or a flatterer. Rather, it is uncertainty about the moral system itself: whether the distinction between the friend and the flatterer is in fact as rigid as it is insisted upon within the "moral system."

We should conclude that according to Plutarch the flatterer is dangerous not only to the individual whom he tries to flatter, but also to the "moral system" as such and to the very concept of friendship.

[6] There is perhaps not much reason to wonder why Plutarch has worked all this out so strongly, if one thinks of what we took to be his aim in writing. As a philosopher, he will have been wedded to the "moral system" right from the beginning. He therefore impresses upon his addressee the risk that the flatterer represents to that system taken as a whole. As we saw, however, the really interesting question is why all this should have actually impressed *his* *addressee*, who need not have been wedded to the "moral system" in a similarly strong way. Or, if we think that he was, why was he? The question should therefore be: What features of the "moral system" does Plutarch appeal to in order to bring out the *attractiveness* of that system, to anybody and particularly to his addressee?

[a] There is first the theme of distrust (ἀπιστία).

[6.a.i] Chap. 4: Hidden flattery infects even true friendship with distrust (50F).

[6.a.ii] Chap. 9: While having this effect the flatterer himself aims to appear as both pleasant and at the same time also trustworthy (πιστός, 53E, cf. πιθανός in 51C).

[6.a.iii] Chap. 8: Similarly, when a flatterer imitates the person whom he is trying to flatter with regard to the latter's beliefs about a third party, he may say either "You have been slow in *detecting* that man's character" (the term is φωρᾶν, catch him out) or "I too share your pleasure in him and *trust* him" (πιστεύειν, 53A).

[b] Then there are the two themes of simplicity, frankness, or sincerity (ἁπλότης) and permanence or constancy.

[6.b.i] Chap. 7: In trying to expose a flatterer, one must "observe the uniformity and permanence of his tastes, whether he always takes delight in the same things, and commends always the same things, and whether he directs and ordains his own life according to one pattern, as becomes a free-born man and a lover of congenial friendship and intimacy; for such is the conduct of a friend." The flatterer, by contrast, "has no abiding-place of character (ἑστίαν ἤθους) to dwell in, nor does he lead a life of his own choosing but another's, moulding and adapting himself to suit another, and he is not simple, not one, but variable and many in one." In fact, he resembles an ape (52AB).

[6.b.ii] Chap. 8: Or else he resembles a cuttlefish that is changing all the time. He is nowhere constant, nor has he got a character of his own, nor does he love and hate, rejoice and grieve with a feeling of his own (52F–53A).

[c] This theme fits in closely with Plutarch's emphasis throughout the treatise on character, ἦθος.

[6.c.i] Chap. 6: Friends have the same character, disposition and nature (51DE).

[6.c.ii] Chap. 7: As opposed to an archflatterer like Alcibiades, moral models like Epameinondas or Agesilaus maintained everywhere their own proper character (52EF).

[6.c.iii] Chap. 12: A person's disposition and character are the seed from which his actions spring, the very first principle and fountainhead of living (56B).

[6.c.iv] Chap. 27: Finally, even though friends may on occasion employ jest and laughter, frank criticism between them should have seriousness and character. And if it concerns matters of greater importance (as it should), the words employed in frank criticism should be characterized by "such feeling, have such a form and be spoken with such earnestness of voice" (presumably *reflecting* the frank critic's character) "that they claim credence" (are ἀξιόπιστοι) "and make an impression" (are κινητικοί, chap. 27, 68C).

[d] Finally, there is the recurrent emphasis on truth and truthfulness.

[6.d.i] Chap. 8: "I have no use for a friend who shifts about together with me and nods assent together with me (for my shadow better performs that function), but I want one who tells the truth together with me and makes up his own mind together with me" (53B).

[6.d.ii] Chap. 18: When flatterers take on the role of a genuine friend, they say that as free men they ought to use frank criticism and not to dissemble or refrain from discussing anything that might be for the general good (60C).

[6.d.iii] Chap. 22: In fact, however, the flatterer's activity shows no sign of "honesty, truth, straightforwardness, or generosity" (δίκαιον, ἀληθινόν, ἀπλοῦν, ἐλευθέριον, 63F).

[6.d.iv] Chap. 24: And as we know, the flatterer is "false, spurious, and debased" (ψευδής, νόθος, ὑπόχαλκος, 65B).

[7] The attractiveness of the "moral system."

We may conclude that Plutarch is appealing to the possibility of trusting somebody, to the need for simplicity and permanence in a person, which is a matter of his having a certain settled character, and to the need for truthfulness in those with whom one is involved. Why will that have made an impression on his addressee?

Before turning to that question I will try to sort out the logical relationship between friendship, frank criticism and flattery. Friendship seems to be conceived of by Plutarch as an end, something good in itself. Friendship is also intimately connected with the "moral system" as a whole. It is, as it were, the apogee of that system: the place where that system is realized. In all this Plutarch is faithfully repeating the moral philosophical tradition of a Peripatetic and Stoic kind. But he also means it: friendship, that is, his and Philopappus', *is* an end. And we must consider why.

Frank criticism is not an end, but a means to bringing about the realization of the "moral system." It belongs within the sphere of *progress towards* virtue (cf. *How a Man May Become Aware of His Progress in Virtue* 82A). By helping to realize the "moral system" in a person, it also helps to bring about friendship. However, frank criticism also *presupposes* a setting of friendship for its psychological efficacy. Is there not a problem here? No, for there may be degrees of friendship. Some degree of friendship is required for frank criticism to become operative. With the help of frank criticism the "moral system" may then be realized in a person and so full friendship become possible.

So, friendship is the supreme value. Frank criticism is mainly ancillary, but also an expression of friendship.

How about flattery? It is specifically tied to friendship, which it attempts to *imitate*. And here frank criticism comes in because it is the very voice of friendship. For this reason the flatterer will imitate the person who uses frank criticism, too.

The main contrast, however, is between friendship and flattery, between the real thing and the counterfeit one. Why was this contrast felt to be such an important one? Plutarch, we remember, appeals to four basic values (trust, simplicity, permanence of character, truthfulness). Why will that have made an impression on his addressee?

Somebody might find the answer obvious. If we cannot trust a person and feel certain that he is truthfully expressing his own stable way of looking at things, then we cannot live with him. If all people were like that, if the "moral system" was not basically in place, life would be unlivable. Still, there appears to be an important difference between the way we might argue this point as members of contemporary culture and the way we should understand it in terms of ancient cultural perceptions.

Here is my suggestion. With his invocation of trust, sincerity, permanence and truthfulness Plutarch is appealing to a set of values and a way of life which was in constant danger of being done away with in ancient society since it stood in more or less direct contrast to a different set of values that was so pervasive that nobody could be said to stand outside it. What I have in mind is the set of values implicit in the very strong consciousness of social and personal status that is characteristic of ancient society. Everybody had a strong sense of where he or she belonged in a status-hierarchy (no matter how we will more specifically define this) and everybody wanted so far as possible to get out on the top. Conversely, everybody was afraid of losing status and moving down in the hierarchy.

However, as part of this all-pervasive setting there also was an idea of a sort of counter-existence, in which people (some people, a few people) might live together without being constantly concerned about status issues. That, I suggest, is the idea of friendship, as Plutarch develops it, and as the philosophers had developed it. Friendship of this sort was felt to be a sort of breathing space where you could be entirely open in your relationship with a few others without risking any loss of status and hence without needing to be concerned about it. That, however, was only possible if you could be certain that you would not later be betrayed by those few other people. And that is what friendship based in the "moral system" ("friendship of character" in the Aristotelian and Stoic tradition) gave you.

Against this background we can see why precisely flattery of the skillful kind discussed by Plutarch should be perceived as being so dangerous. For it threatened to close that breathing space just because it constituted a frontal attack on those values (trust, sincerity, permanence, truthfulness) that made it possible.

What I am suggesting, then, is that Plutarch is implicitly appealing throughout the treatise to his addressee's desire to be able to live in a genuine friendship. That requires that he draw the vital distinction between flatterers and a true friend. And once he does this, he will dismiss those fake friends who surround him and turn instead to the true one, Plutarch. If, by contrast, he does not draw the distinction, he will abolish friendship altogether. And that is not a desirable situation. For friendship, the apogee of the "moral system," is something strongly desired by everybody.[10]

Note that seeing friendship as a breathing space in a society permeated by a concern about status distinctions is an attempt to locate not only friendship, as it had been developed in the philosophical tradition, but also the "moral system" itself. For within that tradition, friendship in its genuine form, so-called "character friendship," is precisely the apogee of the "moral system." It takes up the place where the "moral system" is realized.

We may add the following observation. I have argued that friendship, as conceived by Plutarch, and by implication the "moral system" as a whole, should be understood as formulating a set of countervalues vis-à-vis those present in society at large. Now these latter values found expression in the system of patronage, which we know to have been such an important one in ancient society, certainly in the Roman period if not earlier.[11] But we also know that the

---

[10] In addition, it should be noted that Plutarch also appeals to the more tangible benefits that may be obtained through friendship. Cf. his remark in chap. 5 (51B) that "graciousness (χάρις) and usefulness (χρεία) go with friendship."
[11] Compare the important collection of papers, *Patronage in Ancient Society* (ed. Andrew Wallace-Hadrill; London and New York: Routledge, 1989). It is noteworthy

relationship between patrons and clients was very often designated as being one of friendship (whether φιλία or *amicitia*).[12] So is there not a contradiction here? Not at all. For that designation should be seen as a sham. It reflects an attempt to conceal the real ties, which were strongly hierarchical and status-determined. And so this sham employment of friendship terminology actually supports the picture I have sketched instead of undermining it.

Still, what are the arguments for extracting that picture from Plutarch's *Adulator*? The primary argument lies in the progressive deepening in Plutarch's description of the dangers inherent in flattery that I have catalogued as points [4]–[6] in this section. There is a forcefulness in the metaphors used by Plutarch to depict the perversion of flattery that must have served a purpose. This purpose must have been to impress upon Plutarch's reader that a world in which there is no trust, sincerity, permanence of character and truthfulness, in short no room for genuine friendship, is impossible to live in.

In addition, there are other minor indications that the world within which friendship and frank criticism constitute a counter-value is a world ridden by a concern over status.

[7.i] Chap. 10: Plutarch claims that among true friends there is neither emulation (ζῆλος) nor envy (φθόνος, 54C). Here, then, the concern over status is defused.

[7.ii] Chap. 32: Plutarch also explicitly advises against employing frank criticism in public because it touches directly on the criticized person's concern about his own status (71C).

[7.iii] Chaps. 26ff.: Finally, all the problems with frank criticism that Plutarch's advice in chaps. 26ff. is intended to solve or alleviate stem from the fact that criticism was felt to be an attack on the criticized person's status. It is for this reason that the ancients were so highly conscious of the many problems that surrounded praise and, especially, blame—more conscious, one suspects, than we tend to be.

---

that this treatment concentrates on the Romans. This is partly due to the state of the historiography of the subject, but partly also to what is apparently a sharp contrast between Greek and Roman society in this respect. (Cf. Wallace-Hadrill's introduction, pp. 8–9, and Paul Millett's chapter on "Patronage and Its Avoidance in Classical Athens," pp. 15–47.) Plutarch, of course, lived in a "Roman" world with a circle of Roman friends; cf. C. P. Jones, *Plutarch and Rome* (Oxford: Clarendon, 1971) 39–64, and Ziegler, "Plutarchos," cols. 687–94.

[12] See Richard Saller, "Patronage and Friendship in Early Imperial Rome: Drawing the Distinction," *Patronage*, 49–62.

Note also how Plutarch pays special attention to the question of how frank criticism should be applied to people who are "down" in social terms (chap. 28).

Conclusion

I have argued that *Adulator* is not just a general, "ethical" essay. Rather, it directly concerns the situation of its author and addressee. This (and, I think, this alone) gives us the necessary background for seriously asking the question why, as Plutarch seems to assume throughout, the addressee of the work should have been attracted to the "moral system" on which Plutarch builds his whole argument. In answering this question, I have argued that throughout the treatise Plutarch is appealing to the kinds of value which underlie the "moral system" and its apogee, friendship: trust, sincerity, permanence of character and truthfulness. These are also values which are presupposed, on Plutarch's analysis, in frank criticism, but it is precisely these values which are done away with in flattery. In fact, flattery is a frontal, though by definition insinuating, attack on them. The nexus of friendship, flattery and frank criticism is therefore a tight one and it is centered on those values, trust, sincerity, permanence of character and truthfulness.

What has all this to do with early Christianity? The simple, and I think also correct, answer is that whenever early Christian writers make use of concepts belonging within the nexus of friendship, flattery and frank criticism that I have discussed, they too betray a concern about the status system and a set of counter-values. To the extent, therefore, that their use of those concepts enters directly into the formulation of their own religious message (as I think it often does), that message too will be partly *about* the status system and a set of counter-values. And so work on friendship, flattery and frank criticism will tell us more about the meaning of the religious message itself. The point of the Greek philosophical "moral system" (or rather one of its points) helps to elucidate the meaning of the Christian message.

PART TWO

FRIENDSHIP LANGUAGE IN PHILIPPIANS

PHILIPIANS, ESPECIALLY CHAPTER 4, AS A "LETTER OF FRIENDSHIP": OBSERVATIONS ON A CHECKERED HISTORY OF SCHOLARSHIP

John Reumann

While some (like Berry)[1] stress friendship language in Phil 4:10–20, others apply "letter of friendship" to all four chapters. Hence the title "Philippians, Especially Chapter 4." We shall concentrate on (1) a *Forschungsbericht* about the relatively brief history of research on Philippians as a letter of friendship, a history which turns out to be rather checkered at points; (2) more briefly, an area for investigation where one might expect to find the letter designated as φιλικὴ ἐπιστολή ("friendly letter"), namely in the patristic writers, some of whom were professional rhetoricians before embracing Christianity. If such commentators of the fourth or fifth centuries saw Philippians in the terms used by scholars in recent years, it would be strong confirmation that we are on the right track. Finally, we shall offer (3) conclusions and suggestions. The aim is to stir up questions in an area where some see friendship perhaps excessively, as did Sir Thomas Browne, when he began looking for quincuncial arrangements—five things, one in each corner with the fifth in the center—and found, as Coleridge said, "Quincunxes in the heaven above, quincunxes in the earth below, quincunxes in the mind of man, in optic nerves, in roots of trees, in leaves, in everything."[2] For the concepts of "Paul and friends" and his epistles as "letters of friendship" are very attractive. We are tempted to apply the principle, especially with regard to the joyous letter to the Philippians, that Paul *could* have written it as a letter of friendship (*potuit*); it is *fitting* that he did (*decet*); ergo he *did* (*fecit*). But that is what needs testing. Did he?

---

[1] Ken L. Berry, "The Function of Friendship Language in Philippians 4:10–20" (paper presented to the Hellenistic Moral Philosophy and Early Christianity Group at the annual meeting of the Society of Biblical Literature, San Francisco, CA, November, 1992). A slightly revised version of this paper appears as Chapter Five of this volume.

[2] As quoted in A. R. Thompson, *The Dry Mock* (Berkeley: University of California Press, 1948) v.

What has been Proposed in the History of Scholarship

The importance of φιλία and *amicitia* in the Greco-Roman world has long been known to classicists. When reading Aristotle's *Ethics* in graduate school, I was attracted to do a paper in *Motifsforschung*, comparing φιλία with Anders Nygren's analysis of ἀγάπη and ἔρως. Occasionally scholars of yesteryear have linked such ideas with the NT. For example, James Moffatt, after noting the "kindred origin of the epistle and the oral address" (in a way that anticipates some observations over fifty years later by Klaus Berger about elements of rhetoric in letters where Paul wrote what he would have said, if present),[3] went on to claim that

> the epistolary literature of the early Christians, in fact, almost exemplifies the threefold division made by Cicero [*ad Fam.* 6.10.4; 4.13.1 and 2.4] into (*a*) epistles as letters which convey instruction or information, (*b*) playful and familiar notes to one's friends, and (*c*) letters of consolation.[4]

The dissertation by Francis X. J. Exler in 1923, *The Form of the Ancient Greek Letter*, spoke of communications between family members and friends as "familiar letters,"[5] and Heikki Koskenniemi's 1956 study made a similar emphasis on "family letters."[6]

The "friendly type" of letter was made more accessible to NT studies when in 1977 Abraham Malherbe published texts and translations of "Ancient Epistolary Theorists," including specifically the first of twenty-one kinds of letters in Pseudo-Demetrius.[7] This type of letter was said to be written "by a friend to a friend," or by those of prominence to inferiors or equals, even to persons personally unknown but in a friendly manner to get the person to heed what is written. The example of a letter written "as though ... to a friend" runs,

---

[3] K. Berger, "Apostelbrief und apostolische Rede / Zum Formular frühchristlicher Briefe," *ZNW* 65 (1974) 190–231.

[4] J. Moffatt, *An Introduction to the Literature of the New Testament* (International Theological Library; New York: Charles Scribner's Sons, 1921) 49.

[5] F. X. J. Exler, *The Form of the Ancient Greek Letter: A Study in Greek Epistolography* (Washington, D.C.: Catholic University of America, 1923).

[6] H. Koskenniemi, *Studien zur Idee und Phraseologie des griechischen Briefes bis 400 n. Chr.* (Helsinki: Suomalainen Tiedakatemia, 1956) 110ff.

[7] A. J. Malherbe, "Ancient Epistolary Theorists," *OJRS* 5 (1977) 3–77. Reprinted as *Ancient Epistolary Theorists* (SBLSBS 19; Atlanta: Scholars Press, 1988).

Even though I have been separated from you for a long time, I suffer this in body only. For I can never forget you or the impeccable way we were raised [reared] together from childhood up. Knowing that I myself am genuinely concerned about your affairs, and that I have worked unstintingly [unhesitatingly] for what is most advantageous (τὸ συμφέρον) to you, I have assumed that you, too, have the same opinion of me, and will refuse me in nothing. You will do well, therefore, to give close attention to the members of my household lest they need anything, to assist them in whatever they might need, and to write us about whatever you should choose.[8]

Cf. Pseudo-Libanius, *Epist. Char.* 11: the seventh style of letter is the φιλική, exhibiting "simple friendship only";[9] and as an example,

Since I have many sterling letter carriers available, I am eager to address your intelligent mind. For it is a holy thing to honor genuine (γνησίους) friends when they are present, and to speak to them when they are absent.[10]

The analysis of some 117 ancient letters by John L. White in 1986 not only summarized these references[11] but also provided examples of three epistolary types: 1) letters of introduction and recommendation; 2) of petition; and 3) family letters, out of which, he says, "the cultivated letter of friendship" grew.[12] Some 15 or more of the 117 letters, depending on how one counts, are to friends (#71, e.g.) or family (##95–98, 101–105, 106–108); cf. index, s.v. "family/friendship". These papyrus examples cannot be said to conform to the handbook models, nor was application of the category to NT letters made as yet by White in 1986.

Discussion of the topic in German literature was perhaps more extensive in classical studies and will appear in commentaries on Philippians as a *Freundschaftsbrief* about at the same time as in American scholarship. Certainly the 1970 monograph by Klaus Thraede, *Grundzüge griechisch-römischer Brieftopik*, was a factor; it traced out classical and Christian examples for the philophronetic letter type under

---

[8] Ps.-Demetrius, *Typoi Epist.* 1. See Malherbe, "Ancient Epistolary Theorists," 30–31 = *Ancient Epistolary Theorists*, 32–33, with Malherbe's 1977 translation given in brackets.

[9] Malherbe, "Ancient Epistolary Theorists," 64–65 = *Ancient Epistolary Theorists*, 68–69.

[10] Ps.-Libanius, *Epist. Char.* 58. See Malherbe, "Ancient Epistolary Theorists," 70–71 = *Ancient Epistolary Theorists*, 74–75.

[11] J. L. White, *Light from Ancient Letters* (FFNT; Philadelphia: Fortress, 1986) 200–03.

[12] Ibid., 193–96; cf. 191, 193, 200.

the leitmotif of "unity in friendship."[13] The letter, at least in certain church fathers, becomes an example of friendship (δεῖγμα φιλίας, Chrys. *Ep.* 58, 66, 178), expressing "the bond of love." The interrelation of φιλία and ἀγάπη, foreshadowed in Aristotle's occasional use of ἀγαπᾶν in his *Nicomachean Ethics* (8.3.1; 9.3.1, "befriend"; 9.12.2; 9.7.3; 9.8.6; with φιλεῖν at 9.7.2), came to the fore in the patristic writers,[14] at times as a contrast, for ἀγάπη now becomes the basis for friendship among Christians.[15] Klaus Berger's magisterial treatment of Hellenistic *Gattungen* in the NT viewed the letter of friendship as a series of *topoi*, not a *Gattung.*[16] The themes include letters as (1) an expression of friendship (φιλοφρόνησις), with terms like "dearest" (φίλτατος), "most honorable" (τιμιώτατος, γλυκύτατος), or "my own" (ἴδιος), and (2) as a substitute for absence. But "the Pauline letters are not, for these reasons, to be declared 'letters of friendship,'" he concluded, and (contra Thraede)[17] 1 Cor 5:3 is not to be explained as an epistolary motif (present in spirit, absent physically), for here apostolic power must be reckoned with.[18]

On the world scene, voices from Australia were also significant. In a 1974 essay E. A. Judge was already suggesting why Paul avoided friendship terms, namely because of their patronal status implications.[19] When in 1987 Peter Marshall published his 1980 Macquarrie University dissertation, its treatment of friendship, as a backdrop to enmity, acknowledged debts to Judge and Robert Banks,[20] as well

---

[13] K. Thraede, *Grundzüge griechisch-römischer Brieftopik* (Zetemata 48; Munich: C. H. Beck, 1970) 125–45. Cf. also Thraede's discussion of φιλία and women in "Ärger mit der Freiheit: Die Bedeutung von Frauen in Theorie und Praxis der alten Kirche," *"Freunde in Christus werden . . .": Die Beziehung von Mann und Frau als Frage an Theologie und Kirche* (ed. Gerta Scharffenorth and K. Thraede; Kennzeichen 1; Gelnhausen and Berlin: Burckhardthaus-Verlag; Stein: Laetare-Verlag, 1977) 54, 58–59, 100, 140.

[14] Thraede, *Grundzüge*, 132–35.

[15] Ibid., 135–43.

[16] K. Berger, "Hellenistische Gattungen im Neuen Testament," *ANRW* 25.2 (1984) 1031–1432, especially 1389.

[17] Thraede, *Grundzüge*, 97–102.

[18] Berger, "Hellenistische Gattungen," 1329–30 n. 354; see also the comments in Berger's *Formgeschichte des Neuen Testaments* (Heidelberg: Quelle & Meyer, 1984) 216.

[19] E. A. Judge, "Paul as a Radical Critic of Society," *Interchange* 16 (1974) 191–203.

[20] Robert Banks, *Paul's Idea of Community: The Early House Churches in their Historical Setting* (Grand Rapids: Eerdmans, 1980). See now the rev. ed., *Paul's Idea of Community: The Early House Churches in their Cultural Setting* (Peabody, MA: Hendrickson, 1994).

as to Malherbe, but Thraede and for that matter Berger are not mentioned.[21]

Tracing the lines of development for influences among scholars on φιλία as a *topos* or letter form is thus by no means a clear process. Applications to the NT likely arose simultaneously and without borrowings, simply because we all read some of the same ancient sources. But that also means that to find the phrase "letter of friendship" or *Freundschaftsbrief* by no means implies a common definition, let alone agreed reasons for it.

In any case, in the mid-1980's a number of treatments of Philippians began to refer to all or parts of the document as a letter involving friendship. In 1984, e.g., Wolfgang Schenk's *Philipperbriefe*, in commenting on 4:15, called attention to friendship "as the highest expression of fellowship" in the Greek world, an ideal which includes "a considerable readiness to share material possessions," though this is actually a quotation from Hauck's 1938 *TWNT* article on κοινός, κτλ.;[22] but Schenk added evidence as to how Cynic, Stoic, and Neopythagorean theories hold here for Paul and his addressees.[23] We shall return later to a further suggestion growing out of Schenk's work.

In Rudolf Pesch's 1985 treatment of Philippians as three letters to Paul's *Lieblingsgemeinde*, he spoke of 4:10–18 as reflecting the style of the *Freundschaftsbrief* or philophronetic letter.[24] A similar treatment was given by J. Schoon-Janssen in 1991.[25] While the term is not invoked in the commentaries of G. Hawthorne (but note his reference to Paul's "friends at Philippi")[26] and of M. Silva,[27] Peter T. O'Brien's NIGTC volume treated κοινωνεῖν εἰς λόγον δόσεως καὶ λήμψεως at 4:15 as "an idiomatic expression indicating friendship," citing Peter Marshall.[28] Thus far, a *philia topos* but not a letter of friendship.

---

[21] P. Marshall, *Enmity in Corinth: Social Conventions in Paul's Relations with the Corinthians* (WUNT 2.23; Tübingen: Mohr-Siebeck, 1987).

[22] F. Hauck, "κοινός, κτλ" *TDNT* 3.798.

[23] W. Schenk, *Die Philipperbriefe des Paulus: Kommentar* (Stuttgart: Kohlhammer, 1984) 62; cf. 63–65 on how the "Hellenistic *philia*-concept lies clearly in the background of *koinonia*-terminology."

[24] R. Pesch, *Paulus und seine Lieblingsgemeinde: Paulus—neu gesehen. Drei Briefe an die Heiligen in Philippi* (Freiburg: Herder, 1985) 63–64.

[25] Johannes Schoon-Janssen, *Umstrittene "Apologien" in Paulusbriefen* (GTA 45; Göttingen: Vandenhoeck & Ruprecht, 1991) 136–38.

[26] Gerald F. Hawthorne, *Philippians* (WBC 43; Waco: Word, 1983) 206.

[27] Moisés Silva, *Philippians* (Wycliffe Exegetical Commentary; Chicago: Moody, 1988).

[28] P. T. O'Brien, *The Epistle to the Philippians* (NIGTC; Grand Rapids: Eerdmans, 1991) 514, 534.

Next, two volumes in the "Library of Early Christianity" are relevant. Stanley K. Stowers, *Letter Writing in Greco-Roman Antiquity*, has separate chapters on "Letters of Friendship" (58–70) and "Family Letters" (71–76).[29] In the former, NT verses are related to pseudo-Demetrius' definition of φιλικαὶ ἐπιστολαί (1 Cor 5:3, 1 Thess 2:17, and Col 2:5 are compared for the theme "absent physically but united in mind and heart"),[30] but the conclusion reached is that "although there are no letters of friendship in the New Testament, some letters employ commonplaces and language from the friendly letter tradition."[31] Two instances are cited from Philippians where such commonplaces "possibly appear": 1:7–8, "yearning for the loved one"; and 2:17–18, "sharing in one another's feelings."[32] David Aune's treatment of the NT's literary environment, which appeared in the same series the next year, summarized Stowers' sixfold epistolary typology,[33] without referring to letters of friendship; but Aune does refer to "letters of recommendation" as a "utilitarian aspect" of the Roman concept of friendship[34] and summarizes Thraede's work on *topoi*, including friendship;[35] *topos* "is not a literary form," however, we are warned, but a "common theme."[36] Philippians is termed "a letter of gratitude and paraenesis."[37]

It is about this time that designation of Philippians as a letter of friendship becomes overt. Luke T. Johnson's literary introduction to the NT saw in Philippians "the rhetoric of friendship," used by Paul "to invoke appropriate response in his readers."[38] The argument depends chiefly on vocabulary (σύν words, like συνεργός, 2:25; ἰσότης; μία ψυχή, 1:27; τὸ αὐτὸ φρονεῖν, 1:6, 30; 2:2, 18; 4:3) and instead of φιλία the term κοινωνία. Without referring to this material, Pheme Perkins, noting features of the "*family* letter" in Philippians as well as friendship imagery (in 1:3, 7–8; 4:15–17), titled her presentation to

---

[29] S. K. Stowers, *Letter Writing in Greco-Roman Antiquity* (LEC 5; Philadelphia: Westminster, 1986).

[30] Ibid., 58.

[31] Ibid., 60.

[32] Cf. also pp. 94–97 on friends and paraenesis.

[33] D. E. Aune, *The New Testament in Its Literary Environment* (LEC 8; Philadelphia: Westminster, 1987) 161–62.

[34] Ibid., 166–67.

[35] Ibid., 172–73.

[36] Ibid., 173. Cf. 189 on *topoi* in NT letters (friendship is not mentioned).

[37] Ibid., 210–11.

[38] L. T. Johnson, *The Writings of the New Testament: An Interpretation* (Philadelphia: Fortress, 1986) 341–44.

the SBL "Pauline Theology Group" in 1987, "Christology, Friendship, and Status."[39] But in the revision of this essay for 1991 publication in *Pauline Theology* the "friendship" emphasis totally disappears.[40]

There was a counterbalancing shift, however, in that Stowers, who in the 1986 book had said "there are no letters of friendship in the New Testament,"[41] now seemingly reversed his opinion in an essay for the same SBL group.[42] Stowers here speaks of "a massive, almost overwhelming number of connections with ancient, especially Greek, friendship motifs," and of how "scholars of ancient letter writing have long identified Philippians as a letter of friendship."[43] In citing Koskenniemi, Thraede, and his own 1986 book, Stowers means, I think, that the φιλικὸς τύπος letter has long been discussed by scholars, but without necessarily citing Philippians as an example. Indeed, the "only commentator" Stowers says he discovered "who employs friendship in Philippians" is L. M. White, whose article in the 1990 Malherbe Festschrift will loom significant.

Stowers contends that "Philippians is clearly a letter of friendship" even if φιλία terms are not used,[44] a "hortatory or psychagogic letter of friendship," akin to Seneca's *Letters to Lucilius*, though in Paul's case addressed to a community, not to an individual. As evidence, the presence/absence theme is cited; yearning to be with friends (1:7–8; 4:1; 2:26); common projects (κοινωνία, suffering; 1:7; 2:17–18; 4:14); giving and receiving (4:15; cf. P. Marshall); "one spirit" (1:27), thinking the same thing (2:2); and living in a manner governed by the heavenly commonwealth (3:20), in contrast to enmity (chap. 3; cf. P. Marshall). The further claim is made that Philippians is built around "antithetical models" of friends and enemies (1:15–17, where "envy" and "rivalry" are Paul's terms; and 3:1–21, where ἐχθροί is used at 3:18, but φίλοι not). The attempt is then made to soften βλέπετε at 3:2 to mean "reflect upon" the Judaizers as a negative example. Christ is termed "friend," though the term is not, of course, found in

---

[39] P. Perkins, "Christology, Friendship, and Status: The Rhetoric of Philippians," *SBL Seminar Papers* (SBLSP 26; Atlanta: Scholars Press, 1987).

[40] P. Perkins, "Philippians: Theology for the Heavenly Politeuma," *Pauline Theology, Volume I* (ed. J. M. Bassler; Minneapolis: Fortress, 1991) 89–104.

[41] Stowers, *Letter Writing*, 60.

[42] S. K. Stowers, "Friends and Enemies in the Politics of Heaven: Reading Theology in Philippians," *Pauline Theology, Volume I* (ed. J. M. Bassler; Minneapolis: Fortress, 1991) 105–21.

[43] Ibid., 106–07.

[44] Ibid., 119 n. 45.

Philippians. Finally and above all, 2:6–11, it is suggested, "would have recalled to its ancient readers stories about those who gave up their lives for their friends," as in Lucian's *Toxaris*—though it would be a "novel" or "un-Greek" twist to suffer on behalf of unequals.

In connection with the now emerging view on Philippians as a letter of friendship, detailed monographs by classicists are cited by Stowers to support the important point that "ancient friendship has very little in common with the modern institution of private or personal friendship."[45] These treatments include (1) Gabriel Herman, *Ritualized Friendship and the Greek City*,[46] on how networks of personal alliances for ξενία or guest-friendship continued in the *polis*, through a pattern of favor (εὐεργεσία), pledges (πιστά; a handshake, δεξιά), ritual declaration, and perhaps letters to renew the hospitality relationship or letters of recommendation (cf. Phlm 22); (2) Richard P. Saller, *Personal Patronage under the Early Empire*,[47] on the network of patron and friends or clients, involving the emperor and imperial aristocracy, for reciprocal exchange of goods and services, often asymmetrically; cf. *amici Caesaris* as persons with access to higher-ups (and possibly Phil 4:22, οἱ ἐκ τῆς Καίσαρος οἰκίας and 1:13 πραιτώριον); and (3) Horst Hutter, *Politics as Friendship*,[48] on "friendship systems," such as "union of friends" for political purposes, sometimes including homosexual ἔρως and hetaery. But none of these monographs applies the theme of friendship to letters very directly, let alone to Philippians specifically.

Given Stowers' emphasis on it, L. M. White's 1990 article calls for careful analysis. Philippians is presented as "a paradigm of friendship" (subtitle) as Paul stands "between two worlds," Jewish and Greek, and that in terms of "morality."[49] Paul here is seen to adopt "more a Greek than a Jewish way of shaping moral identity,"[50] via "a communal ideal of virtue in Christ Jesus, a Pauline adaptation of the

---

[45] Ibid., 107 and n. 8.

[46] G. Herman, *Ritualized Friendship and the Greek City* (Cambridge: Cambridge University Press, 1987).

[47] R. P. Saller, *Personal Patronage under the Early Empire* (Cambridge: Cambridge University Press, 1982).

[48] H. Hutter, *Politics as Friendship: The Origins of Classical Notions of Politics in the Theory and Practice of Friendship* (Waterloo, Ont.: Wilfrid Laurier University Press, 1978).

[49] L. Michael White, "Morality between Two Worlds: A Paradigm of Friendship in Philippians," *Greeks, Romans, and Christians: Essays in Honor of Abraham J. Malherbe* (ed. D. L. Balch, E. Ferguson, and W. A. Meeks; Minneapolis: Fortress, 1990) 201–15.

[50] Ibid., 204.

Hellenistic moral paradigm of φιλία."[51] The argument is on good grounds in stating that Philippians contains "little that is Jewish in its content, its tone, or its ethical exhortation."[52] It is on less solid ground, in my judgment, in stating that Philippians "is primarily a friendly hortatory letter [why only "primarily"?] and holds to conventions seen in the epistolary theorists." Of the references cited—Malherbe, *Ancient Epistolary Theorists*; Stowers, *Letter Writing*, and Malherbe, *Paul and the Thessalonians*[53]—the chief appeal seems to be to 1 Thessalonians as a "paraenetic letter"[54] and the position that friendly letters seek to maintain friendship, expressed in exhortation.[55]

White appeals particularly to 2:6–11 as a reflection of "two worlds," the "Jewish *Vorlage*" [= ? is "Aramaic original" meant, cf. n. 30? or does he mean that Isaiah 53 is reflected? or that there was a Jewish or Jewish-Christian composition behind our Greek "hymn"?) being overwhelmed in its Hellenistic "moralizing context."[56] Here one must come to terms with "social context." Paul Sampley had earlier rejected theories about a business partnership between Paul and Lydia or Paul and the Philippians in a commercial venture, and had argued for κοινωνία in Philippians as a consensual agreement, along quasi-legal lines of the Latin *societas*, for mission purposes.[57] White now sets this aside for a broader semantic field, that of friendship (φιλία), which involves hospitality (φιλοξενία), patronage/benefaction (εὐεργεσία), and letter-writing (συστατικαὶ ἐπιστολαί, recommendations). Then the friendship language is invoked to claim "friendship" is "the code word for the moral paradigm," expressed in the soteriological drama of 2:6–11. *Toxaris* is claimed to illustrate "an all-surpassing act of selfless love" as "the supreme virtue of friendship."[58] But it is added that in 4:10–12 the tone suggests the bonds of friendship with the Philippians "had become strained either by Paul's or Epaphroditus's situation."[59] I am personally dubious of the notion

---

[51] Ibid., 201.

[52] Ibid., 205.

[53] A. J. Malherbe, *Paul and the Thessalonians: The Philosophical Tradition of Pastoral Care* (Philadelphia: Fortress, 1987).

[54] See A. J. Malherbe, "Hellenistic Moralists and the New Testament," *ANRW* 2.26.1 (1992) 267–333, esp. 278–93.

[55] Malherbe, *Paul and the Thessalonians*, 69–70.

[56] White, "Morality between Two Worlds," 208.

[57] P. Sampley, *Pauline Partnership in Christ: Christian Community and Commitment in Light of Roman Law* (Philadelphia: Fortress, 1980).

[58] White, "Morality between Two Worlds," 213.

[59] Ibid., 214.

advanced in a footnote that the crisis was created when a house church patron, perhaps Euodia or Syntyche, "decided no longer to support Paul."[60] All in all, White's is a case for a *relationship* of friendship, within a Greek *topos*, illustrated by 2:6–11, within 2:1–18 as moral teaching. "Letter of friendship" here (p. 206 is as close as White comes to using the term) means a hortatory letter between friends. We may add that 2:1–4 and 12ff. might better have been invoked in the argument.

The position emerging in the articles of L. M. White and Stowers is, if anything, escalated by John T. Fitzgerald's *ABD* article on Philippians (published in 1992, but no doubt completed too early to cite White's 1990 article).[61] He holds that Paul's letter "is essentially a letter of friendship,"[62] as is to be seen from its language and concerns drawn from the *philia topos* and from the antithesis with enmity in chap. 3. One praises friends but ridicules enemies.[63] Paul is encouraging the Philippians "to be a community that is characterized by friendship (1:27–2:11; 4:2–9)."[64] The use of "friendship language throughout" the four chapters establishes for Fitzgerald the literary integrity of Philippians as a unity.[65] 4:10–20 is the climax of the whole letter, we are told, not primarily as thanks for a gift but rather as a commentary upon Paul's long-standing relationship with the Philippians, with the gift viewed as "proof of their continuing friendship."[66] But in rhetorical studies there has scarcely been agreement about the genre of Philippians. Schenk[67] had termed chap. 3 "juridical"; Kennedy[68] called the entire letter "epideictic"; Watson[69] preferred "deliberative rhetoric." Dormeyer, in responding to Schenk, termed Phil 3:2–4:3, 8–9 (Letter C) a "classical friendship-letter," of a "mixed sort" and "on a level above the basic genre of Aristotelian rhetoric."[70]

---

[60] Ibid., 214 n. 59.

[61] J. T. Fitzgerald, "Philippians, Epistle to the," *ABD* 5 (1992) 318–26.

[62] Ibid., 320.

[63] Ibid., 321.

[64] Ibid., 320.

[65] Ibid., 321.

[66] Ibid., 322.

[67] Schenk, *Philipperbriefe*, 279–80.

[68] George A. Kennedy, *New Testament Interpretation through Rhetorical Criticism* (Chapel Hill NC: University of North Carolina Press, 1984) 77.

[69] Duane F. Watson, "A Rhetorical Analysis of Philippians and its Implications for the Unity Question," *NovT* 30 (1988) 57–88.

[70] Detlev Dormeyer, "The Implicit and Explicit Readers and the Genre of

If L. M. White's analysis depends, with Malherbe, on the paraenetic or "moral virtue" emphasis, H.-J. Klauck points in a somewhat different direction, that of ecclesiology.[71] Klauck treats 3 John (v. 12, the recommendation of Demetrius); disciples as φίλοι of Jesus (John 15:12–15); Luke's use and correction of friendship ethics; and Paul's applications of the theme (with Rom 5:6–8 as a christological corrective; *Toxaris* revisited?). But there is also an awareness of a move by Paul from natural kinship as a factor in friendship to a fictive one.[72] Hence, "brother/sister" terminology is preferred by Paul over that of "friends,"[73] and these Christian ἀδελφοί are not friends in the Greek sense but *Geschwister* by baptism into Christ's body, transcending Jew and Greek, slave and free, male or female. Further, if Gal 4:12–20 is rightly said to reflect the friendship *topos*, it may be derived via Hellenistic Judaism, rather than from the Greek world directly.[74]

Klauck's pupil, Martin Ebner, treated Phil 4:10–20, on the relation of friendship and autarchy, in his dissertation on *Peristasenkataloge*.[75] Paul can be said to have developed a concept of friendship with his communities which is seen in Galatians through the reference at 6:6 about sharing in "all good things" by teacher and learner; in Philippi, where friendship language is especially frequent; and less so in Corinth, where Paul had to learn to refrain from Corinthian support in favor of self-sufficiency. That Phil 4:10–20 also includes the language of

---

Philippians 3:2–4:3, 8–9: Response to the Commentary of Wolfgang Schenk," *Semeia 48: Reader Perspectives on the New Testament* (ed. E. V. McKnight; Atlanta: Scholars, 1989) 152–53.

[71] Hans-Josef Klauck, "Kirche als Freundesgemeinschaft? Auf Spurensuche in Neuen Testament," *MTZ* 42 (1991) 1–14.

[72] Ibid., 10–13. See also Alan C. Mitchell, "'Greet the Friends by Name:' New Testament Evidence for the Greco-Roman Topos on Friendship" (paper presented to the Hellenistic Moral Philosophy and Early Christianity Consultation at the annual meeting of the Society of Biblical Literature, Kansas City, MO, November, 1991) n. 7. A slightly revised version of Mitchell's paper will appear in *Greco-Roman Perspectives on Friendship* (ed. J. T. Fitzgerald; SBLRBS; Atlanta: Scholars Press, forthcoming).

[73] Klauck, "Kirche als Freundesgemeinschaft?" 10–11; Mitchell, "Greet the Friends by Name," 22.

[74] Klauck, "Kirche als Freundesgemeinschaft?" 8–9; cf. Hans Dieter Betz, *Galatians* (Hermeneia; Philadelphia: Fortress, 1979) 221. See also Klauck's "Brotherly Love in Plutarch and in 4 Maccabees," *Greeks, Romans, and Christians: Essays in Honor of Abraham J. Malherbe* (ed. D. L. Balch, E. Ferguson, and W. A. Meeks; Minneapolis: Fortress, 1990) 144–56.

[75] Martin Ebner, *Leidenslisten und Apostelbrief: Untersuchungen zu Form, Motivik und Funktion der Peristasenkataloge bei Paulus* (FB 66; Würzburg: Echter, 1991). A summary of his treatment of friendship is given by Mitchell, "Greet the Friends by Name," 7–9.

accounting (4:15) and of money-lending (4:17–18, debt and credit) is no problem, since friendship in the world of the day was utilitarian.[76] The financial (4:15) and the ethical (4:14) can then both be said to be involved in a community of friends.[77] But Paul seems involved in two different roles: in vv. 14–16, that of partner, using language of friendship; in 17–19, that of banker, crediting profit to them (v. 17) and, in 18b, Ebner suggests, also as a priest offering their sacrifice. Vv. 14–17 thus have to do with friendship among human beings; v. 18 with friendship with God, who will fulfill all their needs. This brings God into the picture, but a God about whom Paul can testify from personal experience (v. 13) on what this Lord can do. God enabled Paul's self-sufficiency and will fulfill that of the Philippians too.[78] In this way Paul moves beyond a friendship *topos* about himself with the Philippians toward a κοινωνία of community and God–ecclesiology, that is, not only morality.[79]

We must now ask, with Mitchell,[80] how White's "moral paradigm" of friendship in Philippians accords with Ebner's point that Paul needed "to assert his self-sufficiency to correct the Philippians' idea of friendship"; for the two are "incompatible"; Paul's "asserting his autonomy [in chap. 4] goes against the ethics of self-emptying friendship" in Philippians, esp. 2:6–11. Mitchell suggests, through rhetorical questions, that the matter of the letter's literary integrity may need to be reopened, and that the conflict may be due to more than "the harsh lesson Paul learned at Corinth."[81] For the contemporary rules about friendship and enmity easily produced factions. Must the apostle not be free from the conventions of such friendship, in order to preach the gospel? Paul must reshape current ideas of φιλία in Philippi.

We may go one step further. The phrase φρονεῖν ὑπέρ + the genitive, found at Phil 1:7 and 4:10, has been widely identified as friendship language.[82] With Schenk we may claim it was being *quoted* by Paul at 4:10 from an earlier Philippian letter of friendship to Paul.[83] The

---

[76] Ebner, *Leidenslisten und Apostelbrief*, 345–53.

[77] Ibid., 352–58.

[78] Ibid., 358–63.

[79] Ibid., 363–64.

[80] Mitchell, "Greet the Friends by Name," 22–23.

[81] Ibid., 23.

[82] G. Stählin, "φιλέω, κτλ" *TDNT* 9.161–62; Schenk, *Philipperbriefe*, 60, 63–65, 336; Paul Ewald, *Der Brief des Paulus an die Philipper* (KzNT 11; Leipzig: Deichert, 1908) 211 n. 1 = 4th ed. by Gustav Wohlenberg (Leipzig: Deichert, 1923) 227 n. 1.

[83] John Reumann, "Contributions of the Philippian Community to Paul and to

Philippians used the phrase, "to be mindful of Paul," "forget him not," as a slogan of solidarity between community and their apostle. The Philippians employed it in their cover letter that accompanied the gift to Paul, sent through Epaphroditus. He quotes it back to them at 4:10, in his first letter (Letter A, now in 4:10–20) and later echoes it in Letter B to them in what is now 1:7. This fits with references in Klauck, to "the *Philippians'* idea of friendship," a perfectly natural one for such a Roman *colonia* in northern Greece, without even a synagogue. Paul does not reject such expressions of friendship but begins to nuance the idea and to differentiate himself from the patron/client relationship by reference to his being αὐτάρκης at 4:11— much as he accepts 2:6–11 as a Philippian composition on how to witness to the Roman world but corrects it christologically, at least by the addition in 2:8c of θανάτου δὲ σταυροῦ.[84]

It is worth considering that the *philia topos* was therefore one Paul encountered at several times and places. He at times employed some of its language. But he did not create a special ecclesiology out of it with the Philippians, as he struggled to maintain apostolic independence amid the social pressures of the implied patron-client relationship in contemporary friendship networks.

Some of the attention to friendship with regard to Phil 4:10–20 has revolved around the fact that the verses nowhere use any form of εὐχαριστεῖν and therefore, whether as the body of Letter A or the last major section of a four-chapter epistle, are a "thankless thanks" to the Philippians for their gift(s). Among the solutions proposed is that of G. W. Peterman in 1991, appealing to "social convention" involving friendship.[85] It draws on his 1992 University of London dissertation (*non vidi*).[86] In a 1991 paper Peterman called attention to PMert I 12,[87] where a well-educated man writes to a physician-friend that he is going to "dispense with writing to you with a great show

---

Earliest Christianity," *NTS* 39 (1993) 440–41. For the parallel case of the Thessalonians writing to Paul, see A. J. Malherbe, "Did the Thessalonians Write to Paul?" *The Conversation Continues: Studies in Paul and John in Honor of J. Louis Martyn* (ed. R. Fortna and B. R. Gaventa; Nashville: Abingdon, 1990) 246–57.

[84] Reumann, "Contributions of the Philippian Community."

[85] Gerald W. Peterman, "'Thankless Thanks': The Epistolary Social Convention in Philippians 4:10–20," *TynBul* 42 (1991) 261–70.

[86] G. W. Peterman, "Social Reciprocity in Paul: Aspects of Graeco-Roman Social Conventions in Selected Texts" (Diss., King's College, University of London, 1992).

[87] Text and translation available in White, *Light from Ancient Letters*, #93; translation only in Stowers, *Letter Writing*, 61–62.

of thanks (μεγάλας εὐχαριστίας), for it is to those who are not friends that we must give thanks in words (διὰ λόγων εὐχαριστεῖν). ..." The claim by Peterman is that "verbal gratitude is misplaced among those who are intimate" friends, though material gratitude is required; any verbal gratitude means "an expression of debt or of one's intention to repay"; cf. for support Seneca *Ben.* 2.24.4.[88] Some twenty-five other papyrus letters were then examined. One may compare the "thankful ([ἀπ]ευχαριστικός) type" of letter in Pseudo-Demetrius and Pseudo-Libanius.[89] From all this, Peterman concludes that in Phil 4:10–20 *verbal* thanks should not be expected among friends, and that there is no pledge by Paul to repay because "God will discharge Paul's debt by supplying their every need."[90]

Capper, who heard Peterman's paper presented in 1991, found the proposed social convention from intimate friendship did "not provide a complete explanation."[91] D. Peterlin was sympathetic but declared the explanation "somewhat stretched."[92] Witherington was more favorable to the dissertation.[93] Capper's own analysis agreed more with Sampley about a contractual obligation on the part of the Philippians to support Paul ("nascent canon law" Capper terms it) but argues there was a dispute caused by the fact that Paul's imprisonment meant he could not preach the gospel for them and so was "in breach of his contract." Paul's "receipt" for their gift in 4:10–20 represented a negotiated settlement, but Phil 1–2 presents Paul's argument that his imprisonment "actually serves the Gospel (1:12–14)" and so the Philippians should remain reciprocally faithful (1:17–30) and desist from grumbling (2:12–15).[94] There may be some language (like φρονεῖν) that friends and partners in a *societas* would use, but Capper does not suggest that we are dealing here with a *topos* from, or a letter of, friendship.

---

[88] Peterman, "Thankless Thanks," 264.

[89] Ps.-Demetrius, *Typoi Epist.* 21 (Malherbe, "Ancient Epistolary Theorists," 39 = *Ancient Epistolary Theorists*, 41) and Ps.-Libanius, *Epist. Char.* 57 (Malherbe, "Ancient Epistolary Theorists," 71 = *Ancient Epistolary Theorists*, 75).

[90] Peterman, "Thankless Thanks," 268–70.

[91] Brian J. Capper, "Paul's Dispute with Philippi: Understanding Paul's Argument in Phil 1–2 from his Thanks in 4.10–20," *TZ* 49 (1993) 208 n. 33.

[92] Davorin Peterlin, "Paul's Letter to the Philippians in the Light of Disunity in the Church" (Diss., Aberdeen, 1992) 299. The dissertation is now available as vol. 79 of NovTSup (Leiden: Brill, 1995).

[93] Ben Witherington, III. *Friendship and Finances in Philippi: The Letter of Paul to the Philippians* (The New Testament in Context; Valley Forge, PA: Trinity Press International, 1994) 147 n. 71; 168 n. 11.

[94] Capper, "Paul's Dispute with Philippi," 196–97.

The 1992 dissertation on Philippians by Peterlin, written at Aberdeen under I. Howard Marshall, does not take up the (letter of) friendship theme particularly, but sketches a church more divided than in most analyses. Issues involved continued financial support for Paul, and when the latest fund-raising fell short, Epaphroditus went at his own expense to make up that was lacking in service to Paul. The apostle writes in 4:10–20, therefore, "with a considerable degree of unease" but with great impartiality amid the factions in Philippi.[95]

The 1993 dissertation by Lukas Bormann on the city and church at Philippi at the time of Paul, written at Frankfurt under Dieter Georgi, moves away from the friendship paradigm to emphasize *beneficia* within a patron-client relationship, as seen in Roman writers like Seneca. Bormann first reexamines the sources on Philippi and underscores the Romanness of the city, its inhabitants, religion, and culture.[96] As a *colonia*, it is part of the Julio-Claudian patronage system, from the Princeps down. Its soldiers and veterans, *familia Caesaris*, and rural laborers were part of a structure, the propaganda for which, Dionysius of Halicarnassus was saying (*Ant. Rom.* 2.9.11),[97] went back to Romulus. Bormann regards 4:10–20, where there is friendship language, as the key to Paul's relationship with the Philippians (and as Letter A, 4:10–23, in a three-letter sequence).[98] In his analysis of these verses, in light of Roman-Hellenistic social conventions, Bormann finds less helpful Sampley's *societas* theory[99] and L. M. White's use of φιλία,[100] though the latter had referred to "patronage/benefaction (εὐεργεσία)."[101] Bormann looks instead to Seneca (*De beneficiis* and *Epistolae morales*)[102] as background in Roman Philippi.

---

[95] Peterlin, "Paul's Letter to the Philippians," 327.

[96] L. Bormann, *Philippi: Stadt und Christengemeinde zur Zeit des Paulus* (NovTSup 78; Leiden: Brill, 1995) 11–84.

[97] The passage is not, unfortunately, discussed by David L. Balch, "Friendship in the Historian Dionysius of Halicarnassus" (paper presented to the Hellenistic Moral Philosophy and Early Christianity Consultation at the annual meeting of the Society of Biblical Literature, Kansas City, MO, November, 1991). A slightly revised version of Balch's paper will appear in *Greco-Roman Perspectives on Friendship* (ed. J. T. Fitzgerald; SBLRBS; Atlanta: Scholars Press, forthcoming).

[98] Bormann, *Philippi*, 85–160.

[99] Ibid., 206–07, cf. 181–85; cf. also Veronica Korperski, "Feminist Concerns and the Authorial Readers in Philippians," *LS* 17 (1992) 286–89.

[100] Bormann, *Philippi*, 167–68 n. 25.

[101] White, "Morality between Two Worlds," 211.

[102] Cf. S. C. Mott, "The Power of Giving and Receiving: Reciprocity in Helle-

On this reading the Philippians operated with a *do-ut-des* principle of reciprocity: in a patron-client relationship, A gives to B, but B is expected to give back (more) in return.[103] Such patronage "is a father-son relationship, a partnership, not brotherhood or friend-ship."[104] White had spoken of Paul as "spiritual patron," the Philippians as "economic patron."[105] According to Bormann, Paul does not wish to be their patron or "religious hero" or to further any notion that *he* will repay them for what they have given him.[106] Nor does he wish to be client to their patronage. In 4:10–20 he introduces "retarding factors" in vv. 11 and 17 ("not that I . . .") and in the prayer of 19–20. The *peristasis*-catalogue in 11–13 undercuts the idea of "religious hero" with a picture of himself as itinerant proclaimer whom God sustains. In 17–18 Paul moves the exchange between them to include God, and in 19–20 asserts that it is God who will fulfill their need, eschatologically.

Into this exposition of how Paul is seeking to wean the Philippians from their (Roman) idea of *amicitia* (or *beneficia*), Bormann weaves the further suggestion that Paul wished to create an "emancipated clien-tele" in the Philippian Christians.[107] While Paul goes part way with views drawn from his converts' social world, he is in basic conflict with the patron system of the Empire (1:12–17, cf. 1 Thess 2:2; 1:27–30; Acts 16:20–21, though probably Lucan reconstruction). What gives "additional brisance" to the controversy is that the Julio-Claudian house (Nero, A.D. 54–68) was patron over Philippi. Here Paul's εὐαγγέλιον stands in ultimate opposition to the εὐαγγέλια or "good tidings" about the emperor and a religio-political ideology (Dionysius of Halicarnassus).[108] Philippians, then, is no "letter of friendship" but engages critically the *topos* of *amicitia* as understood and practiced in Roman Philippi.

The title *Friendship and Finances in Philippi*, by Ben Witherington III, suggests that there will be considerable attention to φιλία, espe-cially when the author calls his volume "a socio-rhetorical commen-

---

nistic Benevolence," *Current Issues in Biblical and Patristic Literature* (ed. G. F. Hawthorne; Grand Rapids: Eerdmans, 1975) 60 and passim on "giving and receiving."
  [103] Bormann, *Philippi*, 161–224.
  [104] Ibid., 205.
  [105] White, "Morality between Two Worlds," 215 n. 59.
  [106] Bormann, *Philippi*, 212–13.
  [107] Ibid., 206–07.
  [108] Ibid., 217–24.

tary."[109] There is emphasis on the Roman nature of Philippi[110] and on Paul "as a well-educated Roman citizen . . . a person of high status."[111] The exegesis stresses how Paul is trying in the letter "to de-culturate his audience" from values of the Greco-Roman world, such as what constitutes "honor" and "boasting," in favor of "a *counter-culture*,"[112] detaching them "from the values of imperial eschatology and Roman citizenship."[113] One may ask whether this "transvaluation of values"[114] might have applied to contemporary concepts of friendship too. Witherington's introduction on "social concerns" asks whether Paul's monetary links with the Philippians reflects a *societas* relationship (Sampley) or "'friendship' (*amicitia*) . . . involving 'giving and receiving.'"[115] But little is then said about friendship in the commentary, and the notion of a letter of friendship is not broached. With regard to finances it is urged that Paul turned down all offers of patronage[116] and gifts with "strings attached,"[117] aiming instead at parity[118] and reciprocity with the Philippians,[119] though the apostle had initiated the relationship and set the terms as "the ambassador of their Benefactor."[120] Why so little is said about φιλία and why the letter is classified as primarily deliberative rhetoric,[121] with no reference to letters of friendship, is clarified in an excursus on "Paul and the Philippians—Partners, Friends, or Family?"[122] L. M. White's proposal of "a paradigm of friendship" is regarded as having "more to commend it than Sampley's"[123] on *societas* partnership, but arguments are listed against both views. The preference is for a "family" relationship, involving something of hierarchy and something of, but not absolute, parity. Is Philippians then a "family letter," as Loveday Alexander argued?[124] Witherington's treatment shows how "friendship"

---

[109] Witherington, *Friendship and Finances*, 5.
[110] Ibid., 12, 20–22, 98–99, 129, 132–33, 151 n. 2.
[111] Ibid., 168 n. 24; cf. 2–4.
[112] Ibid., 47–49.
[113] Ibid., 100–02.
[114] Ibid., 70.
[115] Ibid., 23.
[116] Ibid., 123–24.
[117] Ibid., 127.
[118] Ibid., 123.
[119] Ibid., 126–27, 130–31, citing Peterman's dissertation.
[120] Ibid., 126.
[121] Ibid., 13, 16.
[122] Ibid., 118–21.
[123] Ibid., 119.
[124] Loveday Alexander, "Hellenistic Letter-Forms and the Structure of Philippians,"

has received a place in commentary treatment in English, but lacks the specificity (with regard especially to 4:10–20) found in Pesch and Schenk a decade earlier.

Patristic Witness to Friendship and to Philippians

One way in which to test perceptions of ancient epistolary and rhetorical forms and *topoi* in a Pauline letter is to ask how the church fathers in subsequent centuries may have perceived the NT documents. After all, writers like Augustine, Tertullian, Cyprian, Arnobius, and Lactantius had been professional rhetoricians before their years as Christian theologians. The Cappadocians, Gregory Nazianzus, Gregory of Nyssa, and Basil of Caesarea, all wrote letters of friendship.[125]

The Oxford *Patristic Greek Lexicon* is, however, not particularly helpful under φιλία (but cf. Clem. Al. *Str.* 2.19 for reflections of Aristotle, and Greg. Naz. *Ep.* 15, φιλία consists in doing all things in common, both sorrow and joys); nil under ἐπιστολή, τύπος, or φιλίκός. But the editors, G. L. Prestige and G. W. H. Lampe, did not necessarily think in rhetorical terms. We can, however, look for help in patristic monographs like Caroline White's *Christian Friendship in the Fourth Century* (in East and West; pagan theory and Christian ideas)[126] and in encyclopedia articles (*RAC; TRE*).

None of the rhetoricians-turned-Christian mentioned above have left commentaries on Philippians. But in the patristic commentaries and homilies that are extant, probes can be made into treatments of Philippians and other letters which are termed "letters of friendship" today. I take as an example the Homilies by John Chrysostom, likely delivered in Constantinople, between 398 and 407.[127]

JSNT 37 (1989) 87–101. The argument is based chiefly on POxy 12.1481 (text and translation in White, *Light from Ancient Letters*, #102). Cf. Peter Wick, *Der Philipperbrief: Der formale Aufbau des Briefs als Schlüssel zum Verständnis seines Inhalts* (BWANT 7/15 [135]; Stuttgart: Kohlhammer, 1994) 152–60.

[125] Cf. Ruth Majercik, "Rhetoric and Rhetorical Criticism in the Greco-Roman World," *ABD* 5 (1992) 710–12; Malherbe, "Ancient Epistolary Theorists," 56–57 = *Ancient Epistolary Theorists*, 58–61; Greg. Naz. *Ep.* 51, to Nicobulus; Thraede, *Grundzüge*.

[126] C. White, *Christian Friendship in the Fourth Century* (New York: Cambridge University Press, 1992).

[127] F. C. Baur dated them earlier, in Antioch. Text: *PG* 62:177–298; translation: NPNF 1st Series, 13.173–255, columns indicated as a or b. See J. Quasten, *Patrology* (3 vols.; Westminster, MD: Newman, 1951–60) 3:449–50.

According to Chrysostom, φιλία, which exists even among the wicked, is not to be undervalued but cultivated with greatest care; but ἀγάπη, produced by sincere faith, stands somewhat in contrast (Homily on 1 Tim 1:5–7; PG 62.509.20–60 = NPNF 13.412ab). With regard to 1 Thess 2:7–8, where Paul said that, "gentle like a nurse among you," we "shared with you the gospel of God and our own selves," Chrysostom states that the person who loves (φιλοῦντα) ought not to refuse his very soul, just as Paul with the Thessalonians would willingly have given his soul, for nothing is sweeter than such ἀγάπη. "A φίλος πιστός (faithful friend) is a medicine of life" (quoting Sir 6:16) and "a strong defense" (Sir 6:14). Nothing is comparable to a genuine φίλος. Φιλία is in itself a great delight, friend knit to friend κατὰ τὴν ψυχήν. But this refers to genuine φίλοι, who are ὁμόψυχοι and who even die for each other, who love (φιλεῖν) warmly, not those who are mere table companions (κοινωνοὺς τῶν τραπεζῶν). One prays for the same things for a friend as for oneself. Genuine friends who ask for and receive favors (χάριν) are more longed for than the light. But that means spiritual (πνευματικοί) friends, such as Paul was, φίλοι κατὰ Χριστόν. Acts 4:32 and 35 are here cited as an example of believers who were "of one heart and soul." This is φιλία, that someone not consider his own things but those of the neighbor (cf. Phil 2:4). Such friends who love are commanded and ruled rather than themselves giving commands or ruling; they bestow favors and reflect the way God gave his Son for us. Where there is φιλία, we hide our own well-doing and make our great deeds appear small. The friendship that excels is like something from heaven. With a friend, one endures banishment; but without a friend one would not choose to live in one's own land. A friend is "another self" (ἄλλον ἑαυτόν). The reward of friendship is that we love (φιλῶμεν) one another (62.403.20–406.28 = NPNF 13.330–32).

The Colossians, like the addressees in Romans (and Hebrews), were people Paul had not seen, but more important is their friendship in the Spirit (62.300.18–19 = NPNF 13.257). In connection with Col 1:8, "love in the Spirit," Chrysostom (62.302.57–309 = NPNF 13.259–63) speaks of the causes producing φιλία: those that are natural (φυσικαί) and those arising out of relationships in life (βιωτικαί). The latter include a friend inherited from forebears, or table-companions, neighbors, or those in the same trade; the former, family relationships, or that of husband and wife. But πνευματικὴ ἀγάπη (spiritual love) is higher than all these. Nothing is so strong as the bond of the

Spirit. Let us therefore, he urges, follow the friendships which are of the Spirit (φιλίας τὰς ἀπὸ τοῦ πνεύματος), not those that arise from the table (ἀπὸ τῶν τραπεζῶν). Then comes the comparison of two tables, one for the blind, halt, and maimed, the other for governors, generals, etc. One should choose the first table, with Christ; not the coldness of men who are made friends at table, but friendship with God (φιλία . . . πρὸς τὸν θεόν).

The Philippians, Chrysostom says, were lovingly (ἀγαπητικῶς) disposed toward Paul and sent money to him with Epaphroditus (62.179.17 = NPNF 13.181b). Although the Philippians were not all of one mind, he wrote them in a generally positive way, like a teacher (62.179.48–180.9 = NPNF 13.182a). That Paul loved them greatly (ἐφίλει) is apparent from 2:20 and 1:7 (62.180.30–34 = 182b). Chrysostom then appeals, toward the close of his introductory discourse, for his hearers to despise wealth and give alms, on the basis of the Philippians' example.

With regard to Phil 1:5, about the Philippians' participation in the gospel, Chrysostom quotes Luke 16:9, on making friends through unrighteous mammon. But later (62.188.33 = 187b) Luke 14:12 is quoted, about not inviting one's φίλοι to dinner but the maimed, lame, and blind (cf. above, on Col 1). In discussing Phil 1:7 Chrysostom says that "spiritual ἔρως" is so imperial (τυραννικόν) "that it possesses the soul of him who loves (φιλοῦντος)," even amid trouble and pain. So φιλία "keeps the soul of the one who loves (ἀγαπῶντος) and pleases God" (62.186.29 = 186ab). On 1:8, the term σπλάγχνοις is deemed a warmer term than even ἀγάπη; the full phrase "affections of Christ" means "according to Christ" or "since you love (φιλεῖτε) Christ" (62.189.36–44 = 188ab).

The comment on 1:9, "that you may abound in knowledge and all discernment," is that Paul "does not extol φιλία merely or ἀγάπη merely, but that which arises out of ἐπίγνωσις," i.e., with judgment, reason, perception. Those who love (φιλοῦντες) without reason end up with mere or simple (189a "weak") friendship, or are spoiled by the ἀγάπη of heretics. The advice is even set forth, Love (ἀγαπᾶτε) so as not to be harmed by φιλία (62.191.10 = 189; cf. Rom 12:18). For friendships often harm many persons (191.14–15). Friendships are also mentioned among the ways to avoid sin (62.210.11 = 201a). It is, however, a mark of boldness and courage to despise friendships in favor of what is pleasing to God (62.218.16 = 206a). In connection with Phil 2:4 it is noted that Paul did not refer to servants being subject to masters but to persons of equal honor subjecting themselves to each other; φιλία is not mentioned, however, at this point (though cf. the reflection of 2:4 above, in connection with 1 Thess 2).

Paul in Rome (his place of imprisonment, according to Chrysostom) is said to represent the *city* of the Philippians as ambassador, not the church there or "friends" (62.249.52–55 = 226a). On 4:2–3, the προστασία or protection, as Euodia and Syntyche labored with Paul in the gospel, came not from the household (οἴκοθεν) or from φιλία but from right actions (κατορθωμάτων), including the zeal of these women (62.280.10–11 = 244). The judgment, "This is genuine and spiritual φιλία" (62.290.4 = 250b), is spoken with regard to 4:12, reflecting how Paul both removes himself from the Philippians and unites himself with them.

All this evidence allows one to say Chrysostom saw Paul as reflecting friendship terminology, perhaps even a *topos* on friendship, but evidence is lacking that Chrysostom viewed any of the epistles or parts of them as "letters of friendship." Even in Phlm 22 the request for ξενία, a lodging, evokes no reference in the homily to a link of friendship; rather, Chrysostom claims that the request reflects Paul's confidence and the hint that Paul's coming would ensure the favor he had requested for Onesimus, for he would be there to check on things. It would be an honor for the hosts to have Paul visit, not a sign or convention of φιλία. While "friend(s) of God" or of Christ is not uncommon in patristic literature (*PGL* 1480b–1481a), I note at least one christological use, in connection with 2 Thess 2:14, about "the Friend of man" (φιλάνθρωπος, 62.488.26 = 390a; cf. 62.224.30 = 210a and the comment on Phil 3:20–21, "an act of [God's] kindness and love toward humanity (φιλανθρωπία)," 62.280.33 = 244b). But no designation of letters as ἐπιστολαὶ φιλικαί.

The same sort of findings are provided by similar but very preliminary probes into the commentaries on Philippians by John of Damascus (ca. 657–749; *PG* 95); Theodoret of Cyprus (ca. 393–466; *PG* 82); Servian of Gabala (School of Antioch, died after 408; ed. K. Staab 1933); Theodore of Mopsuestia (ca. 350–428; ed. H. Swete); Theophylact (11th cent; *PG* 124); and Pseudo-Oecumenius of Trica (*PG* 118). In these writers, vocabulary related to friendship sometimes appears, suggesting a *topos* known to them, but no reference to letters of friendship as a form. But much more detailed work is needed, as also in Latin writers like Ambrosiaster (4th cent.; *PL* 17); Jerome (ca. 342–420; *PL* 30); Cassiodorus (ca. 485–580; *PL* 70); Pelagius (fl. 410–18; *PL* Sup. 1); and Victorinus (280–363, *PL* 8).

An interesting test case among the medieval fathers is Thomas Aquinas (ca. 1225–1274), since the Thomistic account of friendship was influenced by Aristotle's *Nicomachean Ethics* (Book VIII). Paul J. Wadell, moreover, takes *charitas* in Aquinas to be "friendship with God," in service to which the virtues and gifts of the Spirit stand.[128] In commenting on Phil 4:8, Aquinas understands "whatever is lovely" to refer to what leads to "mutual friendship," citing verses about visiting the sick (Sir 7:35) and "a friend who sticks closer than a brother" (Prov 18:24). But does Aquinas' use of Aristotle on friendship, in commentary on Paul or in his own theology, represent a continuous exegetical tradition or a rediscovery of Aristotle in the West?

Among the Reformers, Philipp Melanchthon offers promising references to rhetoric,[129] though the work on Philippians (*CR* 15:1283–94) is perhaps that of his colleague Georg Major.

I have not found evidence of letters of friendship in Bernhard Weiss's history of the interpretation of Philippians.[130]

Another avenue of testing is to proceed as Henry Cadbury did with William Hobart's evidence for Luke's medical profession on the basis of alleged medical vocabulary in Luke-Acts. Cadbury, the joke ran, got his Ph.D. by taking away Luke's M.D., vocabularywise. Indeed, as far as vocabulary goes, Luke might just as well have been a horse doctor as an M.D. Or, as we now put it, Luke uses vocabulary such as any educated person of his day might have employed. Analogy: is our "vocabulary of friendship" as strikingly distinctive as we think, or does it reflect a number of other areas; e.g., in Phil 4, commerce and banking?

Of course, one can answer such problems by pointing to how the φιλία concept in antiquity involved an economic, political old-boys network, conferring favors. So commercial terminology might be closely linked with it. But is such a social/economic/political world the

---

[128] P. J. Wadell, *Friends of God: Virtues and Gifts in Aquinas* (American University Studies, Series 7; Theology and Religion, Vol. 76; New York: Peter Lang, 1991) 5–15.

[129] So C. Joachim Classen, "St Paul's Epistles and Ancient Greek and Roman Rhetoric," *Rhetoric and the New Testament: Essays from the 1992 Heidelberg Conference* (ed. S. E. Porter and T. H. Olbricht; JSNTSup 90; Sheffield: JSOT Press, 1993) 271–79.

[130] B. Weiss, *Philipper-Brief . . . Geschichte seiner Auslegung* (Berlin: Hertz, 1859).

analogy we want or that is correct for Paul and friends, a world of patron and clients and faction leaders?[131]

Finally, there is the judgment of others engaged in NT rhetorical criticism that Philippians is not a "letter of friendship" but an "administrative letter"; that 4:10–20 is akin to 2 Cor 8 and 9.[132]

Conclusions and Suggestions

1. The chief finding from the history of research and patristic references is that the notion of influence from the vocabulary of φιλία or a friendship *topos* on Paul is better supported than a literary category of ἐπιστολὴ φιλική. There is something of a jump from the mood created by certain words and phrases to a proposed letter form. Philippians ill fits the examples of such a letter type in the theorists' handbooks, and one wonders if such letters ever were written and were not simply for schoolboy exercises and a classification scheme seldom found in "pure" form. The case for a letter of friendship is chiefly argued from the vocabulary that appears in letters from friend to friend in the Greco-Roman world.

2. The starting point in American research seems to have been Malherbe's designation of 1 Thessalonians as a friendly letter marked by paraenesis. The genre of 1 Thessalonians can, of course, itself be subject to some debate. Philippians may reflect friendship language more—or less—than 1 Thessalonians. At issue is whether paraenesis is a sufficient criterion and is to be explained from a "friendly relationship" between writer and addressee or involves a further relationship of teacher and pupils, or founding father and community, or apostle and church.

3. The damaging absence of φιλία terms in Paul has produced several explanations—theologically, that φιλία was too anthropocentric for Paul to use;[133] or sociologically, that Paul desired to avoid

---

[131] Cf. Carl Landé's introduction and comments in *Friends, Followers, and Factions: A Reader in Political Clientism* (ed. S. W. Schmidt et al.; Berkeley: University of California Press, 1977) xiii–xxxvii and 506–09; Jeremy Boissevain, *Friends of Friends: Networks, Manipulators and Coalitions* (New York: St. Martin's Press, 1974); and Bruce Malina, "Patron and Client," *Forum* 4 (1988) 2–32.

[132] So Hans Dieter Betz, *2 Corinthians 8 and 9* (Hermeneia; Philadelphia: Fortress, 1985) 139; cf. 93 n. 27; 118 n. 29).

[133] So J. N. Sevenster, *Paul and Seneca* (Leiden: Brill, 1961).

the status implications of patronal friendship.[134] One would have more confidence in the theory if there were an occasional example in Paul, rather than having to explain why he has transmuted φιλία into something else, like κοινωνία (itself a multivalent term).[135]

4. In any case, the usual Greek "rules of friendship" are lacking in the NT, except possibly at Luke 16:9.[136]

5. The fuller social-world sense of friendship in antiquity makes the usability of the *philia topos* questionable for Paul. It did not fit his role or self-understanding as apostle. Is that why he fails to use the terms or cite the rules? A "society of friends," Greco-Roman style, is not Pauline ecclesiology.

6. Worth investigating is the suggestion that φιλία concepts confronted Paul from the house churches and their leaders which his mission created in the Greco-Roman world. This is to suggest that at least some Philippians and Corinthians saw their relation to the itinerant preacher as that of patron and client—they the patrons, Paul and others the clients. Or they the clients, Paul the patron. Paul was then engaged in a delicate operation of affirming what was useful and of delimiting what was dangerous to his apostolic work in such an arrangement. The Philippians with their gift may have forced his assertion of independence and self-sufficiency or, better, sufficiency from God, to which he wished them also to come. This affirmation and distancing process can possibly be traced though his relationships with the Aegean congregations and their leaders.

---

[134] So Judge, "Paul as a Radical Critic of Society."

[135] John Reumann, "Koinonia in Scripture: Survey of Biblical Texts," *On the Way to Fuller Koinonia* (ed. T. F. Best and G. Gassmann; Faith and Order Paper no. 166; Geneva: WCC Publications, 1994) 37–69.

[136] K. Berger, *Formgeschichte des Neuen Testaments*, 156. But cf. Mitchell, "Greet the Friends," and "The Social Function of Friendship in Acts 2:44–47 and 4:32–37," *JBL* 111 (1992) 255–72.

THE FUNCTION OF FRIENDSHIP LANGUAGE IN PHILIPPIANS 4:10–20

Ken L. Berry

In Phil 4:10–20 Paul acknowledges and responds to the gift from the Philippians which had recently been delivered to him by Epaphroditus (4:18). The passage has often been described as Paul's thank you note and/or receipt for the gift.[1] The position of this response to their gift at the end of the canonical form of the letter has prompted many scholars to argue that it was originally a separate letter of thanksgiving written shortly after Epaphroditus arrived with the gift.[2] On the other hand, some have felt that Paul is so restrained in expressing his appreciation that they call it a "thankless thanks."[3] Such observations suggest the need for further investigation of the purpose and function of this passage.

Paul refers to the recent gift at three points in this passage (vv. 10, 14, 17–18). He does not explicitly thank them for the gift itself, but it is something of an overstatement to describe this section as thankless.[4] His appreciation comes through clearly enough as he relates his great joy (v. 10: Ἐχάρην . . . μεγάλως), commends their action (v. 14: καλῶς ἐποιήσατε), and describes his resulting state of abundance (v. 18: περισσεύω, πεπλήρωμαι). Also, it was considered acceptable for

---

[1] For example, by J. P. Sampley, *Pauline Partnership in Christ* (Philadelphia: Fortress Press, 1980) 52, and G. F. Hawthorne, *Philippians* (WBC 43; Waco: Word, 1983) 194.

[2] See, e.g., F. W. Beare, *A Commentary on the Epistle to the Philippians* (HNTC; 2d ed.; New York: Harper & Row, 1969) 150; B. D. Rahtjen, "The Three Letters of Paul to the Philippians," *NTS* 6 (1959–60) 167–73; H. Koester, "Philippians, Letter to the," *IDBSup* (1976) 665–66; J.-F. Collange, *The Epistle of Saint Paul to the Philippians* (London: Epworth, 1979) 5–6; W. Schenk, *Die Philipperbriefe des Paulus* (Stuttgart: Kohlhammer, 1984) 334–36.

[3] See, e.g., M. Dibelius, *An die Thessalonicher I–II. An die Philipper* (3d ed.; Tübingen: Mohr, 1937) 95; E. Lohmeyer, *Der Brief an die Philipper* (MeyerK 9.1; 11th ed.; Göttingen: Vandenhoeck und Ruprecht, 1956) 178; and J. Gnilka, *Der Philipperbrief* (HTKNT 10.3; Freiburg: Herder, 1976) 173.

[4] Jouette Bassler, *God and Mammon: Asking for Money in the New Testament* (Nashville: Abingdon, 1991) 77, suggests that Paul does not express his thanks directly because the Philippians then would have been obligated to give to Paul again, which Paul did not want them to do. Therefore he expressed his appreciation in somewhat indirect ways.

close friends to forego certain social conventions, such as a formally expressed statement of thanks.[5] However, it is striking that as much if not more space is devoted to explaining that he could have gotten along well enough without the gift (vv. 11–13) and that he does not seek their gift (vv. 17–18), as well as to recounting their relations in the past (vv. 15–16). These features make this passage rather different from a typical thankful letter, such as the example in one epistolary handbook which stresses the recipient's great debt and complete inability to do anything that would be an adequate return of thanks.[6] The function of 4:10–20 would appear to be other or more than simply expressing thanks.

The Philippians' recent gift sent to help Paul during his time of hardship in prison was typical of the kinds of services and benefits which were considered an important part of friendship.[7] The benefits offered by friends could involve a wide variety of material goods or personal services, including hospitality, provision of food and shelter, rescue from danger or death, ransom from captivity, assistance in business or legal affairs, loans or gifts of money or other material resources to cover such needs as travel expenses, debts, or reestablishment after a catastrophe.[8] The Philippians would naturally have

---

[5] Cf., e.g., PMert I 12: γράφειν δέ σοι μεγάλας εὐχαριστίας παρετέο(ν)·δεῖ γὰρ τοῖς μὴ φίλοις οὖσι διὰ λόγων εὐχαριστεῖν: "I may dispense with writing to you with a great show of thanks; for it is to those who are not friends that we must give thanks in words" (trans. by S. K. Stowers, *Letter Writing in Greco-Roman Antiquity* [Philadelphia: Westminster, 1986] 61). For other examples of the commonplace of friends dispensing with formalities, see R. P. Saller, *Personal Patronage under the Early Empire* (Cambridge: Cambridge University Press, 1982) 13 n. 28. Since writing the earlier version of this paper, I have discovered a recent article by G. W. Peterman in which he also points to PMert I 12, as well as to some twenty-two other papyri, in explaining the absence of an explicit "thank-you" in Phil 4:10–20 ("'Thankless Thanks': The Epistolary Social Convention in Philippians 4:10–20," *TynBul* 42 [1991] 261–70).

[6] Ps.-Demetrius, *Typoi Epist.* 21 (text and translation in A. J. Malherbe, *Ancient Epistolary Theorists* [SBLSBS 19; Atlanta: Scholars Press, 1988] 40–41): "The thankful type calls to mind the gratitude that is due (the reader). For example: I hasten to show in my actions how (well) disposed I am to you for the kindness you showed me in your words. For I know that what I am doing for you is less than I should for even if I gave my life for you, I would still not be giving adequate thanks for the benefits I have received. If you wish anything that is mine, do not write and request it, but demand a return. For I am in your debt."

[7] Cf. the account of how a certain Demetrius attended to his imprisoned friend Antiphilus in Lucian, *Tox.* 30–33.

[8] Other benefits would include recommendations, assisting a friend's protégés, friends, or clients, caring for family members, attending family ceremonies such as weddings or funerals, and, in addition, goodwill, affection, companionship, and advice. The following passages include lists of friendly services and benefits: Sen. *Ben.* 1.2.4;

viewed their gift to Paul in this context.[9] With a view to this act of friendship by them, Paul here uses many of the themes common in discussions of friendship in acknowledging their gift and in describing and clarifying his relationship to them.

Paul relates the great joy[10] that he felt upon receiving new evidence of their concern for him (v. 10).[11] Such descriptions of the joyful experience of receiving a letter or news are commonplace in friendly letters.[12] Paul's indication that this renewed demonstration of concern came after a long interval of time (ἤδη ποτέ, "now at length") might be taken as a veiled rebuke. Discussions of the bestowal of such benefits gave careful consideration to their timing. One should not delay too long in bestowing a benefit or returning a favor,[13] although one was not responsible if lack of opportunity or means prevented carrying out one's intention.[14] However, writers of

---

1.11–12; 3.21, 23; 6.29–30; Cic. *Off.* 1.7.22; 1.17.56; 2.15.52–55; Plut. *De am. mult.* 95C. See P. Marshall's discussion of friendship as giving for a return in chap. 1 of *Enmity at Corinth: Social Conventions in Paul's Relations with the Corinthians* (WUNT; Tübingen: Mohr [Siebeck], 1987) 1–34, esp. 31–32, for a list of typical services. See also G. Herman's discussion of the circulation of resources among friends and their obligation to provide various services in *Ritualised Friendship and the Greek City* (New York: Cambridge University Press, 1987) 73–142. Cf. Mary Whitlock Blundell, *Helping Friends and Harming Enemies* (New York: Cambridge University Press, 1989) 32–33, *passim*; H. Bolkestein, *Wohltätigkeit und Armenpflege im vorchristlichen Altertum* (Utrecht: A. Oosthoek, 1939) 95–102, 219–223; J. Michel, *Gratuité en droit romain* (Brussels: Université Libre de Bruxelles, 1962) 502–54; Saller, *Personal Patronage*, 13, *passim*; J. Hellegouarc'h, *Le vocabulaire latin des relations et des partis politiques sous la république* (Paris: Les Belles Lettres, 1963) 152–70; A. R. Hands, *Charities and Social Aid in Greece and Rome* (London: Thames & Hudson, 1968) chap. 3: "Giving for a Return," 26–48, esp. 31.

[9] Some of the Philippians may also have viewed their assistance to Paul as a form of patronage, which would have certain status implications for them.

[10] Paul says that he rejoiced "in the Lord." This phrase may indicate the ultimate ground for his joy or the sphere in which his joy thrives, or simply that his joy is thoroughly Christian in character, free from any resentment or ingratitude. Cf. P. T. O'Brien, *The Epistle to the Philippians* (NIGTC; Grand Rapids: Eerdmans, 1991) 516; BAGD, 259. Collange comments that the renewed brotherly concern shown by the Philippians toward Paul testifies to Christ's Lordship over the church (*Philippians*, 149).

[11] Hawthorne takes ἐχάρην as an epistolary aorist referring to Paul's joy at the time of writing (*Philippians*, 196). But the usage of the phrase ἐχάρην . . . μεγάλως elsewhere makes it more likely that the verb is a true past tense.

[12] Cf. PMert I 12; Julian, *Ep.* 77; Fronto, *Ep.* 2.2; POxy 3069; PYale 42; BGU II 632. Instead of ἐχάρην . . . μεγάλως, one sometimes finds λίαν ἐχάρην or μεγάλην ἐχάρην. Cf. H. Koskenniemi, *Studien zur Idee und Phraseologie des griechischen Briefes bis 400 n. Chr.* (Helsinki: Suomalainen Tiedeakatemian, 1956) 75–77; and R. Funk, "The Form and Structure of II and III John," *JBL* 86 (1967) 426.

[13] Sen. *Ben.* 2.1.2; 2.5.2–3, 4.

[14] Sen. *Ben.* 4.40.3; 2.32.2.

friendly or family letters often feigned hurt at not receiving letters or communications more promptly,[15] and as Stanley Stowers notes, such grousing was itself considered to be a demonstration of affection.[16] As here, such a reference to the long time between letters or communications might occur alongside an expression of joy over the reception of news or a letter.[17] Paul moves quickly to counter any sense of rebuke by acknowledging that the delay was not their fault since they had been without opportunity (v. 10b). In any case, since the passage of time without communication is naturally a test for any friendship,[18] one may suspect that it had caused Paul some anxiety about whether they still remembered him and his teaching. Such remembrance is necessary for maintaining friendship during periods of separation and is especially important if a teacher's instruction and exemplary life are to continue to guide his students' moral and spiritual development.[19] And for Paul, his life was inseparable from the gospel, so that if the Philippians forgot him, their faith would be in danger. Thus the renewal of contact after a long interval understandably gave Paul great joy, as it gave an indication that they remembered him, and more importantly, the gospel that he had proclaimed among them.

Paul's expression of joy focuses on their thoughtful concern for him without referring explicitly to the material gift. The word here for concern (φρονεῖν), found often in this letter with varied nuances (1:7; 2:2, 5; 3:15, 19; 4:2, 10), can be used as a synonym for friend-

---

[15] See, e.g., Cic. *Fam.* 2.1: "Though I am sorry you should have suspected me on the score of 'neglect,' still I am more pleased that you missed my attentions than put out that you should accuse me of any remissness, especially since in so far as your charge went, I was in no sense to blame, while in so far as you implied that you longed for a letter from me, you openly avowed an affection for me, which, well as I knew it before, is none the less delightful and desirable" (trans. by W. G. Williams in the LCL). Letter writers often express surprise at the recipient's failure to maintain contact, or disappointment that many letters have gone unanswered. Such statements indicate a desire to maintain the relationship. Cf. PMich III 221.4ff.; VIII 466.4ff.; 479.4ff.; 484.3ff.; SelPap I 121.6ff.; BGU IV 1079.2–3; POxy IX 1216.4ff.

[16] Stowers, *Letter Writing*, 63.

[17] Cf., e.g., PYale 42.5ff.

[18] Arist. *Eth. Nic.* 8.5.1.

[19] For an example of the attitude of a recent convert to philosophy toward his absent teacher, see Lucian, *Nigr.* 6–7. See also Seneca's recommendation that the student always keep his teacher or some hero in his thoughts as a model and guardian (*Ep.* 11.8–11). A. J. Malherbe treats the theme of remembrance of the teacher with reference to 1 Thess 3:6–10 in *Paul and the Thessalonians* (Philadelphia: Fortress, 1987) 66–68.

ship.[20] The primary significance of the Philippians' gift for Paul is its demonstration that they are still concerned about him and remember him, keeping their relationship with him intact. Philosophers discussing the gifts or benefits conferred by friends often said that the intention or goodwill behind a gift was more important than the gift itself. For example, Cicero reflects this attitude when he says that "it is not so much the material gain procured through a friend as it is his love and his love alone that gives us delight; and that advantage which we derive from him becomes a pleasure only when his service is inspired by an ardent zeal" (*Amic.* 51).[21] Cicero makes this statement in the course of arguing that friendship is not based on utility or cultivated because of need. Paul appears to go on to make a similar point in the verses that follow.

In v. 11 Paul qualifies what he has just said in order to avoid misunderstanding. Paul has not been prompted to speak of his joy over the Philippians' renewed concern for him[22] because of some need or deficiency (καθ' ὑστέρησιν) which they had been able to fill, for he has learned to be content or self-sufficient (αὐτάρκης) whatever his circumstances (vv. 11–12). It may be, as Abraham Malherbe has suggested, that in an accompanying letter the Philippians had described their latest gift as one intended to fulfill his needs.[23] Paul wants to make clear that he is not motivated by need-fulfillment in his relationship with them. The related issues of need and self-sufficiency which are mentioned here by Paul were prominent in the classical discussions of friendship and may be stated in the form of two questions. First, do friendships have their ultimate origin or basis in the practical needs of life and the utility of others in filling those needs or deficiencies? And second, is it consistent to say that the wise or good person is self-sufficient, and also that the wise are friends to one another?

As to the first issue, Aristotle calls attention to the common utilitarian view when he says, "most people think of friends as being those who are useful to us" (*Eth. Nic.* 9.9.4). The Epicureans were

---

[20] Schenk, *Philipperbriefe*, 65; cf. 2 Macc 14:8, 26; 1 Macc 10:20; Esth 8:12b (LXX).

[21] Cf. also Sen. *Ben.* 1.5.5; 1.6.1; Arist. *Eth. Nic.* 9.1.7.

[22] Collange understands Paul to be referring to an earlier request for aid that was not motivated by need (*Philippians*, 149–50). But the present tense verb λέγω would seem to refer to what Paul had just said or was in the process of saying.

[23] "Did the Thessalonians Write to Paul?" *The Conversation Continues: Studies in Paul & John in Honor of J. Louis Martyn* (ed. R. T. Fortna and B. R. Gaventa; Nashville: Abingdon, 1990) 257 n. 44.

the philosophical school most closely associated with a utilitarian view of friendship. Epicurus taught that friendship had its basis in such needs as help, protection, and security (*SV* 23; cf. Diog. Laert. 10.120).[24] In Aristotle's theory there were three kinds of friendship: friendships of utility, friendships of pleasure, and friendships of virtue. He ranked friendships of utility as the lowest class, while he considered friendship based on virtue the perfect form of friendship (*Eth. Nic.* 8.3.1–9). Stoics rejected a utilitarian view of friendship and saw its origin in nature. Seneca, for instance, said that the sage is drawn into friendship not by his own selfish needs, but by natural promptings and friendship's own inherent attractiveness (*Ep.* 9.17). One may seek it as "an object of great beauty, not attracted to it by desire for gain, nor yet frightened by the instability of fortune" (*Ep.* 9.12). Cicero, perhaps the most vocal critic of Epicurean or utilitarian views on friendship, put it this way:

> friendship springs rather from nature than from need, and from an inclination of the soul joined with a feeling of love rather than a calculation of how much profit (*utilitas*) the friendship is likely to afford. . . . love arises when we have met someone whose habits and character are congenial with our own; because in him we seem to behold a sort of lamp of uprightness and virtue (*Amic.* 27–28).

Cicero notes that a corollary to the idea that friendship has its basis in need would be that one's fitness for friendship would be in direct proportion to one's weakness or poverty. However, Cicero argues that the opposite is actually the case.

> For to the extent that a man relies on himself and is so fortified by virtue and wisdom that he is dependent on no one and considers all his possessions to be within himself, in that degree is he most conspicuous for seeking out and cherishing friendships (*Amic.* 30).

As Cicero indicates, the issue of friendship and utility is closely related to that of friendship and self-sufficiency.[25] Although self-sufficiency was a widely promoted virtue in Greek and Roman philosophy, it was understood differently by different schools or au-

---

[24] See A.-J. Festugière, *Epicurus and His Gods* (Oxford: Basil Blackwell, 1955) 37; J. M. Rist, "Epicurus on Friendship," *CP* 75 (1980) 121–29; P. Mitsis, *Epicurus' Ethical Theory: The Pleasures of Invulnerability* (Ithaca: Cornell University Press, 1988) chap. 3: "Friendship and Altruism," 98–128; D. K. O'Connor, "The Invulnerable Pleasures of Epicurean Friendship," *GRBS* 30 (1989) 165–86.

[25] Cf. Xen. *Mem.* 2.3.22–23; Arist. *Eth. Nic.* 9.9.1; Sen. *Ep.* 9; Diog. Laert. 6.11.

thors.[26] For Plato, self-sufficiency was impossible in the physical sphere (*Resp.* 2.369B) but was attainable for the virtuous person on the moral level. The Good is perfect and lacks nothing (*Phlb.* 20E.6), and so the person who possesses the Good has within himself all the resources for a good life and needs nothing else, not even friends (*Ly.* 215A.6–215C).

In the view of Aristotle, self-sufficiency was not possible on the practical level, since humans are social organisms. In fact, only the community can aim at self-sufficiency (*Eth. Nic.* 1.7.6–7). Self-sufficiency is possible for the individual only in a limited sense on the level of pure contemplation, but even then that person will not be self-sufficient in the physical sense (*Eth. Nic.* 10.7.4; 10.8.9). Access to an adequate supply of material goods was necessary for happiness.

The Epicureans aimed at self-sufficiency by eliminating all desires but those that were both natural and necessary. Their aim was not to make do always with little, but to find a little sufficient, if one does not have a lot. One should be satisfied with a simple life, but one can still enjoy luxuries on those occasions when they present themselves.[27]

For the Cynic Diogenes, self-sufficiency involved contentment with the bare necessities of basic food, clothing and shelter on the physical level (Diog. Laert. 6.104), and complete detachment from the world and worldly values on the spiritual plane. The means to this end were ἄσκησις and πόνος, discipline and hardship. Some later Cynics, such as Bion[28] and Teles,[29] advocated a less rigid form of self-sufficiency that involved adaptation to the world and changing

---

[26] Cf., e.g., A. W. H. Adkins, "'Friendship' and 'Self-Sufficiency' in Homer and Aristotle," *CQ* 13 (1963) 30–45; A. N. M. Rich, "The Cynic Conception of αὐτάρκεια," *Mnemosyne* 9 (1956) 23–29; K. Gaiser, "Das griechische Ideal der Autarkie," *Acta Philologica Aenipontana, III* (ed. R. von Muth; Innsbruck: Universitätsverlag Wagner, 1976) 35–37; R. Nickel, "Das Verhältnis von Bedürfnis und Brauchbarkeit in seiner Bedeutung für das kynostoische Ideal der Bedürfnislosigkeit," *Hermes* 100 (1927) 42–47; M. Billerbeck, *Der Kyniker Demetrius* (Philosophia Antiqua 36; Leiden: E. J. Brill, 1979) 20ff.; H. Niehues-Pröbsting, *Der Kynismus des Diogenes und der Begriff des Zynismus* (Munich: W. Fink, 1979) 125ff., 149ff.; H. D. Betz, *Der Apostel Paulus und die sokratische Tradition: Eine exegetische Untersuchung zu seiner Apologie 2 Korinther 10–13* (BHT 45; Tübingen: J. C. B. Mohr [Paul Siebeck], 1972) 108ff.; M. Ebner, *Leidenlisten und Apostelbrief: Untersuchungen zu Form, Motivik und Funktion der Peristasenkataloge bei Paulus* (FB; Würzburg: Echter, 1991) 338–43.

[27] Epicurus, *Ep.Men.* in Diog. Laert. 10.130–31.

[28] Stob. *Ecl.* III.1 (pp. 37–49).

[29] Cf. Teles, Frg. II (Περὶ αὐταρκείας). Text and translation in E. N. O'Neil (ed./trans.), *Teles (The Cynic Teacher)* (SBLTT 11; Missoula: Scholars Press, 1977) 6–19.

circumstances, rather than a stern renunciation of the world that always existed only on the barest of necessities.[30]

For the Stoics, virtue was sufficient in itself for happiness (Diog. Laert. 7.127; Sen. *Ep.* 85.1). All external things were morally indifferent. Through self-discipline and toil one could develop one's inner resources and become detached from everything external to oneself. Such detachment would not allow any external circumstance to affect one's inner tranquility. Thus standing above circumstances, one could gladly accept whatever Fate decreed.

While some found an inconsistency in claiming that the wise or good man is self-sufficient while speaking of friendship between wise or good men,[31] others held to both ideas,[32] and some offered explanations to resolve the tension in various ways. Seneca, for example, explained that the wise man is self-sufficient in that he can do without friends, not that he desires to do without them (*Ep.* 9.5). He craves as many friends as possible, not, however that he may live happily, for he will live happily even without friends. For the supreme good and happiness are to be developed and sought entirely within oneself and not in external things which are subject to the changes of fortune (*Ep.* 9.15). One reason he desires friends is for the purpose of practicing friendship (*Ep.* 9.8). Similarly, Aristotle argued that the supremely happy man, the good man, does not have need of useful or pleasant friends, but does need friends for objects of his own beneficence, for the contemplation of others' good actions, and for the training in virtue which such association provides (*Eth. Nic.* 9.9.4–7).

Paul seems to want to make clear that the fundamental basis of his relationship with the Philippians is not utilitarian. In other words, his friendly relations with them were not based on their utility to him or any material gain which he might derive from them.[33] His positive feelings toward them are not caused by any lack which he has felt (4:11). He could have gotten along without their gift. Paul

---

[30] Rich, "The Cynic Conception of αὐτάρκεια," 23.

[31] For example, according to Diogenes Laertius (2.98), Theodorus was such: "Friendship he rejected because it did not exist between the unwise nor between the wise; with the former, when the want is removed, the friendship disappears, whereas the wise are self-sufficient and have no need of friends." Cf. also Socrates in Pl. *Ly.* 215A.

[32] Antisthenes, for example, according to Diog. Laert. 6.11–12.

[33] Cf. 1 Thess 2:5; 2 Cor 11:14–18.

does not deny that he has been in adverse circumstances but asserts that he has learned how to cope with such (vv. 11–12). In fact, he had learned how to live in circumstances at both extremes of the spectrum: abasement (ταπεινοῦσθαι) and abundance (περισσεύειν),[34] being full and being hungry, experiencing abundance (περισσεύειν) and deprivation (ὑστερεῖσθαι).[35] As in the case of Cynics like Teles, Paul has learned to adapt to his circumstances. Paul's self-sufficiency is not grounded in the strength of his own inner resources, as for most Stoics, but in a power which comes from an agent beyond himself (ἐν τῷ ἐνδυναμοῦντί με, v. 13), God (or Christ).[36] And it is in Paul's varied circumstances that this power becomes effective. In sharing the humiliation of the one who humbled himself (cf. ἐταπείνωσεν, 2:8) and sharing his sufferings, Paul also experiences the power (δύναμις) of his resurrection (3:10).

Paul's affirmation of his self-sufficiency or independence could serve a number of possible functions. It underscores the genuineness of his goodwill toward them. He is not motivated by greed or selfish interests. Rather, Paul models the proper attitude of unselfishness and contentment. Perhaps there were people in Philippi who questioned Paul's motives, or perhaps Paul expects that rival teachers might do so. Not only does the affirmation of self-sufficiency clarify Paul's motives, but it also serves to uphold Paul's independence and ensure that the Philippians not come to view their support of Paul in a way that enhanced their own status, so that they considered themselves superior to Paul as his patrons. Since Paul was self-sufficient, he could not be viewed as dependent on them as their client or employee.[37]

---

[34] Ταπεινοῦσθαι and περισσεύειν should be understood primarily here as economic abasement and abundance, as the following pairs indicate, rather than spiritual conditions. See Marshall, *Enmity at Corinth*, 235 n. 227, and O'Brien, *Philippians*, 523–24.

[35] The series of paradoxical statements in which Paul elaborates the nature of his ability to cope with all circumstances finds an interesting parallel in Cicero who says that friends "though in need, yet abound; though weak, are strong" (*Amic.* 23). Whereas for Cicero friends or even their memory provide strength or resources to those in adversity, for Paul it is God who is the source of such strength.

[36] Some Stoics, however, would see their inner strength as a gift from God; cf. Epict. *Diss.* 1.6.14–15. On the role of the divine in regard to human suffering and the attainment of virtue, in both Paul and the philosophers, see J. T. Fitzgerald, *Cracks in an Earthen Vessel: An Examination of the Catalogues of Hardships in the Corinthian Correspondence* (SBLDS 99; Atlanta: Scholars Press, 1988) 70–87 ("Fortune, God, and Free Will"), 169–72, 204–05.

[37] This kind of concern may partly explain Paul's persistent refusal to accept

Paul's strong affirmation of his independence could be understood by the Philippians as calling their friendship into question, or indicating that Paul did not appreciate their gift. So, in v. 14 Paul again takes care to avoid giving the wrong impression and qualifies what he has just said. Although Paul was self-sufficient or independent, and so his friendship with them was not based on need or desire for material gain, he acknowledges that what they had done was good and appropriate (καλῶς ἐποιήσατε),[38] and that they had benefited him in his difficult situation (ἐν θλίψει). Paul maintains a balance between denying that need or utility is the basic motivation in friendship and affirming that assistance to a friend in need is a natural and desirable result of friendly relations. In a similar fashion, such people as Cicero who rejected a utilitarian origin for friendship could still acknowledge that many benefits or advantages ensued from friendship. In fact, Cicero was inclined to think that it was not well for friends never to need anything at all (*Amic.* 51). However, he stressed that friendship was not sought in the first place because of material need or for the sake of material gain (*Amic.* 30). It is not the case that friendship attends upon advantage, but, on the contrary, that advantage attends upon friendship (*Amic.* 51).[39]

By insisting on his self-sufficiency in vv. 11–13, Paul affirmed the genuineness of his friendship. In v. 14 he acknowledges the genuineness of their friendship. They had proven this by sharing with him in his affliction in prison through their gift.[40] Again, rather than referring simply to the material gift, Paul speaks of the spiritual or

---

financial support from the Corinthians. Paul's experience with the Corinthians may account for his concern to clarify his relationship with the Philippians here. On Paul's relations with the Corinthians, see Marshall, *Enmity at Corinth.*

[38] The phrase used in 4:14 to commend their recent act of kindness toward Paul corresponds to the formulaic epistolary phrase used to introduce a polite request, καλῶς ποιήσεις. Cf. e.g., 3 John 6; PMich I 6; I 48; III 201; PCairZen II 59251; SelPap I 101; PTebt I 56; PPrinc III 160; PRyl II 231; PLond III 893. The use of this phrase in the aorist occurs in Acts 10:33 where Cornelius indicates his pleasure that Peter came at his request, and also in Ign. *Smyrn.* 10:11. One could argue from the use of this phrase in Phil 4:14 that there had been a request for support, either explicit or implicit, from Paul to the Philippians. However, the phrase can simply be taken as an expression of appreciation for an unsolicited gift.

[39] Epicurus, although advocating a utilitarian theory of friendship, demonstrates a similar balance or tension when he says that one should neither continually ask for help nor never associate help with friendship (*SV* 39).

[40] Epicurus held that it was as painful to have one's friend tortured as to be tortured oneself (*SV* 56).

moral significance of their gift, their sympathetic participation in his hardship. Their gift was a sign of their spiritual fellowship or unity with Paul and their desire to be present with him. Cicero says that friendship "lessens the burden of adversity by dividing and sharing it" (*Amic.* 22),[41] as the Philippians had done for Paul. Such times of adversity may serve as tests to demonstrate who one's real friends are.[42] Isocrates exhorted Demonicus, "Prove your friends by means of the misfortunes of life and of their fellowship in your perils" (*Demonicus* 26).[43] The false friend or flatterer disappears when trouble or hardship comes, but true friends share both joys and sorrows and offer unlimited help in time of need.[44]

The genuineness of their friendship is demonstrated not only by this latest gift, but by a series of such gifts intended to meet Paul's needs stretching back to when he first departed from them. By recalling these Paul underlines the continuity between their past association and the present. The philosophers stressed the importance of loyalty in friendship[45] and noted that true, steadfast friends are rare,[46] and such were the Philippians for Paul. Their friendship has been a long one, and he still remembers their earlier benefits. When he first left Macedonia, they alone entered into partnership with him in an account of giving and receiving (ἐκοινώνησεν εἰς λόγον δόσεως καὶ λήμψεως, v. 15).

Paul's use of the words συγκοινωνήσαντες and ἐκοινώνησεν in this context calls to mind the well known proverb, κοινὰ τὰ φίλων, "Friends have all things in common."[47] Friendship is also often defined as

---

[41] Cf. also Plut. *De am. mult.* 94C, 96A, C–D; Lucian, *Tox.* 7.

[42] Xen. *Mem.* 2.4.3; Arist. *Eth. Nic.* 8.1.2; Sen. *Ep.* 9.8; Cic. *Amic.* 63–64; Isoc. *Demonicus* 24–25; Plut. *Adulator* 49C–D, 68F–69A.

[43] Some authors advised making preliminary tests of potential friends before becoming too intimate with them. Thus Plutarch urges, "One's friend, like a coin, should have been examined and approved before the time of need, not proved by the need to be no friend" (*Adulator* 49DE).

[44] Xen. *Mem.* 2.4.3; 2.7.1ff.; 2.10.1ff.; Arist. *Eth. Nic.* 8.1.2; 8.3.8; *Eth. Eud.* 7.2.9ff.; Plut. *Adulator* 68F–69A; *De am. mult.* 94B; Epict. *Diss.* 2.22.12; Lucian, *Tox.* 18; Dio Chrys. *Or.* 3.100; Cic. *Amic.* 26; Sen. *Ep.* 6.6; 9.9.

[45] Cf. F.-A. Steinmetz, *Die Freundschaftslehre des Panaitios: Nach einer Analyse von Ciceros "Laelius de amicitia"* (Palingenesia 3; Wiesbaden: Steiner, 1967) 116–23; Cic. *Amic.* 64–65; Arist. *Eth. Nic.* 8.8.4; Plut. *Adulator* 52A–53B; *De am. mult.* 95A–B, 97B; *Aqu. an ign.* 955F; Epict. *Diss.* 2.22.25.

[46] Cf. Plut. *De am. mult.* 93F, 97B; Cic. *Amic.* 64.

[47] Pl. *Ly.* 207C; *Resp.* 449C, 449D, 450C; Arist. *Eth. Nic.* 9.8.2; Plut. *Adulator* 65A; *De am. mult.* 94C, 96D; Diog. Laert. 8.10; Cic. *Off.* 1.51 (cf. Cic. *Amic.* 103); Sen. *Ben.* 7.12.1; *Ep.* 3, 6.3; Ps.-Crates, *Ep.* 26; Iambl. *VP* 17.72; Julian, *Or.* 8.245 A–B.

κοινωνία.[48] Κοινωνέω and its cognates occur quite frequently in this letter (1:5, 7; 2:1; 3:10; 4:14, 15), and all but one case involve social relations. In 1:5 Paul expresses thanks to God for the Philippians' κοινωνία in the gospel from the first day until the present. Κοινωνία is probably best understood in this case as referring in the broad sense to their "cooperation" in promoting the gospel, with their recent gift being the instance foremost in Paul's mind.[49] In 1:7 Paul notes that they had been his συγκοινωνοί, "partners" or "fellow-sharers" in God's grace both in Paul's imprisonment and in his defense of the gospel. In 2:1 Paul appeals for unity and harmony on the basis of their experience of κοινωνία πνεύματος, i.e., either their "joint-participation" in the Spirit or their "fellowship" created by the Spirit.

J. Paul Sampley understands the use of κοινωνέω in 4:15 and related commercial language in 4:10–20 as evidence that Paul and the Philippians had a formal contractual partnership or *societas*, in which the Philippians were to reimburse Paul for his expenses in his evangelistic endeavors as their representative.[50] However, the language which Sampley sees as the technical terminology of legal partnerships is used with reference to the broader range of social relations encompassed by φιλία and *amicitia*.[51] It is not necessary to see Paul's "partnership" with the Philippians as being in the nature of a formal, legal contract. The phrase "giving and receiving" is common accounting terminology for payments and receipts or credits and debits, and is often understood strictly in such terms here as a reference to the financial transactions between the Philippians and Paul.[52] But this phrase and similar commercial terminology are also used to refer to the reciprocity or mutuality in friendship and the exchange of favors and benefits between friends.[53] According to those with a

---

[48] Arist. *Eth. Nic.* 8.9.1; 8.12.1; 9.12.1; Lucian, *Tox.* 5–6; Max. Tyr. *Or.* 20.6.

[49] J. B. Lightfoot, *St. Paul's Epistle to the Philippians* (London: Macmillan, 1894) 81; O'Brien, *Philippians*, 62.

[50] Sampley, *Pauline Partnership*, 51–62. Cf. H. A. A. Kennedy, "The Financial Colouring of Phil. iv, 15–18," *ExpT* 12 (1900–01) 43–44. Kennedy notes that John Chrysostom had called attention to the financial terminology.

[51] L. M. White, "Morality between Two Worlds: A Paradigm of Friendship in Philippians," *Greeks, Romans, and Christians: Essays in Honor of Abraham J. Malherbe* (ed. D. L. Balch, E. Ferguson, and W. A. Meeks; Minneapolis: Fortress, 1990) 210–11.

[52] Lightfoot, *Philippians*, 165; Sampley, *Pauline Partnership*, 57; Hawthorne, *Philippians*, 204; Schenk, *Philipperbriefe*, 63.

[53] See Marshall, *Enmity at Corinth*, 155–59, *passim*; Arist. *Eth. Nic.* 2.7.4; 4.1.24; 8.13.8–9; 8.14.3; 9.2.3; Cic. *Amic.* 26, 28–29, 58; *Off.* 1.15.47–48; 2.17.59; Sen. *Ep.*

utilitarian view of friendship, such reciprocity or the giving and receiving of benefits and services is what people primarily desire from friendship. But even those such as Cicero who reject a utilitarian view admit that this mutual interchange is really inseparable from friendship (*Amic.* 26; cf. Sen. *Ep.* 81.12), and that long association and the giving and receiving of kindnesses increase mutual affection and further strengthen friendship (Cic. *Amic.* 29; *Off.* 1.56). In addition to their shared mutual concern and affection for one another, the Philippians had benefited from Paul's proclamation of the gospel and his teaching and direction while he was with them, and they reciprocated in the form of financial contributions to him after he left.[54] By pointing to such shared experiences and reviving such memories, their friendship is strengthened even further.

Lest his rehearsal of their past generosity make them think he sets his heart on their gifts, Paul once more moves to correct such an idea (4:17).[55] He clarifies what he seeks or desires from their relationship by means of an antithetical statement. He first states negatively what is not his aim. He does not seek τὸ δόμα. In this context τὸ δόμα could have its usual meaning, "the gift," such as the benefits given by friends. Or it could be taken in the more technical sense of "payment," or "interest payment."[56] Paul then states in a positive way what his real desire is. He is intent on the "fruit that increases to their account." The use of commercial language in this latter part of the verse is quite clear. Καρπός, literally "fruit," can mean the interest or profit accruing from a business transaction. Πλεονάζειν can be used for the accruing or compounding of interest in an account. To speak of "profit" or "interest" in the context of friendly relations, as Paul does here, was not unusual. A gift made in return for a friend's earlier gift was considered payment of a debt, and one was expected to make that payment with interest, so that the value of the return gift exceeded that of the initial gift. From the viewpoint of the initial giver, benefits to friends were often considered investments

---

81.12; *Ben.* 1.4.2; 2.30.2; cf. 4.21.1-3; 5.4.1-2; Dio Chrys. *Or.* 3.110. See also J. Hainz, *Koinonia* (BU 16; Regensburg: Pustet, 1982), 113-14.

[54] Similarly in philosophical circles, teachers and students both derived and conferred benefits and affection; cf. Sen. *Ep.* 6.6. See also Gal 6:6.

[55] Aristotle says that it is not noble to appear eager to receive benefits, yet one must be careful not to appear rude when a service is offered (*Eth. Nic.* 9.11.6).

[56] Gnilka, *Philipperbrief*, 179; Sampley, *Pauline Partnership*, 54; Ebner, *Leidenlisten und Apostelbrief*, 333. One might then take the phrase in the sense of "demand interest payment."

which one would receive back with interest.[57] Different suggestions
have been made as to precisely what this "profit" or "interest" is in
v. 17. Usually this is taken to be a profit or credit accruing to their
heavenly account as a result of their giving, from which they then
receive in the form of present blessings or a future reward from God.
Martin Ebner offers a different understanding. In his view, Paul is
calling for a change in their relationship. For the future, he no longer
seeks in return for his teaching them payment in the form of monetary gifts, as they have made in the past. Rather, he seeks from
them spiritual "fruit" or "interest" on his earlier investment. He does
not seek this interest so that he might enjoy it himself, but that it
might be credited to their account.[58] Whether the interest is the return
on the work Paul invested in the Philippians which he then transfers
to their account, or whether it is the return from the Philippians'
own giving, Paul makes clear that he does not seek his own personal
gain, but what will profit them.[59]

In v. 18 Paul gives a formal acknowledgement or receipt for the
things from them that Epaphroditus had delivered. Ἀπέχω often occurs
in the papyri in receipts acknowledging payment in full.[60] Whatever
debt they owed him has been settled, and due to their gift he now
enjoys a state of abundance. He has been filled (πεπλήρωμαι) and
has more than he needs (περισσεύω). Friends are said to fill up what
one lacks.[61] Someone with loyal friends may be called rich because
of the benefits which overflow as needs are met by friends.[62] However, Paul moves to broaden their understanding of the relationship.
Paul is not the only or the ultimate recipient of their gift. Their
gift involves not only their relationship to Paul, but also their
relationship to God. More important than the fact that Paul had
been enriched by their gift is the fact that it is a sacrifice pleasing to
God (4:18). Paul goes on to say that God will respond to their sacrifice (v. 19).

---

[57] Cf. Marshall, *Enmity at Corinth*, 9–12; S. C. Mott, "The Power of Giving and
Receiving," *Current Issues in Biblical and Patristic Interpretation* (ed. G. F. Hawthorne;
Grand Rapids: Eerdmans, 1975) 61–64.

[58] Ebner, *Leidenlisten und Apostelbrief*, 354–55.

[59] Cicero says that a friend prefers the advancement of friends to his own (*Amic.*
64).

[60] Cf., e.g., BGU II 584.5–6; 612.2–3. See also MM, 57. For the NT, cf. Matt
6:2, 5, 16; Luke 6:24.

[61] E.g., Xen. *Mem.* 2.4.6; 2.6.23.

[62] Cic. *Amic.* 22–23, 58; Xen. *Hier.* 3ff.

Having acknowledged that they have given attention to his needs (vv. 16, 17), Paul now turns his attention to and speaks explicitly of their needs.[63] Paul is not in a position to fulfill their needs, but God is. Paul's use of the genitive pronoun μου, "my God," suggests that he conceives of God reciprocating on his behalf, acting as his patron, as it were.[64] God will fulfill every need of theirs (v. 19), as they have filled Paul's needs (vv. 16, 18). What needs of the Philippians are in view here? The references to the Philippians' attention to Paul's material needs might suggest that Paul is here giving assurance that God will provide their material needs. However, the use of the phrase "*every* need" would seem to point toward a broader application. It is probably not to be limited to their physical needs, as in Paul's case, but may embrace as well all the spiritual and moral concerns or problems that Paul has tried to address in the letter.[65]

Thus acts of friendly kindness are performed not simply in return for past benefits, or in anticipation of future ones, or even from some innate feeling of love, but as part of a manner of life that seeks to please God and that recognizes him as the ultimate supplier of every need. As Jouette Bassler says, "Paul views the Philippians' gift as part of a much larger pattern of reciprocity that embraces Paul, the Philippians, the gospel, and God."[66] The Philippians received the message of God's grace, which led to their support of Paul's further evangelistic work. This giving resulted in credit accumulating in their account, which will lead to further blessings from God.

Phil 4:10–20 has numerous ties to themes or concerns in earlier sections of the canonical form of the letter which I believe count as evidence weighing in favor of the original unity of the letter.[67] I also believe that these connections indicate that this section serves to further the overall aims of the body of the letter.

---

[63] Friendly letters frequently close with requests for or offers of attention to whatever needs the friends may have. Cf. Ps.-Demetrius, *Typoi Epist.* 1; PCairZen I 59015; PCairZen V 59804; PCairZen II 59251; PMich I 6; PMich I 10; PCol III 9; PTebt I 59.

[64] G. Wiles, *Paul's Intercessory Prayers* (SNTSMS 24; Cambridge: University Press, 1974) 103.

[65] Wiles, *Paul's Intercessory Prayers*, 104.

[66] Bassler, *God and Mammon*, 77. On divine-human reciprocity or friendship, cf. Mott, "Giving and Receiving," 64–67; Blundell, *Helping Friends*, 46–47.

[67] For the use of friendship language throughout Phil 1–4 as an argument in support of the integrity of the letter, see J. T. Fitzgerald, "Philippians, Epistle to the," *ABD* 5 (1992) 318–26.

The opening and closing sections of a letter are often dominated by philophronetic elements which serve to maintain and strengthen the relationship between the sender and recipients. This is true in the case of Philippians not only in a general way, but also in such specific terms and themes which occur in both sections that one may speak of an *inclusio*.[68] In the opening verses of the letter Paul gives thanks for their partnership in the gospel from the first day until then (1:5). In 4:15 he recalls with appreciation how "in the beginning of the gospel" they had entered into a partnership of giving and receiving with him. As in the opening he reveals how he thinks about them (φρονεῖν ὑπέρ, 1:7), in the closing he rejoices over evidence of their thoughtful concern about him (ὑπὲρ . . . φρονεῖν, 4:10). In 1:9–11 he prays that their love may abound (περισσεύῃ) in knowledge and discernment and that they may be filled (πεπληρωμένοι) with the "fruit" (καρπόν) of righteousness. In 4:17–19 he expresses his wish for the "fruit" (καρπόν) that increases (πλεονάζοντα) in their spiritual account through their giving, and assures them that God will fulfill (πληρώσει) every need of theirs. In both of these sections Paul strengthens the relationship with them by speaking of the joy that it brings him and by affirming or clarifying the basis of their relationship. He emphasizes his goodwill and affection toward them and his desire for their spiritual and moral enrichment.

Paul's presentation of himself in 4:10–20 as one who is αὐτάρκης in all circumstances through God's power and who is concerned for their advantage and not his own is consistent with the attitude displayed in 1:12–26 where he relates news regarding his own situation. In spite of imprisonment and opposition, Paul can find reason for joy because the cause of the gospel is advancing. Paul is ready to forego what might be in his own best interests (i.e., death and closer union with Christ), for the sake of what will promote the advance of the Philippians' faith and joy.

Paul's self-presentation in 4:10–20 adds further specificity to his example that he urged them to imitate in 3:17 and 4:9. He displays in this final section the kind of selfless and altruistic friendship that was the focus of his exhortation to the Philippians in 2:1–5, and that was exemplified by Christ (2:5–11), as well as by Timothy and Epaphroditus (2:19–30). In addition, the Philippians themselves had exemplified in their relations with Paul the kind of friendly disposi-

---

[68] W. J. Dalton, "The Integrity of Philippians," *Bib* 60 (1979) 101.

tion and behavior that he wants to characterize relations among the Philippians themselves. So, in rehearsing the story of their relationship with him, Paul reinforces his direct exhortation to unselfish service given earlier in the letter (2:1–4) by recalling their own past example—an effective strategy in friendly paraenesis.[69]

Paul's focus on strengthening the relationship with the Philippians in 4:10–20 has its counterpart in chapter 3 where he seeks to neutralize the influence of rival teachers. Paul's self-sufficiency and his concern about the Philippians' needs stand in contrast to the enemies of the cross whose god is their own belly and who have their minds set (φρονοῦντες) on earthly things (3:18–19).

In 4:4–7 Paul exhorts the Philippians not to be anxious but to make their requests known to God. Corresponding to this, Paul's self-description in 4:11–13 provides an example of contentment and trust in God's power whatever the circumstances, and in 4:19 Paul provides further assurance that God will provide for all their needs.

In summary, in 4:10–20 Paul strengthens the renewed relationship with the Philippians by expressing his positive feelings for them in response to their recent display of concern for him and by recalling their long association. Their concern for him is important to him. But he clarifies the nature of their relationship, stressing that he is not involved in it for his own personal gain, unlike others such as the rival teachers in chapter 3 who may be motivated by self-interest. Paul also carefully maintains his independence, in case some of the Philippians might be tempted to become proud in supposing Paul was dependent on their patronage. Paul also reinforces his exhortations in the rest of the letter by pointing to their own example of selfless service to Paul and partnership in the gospel and by providing in his own life a model of self-sufficiency and concern for others without thought for personal gain. Paul wants the Philippians to see their friendship in the broader context of their relationship to God, to whom their acts of thoughtful concern and generosity are pleasing sacrifices, and who will fulfill all their needs.[70]

---

[69] Plut. *Adulator* 72C–D, 73C–D.

[70] After completing this paper I discovered the recent article by B. J. Capper, "Paul's Dispute with Philippi: Understanding Paul's Argument in Phil 1–2 from his Thanks in 4.10–20," *TZ* 49 (1993) 193–214. Capper follows Sampley in understanding the commercial terminology in 4:10–20 as evidence of a formal, contractual agreement or partnership between Paul and the Philippians. Capper goes on to argue that Paul had been in dispute with them because of his imprisonment. Since

his traveling ministry had ceased and his preaching had been curtailed through his arrest, he was in breach of his contract, and the Philippians withheld his support. Paul had negotiated a settlement to the dispute, and they resumed their support, but in Phil 1–2 Paul seeks to argue that his imprisonment was not a breach of his contract or a failure to serve Christ but was in keeping with the story of Christ in the gospel. The Philippians, with their rebellious attitude of grumbling and questioning toward Paul, needed to imitate the humility of Christ in his death on the cross. I can only make a brief response here. Regarding the "contractual" language, see the response to Sampley above regarding the use of such terms with reference to friendship. I have noted above that the "thankless" tone of 4:10–20 is probably overstated, and that social conventions of the time help explain the absence of an explicit "thank-you." I fail to find clear evidence for the kind of dispute that Capper suggests. In 4:10 Paul acknowledges that the Philippians' concern for him had been constant and that the interruption in their support was due to a lack of opportunity; it was not the result of their own decision or that of their leaders (so Capper).

Finally, I was unable to obtain the new work by Ben Witherington III, *Friendship and Finances in Philippi: The Letter of Paul to the Philippians* (Louisville: Westminster/John Knox, 1994), which will obviously be of interest to readers of this volume.

PAUL'S SELF-SUFFICIENCY (PHILIPPIANS 4:11)

ABRAHAM J. MALHERBE

This paper deals with Philippians 4:11, specifically, with Paul's statement that he was αὐτάρκης in all things. I wish to argue that the statement should be understood in the context of ancient discussions of friendship and not the technical Stoic idea of αὐτάρκεια. It is quite popular to say that αὐτάρκεια is a Stoic term, but there is considerable difference of opinion on the degree to which and the manner in which Paul is thought to appropriate the Stoic notion.

For example, E. N. O'Neil, in speaking of the term, says of the text in which it occurs in Philippians, "the whole passage (vss. 11–13) must be considered. These words of Paul could just as easily have been uttered by Antisthenes, Diogenes, Crates, or even Teles."[1] That, of course, is gross overstatement.

Rudolf Bultmann is more interesting. First, he portrays what he considers the Stoic view. According to Bultmann, the Stoic must free himself from his emotions. "For these seek to attach him to 'alien things'. He must strive after self-sufficiency (αὐτάρκεια), both within and without. He must cultivate renunciation and endurance. For then he will be free and happy, and nothing can assail him. . . . He withdraws into himself and with clarity of mind perceives the divine, universal law, which, when all is said and done, he cannot alter."[2] Bultmann then interprets Paul in light of this view of self-sufficiency. Paul's freedom is said to be his radical openness for the future. "Such a conception of freedom," says Bultmann, "seems to bring Paul very close to Stoicism. Indeed, the very fact that he defines genuine human existence in terms of freedom, a concept unknown to the Old Testament and Judaism, is itself sufficient to suggest an affinity between Paul and the Stoics, to say nothing of the actual vocabulary he uses. The Stoic wise man is, like Paul, free from all external

---

[1] Edward N. O'Neil, "De cupiditate divitiarum (Moralia 523C–528B)," *Plutarch's Ethical Writings and Early Christian Literature* (ed. H. D. Betz; SCHNT 4; Leiden: E. J. Brill, 1978) 312.

[2] Rudolf Bultmann, *Primitive Christianity in Its Contemporary Setting* (Cleveland: Collins, 1956) 138.

necessitites and claims from the outside world, its conventions, judgements and values."[3]

In Bultmann's interpretation, then, Phil 4:11 describes Paul's interior detachment. "Like Paul, the Stoic could say: 'I know both how to be abased, and I know how to abound'. . . . But he would not continue: 'I can do all things through Christ who strengtheneth me' (Phil. 4:12f.). This is just where the difference lies. The Stoic is free because of his reason. He concentrates on reason by turning his back on all encounters and claims from the outside world. This makes him free *from* the future. He is enabled to escape from the toils of life in time. Paul, on the other hand, is free because he has been made free by the grace of God, and has surrendered freely to his grace. He has been freed from all the claims which seek to bind him to all reality, present, transitory and already past. He has become free *for* the future, for encounters in which he will experience God's grace ever anew as a gift from the outside."[4]

Other commentators, without Bultmann's originality, have also drawn attention to the Stoic use of the term but have been careful to point out that Paul was quite un-Stoic in claiming that it was Christ who supplied the power by which Paul could live as he did. Yet others have recognized that, while the term was used by Stoics (and Cynics), it "had a wider currency than simply that of a technical expression in the Cynic-Stoic (*sic*) school," and that Paul transformed the term.[5] These interpretations generally focus on the word, rather than the larger context of the text in Philippians. And they almost never give serious attention to the fact that αὐτάρκεια frequently appeared as part of larger complexes of ideas, some of which are also present in Paul's discussion here. One of the commonplace discussions in which self-sufficiency was often taken up was that of friendship.

Friendship Language in Philippians

The importance of friendship in ancient society needs no extended discussion, and its importance has become increasingly clear to NT

---

[3] Ibid., 185.
[4] Ibid., 186.
[5] Ralph P. Martin, *Philippians* (NCB; London: Marshall, Morgan & Scott, 1976)

scholars in recent years. For instance, a group in the Society of Biblical Literature, recently organized by John T. Fitzgerald to study hellenistic moral philosophy and early Christianity, in its 1991 session devoted seven hours to the examination of friendship in a wide selection of ancient writers and documents,[6] and in 1992 devoted three papers to Phil 4:10–20 from the perspective of ancient discussions of friendship.[7] I shall draw attention to the language of friendship in Phil 4:10–20, but before doing so, I briefly point to the occurrence of such language in other parts of the letter. Paul's use of this language is in fact at the heart of his strategy in dealing with the problems faced by his readers.[8]

Two short definitions of friendship, occurring already in Aristotle, are used by Paul in Philippians: friends are people of one soul (1:27; cf. 2:2), and they think the same thing (2:2; 4:2); a third one, that friends have all things in common, is reflected in Paul's repeated concern with sharing in the letter (1:5, 7; 2:1).[9] In addition, numerous clichés from the literature on friendship are scattered throughout the letter: friends rejoice together (1:4, 18, 25; 2:2, 28, 29; 3:1; 4:1, 4, 10),[10] have confidence in each other because of their constancy

---

162, referring to J. N. Sevenster, *Paul and Seneca* (NovTSup 4; Leiden: E. J. Brill, 1961) 113f. See also M. Vincent, *The Epistles to the Philippians and to Philemon* (ICC; Edinburgh: T. & T. Clark, 1897) 143; W. Michaelis, *Der Brief des Paulus an die Philipper* (THKNT 11; Leipzig: Deichert, 1935) 70; F. W. Beare, *The Epistle to the Philippians* (HNTC; New York: Harper & Brothers, 1959) 152–53.

[6] See John T. Fitzgerald (ed.), *Greco-Roman Perspectives on Friendship* (SBLRBS; Atlanta: Scholars Press, forthcoming).

[7] Ken L. Berry, "The Function of Friendship Language in Philippians 4:10–20"; John T. Fitzgerald, "Philippians 4 in Light of Some Ancient Discussions of Friendship"; and John Reumann, "Philippians, Especially Chapter 4, as a 'Letter of Friendship'" (papers presented to the Hellenistic Moral Philosophy and Early Christianity Group at the annual meeting of the Society of Biblical Literature, San Francisco, CA, November, 1992). Revised versions of all three papers are published in the current volume. I am particularly indebted to Berry, who deals with some of the same material I do.

[8] See also L. Michael White, "Morality Between Two Worlds: A Paradigm of Friendship in Philippians," *Greeks, Romans, and Christians: Essays in Honor of Abraham J. Malherbe* (ed. D. L. Balch, E. Ferguson, and W. A. Meeks; Minneapolis: Fortress, 1990) 201–15.

[9] Clichés describing friendship are conveniently collected by G. Bohnenblust, "Beiträge zum Topos Περὶ Φιλίας" (Inaug. Diss., Univ. Bonn; Berlin: Gustav Schade [Otto Francke], 1905). μία ψυχή: Arist. *Eth. Nic.* 9.8 (1168b6ff.); Diog. Laert. 5.20; Plut. *De am. mult.* 96E; cf. Acts 4:36; τὸ αὐτὸ φρονεῖν: Cic. *Amic.* 15, 16, 21; Dio Chrys. *Or.* 34.20; Dion. Hal. *Ant. Rom.* 4.20.4,2; 7.59.7.5,9; 8.15.1.6; κοινὰ τὰ φίλων: Pl. *Ly.* 207C; Cic. *Off.* 1.51; Diog. Laert. 8.10; cf. Acts 4:32.

[10] On this commonplace in letters, see Stanley K. Stowers, *Letter Writing in*

and loyalty (1:6, 14, 25; 2:24),[11] defer to each other (2:8, 17, 27, 30),[12] and engage in mutual enterprises (note the cognates with σύν: συνεργός, 2:25; 4:3; συναθλέω, 1:27; 4:2; συστρατιώτης, 2:25; σύζυγος, 4:3; συγκοινωνός, 2:8, 17, 27, 30). The point is that 4:10–20 is not unique in using friendship language, but is in fact the culmination of a letter that employs such language from its very beginning.

Friendship Language in Philippians 4:10–20

Modern scholarship has interpreted 4:10–20 as Paul's thank you note for a financial contribution he had received from the Philippians, but has then found it difficult to fit this text into the remainder of the canonical letter or the historical situation that the canonical letter may be taken to presuppose. The frustration caused by Paul's "danklose(r) Dank,"[13] expressed so late in the letter, has contributed to a preparedness to view these verses as a thank you note written on an earlier occasion, which a later redactor combined with a number of other fragments to compose the letter in the form in which we now have it.[14] I do not wish here to address in detail the matter of the letter's integrity; suffice it to say that I think the letter in its present shape makes perfectly good sense. My interest is rather to point out that 4:10–20 contains a number of the clichés of friendship also found elsewhere in the letter, and that it is reasonable to attempt to understand the passage in light of Paul's playing on the theme of friendship. Let me just note a few of those themes which will assist us in gaining a firmer grasp on Paul's intention.

Greco-Roman Antiquity (Philadelphia: Westminster, 1986) 61, 65, 83, 99, who provides examples.

[11] Cic. *Amic.* 33–34, 64–65; Plut. *De am. mult.* 95AB; *Adulator* 52A–53B. See, further, Fritz-Arthur Steinmetz, *Die Freundschaftslehre des Panaitios: Nach einer Analyse von Ciceros 'Laelius de amicita'* (Palingenesia 3; Wiesbaden: Steiner, 1967) 116–23.

[12] Cic. *Amic.* 34, 69–73.

[13] A description by Martin Dibelius, *An die Thessalonicher I–II. An die Philipper* (HNT 11; Tübingen: J. C. B. Mohr [Paul Siebeck], 1937) 95, often repeated, most recently by Markus Schiefer Ferrari, *Die Sprache des Leids in den paulinischen Peristasenkatalogen* (SBB 23; Stuttgart: Katholisches Bibelwerk, 1991) 271. Gerald W. Peterman, "'Thankless Thanks': The Epistolary Social Convention in Philippians 4:10–20," *TynBul* 42 (1991) 261–70, has suggested that Paul follows a convention according to which one withheld verbal gratitude from social intimates. Stowers, *Letter Writing*, 61, refers to the commonplace that friends need not verbally express their thanks.

[14] For discussion, see John T. Fitzgerald, "Philippians, Epistle to the," *ABD* 5.318–26.

Basic to ancient friendship was the notion of sharing, including sharing the adversity encountered by a friend. Cicero says, ". . . friendship adds a brighter radiance to prosperity and lessens the burden of adversity by dividing and sharing it" (*Amic.* 22); one may have pride in aiding a friend and sharing his dangers (Lucian, *Toxaris* 7).[15] So Paul speaks of the Philippians as sharing his affliction (4:14).

Friends also shared benefits, including those of a material sort, and this "mutual interchange is . . . inseparable from friendship" (Cic. *Amic.* 26). Commercial language, for example, that of credits and debits, taken from the terminology of accountancy, was used to describe this interchange (Cic. *Amic.* 26). The obligation to share could result in cold calculation, however, and Cicero warned against it: "It surely is calling friendship to a very close and petty accounting to require it to keep an exact balance of credits and debits (*ratio acceptorum et datorum*). I think that true friendship is richer and more abundant than that and does not narrowly scan the reckoning lest it pay out more than it has received" (*Amic.* 58). Paul uses exactly the same language when in 4:15 he writes of the Philippians who had shared with him in giving and receiving (λόγος δόσεως καὶ λήμψεως = *ratio acceptorum et datorum*).

Seneca reflects another concern about sharing one's friendship when he considers when one should return a benefit. There is a fine line to be drawn. One does not want to be gauche and return a benefit too promptly. "He who hastens at all odds to make a return shows the feeling, not of a person that is grateful, but of a debtor. And, to put it briefly, he who is too eager to pay his debt is unwilling to be indebted, and he who is unwilling to be indebted is ungrateful" (*Ben.* 4.40.5). That does not mean, however, that one should delay in returning a benefit. Seneca again: "No gratitude is felt for a benefit when it has lingered long in the hands of him who gives it. . . . Even though some delay should intervene, let us avoid in every way the appearance of having deliberately delayed; hesitation is the next thing to refusing, and gains no gratitude" (*Ben.* 2.1.2). But it is otherwise when circumstances prevent one from reciprocating: "I am not responsible for the delay if I lack either the opportunity or the means" (*Ben.* 4.40.3).

---

[15] For this paper, the translations found in the Loeb Classical Library, where available, have been used, sometimes in a slightly modified form.

I suggest that it is in the context of such discussions of friendship that we should understand Phil 4:10. The understanding of vs. 10 reflected by the Revised Standard Version has led to the consternation about the verse. That translation reads, "I rejoice in the Lord greatly that now at length you have revived your concern for me; you were indeed concerned for me, but you had no opportunity." Ralph Martin illustrates the difficulties commentators have with the verse. He thinks vs. 10a is a "roundabout and oblique allusion to the church's gift" which has caused scholars to describe it as Paul's "thankless thanks."[16] Martin surmises that Paul wrote in this way because he "felt a certain embarrassment over money matters, and that his ambiguous way of writing reflects something of a conflict between his desire to express gratitude for the gift received both recently and earlier (v. 15) and a concern to show himself superior to questions of depending on others for financial support."[17]

I wish to argue that once one recognizes the conventions about friendship with which 4:10–20 is replete, Paul is not roundabout or oblique, nor does he write a thankless thanks, nor is he embarrassed about money matters. What he does, rather, is to draw out, with the aid of such conventions, the significance of the gift as an act by which he and his readers had been drawn more closely together.

To begin with, Paul affirms that the Philippians had been concerned for him, had shown that concern on more than one occasion, and done so concretely from the time of his earliest association with them (vss. 15–16). Furthermore, he interprets the delay in their most recent contribution as due to a lack of opportunity, thus letting them know that he does not think they had deliberately delayed or hesitated. Seneca had said that no gratitude was felt for a benefit when it was long delayed. Paul, on the other hand, presuming that there was good reason for the delay, rejoiced greatly for their expressed concern. So, delay there had been, but rather than chiding them for it, Paul interprets it as failing to thwart the friendly intentions of his readers.

The positive way in which Paul interprets the Philippians' action is further evident in his use of ἀναθάλλειν, translated "revive" in the RSV ("now at length you have revived your concern for me"). I

---

[16] Martin, *Philippians*, 160.
[17] Ibid., 161.

choose to translate ἀνεθάλετε τὸ ὑπὲρ ἐμοῦ φρονεῖν as "you have bloomed again, so far as your care for me is concerned." Commentators and lexicographers agree that this rendering is possible, even if most of them prefer another. My translation is influenced by my perception of the language of friendship in this letter. It is not unusual in such language to use agricultural or horticultural metaphors in describing friendship and its benefits. So Cicero says that friendship is "desirable, not because we are influenced by the hope of gain, but because its entire fruit is in the love itself" (Amic. 31). And the response to an unsought kindness, he says elsewhere, should be to "imitate the fields, which return more than they receive" (Off. 1.15.48). Such language describes the generosity and lack of calculation with which true friends render benefits to each other. If understood thus, Paul's use of ἀναθάλλειν is intended as a compliment of the spontaneity and good will with which the Philippians made the contribution rather than as chiding for finally having ceased their neglect of him. In other words, rather than continuing to draw attention to the timing of the gift, as he had with ἤδη ποτέ ("now finally"), Paul prefers to drive to the disposition that led to the contribution. The same thing is seen in his affirmation in vs. 17 that rather than seek the gift, he seeks the fruit that accrues to their credit.[18] So, rather than beginning the discussion of the Philippians' gift in the awkward fashion often attributed to him, Paul in fact does so positively, in a complimentary manner indebted to the discussions of friendship. Such discussions also inform vss. 11–13, the immediate context for his claim in vs. 11 that he is αὐτάρκης.

A more general view of AYTAPKEIA

Before examining Philippians 4 more closely, I wish to draw attention to the idea of self-sufficiency, particularly in its non-technical meaning. I confine myself to the Cynics and Pythagoreans, who are adequate for my argument.[19]

---

[18] Attention has already been drawn to this type of language by Martin Ebner, *Leidenslisten und Apostelbrief: Untersuchungen zu Form, Motivik und Funktion der Peristasenkatalogen bei Paulus* (FB 66; Würzburg: Echter, 1991) 349 n. 118, who also points (348 n. 102) to καρπός (sc. *fructus*) in Cic. *Fam.* 13.22.2; 50.2; 65.2; *Amic.* 31 (see also 22); Arist. *Ep.* 3.

[19] The literature on self-sufficiency is immense. Useful general discussions are

Audrey Rich summarizes the Cynic view as follows:

> To Diogenes the Cynic, αὐτάρκεια meant, broadly speaking, two things:
> on the physical plane, contentment with the bare necessities of life;
> and on the spiritual level, complete detachment from the world and
> worldly values. The αὐτάρκης was the man who had dispensed with
> the superfluous in every department of life and reduced his needs to a
> minimum. All that he required for his material well-being was food,
> shelter and clothing of the meanest sort; his spiritual needs could be
> satisfied by virtue alone, the possession of which was sufficient to en-
> sure happiness. The Cynic, then, had no desire for wealth, knowledge,
> pleasure or friendship. In his mind all these would be classed together
> as unnecessary luxuries. Nothing, in fact, that was to be derived from
> any source external to himself had any value for him or could affect
> him in any way. The Cynic aimed at αὐτάρκεια as it was exemplified
> in Diogenes, and his motive in doing so was obvious. Self-sufficiency
> alone, in the Cynic view, can give security and immunise man against
> the ills inflicted by Fortune.[20]

Self-sufficiency in its most uncompromising form continued to be the
ideal of many Cynics. A few examples illustrate this attitude. The
Cynic in the pseudo-Lucianic *Cynicus* (15) prays: "I pray that I may
not need bedclothes any more than the lions, nor expensive fare
than the dogs. But may I be αὐτάρκης in having for my bed the
whole earth, may I consider the universe my house, and choose for
food that which is easiest to procure. Gold and silver I do not need,
neither I nor any of my friends. For from the desire of these grow
up all men's ills—civic strife, wars, conspiracies and murders. All
these have as their fountainhead the desire for more. But may this

---

P. Wilpert, "Autarkie," *RAC* 1 (1950) 1039–50; H. Rabe, "Autarkie, autark," *Historisches
Wörterbuch der Philosophie* (ed. J. Ritter et al.; Basel: Schwabe, 1971) 685–91; R. Vischer,
*Das einfache Leben: Wort- und motivgeschichtliche Untersuchungen zu einem Wertbegriff der antiken
Literatur* (Göttingen: Vandenhoeck & Ruprecht, 1965) 60–87; Ebner, *Leidenslisten und
Apostelbrief*, 338–43. For the Cynics, see Heinrich Niehues-Pröbsting, *Der Kynismus des
Diogenes und der Begriff des Zynismus* (Munich: Wilhelm Fink, 1979) 148–206, esp. 155–
58, 184–98. While it is always important to do justice to the differences between
philosophical schools on a particular matter, there was nevertheless a tendency toward a vulgarization of philosophical ethics. On the phenomenon, see A. J. Malherbe,
"Hellenistic Moralists and the New Testament," *ANRW* 2.26.1 (1992) 332. It may
be that people were no longer interested in the philosophical foundations of such
moral topics (thus Albrecht Dihle, "Ethik," *RAC* 6 [1966] 666, cf. 652ff.), yet their
philosophical allegiances nevertheless provided distinct perspectives on the common
coin of moral discourse. It is sufficient for my immediate purpose to draw attention
to common elements in that discourse.
[20] A. N. M. Rich, "The Cynic Conception of AYTAPKEIA," *Mnemosyne* Ser. 4.9
(1956) 23–29.

desire be far from us, and never may I reach out for more (πλεονεξία) than my share, but be able to put up with less than my share."

Another example is provided by the rigorous Cynic Demetrius, the friend of Seneca, and thus a contemporary of Paul. According to Seneca, Demetrius used to scorn theory and scientific speculation because they served no practical purpose. For example, Demetrius claimed that people given to gluttony and lust could not know true pleasure. True pleasure, he said, comes, not from the hedonistic life, but comes from on high and is "constant, serene, always unclouded, (and) is experienced by the man who is skilled in the laws of gods and men. Such a man rejoices in the present, and puts no faith in the future; for he who leans upon uncertainties can have no sure support. Free, therefore, from the great anxieties that rack the mind, there is nothing that he hopes for or covets (*cupit*), and, content (*contentus*) with what he has, he does not plunge into what is doubtful. And do not suppose that he is content with a little, for all things are really his as a wise man."[21]

A reaction against the austere Cynicism represented by Demetrius had already set in two centuries earlier. Bion of Borysthenes represented this milder strain of Cynicism. The term αὐτάρκεια does not occur in the surviving fragments of his work; of greater significance is that he represents the attitude of this type of Cynicism toward the world which became widespread. For such Cynics, αὐτάρκεια was not so much a stern renunciation of the world as an attempt to adapt oneself to the world and changing circumstances just as an actor adapts himself to the varied roles he has to play.[22] Here self-sufficiency becomes synonymous with the widely used phrases ἀρκεῖσθαι τοῖς παροῦσιν, "to be satisfied with what is at hand," and χρᾶσθαι τοῖς παροῦσιν, "to make do with what is at hand."[23]

How self-sufficiency was understood in this sense appears from the tractate Περὶ Αὐταρκείας by Teles, in which Teles is primarily

---

[21] Sen. *Ben.* 7.2.4–5. For Demetrius' freedom from want, see Margarethe Billerbeck, *Der Kyniker Demetrius. Ein Beitrag zur Geschichte der frühkaizerzeitlichen Popularphilosophie* (Philosophia Antiqua 36; Leiden: E. J. Brill, 1979) 20–31, and further, on his philosophy, Jan Fredrik Kindstrand, "Demetrius the Cynic," *Philologus* 124 (1980) 83–98.

[22] See the discussion in Jan Fredrik Kindstrand, *Bion of Borysthenes* (AUU; Studia Graeca Upsaliensia 11; Uppsala: Almqvist & Wiksell, 1976) 64–67.

[23] For ἀρκεῖσθαι τοῖς παροῦσιν, see Xen. *Symp.* 4.42; Teles, Frg. IVA (38,10–21; 41,12 Hense); Epict. *Diss.* 1.1.27; cf. Heb 13:5; 1 Tim 6:8. For χρᾶσθαι τοῖς παροῦσιν, see Philo, *Prob.* 122; Dio Chrys. *Or.* 30.33; Plut. *De exil.* 606D.

concerned with the wise man's attitude toward poverty. Teles develops the theme that the wise man adapts himself to circumstances, and that he is not really in want of things since he has learned to be satisfied with what is at hand. As the good actor performs well whatever part the poet assigns him, so the good man acts well whatever role Fortune should lay upon him. The good man therefore does not fight poverty, for it does not really deprive him of the necessities of life. The hungry man, for instance, eats with greater relish than the man who habitually stuffs himself. The good man does not blame the circumstances in which he finds himself, nor does he attempt to change them, but prepares himself to adapt to them, just as sailors prepare themselves for the sea. They do not attempt to change the wind and sea, but prepare themselves to turn with them. In the same way, the good man uses what is at hand and so is self-sufficient. He lives with the circumstances allotted to him. If he deals with them in one way they will appear favorable and easy, but if in another, they will appear harsh. This αὐτάρκεια, then, is not a withdrawing into oneself, but an acceptance of one's circumstances and a concern to discover value in them.[24]

Characteristic of these Cynic attitudes is their individualism; only very seldom is the focus wide enough to include anyone else. Other philosophers, however, did take into consideration the social dimension. Note, for example, the way the ideal king, who is taken to be the paragon of self-sufficiency, is described in a tractate on kingship attributed to the Pythagorean Ecphantus:

> In so far as (the ideal king) has a sacred and divine mentality he will cause all good things, but nothing that is evil. And he will clearly be just, one who has κοινωνία with all. For κοινωνία consists in equality (ἰσότης), and while in the distribution of equality justice plays the most important part, yet κοινωνία has its share. For it is impossible to be unjust while giving a share of equality, or to give a share of equality and not be κοινωνός. And could anyone doubt that the self-sufficient man is self-controlled? For extravagance is the mother of self-indulgence, which in turn is the mother of insolence (ὕβρις), from which most human ills arise. But self-sufficiency does not beget extravagance or her brood. Rather, self-sufficiency, being a primal entity, leads all things, but is itself led by nothing, and precisely this is a property alike of God and the king himself, to be the ruler, but to be ruled by no

---

[24] Frg. II; text and translation in Edward N. O'Neil, *Teles (The Cynic Teacher)* (SBLTT 11; Missoula: Scholars Press, 1977) 6–19. See also Frg. IVB (pp. 48–53).

one. . . . In ruling over men and in controlling his own life he uses one and the same virtue, not amassing acquisitions on account of any lack, for his personal service, but doing as one does in a life of action according to nature. For although κοινωνία exists, each man nevertheless lives sufficient unto himself. For in conducting his life the self-sufficient man needs nothing outside himself; and if he must live an active life, and take other factors into account, he nonetheless will keep his self-sufficiency. For as he will have his friends as a result of his own virtue, so in making use of them he acts in accordance with no other virtue than what he uses also in his own life.[25]

For our purpose, it is important to notice that αὐτάρκεια has become widely used, by people of many persuasions, most frequently without the intellectual or psychological baggage of Stoicism. It is also of interest that the non-Cynic self-sufficient man is concerned with κοινωνία, φιλία, and virtue, and that in his social relations his self-sufficiency consists in equality. As self-sufficient, he lacks nothing. He takes into consideration the circumstances under which he lives, but nevertheless remains self-sufficient.

Friendship and Self-Sufficiency

Below the surface of Ecphantus' text shimmers a problem that becomes overt in discussions of friendship: how could a friend claim self-sufficiency and still participate in the exchange of benefits, which, we have noted, was central to friendship? The problem was discussed with great regularity, particularly in connection with the motives or reasons for friendship. A variety of reasons were given, two of which concern us. The highest form of friendship, according to Aristotle, was that which arose between two people because of their similarity in character or virtue (*Eth. Nic.* 8.3.1–9). A less noble reason, advocated by Epicurus and roundly rejected by others, especially the Stoics, was utilitarian, namely, that friendship arises out of need or for the attainment of certain goals, such as happiness or tranquility.[26]

---

[25] This extract of Stobaeus (4.7.66 = 4.278, 23–279, 20 Hense) is printed in Holger Thesleff, *The Pythagorean Texts of the Hellenistic Period* (Acta Academiae Aboensis, Ser. A 30.1; Åbo: Åbo Akademi, 1965) 83, 18–84, 8. For this and other Neopythagorean tractates on kingship, see Erwin R. Goodenough, "The Political Philosophy of Hellenistic Kingship," *YCS* 1 (1928) 52–102.

[26] See Diog. Laert. 10.120; P. Mitsis, *Epicurus' Ethical Theory: The Pleasures of Invulnerability* (Ithaca: Cornell University Press, 1988) 98–128, for the Epicureans. For rejecton of their position, see Cic. *Amic.* 27–28, 30; Sen. *Ep.* 9.17.

Cicero shows us how these two conflicting views had entered non-technical discussion by the first century BC. Virtue, he says, "is the parent and preserver of friendship and without virtue friendship cannot exist at all. To proceed, then, let us interpret the word 'virtue' by the familiar usage of our everyday life and speech, and not in pompous phrase apply it to the precise standards which certain philosophers use; and let us include in the number of good men those who are so considered . . . who satisfy the ordinary standard of life" (*Amic.* 21; cf. 33, 100). "It is far from being true that friendship is cultivated because of need (*indigentiam*); rather it is cultivated by those who are most abundantly blessed with wealth and power and especially with virtue, which is man's best defence; by those least in need of another's help; and by those most generous and most given to acts of kindness. . . . It is not the case, therefore, that friendship attends upon advantage, but, on the contrary, that advantage (*utilitas*) attends upon friendship" (*Amic.* 51).

Friends show goodwill and affection for each other, rejoice with each other, and share the burdens of adversity; ". . . friends, though they be absent, are at hand; though in need, yet abound; though weak, are strong; and—harder saying still—though dead, are yet alive . . ." (*Amic.* 23). All this being so, how can friends be said to be self-sufficient?

Cicero's answer is that "to the extent that a man relies upon himself and is so fortified by virtue and wisdom that he is dependent on no one and considers all his possessions to be within himself, in that degree is he most conspicuous for seeking out and cherishing friendships. Now what need did Africanus have of me? By Hercules! none at all. And I, assuredly, had no need of him either, but I loved him because of a certain admiration for his virtue, and he, in turn, loved me, because, it may be, of the fairly good opinion which he had of my character . . ." (*Amic.* 30).

Yes, "the wise man is self-sufficient. Nevertheless, he desires friends, neighbors, and associates no matter how much he is sufficient unto himself. . . . In this sense the wise man is self-sufficient, that he can do without friends, not that he desires to do without them" (Sen. *Ep.* 9.3, 5).

So, it is on the basis of virtue, understood in the ordinary, general sense, that a friendship is formed. One seeks out the person who is worthy of one's friendship, Plutarch says, and attaches oneself to him (*De am. mult.* 94E). The more fully one understands this, the more fully one grasps the truth that one does not develop friendships because of need; indeed, true friendship does not proceed from need but virtue, the virtuous person seeking a friend who is like himself.

Philippians 4

Now, how does Philippians 4 read in light of all this? We begin with vs. 8, Paul's exhortation that his readers reflect on a list of moral qualities which constitutes the most Greek verse in all of Paul's letters. That ἀρετή, virtue, occurs in the climax of the list should not disconcert us; we remember that Cicero spoke of virtue in an ordinary sense, descriptive of a good person.[27] The qualities Paul enumerates are precisely those which would universally characterize such a person. Parallel to what the Philippians are to reflect on (λογίζεσθε) in vs. 8 is what they are to do (πράσσετε) in vs. 9, and that is what they have learned, received and heard from Paul. Paul, in other words, is to continue to be the paradigm for their moral conduct. While it is not explicitly stated that Paul embodies the virtues enumerated, the list functions to delineate the paradigm he presents. Cicero would say that the quality of character without which friendship could not exist was present in Paul and that the Philippians had accepted him as worthy of their friendship.

In vs. 10, I have argued, Paul compliments them for the friendly disposition with which they had recently shown their friendship to him. Then, in vss. 11–13, he is at great pains to make certain they understand that he did not consider their gift in a utilitarian manner: Paul had rejoiced over their gift, which should not, however, be taken to mean that he rejoiced because his need was met, for he was αὐτάρκης. Self-sufficiency is thus introduced in a discussion of friendly social relations. The circumstances in which Paul learned to be αὐτάρκης are illustrated by a series of six (resp. five) infinitives, which reveal an understanding of self-sufficiency very much like that of Teles:

---

[27] Ἀρετή, understood in the Greek sense of moral achievement or excellence, appears contradictory to Paul's ethics. See Wolfgang Schrage, *The Ethics of the New Testament* (Philadelphia: Fortress, 1988) 217–18, and the literature cited there. Siegfried Wibbing, *Die Tugend- und Lasterkataloge im Neuen Testament und ihre Traditionsgeschichte unter besonderes Berücksichtigung der Qumran-Texte* (BZNW 25; Berlin: Töpelmann, 1959) 103, correctly thinks that Paul uses the word here in a general sense.

whatever the circumstances one encounters, go with them. Paul can do so because Christ empowers him.[28]

There is no Stoic introspection present here despite the long exegetical tradition that has brought the Stoic notion into play. Paul is essentially concerned with personal relationships rather than introspection. His purpose, here in the conclusion of his letter, is to strengthen the tie of friendship that binds him and his readers by raising the matter of their gift to a higher plane, that of friendship. But, in denying that he viewed their gift in terms of need, Paul stresses his sufficiency to such a degree that the value of the gift could be put in question. Anticipating this, Paul qualifies (πλήν) his statement, once more with a cliché of friendship: they nevertheless did well in sharing in his affliction (vs. 14), thus acting in the way friends act.

To say that Paul describes his relations with the Philippians in the clichés of friendship and that he does not indulge in introspection is not to imply that there is no other dimension to that relationship. Vss. 10–20 open with a thanksgiving to the Lord for the Philippians' concern for him (vs. 10), and the section closes with a doxology (vs. 20). Within this *inclusio* Paul expresses the conviction that as he was empowered to be αὐτάρκης in all circumstances, God out of his riches will supply the Philippians' every need (vs. 19). Indeed, what Paul had already received was a sacrificial gift acceptable to God (vs. 18). As he does elsewhere, then, Paul uses the moral philosophical language of his day, but places it within a larger framework quite foreign to the philosophical tradition he uses.[29]

Paul's deft use of the language of friendship shows that he was fully aware of how the subject was being discussed and was able to use the language for his own purpose. What strikes one, however, is that he does not actually use φίλος or φιλία. This omission could only have been deliberate, but why did Paul avoid these words? He does so elsewhere, too, and various reasons have been suggested for the omission.

---

[28] The formal features of Paul's statement heighten the significance of ἐν τῷ ἐνδυναμοῦντί με; see Schieffer Ferrari, *Die Sprache des Leids*, 273–77.

[29] For numerous other examples where he does the same thing, see A. J. Malherbe, *Paul and the Popular Philosophers* (Minneapolis: Fortress, 1989). See also Stanley K. Stowers, "Friends and Enemies in the Politics of Heaven," *Pauline Theology I: Thessalonians, Philippians, Galatians, Philemon* (ed. Jouette M. Bassler; Minneapolis: Fortress, 1991) 117–21, on friendship and theology in the letter.

Paul may in general have avoided these words because of the anthropocentric connotations they carried, whereas in his view Christian relationships were determined by God.[30] There may, however, also have been local circumstances that contributed to his avoidance. He may have omitted them from 1 Thess 5:9–12 because he wanted his readers to avoid social attitudes like those associated with the Epicureans, which were tied up with φιλία.[31] Perhaps he did not use them in his correspondence with the Corinthians because he refused their offer of friendship with its attendant obligations.[32] Something similar may also have been behind his omission in Philippians; it is likely, I think, that Epaphroditus, with the Philippians' contribution had brought a letter from them in which they expressed their desire, as Paul's friends, to meet his needs.[33] Paul's denial that he is speaking καθ' ὑστέρησιν could then mark a move to a yet higher level of discussion that even dispenses with φίλος and φιλία. But the matter deserves closer scrutiny.[34]

---

[30] J. N. Sevenster, "Waarom spreekt Paulus nooit van vrienden en vriendschap?" *NedTTs* 9 (1954/1955) 356–63.

[31] See A. J. Malherbe, *Paul and the Thessalonians: The Philosophical Tradition of Pastoral Care* (Philadelphia: Fortress, 1987) 104.

[32] So Peter Marshall, *Enmity in Corinth: Social Conventions in Paul's Relations with the Corinthians* (WUNT 2.23; Tübingen: J. C. B. Mohr [Paul Siebeck], 1987).

[33] See A. J. Malherbe, "Did the Thessalonians Write to Paul?" *The Conversation Continues: Studies in Paul and John in Honor of J. Louis Martyn* (ed. R. T. Fortna and B. R. Gaventa; Nashville: Abingdon, 1990) 254 and n. 44.

[34] This essay also appears (in a slightly different form) in *Texts and Contexts: Biblical Texts in Their Textual and Situational Contexts. Essays in Honor of Lars Hartman* (ed. T. Fornberg and D. Hellholm; Oslo: Scandinavian University Press, 1995) 813–26.

PHILIPPIANS IN THE LIGHT OF SOME ANCIENT
DISCUSSIONS OF FRIENDSHIP

John T. Fitzgerald

In his correspondence with the church at Philippi, Paul uses a number of terms that belong to the ancient *topos* on friendship.[1] Attention to this fact has been called in several recent studies, the most important of which are those by L. Michael White,[2] Stanley K. Stowers,[3] and Abraham J. Malherbe.[4] The growing recognition of the importance of friendship language in Philippians[5] coincides with the increasing awareness that Paul's letters have a general affinity with ancient letters of friendship, which ancient Greek and Latin rhetoricians regarded as the most authentic type of letter.[6]

Furthermore, recent investigations of friendship in Greco-Roman authors and texts have deepened our understanding of the theory and practice of friendship in the ancient Mediterranean world, making it possible to recognize additional aspects of Philippians that can be illuminated by careful attention to Paul's use of friendship language

---

[1] For Paul's use of the *topos* on friendship and other *topoi* (stock treatments of moral subjects), see A. J. Malherbe, *Moral Exhortation, A Greco-Roman Sourcebook* (LEC 4; Philadelphia: Westminster, 1986) 144–61, esp. 144, and James L. Jaquette, *Discerning What Counts: The Function of the Adiaphora Topos in Paul's Letters* (SBLDS 146; Atlanta: Scholars Press, 1995) 12–13.

[2] L. M. White, "Morality between Two Worlds: A Paradigm of Friendship in Philippians," *Greeks, Romans, and Christians: Essays in Honor of Abraham J. Malherbe* (ed. D. L. Balch, E. Ferguson, and W. A. Meeks; Minneapolis: Fortress, 1990) 201–15.

[3] S. K. Stowers, "Friends and Enemies in the Politics of Heaven: Reading Theology in Philippians," *Pauline Theology, Volume I* (ed. J. M. Bassler; Minneapolis: Fortress, 1991) 105–21.

[4] A. J. Malherbe, "Paul's Non-Stoic *Autarkeia*" (paper presented at the international meeting of the Society of Biblical Literature, Melbourne, Australia, July, 1992). A revised version of this paper appears as Chapter Six of this volume.

[5] For recent treatments of friendship terms and concepts in Philippians, see the survey of scholarship by John Reumann in Chapter Four of this volume. In addition to the studies cited by Reumann, see James L. Jaquette, "A Not-So-Noble Death: Figured Speech, Friendship and Suicide in Philippians 1:21–26," *Neot* 28 (1994) 177–92.

[6] See John L. White, *Light from Ancient Letters* (FFNT; Philadelphia: Fortress, 1986) 191. Similarly, "Greek and Latin rhetoricians regarded the letter, when fully actualizing its potential, as a cultivated expression of friendship whereby the writer's very personality was made present to the recipient" (Ibid., 190).

in the letter.[7] This is so because friendship is not a self-contained topic hermetically sealed off from other subjects. Rather, it is interwoven with a variety of other topics, such as αὐτάρκεια, and cannot be satisfactorily understood apart from its various interconnections. Consequently, the more we learn about friendship in antiquity, the more sensitive we will become to the ways in which the different sections of the letter are linked together.

The present study is based primarily on the research and publications of members of the Hellenistic Moral Philosophy and Early Christianity Group. The purpose of the investigation is three-fold: (1) to comment on the advantages and disadvantages of characterizing Philippians as a "letter of friendship"; (2) to identify terminology in Philippians, especially 4:1–9, that belongs to the *topos* on friendship; and (3) to argue the thesis that one reason why Paul makes such an extensive use of friendship language in Philippians is because he is attempting to correct the Philippians' understanding of friendship.

Philippians as a "Letter of Friendship"

Viewed in terms of ancient epistolary theory, all of Paul's letters are "mixed" in terms of their style and content. None conforms precisely to the epistolary types and styles identified by theorists such as Ps.-Demetrius and Ps.-Libanius. The mixed character of Paul's letters is due not only to their length and complexity but also to the fact the apostle invariably writes with more than one purpose in mind. Theorists, by contrast, were concerned primarily with the identification of simple letters written for a single purpose. In addition, Paul's letters indicate that he was a skilled epistolographer fully capable of combining in one letter a wide variety of styles. Even his opponents in Corinth conceded his skill in this area (2 Cor 10:10).[8]

---

[7] See the eleven studies of friendship contained in John T. Fitzgerald (ed.), *Greco-Roman Perspectives on Friendship* (SBLRBS; Atlanta: Scholars Press, forthcoming).

[8] See the similar judgment by David E. Aune, *The New Testament in Its Literary Environment* (LEC 8; Philadelphia: Westminster, 1987) 203: "Most early Christian letters are multifunctional and have a 'mixed' character, combining elements from two or more epistolary types. . . . Paul in particular was both a creative and eclectic letter writer. The epistolary situations he faced were often more complex than the rhetorical situations faced by most rhetoricians. Many letters therefore exhibit combinations of styles."

An awareness of the mixed and complex nature of Paul's correspondence suggests that the identification of any of Paul's letters in terms of one specific type of letter is an oversimplification. 2 Cor 10–13, for example, is almost invariably referred to as an apology, and the apologetic letter is one of the epistolary types identified by the ancient theorists.[9] In this case, the identification is based chiefly on the apologetic function of these chapters. In reality, however, 2 Cor 10–13 is a mixed letter containing different elements and styles, such as appeals, exhortations, rebukes, threats, attacks, counterattacks, irony, and self-commendation.[10] To characterize 2 Cor 10–13 as "apologetic" has both advantages and disadvantages. The major drawback is that this designation is misleading to the extent that it calls attention to only one feature of the letter and overlooks others. On the other hand, the chief benefit is that it highlights an important feature of these chapters.

A similar situation exists in regard to Paul's letter to the church at Philippi. To refer to it as a *Freundschaftsbrief* or "letter of friendship" is misleading to the extent that such a characterization neglects other features of the letter (such as its rhetorical elements) or suggests that the letter conforms to a particular *Gattung*. Yet this designation is quite useful in calling attention to the presence in the letter of a remarkable number of terms that were associated in antiquity with the topic of friendship. Until recently, modern scholarship paid too little attention to this fact, and the characterization of Philippians as a friendly letter serves both to correct this neglect and to highlight an important feature of the letter.

In his recent introduction to the NT, Udo Schnelle rightly says, "Taken as a whole, Paul's letters stand closest to the ancient

---

[9] Ps.-Demetrius, *Typoi Epist.* 18 (40, 1–16 Malherbe). For the text and a translation, see Abraham J. Malherbe, *Ancient Epistolary Theorists* (SBLSBS 19; Atlanta: Scholars Press, 1988) 40–41. Unless otherwise noted, the translations used in this essay follow, where available, the renderings of the Loeb Classical Library. For the epistolary theorists, Malherbe's translations are used.

[10] For the "mixed" character of 2 Cor 10–13, see esp. J. T. Fitzgerald, "Paul, the Ancient Epistolary Theorists, and 2 Corinthians 10–13: The Purpose and Literary Genre of a Pauline Letter," *Greeks, Romans, and Christians: Essays in Honor of Abraham J. Malherbe* (ed. D. L. Balch, E. Ferguson, and W. A. Meeks; Minneapolis: Fortress, 1990) 190–200, and, for 2 Corinthians as a whole, idem., "The Second Letter of Paul to the Corinthians," *The HarperCollins Study Bible: New Revised Standard Version with the Apocryphal/Deuterocanonical Books* (ed. W. A. Meeks; New York: HarperCollins, 1993) 2164. For the mixed letter type in epistolary theory, see Ps.-Libanius, *Epist. Char.* 45 and 92 (73, 6 and 80, 37–41 Malherbe).

deliberative letters of friendship, yet in no case does Paul hold fast to the ideal types of the ancient rhetoricians and their followers."[11] This judgment is especially true in regard to Philippians. In writing the letter, Paul makes use of what rhetoricians called the "friendly" style and uses terminology from the *topos* on friendship. In addition, one of his likely purposes in writing is to correct the recipients' understanding of friendship. In terms of style, vocabulary, and purpose, therefore, Philippians is *in part*—indeed, in large part—a "letter of friendship," but it is also much, much more. And because Philippians is much more than any one designation—no matter how accurate— can possibly express, its precise classification both literarily and rhetorically will continue to be a matter of scholarly debate.

Friendship Language in Philippians 1–3

Language and ideas traditionally associated with friendship occur not only in chapter four[12] but are present throughout the letter, especially in the first two chapters. This is important, for it means that chapter four marks the *culmination* of friendship language in Philippians, not its inception. Before turning specifically to chapter four, therefore, I wish to begin this section of the essay by briefly noting some of the clearest examples of friendship language used already in chapters 1–3.

First, an extremely common description of friendship in the Greek world is that friends are of "one soul" (μία ψυχή). This characterization of friendship occurs already as a commonplace in Aristotle (*Eth. Nic.* 9.8.2) and continues to be used proverbially in the first century and thereafter (Plut. *De am. mult.* 96F). Basic to this characterization of friendship is the belief that a friend is a person's second self or alter ego. Friends are so similar that they are two bodies, as it were, sharing one soul (Diog. Laert. 5.20).[13] Paul uses this designation of

---

[11] U. Schnelle, *Einleitung in das Neue Testament* (UTB für Wissenschaft: Uni-Taschenbücher 1830; Göttingen: Vandenhoeck & Ruprecht, 1994) 53 n. 63.

[12] On friendship language in Phil 4:10–20, see the essays by Ken L. Berry and Abraham J. Malherbe in Chapters Five and Six of this volume.

[13] In this connection, the image of the "Moliones," the twin brothers Cteatus and Eurytus, sons of Actor (or Poseidon) was occasionally used (Hom. *Il.* 11.749; 23.638). Post-Homeric tradition depicted them as Siamese twins, their bodies conjoined in some way, and this conception may already lie back of Homer's depiction of them as driving the chariot together in *Il.* 23.638. See the comments on them by G. S.

friendship in 1:27, when he exhorts the Philippians to strive side by side "with one soul" (μιᾷ ψυχῇ). In addition to using the typical phrase, he also employs two variants that reflect the same or similar conception. One of these appears in the apostle's description of Timothy in 2:20, when he says that he has no one as ἰσόψυχος as this co-worker. Timothy is thus "of equal soul" with Paul, a description that combines the "one soul" definition of friendship with another ancient definition, viz., that "friendship is equality" (ἰσότης; mentioned together with the "one soul" saying in Arist. *Eth. Nic.* 9.8.2 and *Eth. Eud.* 7.6.9).[14] Paul's second variation of the "one soul" / "equal soul" description of friends appears in 2:2, where he asks the Philippians to be σύμψυχοι, "fellow souls."[15] Finally, in addition to Paul's "one soul" exhortation, he also asks the Philippians in 1:27 to stand (together) "in one spirit (ἐν ἑνὶ πνεύματι)."

Another extremely common ancient understanding of friendship is reflected in the affirmation that friends "think the same thing (τὸ αὐτὸ φρονεῖν)." This understanding of friendship is closely related to the "one soul" characterization. Because friends share one soul, they naturally think the same. It is not surprising, therefore, that this description is both ancient and widespread.[16] Paul uses it twice. The

---

Kirk, B. Hainsworth, and N. Richardson in *The Iliad: A Commentary* (ed. G. S. Kirk; 6 vols.; Cambridge: Cambridge University Press, 1985–93) 1.219–20 (Kirk); 3.304 (Hainsworth); 6.238 (Richardson). See also the note by J. G. Frazer, *Apollodorus, The Library* (LCL; 2 vols.; London: W. Heinemann; Cambridge, MA: Harvard University Press, 1921) 1.248–49. Plutarch depicts them as "one soul making use of the hands and feet and eyes of two bodies" (*Mor.* 478C–D; see also *Mor.* 1083C). For the application of the Moliones to the close union of two friends in Christian tradition, see the comments of Carolinne White, *Christian Friendship in the Fourth Century* (Cambridge: Cambridge University Press, 1992) 63 and 237–38 n. 7, who points to Gregory of Nazianzus' panegyric on his friend Basil. Gregory claims that people looked on the two Christians "as an illustrious pair. Orestes and Pylades were in their eyes nothing to us, or the sons of Molione" (*Or.* 43.22; the translation is that of the *NPNF*. See also Gregory of Nazianzus' statement that Basil and he "had all things in common and a single soul, as it were, bound together our two bodies" (*De vita sua* 228–30; trans. by D. M. Meehan in the FC).

[14] According to Timaeus, Pythagoras was the first to coin this expression. See Diog. Laert. 8.10.

[15] Compare the modern American expression "soul brothers."

[16] See, for example, Cic. *Amic.* 15 ("the whole essence of friendship" lies in "the most complete agreement in policy, in pursuits, and in opinions") and *Planc.* 2.5 ("there is no surer bond of friendship than the sympathetic union of thought and inclination"); Dio Chrys. *Or.* 34.20; Greg. Naz. *De vita sua* 236–37: "There is no such solid bond of union as thinking the same thoughts"; trans. by D. M. Meehan in the FC).

first time is in 2:2, where he exhorts all the Philippians to think the same. The second time is in 4:2, where he asks this of Euodia and Syntyche. In both cases, he is using the cultural idiom to exhort the Philippians in general, and Euodia and Syntyche in particular, to be friends. In addition to these two instances, Paul also uses a close variant in 2:2, where he exhorts the Philippians to think "one thing (τὸ ἓν φρονοῦντες)." All three instances illustrate Plato's insistence that friendship is a matter of ὁμόνοια, of being of the same mind and thus in harmony and concord (*Alc.* 126–27).[17]

Still another ancient understanding of friendship is reflected in the widespread sentiment that "friends have all things in common (κοινὰ τὰ φίλων)."[18] This saying was already proverbial by the time of Plato (*Ly.* 207C) and Aristotle (*Eth. Nic.* 9.8.2), and Aristotle himself argued that κοινωνία is essential to all forms of friendship (*Eth. Nic.* 8.12.1). Paul's emphasis on sharing in his letter to the Philippians should be seen, at least in part, in light of this ancient definition of friendship in terms of κοινωνία. He mentions it for the first time already in his thanksgiving in 1:5, when he expresses his gratitude for the Philippians' κοινωνία in the gospel. It continues throughout the letter, with Paul using κοινωνία and its cognates a total of some 6 times in Philippians (1:5, 7; 2:2; 3:10; 4:14–15). Paul's emphasis on sharing something in common and engaging in mutual enterprises is not restricted, however, to his use of κοινός-language. It is also reflected in other features of the letter. It is seen, for example, in his use some thirteen times of compounds with σύν (1:7, 27; 2:17–18, 25; 3:10, 17; 4:3, 14). Of particular interest in this regard is Paul's statement concerning mutual joy in 2:18–19 (see also 1:4, 18, 25; 2:2, 28–29; 3:1; 4:1, 4, 10). Friends were expected to share both joy and sorrow, to rejoice with those who rejoice and weep with those who weep, as Paul himself says elsewhere (Rom 12:15). Or, as Aristotle says, "it is characteristic of a friend to rejoice for no other reason than because the other is rejoicing" (*Eth. Eud.* 7.6.9). Paul's concern with sharing is also reflected in his use of words such as αὐτός or "same." For instance, he both exhorts the Philippians to have the same love (2:2) and affirms that they share the same ἀγών as he (1:30). All of this, to the ancient Greek, suggested friendship.

---

[17] See also Dio Chrys. *Or.* 34.20; Epicur. *SV* 61 and the comment of C. Bailey, *Epicurus: The Extant Remains* (Oxford: Clarendon, 1926) 385.
[18] See, for example, Cic. *Off.* 1.51 and Diog. Laert. 8.10.

So, too, did Paul's use of the motifs of presence and absence. It was axiomatic to the ancient Greek that true friends desired to be together. Such was not always possible, especially if a person had many friends or traveled often. As is well-known, one of the mechanisms in antiquity for dealing with the problem of absence was the letter, which functioned as a substitute for physical presence. According to the epistolary theorist commonly referred to as Ps.-Libanius, "One will speak in [a letter] as though one were in the company of the absent person" (*Epist. Char.* 2 [66, 8–9 Malherbe]). This is particularly true of friendly letters, which are expressions of friendship (*Epist. Char.* 11 [68, 21 Malherbe]). Ps-Libanius' example of a friendly letter, for instance, expresses the letter writer's eagerness to address the recipient. "For it is a holy thing," he says, "to honor genuine friends when they are present, and to speak to them when they are absent" (*Epist. Char.* 58 [74, 31–33 Malherbe]).

L. Michael White has argued that the hymn in chapter 2 depicts Christ as a friend.[19] Stanley K. Stowers, building upon that insight, has analyzed 1:19–26 in terms of Paul's absence from his friends, from Christ the friend with whom he most desires to be, and from the Philippians, the friends whom he wishes to benefit.[20] This he does in the exhortation found in 1:27–2:13, which is framed by references to presence and absence (1:27; 2:12). Such exhortations and advice as given here and in the rest of the letter are perfectly proper in letters to friends, for, as Stowers also reminds us, friendship provides a fitting context for moral instruction. That is precisely the relationship presupposed, for instance, in the letters of Seneca to his young friend. Paul's letter to the Philippians is thus, like Seneca's letters, a good example of moral instruction designed to further the moral progress (προκοπή: 1:25) of friends. It differs from Seneca's letters, of course, in being directed to a community of friends rather than to an individual friend.

Much more about the use of friendship language in chapters 1–3 could be said, but, for the sake of space, it is appropriate for me to focus the remainder of my comments on chapter four. I shall, however, make reference to chapters 1–3 at certain points in order to flesh out what I see going on in chapter 4.

---

[19] White, "Morality between Two Worlds," 207–15.
[20] Stowers, "Friends and Enemies," 107–21.

Friendship Language in Philippians 4

Because Ken L. Berry's contribution to this volume focuses on 4:10–20,[21] I shall not devote extensive attention to these verses. Instead, I shall concentrate on verses 1–9.

I begin with the observation that all three of the fragments that some scholars have detected in chapter 4 contain friendship language or terms congenial to the depiction of friends. Friendship language occurs in verse 1, which is often assigned to a putative fragment (usually identified as Letter C) that begins in 3:1b or 3:2.[22] It occurs also in verses 2–3, which is sometimes connected along with verse 1 to 3:2–21[23] but is more frequently connected with the fragment claimed to be preserved in 1:1–3:1.[24] The same is true for verses 8–9, which are usually assigned by partition advocates to the main letter of 1:1–3:1, but occasionally to the fragment possibly preserved in 3:2–21.[25] Finally, friendship language occurs in verses 10–20, which is often claimed to be a fragment of a separate letter (Letter A). The presence of friendship language throughout chapter 4 is, in my judgment, a strong argument in favor of the chapter's integrity.[26]

Friendship terminology in chapter 4 commences with the first verse. The terms of affection and longing that occur here are standard in discourses involving friends. Paul twice says that he loves them, doing so both times with ἀγαπητοί. Inasmuch as they are his joy and crown, he yearns to be with them (ἐπιπόθητοι), just as Epaphroditus

---

[21] See Chapter Five of this volume.

[22] Phil 4:1 is usually assigned to Letter C (at least 3:2–4:1) by advocates of the three-letter hypothesis. For a listing of some of those who adopt this position, see J. T. Fitzgerald, "Philippians, Epistle to the," *ABD* 5 (1992) 321.

[23] See, for example, H.-M. Schenke and K.-M. Fischer, *Einleitung in die Schriften des Neuen Testaments* (2 vols.; Gütersloh: Gütersloher Verlagshaus, 1978) 1.125–29, who see remnants of Letter C in 3:2–4:3 and 4:8–9. A convenient synopsis of their reconstruction of the sequence of events and letters to Philippi is available in Fitzgerald, "Philippians," 321.

[24] This connection is made, for instance, by both Joachim Gnilka, *Der Philipperbrief* (HTKNT 10.3; Freiburg: Herder, 1968) 10, 165, who divides canonical Philippians into two letters (Letter A: 1:1–3:1a; 4:2–7, 10–23; Letter B: 3:1b–4:1; 4:8–9), and F. W. Beare, *A Commentary on the Epistle to the Philippians* (New York: Harper & Bros., 1959) 5, 102, 142, who divides canonical Philippians into three letters (A: 4:10–20; B: 1:1–3:1; 4:2–9; 4:21–23; C: 3:2–4:1)

[25] This connection, for example, is made by both Gnilka, *Philipperbrief*, 10, 219, and Schenke and Fischer, *Einleitung*, 1.125–29.

[26] For the use of friendship language throughout canonical Philippians as an argument in favor of the letter's integrity, see Fitzgerald, "Philippians," 321–22. I concede, however, that this argument is not a decisive one.

had yearned to be with them (2:25; see also Rom 1:11; 15:23; 2 Cor 7:7, 11; 9:14; 1 Thess 3:6).

In 4:2–3, Paul not only uses the key phrase "to think the same thing," but also employs four compound words with σύν that are intended to convey the notion of mutual understanding and endeavor. The reason for Paul's desire that there be ὁμόνοια between Euodia and Syntyche, though not explicitly stated, is nonetheless crystal clear. As Aristotle says, "those who agree in mind (οἱ ὁμονοοῦντες) do not quarrel" (*Eth. Eud.* 7.7.7).

To assist Euodia and Syntyche in settling their dispute, Paul appeals to the "true yokefellow (γνήσιε σύζυγε)." Although the name of this anonymous individual can only be the subject of speculation, it may well be the case that the yokefellow was a woman. This is certainly possible grammatically, and the word σύζυγος, at any rate, was most often applied to women in their relationship with men, usually as the wife. What is more important to the argument here, however, is that the word "yoke" was one of the metaphors used to describe the relationship of friends. Cicero, for example, says that "that friendship (*amicitia*) is sweetest which is 'yoked together with' (*coniugavit*) congeniality of character" (*Off.* 1.58).[27] In his *Iphigenia in Tauris*, Euripides has Iphigenia, the daughter of Agamemnon, use the word σύζυγος to describe the relationship between Orestes and Pylades (250). In the Greco-Roman period, of course, these men were celebrated as one of the most famous pairs of friends in history. Lucian, for example, begins his treatment of friendship in the *Toxaris* with the story of this famous pair of friends (1–8). Plutarch, moreover, uses the phrase "yoke of friendship (ζεῦγος φιλίας)" when introducing his list of famous friends, which were Theseus and Perithoüs, Achilles and Patroclus, Orestes and Pylades, Phintias and Damon, Epameinondas and Pelopidas (*De am. mult.* 93E).

This classical and hellenistic usage of yoke to describe the bond of friendship was also used by Christian writers of a later period. Ausonius, for example, accuses Paulinus of Nola of shaking off the "yoke" of friendship:

---

[27] The translation of the LCL has been modified to bring out the literal meaning of the verb that Cicero uses, which is *coniugo*. The verb *coniugo* is a compound formed with *cum* (*com/con* = "with") and *iugo* ("to yoke"; cf. *iugum* = "yoke"). The *OLD* (s.v.) gives this passage from Cicero as an example of the verb used to mean "to form a friendship."

We are shaking off a yoke, Paulinus, which its tried equableness once made easy, a yoke lightly laid and worthy the respect of those it joined, which mild Concord (*Concordia*) used to guide with even reins; ... so gentle, so easy a yoke which both our fathers drew on into old age from the beginning of their life, which, laid upon their duteous heirs, they would have had remain throughout till length of days broke up our lives. ... This yoke so mild Mars' horses would endure with obedient neck. ... Yet it is being shaken off, Paulinus; and that, not through the fault of both, but of one alone—of thee. For my neck will ever bear it gladly. It is the partner of my toil deserts me, and 'tis not so easy for one, when his fellow fails, to carry on alone that which the two bare as comrades.[28]

Ausonius' association of concord (= ὁμόνοια) with the yoke is striking and recalls the way in which Paul moves from an appeal for concord to the request for assistance from the yokefellow.

Paulinus, in response to Ausonius' accusation, denies that he is terminating their friendship and restates the image of the yoke so as to avoid the suggestion that he is Ausonius' literary equal:

You add the additional charge of neglect of friendship. ... You complain that I have shaken off the yoke which joined me to you in literary pursuits. But I maintain that I never shouldered it, for equals undertake a yoke. No man joins a strong partner with a weak, and it is no harmonious pair if those forced together are unevenly balanced. ... Tully and Maro could hardly be equal yoke-fellows with you. If love is the yoke we share, this is the only yoke which I dare boast of sharing with you, for in love the modest can vie with the great, and share its reins. Sweet friendship brings equality through my eternal compact with you, and through our equal observance of perennial love towards each other. No malicious gossip loosens this yoke from our necks; no lengthy absence from my native soil has destroyed it or will destroy it.[29]

That is, Paulinus wishes to remain Ausonius' friend, but he wishes to be yoked with him, no longer in their devotion to the pagan Muses, but in their commitment to Christ. As P. Walsh notes, "he demonstrates how the *amicitia* demanded by Ausonius, that intimacy in social

---

[28] Ausonius, *Ep.* 27 ed. Evelyn White in the LCL = *Ep.* 24 ed. Green.

[29] Paulinus of Nola, *Carm.* 11. The translation is that P. G. Walsh in the ACW. In viewing *Carm.* 11 as Paulinus' response to *Ep.* 27 Evelyn White (= *Ep.* 24 Green), I am following the chronological sequence adopted by M. J. Byrne, *Prolegomena to an Edition of Decimus Magnus Ausonius* (New York: Cornell University Press, 1916) 35–36, P. G. Walsh (trans.), *The Poems of St. Paulinus of Nola* (ACW 40; New York: Newman, 1975) 20–21, and others. Ausonius' *Ep.* 27 is itself a response to Paulinus, *Carm.* 10. For Paulinus' view of friendship, see esp. P. Fabre, *S. Paulin de Nole et l'amité chrétienne* (Paris: E. de Boccard, 1949), and White, *Christian Friendship*, 146–63.

and literary diversions so esteemed by the pagan Romans, is transcended by the new *amicitia* which only Christians can share."[30]

In light of this usage of the word "yoke," it is clear that Paul is addressing someone in Philippi as his "genuine friend."[31] Furthermore, Paul uses the image of the yoke here in close conjunction with the military image of Euodia and Syntyche "fighting at his side (συνήθλησαν)" in the gospel's cause (4:3). The conjunction of the two images occurs already in the *Iliad*, where Homer describes the two Aiantes fighting side-by-side like two yoked oxen:

> But Oileus' son the racing Ajax—not for a moment,
> not at all would he leave his giant brother Ajax,
> shoulder-to-shoulder they fought together here:
> close as a brace of wine-dark oxen matched in power,
> dragging a bolted plow through packed fallow land
> and the sweat rushes up at the roots of both their horns
> and only the width of polished yoke keeps both beasts apart,
> struggling up the furrow to cut the field's last strip.
> So both men stood their ground, bracing man-to-man
> and a flock of comrades, hardened combat veterans
> followed the Great Ajax, ready to take his shield
> whenever sweat and labor sapped his knees.[32]

Although Paul does not use the image of the yoke in connection with the depiction of the battle that the women waged with him for the sake of the gospel, the passage from Homer shows that his move from one image to the other would not have struck any educated Greek as awkward.

The same concern with friendship that is evident in 4:1–3 can also be seen in verses 8 and 9. Verse 8, of course, contains a list of eight virtues, and, as we shall see in a moment, the truest form of friendship was held by the majority of philosophers to be grounded in virtue. Then, in verse 9, Paul presents himself as a model for their imitation. Professor Malherbe has made the persuasive suggestion

---

[30] Walsh, *The Poems of St. Paulinus of Nola*, 24.

[31] Compare 2 Cor 6:14, where Paul uses "yoke" language to advise the Corinthians not to be friends with "unbelievers." For the phrase "genuine friend (γνήσιος φίλος)," see Phoc. 2A (ed. BergK, *PLG*) and the texts cited by C. Spicq in the *TLNT* 1.297.

[32] Hom. *Il.* 13.701–11. The translation is that of Robert Fagles, *Homer, The Iliad* (New York: Penguin, 1990) 364. Great Ajax is the son of Telamon, king of Salamis, and Little Ajax is the son of Oileus, king of the Locrians. Richard Janko comments as follows: "A fine ploughing-simile illustrates the Aiantes' single-mindedness, physical closeness (only the yoke separates the toiling oxen, 706), effort (the oxen sweat, cf. 711) and success (they reach the end of the furrow)." See *The Iliad: A Commentary* (ed. G. S. Kirk; 6 vols.; Cambridge: Cambridge University Press, 1985–93) 4.135.

that the list of virtues in verse 8 serves to delineate the paradigm that Paul presents. That is, in verses 8–9 Paul is presenting himself as a virtuous individual and friend who possesses the virtues which the Philippians are to reflect upon (v. 8) and practice (v. 9).[33]

It is, therefore, as the virtuous friend that Paul discusses the Philippians' gift in verses 10–20. He describes that gift in v. 15 in terms of both κοινωνία and mutual benefaction, and, like Cicero, uses the same commercial language of credits and debits (of "giving and receiving") to do so (*Amic.* 58). Also, like Cicero, he makes use of horticultural metaphors to describe the Philippians' friendly gift. In sending their gift, the Philippians have, Paul says, "bloomed again" (ἀνεθάλετε) as far as their care for him is concerned (v. 10).[34] A second agricultural metaphor occurs in v. 17, where Paul describes the gift's interest as "fruit." Compare Cicero, who says that friendship is "desirable, not because we are influenced by the hope of gain, but because its entire fruit is in the love itself" (*Amic.* 31).

Paul interprets the gift both positively and in terms of their mutual friendship. In doing so, he makes use of the commonplace idea that friends share each other's hardships. This appears in v. 14, where he praises the Philippians for their κοινωνία in his affliction. Again, he interprets the interval between their gifts in a manner that exonerates the Philippians of any blame. Philosophers recognized two legitimate reasons why a friend might be slow in returning a benefit. One was lack of financial ability, and the other was lack of opportunity (Sen. *Ben.* 4.40.3). The latter, Paul says, was the reason for the Philippians' delay, and so, on that basis, he accepts their gift with joy (v. 10). In sum, by removing any basis for censure in v. 10 and by praising the Philippians directly in v. 14, Paul shows that he accepts their gift as an expression of their friendship for him.

Finally, Paul's reference to his αὐτάρκεια, as Malherbe has convincingly demonstrated, should not be understood primarily in terms of the apostle's inner freedom and disposition.[35] The context in which Paul mentions his self-sufficiency is that of his friendship with the Philippians, and his reference should be understood within that context. The relationship between φιλία and αὐτάρκεια had in fact been

---

[33] See Malherbe's essay in Chapter Six.
[34] For this interpretation of ἀνεθάλετε in 4:10, see Malherbe's essay in Chapter Six.
[35] See Chapter Six. The relationship of friendship and self-sufficiency is also treated by Ken L. Berry in Chapter Five.

discussed for centuries by philosophers, including Aristotle, the Stoics, the Neopythagoreans, and others, who tried to find some way to avoid or at least to mitigate the conclusion that friends are necessarily superfluous for the truly self-sufficient individual (cf. Diog. Laert. 2.98). Aristotle, for example, at one point says that "he who lives the best life will have fewest friends, and they will constantly become fewer, and he will not be eager to have friends but will think lightly not only of useful friends but also of those desirable for society" (*Eth. Eud.* 7.12.3). Seneca, on the other hand, sought to preserve the sage's desire to have friends. "In this sense," he says, "the wise man is self-sufficient, that he can do without friends, not that he desires to do without them" (*Ep.* 9.5). Cicero went even further, arguing the paradoxical position that the more self-sufficient a man is, the more conspicuous he will be in "seeking out and cherishing friendships" (*Amic.* 30).

Paul follows in the train of those who want to affirm strongly both αὐτάρκεια and φιλία. On the one hand, he insists that he is αὐτάρκης, demonstrating that by means of the list of vicissitudes that he cites in v. 12. Like a moderate Cynic, he does not sternly renounce the unnecessary luxuries of life but adapts himself to the particular περίστασις in which he finds himself and uses that circumstance to demonstrate his power of self-sufficiency.[36] On the other hand, as we have seen, he accepts the Philippians' gift as an expression of their friendship.[37]

Chapter four is, therefore, replete with terms and ideas connected with friendship. Furthermore, there is a conceptual link between the use of friendship language in chapter 4 and Paul's affirmations at the end of chapter 3 about the heavenly commonwealth, the πολίτευμα (3:20). Aristotle, it should be recalled, stressed the social and political nature of friendship. Because the ἄνθρωπος is by nature a social being,

---

[36] On Paul's use of *peristasis* catalogues, see esp. J. T. Fitzgerald, *Cracks in an Earthen Vessel: An Examination of the Catalogues of Hardships in the Corinthian Correspondence* (SBLDS 99; Atlanta: Scholars Press, 1988). For the catalogue of vicissitudes in Phil 4:11–12, which reckons with both favorable and unfavorable circumstances through fluctuation in fortune, see pp. 45, 203–05.

[37] Elizabeth Asmis, "Philodemus' Epicureanism," *ANRW* 2.36.4 (1990) 2389–90, points out that Philodemus emphasizes the importance of friendship in regard to both prosperity and adversity. "In prosperity, people should gratify both themselves and their friends. In adversity, it is even more important to satisfy our friends' needs than our own" (2389; see Phld. *Oec.* 26). For friendship in prosperity and adversity, see also Cic. *Amic.* 22.

i.e., a πολιτικόν creature (*Eth. Nic.* 1.7.6; 9.9.3; *Pol.* 1.1.9), his or her life should not be that of a recluse, but rather partake of the social life of the πόλις. The setting for friendship is, therefore, that of the πόλις, so that it takes place in this "established collectivity of lives and values."[38] Knowing this, the good ruler promotes civic friendship as the bond of the state and seeks to banish faction, which brings discord (*Eth. Nic.* 8.1.4).

The Epicureans also made this link and described their community of friends as a commonwealth. Numenius, for example, says, "The school of Epicurus resembles a true commonwealth (πολιτεία), altogether free of factionalism, sharing one mind and one disposition" (Eus. *Prep. Ev.* 14.5).[39]

For our purposes, what is important to note is the connection between the πόλις, friendship, and the desire for concord. The same connection appears twice in Philippians and follows a similar sequence. It appears first in the section that begins in 1:27. Here Paul commences by placing his exhortation under the general rubric of "living as citizens (πολιτεύεσθε)." Next, he piles up traditional friendship language to describe their manner of living together. They are to be of one soul, to have κοινωνία of spirit, to think the same, to be fellow souls, and to be one in thinking. These exhortations are accompanied by terms of emotion, "affection (σπλάγχνα)," "sympathy (οἰκτιρμοί)," and "joy (χαρά)." The ideal to which Paul exhorts them is contrasted with the selfish ambition that gives rise to strife (ἐριθεία), the antithesis of friendship. Finally, Paul concludes by setting forth the example of Christ as the model friend. All of this is set over against a reference to the opponents against whom the Philippians are now struggling but who eventually will be destroyed (ἀπώλεια, 1:28).

A similar sequence appears in the latter part of chapter 3 and the first part of chapter 4. Here Paul again uses πόλις-language, this time referring to the πολίτευμα or commonwealth in heaven. What follows in chapter 4 is intended to show how the Philippians' earthly life together is to be governed by that commonwealth to which they belong. He begins the chapter with the same kind of affectionate

---

[38] The expression is that of Frederic M. Schroeder, "Friendship in Aristotle and the Peripatetic Tradition" (paper presented to the Hellenistic Moral Philosophy and Early Christianity Consultation at the annual meeting of the Society of Biblical Literature, Kansas City, MO, November, 1991). A revised version of this paper will appear in *Greco-Roman Perspectives on Friendship* (see note 7).

[39] The translation is that of Stowers, "Friends and Enemies," 113.

language (4:1) that he had used at the beginning of chapter 2. Then, as in 2:2, Paul once again uses the traditional language of friendship, this time addressing Euodia and Syntyche and asking them to have the ὁμόνοια that friendship entails. The peace that he twice wishes for the Philippians can only exist when they cease from strife and become friends (vv. 7, 9). Again, just as 1:27–2:11 concludes with the presentation of Christ as a model friend, so 4:8–20 presents Paul as a paradigm of virtuous friendship. Another similarity is that both sections contain references to opponents whose future destruction (ἀπώλεια, 1:28; 3:19) is avowed by Paul. In chapter one, the reference follows the use of πόλις-language; in chapter three, however, the reference precedes the use of commonwealth imagery. Finally, the similarity of the two sections is further signaled by use of the verbs "stand" (στήκετε, 1:27; 4:1) and "strive side by side" (1:27; 4:3) in both passages. The use of συναθλεῖν in both 1:27 and 4:3 is particularly striking, inasmuch as these are the only two passages in which Paul uses this verb at all.

Finally, given Paul's use of friendship language throughout the letter, it is not surprising that he should also make reference not only to his own παρρησία (1:20) but also to that of the majority of the brothers (1:14).[40] Moreover, just as παρρησία was used by the hellenistic moralists to address the public as well as to correct friends, so also Pauline παρρησία is exercised not only courageously toward non-Christians but also psychagogically toward fellow Christians. Indeed, Paul's letter to the Philippians contains striking examples of frank speech. These include his candid remarks about the improper motives with which some proclaim the gospel (1:15, 17), about the dangers represented by the evil workers (3:2), and about the egoistic orientation of the enemies of the cross of Christ (3:18–19) and their eventual fate (3:19; see also 1:28). True friends, of course, are distinguished from false ones by the sincerity of their motives, and one of their obligations is boldly to warn their friends about entering into a close association with those whose values are dangerous and destructive.[41]

In addition to the preceding instances of boldness, Paul exhibits incredible frankness when he makes a direct appeal to Euodia and

---

[40] On the term παρρησία in the Pauline homologoumena, see David E. Fredrickson's essay in Chapter Eight of this volume.

[41] On these points, see the essays by David Konstan and Troels Engberg-Pedersen in Chapters One and Three of this volume.

Syntyche in 4:2. This passage is all the more remarkable in light of Philodemus' judgment that women, eminent people with resources and reputation, and old people are generally more resentful of frank criticism than are other individuals (*Lib.* cols. 22–24).[42] Euodia and Syntyche belong to at least the first of these three categories (women); they probably belong to the second category (eminent people with resources and reputation) and possibly to third category (old people) as well. That Paul dares to address them directly—and publicly rather than privately—may reflect the severity of the discord that existed between them, or, it may indicate, as Nils A. Dahl has recently suggested, "that the disagreement between Euodia and Syntyche is the chief problem Paul faces and the main reason why his joy over the Philippians is less than complete."[43] In any case, it indicates, as 4:3 suggests, that he has a close personal friendship with both women based on their previous collaboration in the gospel.[44]

Whatever the reason for Paul's use of παρρησία toward these women, the fact that he does so is evidence not only of his verbal boldness but also of his confidence in them that they will respond appropriately. To ensure that they will do so, he asks his own friend— the "true yokefellow"—to assist them toward that end. This request is revealing, for it indicates that the Philippian church will make use of a communal psychagogical approach in addressing its difficulties. The Philippian church thus emerges as a community of friends, a community that is in certain ways strikingly similar to Philodemus' Epicurean community. Both are communities in which παρρησία is exercised openly within the group and the assistance of intimate associates is enlisted, all with a view toward the restoration and maintenance of the kind of friendship that is indispensable to moral/ spiritual progress.[45]

---

[42] On frankness in Philodemus, see the discussion by Clarence E. Glad in Chapter Two of this volume.

[43] N. A. Dahl, "Euodia and Syntyche and Paul's Letter to the Philippians," *The Social World of the First Christians: Essays in Honor of Wayne A. Meeks* (ed. L. M. White and O. L. Yarbrough; Minneapolis: Fortress, 1995) 14.

[44] The use of "one soul" language with the same verb in 1:27 is a strong indication that Paul views these women as personal friends.

[45] As R. L. Hunter, "Horace on Friendship and Free Speech (Epistles 1.18 and Satires 1.4)," *Hermes* 113 (1985) 488, notes, "it was a traditional idea of Greek popular ethics that one had a duty to correct the faults of a friend." This traditional obligation became associated with παρρησία in the Hellenistic period, when παρρησία became "a private virtue exercised among friends" that "was particularly associated with the Epicureans, but was by no means limited to that school." For the public

Paul's Correction of the Philippians' Understanding of Friendship

I conclude with a conjecture based on Paul's list of virtues in 4:8. This list of virtues is not only related thematically to the topic of friendship but also indicates a particular kind of friendship. Aristotle, one should recall, distinguishes three kinds of friendship. The criterion he uses for his classification has to do with the *basis* of friendship. The first is character friendship, which is based on virtue. The second kind of friendship is grounded in pleasure, and the third is based on utility or advantage. True friendship is character friendship, which is altruistic and seeks the friend's good. The other two kinds of friendship are inferior, unstable, and egoistic.

My conjecture, simply put, is this: Throughout Philippians Paul is seeking to elevate the Philippians' understanding of friendship and place it on a higher plane. The Philippians' understanding of friendship seems to have been utilitarian, the third of Aristotle's three types. The Epicureans advocated this kind of friendship, but most agreed with Aristotle in rejecting the claim that true friendship is cultivated because of need. Paul thus sides with the majority of philosophers in basing friendship on virtue. His particular depiction of friendship is both descriptive and prescriptive. Like philosophers who use friendship language to describe utopian communities, Paul uses friendship language to depict the Christian community as it should exist ideally, and he adduces several examples of those who practice the friendship that belongs to this ideal society.

My basis for advancing this conjecture is essentially two-fold. First, Paul consistently describes both people and ideas in terms of friendship based on virtue. There is, as we have seen, the virtue list in 4:8, which includes the key term ἀρετή in its climax. In keeping with this is the striking use of the term ἀξίως ("worthily") in 1:27 to describe

---

and participatory nature of Epicurean psychagogy, where communal παρρησία is essential for moral progress (προκοπή) and where students assist the teacher in helping their peers, see Clarence E. Glad's discussion in Chapter Two. Note that Paul's παρρησία in 4:2 is not only public but that it also follows soon after the mention of his own "progress" in 3:12–14 and his exhortation in 3:17 for the Philippians to follow his example in progressing toward the goal. In short, Paul's friendship with Euodia and Syntyche allows him to utilize the παρρησία that will help his friends make the kind of progress that he himself is making. Therefore, just as Plutarch uses frank criticism to bring about the realization of his "moral system," so also Paul uses it to help the Christian community of friends to realize its goal (3:12–21). For the place of frank criticism within Plutarch's thought, see the essay by Troels Engberg-Pedersen in Chapter Three of this volume.

proper conduct. Such conduct seeks the advantage of Christ (2:21) and of others, not its own advantage (2:4). This non-utilitarian kind of friendship is exemplified by Christ (2:5–11), by Timothy (2:20), and by Epaphroditus (2:30). True friendship is marked by genuineness, which is exhibited by both Timothy (2:20) and the yokefellow of 4:3. A true friend is, moreover, not a new acquaintance. Both time and testing are necessary presuppositions for true friendship (Arist. *Eth. Nic.* 8.3.8; 4.3; *Eth. Eud.* 7.2.46), and people like Timothy are true friends, whose proof is known (2:22). A true friend is thus worthy of one's confidence (Arist., *Eth. Nic.* 8.3.8; *Eth. Eud.* 7.2.40; Phil 1:14). Finally, Paul's treatment of the Philippians' gift is designed to show that his acceptance of it is not based on his own need, though that is why they sent it (4:16). Indeed, as Abraham J. Malherbe has suggested, it is likely that the Philippians sent a letter to Paul in conjunction with their gift, and in that letter they indicated that, as the apostle's friends, they wanted to meet his needs.[46] Because Paul insisted on his αὐτάρκεια, however, he refused to accept the gift on that basis. He nevertheless accepted the benefaction and did so joyfully, because they did well to send it and thereby partake of his affliction (4:14). In short, because theirs is a friendship based on virtue, he joyfully accepts their gift as an act of both friendship and virtue.

Second, the problems Paul addresses in Philippians are those typically associated with friendships based on personal advantage. This is, according to Aristotle,[47] the most common type of friendship (*Eth. Eud.* 7.2.14) and yet the most problematic. Whereas true friends long to be with each other (*Eth. Nic.* 8.5.3; *Eth. Eud.* 7.12.18), utilitarian friends have no desire to associate together (*Eth. Nic.* 8.3.3). Friendships based on utility often involve people of different financial and educational levels, such as the rich and the poor or the learned and

---

[46] A. J. Malherbe, "Did the Thessalonians Write to Paul?" *The Conversation Continues: Studies in Paul and John in Honor of J. Louis Martyn* (ed. R. T. Fortna and B. R. Gaventa; Nashville: Abingdon, 1990) 254 n. 44. See, in addition, W. Schenk, *Die Philipperbriefe des Paulus: Kommentar* (Stuttgart: Kohlhammer, 1984) 60, 63–65, who correctly identifies φρονεῖν ὑπέρ as friendship language and makes the attractive suggestion that Paul is quoting this phrase from a letter sent to him by the Philippians.

[47] In the final section of this essay, I rely chiefly on Aristotle, thus providing an Aristotelian analysis of friendships based on utility. For two recent analyses of Aristotle's understanding of friendship, see Paul Schollmeier, *Other Selves: Aristotle on Personal and Political Friendship* (Albany: State University of New York Press, 1994) and Suzanne Stern-Gillet, *Aristotle's Philosophy of Friendship* (Albany: State University of New York Press, 1995).

the ignorant (*Eth. Nic.* 8.8.6). In short, this is the type of friendship most likely to emerge in the socially, intellectually, and economically diverse gatherings of the early church.[48]

Furthermore, these utilitarian friendships were, according to Aristotle, the ones most liable to give rise to complaints and recriminations. "Complaints and recriminations occur solely or chiefly in friendships of utility, as is to be expected. . . . For here the friends associate with each other for profit, and so each always wants more, and thinks he is getting less than his due; and they make it a grievance that they do not get as much as they want and deserve; and the one who is doing a service can never supply all that the one receiving it wants" (*Eth. Nic.* 8.13.2, 4). This is especially true in friendships of utility that have a moral rather than a legal basis. In this circumstance, one person trusts the other for repayment, but the recipient's obligation to do so is strictly voluntary and not mandated by law. Because the return of the benefit may not be to the recipient's advantage, he may refuse to do so (*Eth. Eud.* 7.10.17). "In a friendship based on virtue," by contrast, "each party is eager to benefit the other . . .; and as they vie with each other in giving and not in getting benefit, no complaints nor quarrels can arise, since nobody is angry with one who loves him and benefits him" (*Eth. Nic.* 8.13.2; see also 8.13.11).

As a result, friendships based on virtue are permanent, whereas those based on utility are easily broken off (*Eth. Nic.* 8.3.3), especially when they are no longer advantageous. "A friendship based on utility dissolves as soon as its profit ceases; for the friends did not love each other, but what they got out of each other" (*Eth. Nic.* 8.4.2). It is also easily dissolved by calumny and suspicion (*Eth. Nic.* 8.4.3), because they do not trust each other and lack the confidence in each other that comes from time and testing.

In short, both Paul's positive description of conduct using terms from character friendship and his attempt to deal with the quarrel

---

[48] The diversity of the Christian community is similar to that of the Epicurean communities, at least in the southern part of Italy (see Glad's discussion in Chapter Two on the socially diverse composition of the Epicurean communities). The social levels of Euodia, Syntyche, and the yokefellow are not mentioned by Paul, but the communal psychagogic practice revealed in 4:2–3 would be particularly interesting if the three came from more than one social class. Philodemus, at any rate, indicates that the Epicureans were sensitive to the problems associated with offering frank criticism to people from a different social class (*Lib.* col. 22–24).

between Euodia and Syntyche (4:2–3) suggest a situation in which the Philippians are treating the relationships within the church on the basis of utility rather than virtue. The grumbling and questioning denounced in 2:14–15 would also fit such a situation. Indeed, it would not be too surprising if the Philippians were like the people described by Aristotle, who "wish to have it both ways at once— they associate together for the sake of utility but make it out to be a moral friendship as between good men" (*Eth. Eud.* 7.10.17). In any case, Paul's goal seems to be that of transforming their relationship with each other, and theirs with him, from one of utility to one of virtue. If the Philippians respond positively to Paul's exhortation, they will think and act in a manner that is appropriate to the utopian community by which their life is to be governed (3:20–21).

PART THREE

ΠΑΡΡΗΣΙΑ IN THE NEW TESTAMENT

ΠΑΡΡΗΣΙΑ IN THE PAULINE EPISTLES

David E. Fredrickson

Introduction

A study of Paul's παρρησία promises to relate his letters to a key concept shared by ancient politics, rhetoric, and philosophy. Abraham Malherbe has shown how a number of texts in Paul's letters, Acts and the Pastoral Epistles are illumined by philosophic παρρησία in particular.[1] Other scholars, however, have argued that Paul shows little interest in ancient traditions concerning free speech.[2] Following Malherbe's lead, the present study aims to deepen appreciation for Paul's engagement with his world of thought and to clarify some of his arguments by placing his references to free speech in Phlm 8–9, 1 Thess 2:1–12, Phil 1:12–20, and 2 Cor 1–7 in a philosophic context.

Before turning to these passages and their philosophic background, a misconception which has hindered modern treatments of Paul's παρρησία must be addressed. In contrast to an ancient definition which understood παρρησία to be boldness in words (τὸ ἐν λόγοις θαρρεῖν),[3] modern exegetes have emphasized the apostle's boldness nearly to the exclusion of his words.[4] For example, the phrase πολλῇ παρρησίᾳ χρώμεθα in 2 Cor 3:12 is frequently translated "we have much

---

[1] See his "'Gentle as a Nurse': The Cynic Background to I Thess ii," *NovT* 12 (1970) 208–17; *Paul and the Thessalonians: The Philosophic Tradition of Pastoral Care* (Fortress: Philadelphia, 1987) 81–94; "'Pastoral Care' in the Thessalonian Church," *NTS* 36 (1990) 375–91; "Antisthenes and Odysseus, and Paul at War," *HTR* 76 (1983) 156–62. For the "philosophic" Paul in Acts, see "'Not in a Corner': Early Christian Apologetic in Acts 26:26," *The Second Century* 5 (1985–1986) 193–210. For παρρησία in moral admonition, see "Medical Imagery in the Pastoral Epistles," in *Texts and Testaments: Critical Essays on the Bible and Early Church Fathers* (ed. W. E. March; San Antonio, TX: Trinity University Press, 1980) 24–31 and "'In Season and Out of Season': 2 Timothy 4:2," *JBL* 103 (1984) 235–43.

[2] S. Marrow, "*Parrhēsia* and the New Testament," *CBQ* 44 (1982) 439, 446.

[3] *Lex. Vind.* Π 100 (A. Nauck, *Lexicon vindobonense* [Petersburg, 1867; reprint. Hildesheim: Olms, 1965] 152). The definition does mention, however, a metaphorical sense.

[4] H. Schlier, "Παρρησία, παρρησιάζομαι," *TDNT* 5 (1967) 883. For the beginning of a course correction, see W. C. van Unnik, "The Christian's Freedom of Speech," *Sparsa Collecta: The Collected Essays of W. C. van Unnik* (NovTSup 29–31; Leiden: E. J. Brill, 1973–83) 2.276. He is not consistent on this point, however;

boldness" or "we are very confident" rather than "we use much bold speech."[5] 2 Cor 7:4 is translated in a similar fashion; πολλή μοι παρρησία πρὸς ὑμᾶς is rendered "great is my confidence in you" rather than "great is my bold speech toward you."[6]

A brief review of the phrase παρρησίᾳ χρῆσθαι warns against equating Paul's παρρησία with confidence and also indicates his familiarity with a commonplace expression for rhetorical activity. Demosthenes, according to Caecilius Calactinus, was "accustomed to use bold speech (παρρησίᾳ χρῆσθαι)."[7] Centuries later Philostratus' description of Menippus shows that the phrase refers to a manner of speaking: "he was by now a qualified disputant and remarkably outspoken (παρρησίᾳ χρῆσθαι δεινὸς ἦν)."[8] The phrase frequently occurs in discussions of the proper method of moral admonition. While Epicurus thought the proclamation of his views on nature was a use of free speech beneficial to the human race,[9] his followers broadened παρρησία to moral exhortation in general.[10] Just as the physician uses medical

---

see his "The Semitic Background of ΠΑΡΡΗΣΙΑ in the New Testament," in *Sparsa Collecta*, 2.296–305.

[5] A. Plummer, *A Critical and Exegetical Commentary on the Second Epistle of St. Paul to the Corinthians* (ICC; New York: Charles Scribner's Sons, 1915) 215; H. Holstein, "La parrêsia dans le Nouveau Testament," *BVC* 11 (1963) 51; G. Scarpat, *Parrhesia: Storia del termine e delle sue traduzione in latino* (Brescia: Paideia, 1964) 79; V. Furnish, *II Corinthians* (AB 32A; Garden City, N. Y.: Doubleday, 1984) 231. Bultmann's assertion that παρρησία is equivalent to πεποίθησις succinctly states the misconception I am seeking to identify (*The Second Letter to the Corinthians* [Minneapolis: Augsburg, 1985] 85).

[6] G. F. C. Heinrici rejected "freedom of speech" advocated by Beza, Luther, and others (*Der zweite Brief an die Korinther* [MeyerK; 7th ed.; Göttingen: Vandenhoeck & Ruprecht, 1890] 216). He has persuaded most subsequent interpreters. See Plummer, *The Second Epistle of St. Paul to the Corinthians*, 215; Windisch, *Der zweite Korintherbrief* (MeyerK; 9th ed.; Göttingen: Vandenhoeck & Ruprecht, 1924) 223; Holstein, "La parrêsia dans le Nouveau Testament," 45–46; D. Smolders "L'audace de l'apôtre selon saint Paul: Le théme de la parrêsia," *Collectanea mechliniensia* 43 (1958) 125. Lexical evidence strongly supports the "bold speech toward" translation. See Dio Chrys. *Or.* 43.7: ἐγὼ δὲ ἔχω παρρησίαν πρὸς ὑμᾶς ὅσην οὐδείς. Note the equivalence of ἔχειν παρρησίαν and χρῆσθαι παρρησίᾳ in Plut. *De exil.* 606B–C. For further examples of παρρησία πρὸς τινά, see Eur. *El.* 1056; Dion. Hal. *Ant. Rom.* 8.74.3; Plut. *Praec. ger. reip.* 805B; Joseph. *AJ* 2.52; *Acts Jo.* 33; Lib. *Or.* 15.12.

[7] Caecilius Calactinus, frg. 139 (E. Ofenloch, *Caecilii Calactini fragmenta* [Leipzig: Teubner, 1907; repr. Stuttgart: Teubner, 1967] 122). Cf. Ps.-Lucian, *Dem. Enc.* 36. See further Pl. *Ep.* 8.354A; Isoc. *Or.* 9.39; Demades, frg. 97; Plut. *Lys.* 22.1; *Reg. et imp. ap.* 190F; *Ap. Lac.* 229C.

[8] Philostr. *VA* 5.43. Cf. Dion. Hal. *Rhet.* 9.15. For the speaker's desire to benefit the state through his use of free speech, see Dion. Hal. *Ant. Rom.* 9.32.7; 10.13.6; 11.56.5; Polyb. 2.8.9; Aristid. Rhetor, *Or.* 3.118.

[9] Epicur. *SV* 29.

[10] Phld. *Lib.* frg. 7.

instruments to treat disease, so the Epicurean leader used παρρησία to treat moral failure.[11] Likewise, Plutarch associates the use of bold words with the treatment of disease.[12] Παρρησία, like a drug employed too frequently, can be entirely used up.[13] The phrase is synonymous with νουθετεῖν, ἐπιτιμᾶν, ἐλέγχειν and other terms denoting moral reproof.[14] Using παρρησία is a matter of speaking the truth in order to treat spiritual ailments.[15]

These passages suggest that the proper way to understand Pauline παρρησία is not to focus on the apostle's consciousness but to describe the character and legitimation of his ministry as a public, rhetorical activity. To do this we must orient ourselves within the philosophic tradition which took very seriously, as Paul did, the ἐν λόγοις aspect of παρρησία.

Free Speech, Freedom, and Friendship

By the time of the Pauline epistles, the nature of free speech was a controversial matter. Was it simply the verbal expression of the sage's freedom or was it also an art to be employed for the improvement of others? As we will see, this tension between expression and art plays a major role in Paul's treatment of his own παρρησία.

The grounding of παρρησία in ἐλευθερία originates in Athens' decision to grant free speech to all of its freeborn, male citizens.[16] As a rule, aliens and slaves were not permitted to speak freely.[17] Loss of

---

[11] Phld. *Lib.* frgs. 64–65; col. VA. The phrase προσφέρειν παρρησίαν also alludes to medical practice. See Phld. *Lib.* frg. 3; Dio Chrys. *Or.* 77/78.45.

[12] Plut. *Adulator* 71D: θεραπευτικῶς χρῆσθαι τῇ παρρησίᾳ. For a full discussion of this treatise by Plutarch, see Troels Engberg-Pedersen's essay in this volume (Chapter Three).

[13] Plut. *Adulator* 73A–B.

[14] Plut. *De aud.* 47A–B; *Adulator* 66A; *Coniug. praec.* 139F; *De exil.* 606C; *Quaest. conv.* 617F; Dio Chrys. *Or.* 51.4; Philo, *Her.* 19; Julian, *Or.* 6.201A–C; *Suda* Π 636.

[15] Dio Chrys. *Or.* 33.7.

[16] For παρρησία in Athenian democracy, see E. Peterson, "Zur Bedeutungsgeschichte von Παρρησία," *Reinhold Seeberg Festberg* (ed. W. Koepp; 2 vols.; Leipzig: D. W. Scholl, 1929) 1.283–84; Schlier, "Παρρησία, παρρησιάζομαι," 871–72. Scarpat's treatment is superior, since he includes synonyms of παρρησία (*Parrhesia*, 11–45). For a rare instance of women claiming this civic right, see Plut. *Com. Lyc. et Num.* 3.5.

[17] Lucian, *Iupp. Trag.* 32. Nevertheless, cities sometimes relaxed the rule. See Dem. *Or.* 9.3; 58.68; Isoc. *Or.* 6.97–98. Greek drama provides evidence that the lack of free speech was the most serious disadvantage of slaves and aliens. See Eur. *Ion* 670–75; *Phoen.* 393; Aesch. *Supp.* 197–203; Stob. *Flor.* 3.13.2, 16, 30.

free speech was considered a grievous misfortune by the freeborn.[18] Euripides has Polyneices put deprivation of free speech at the top of the list of hardships brought about by exile, since without it one was reduced to the lot of a slave.[19] Subjection to a tyrant meant the loss of free speech; rid of him, the citizens regained παρρησία.[20]

Philosophers took the position that the basis of free speech was moral, not civic, freedom. The popular story of the sale of Diogenes portrays the sage whose competence (δύναμις, ἱκανότης) to rule himself gives him the right to rule others.[21] Similarly, Plutarch argued against Polyneices' view that the most vexing aspect of exile was the loss of free speech.[22] Plutarch asserts that baseness alone makes one speak like a slave.[23] The Cynic's self-confident use of παρρησία is an extreme development of this pattern of legitimation.[24] The wise man's absolute moral superiority to a society convulsed with vice and discord accounts for the intensity and self-confidence of Cynic free speech.[25] Although the literature sometimes mentions the cure of human ills as the Cynic's motivation, more often the utterance of bold words aimed at displaying true freedom.[26]

Epictetus and Dio Chrysostom rejected the Cynic view that self-confidence is sufficient authority for bold speech. They proposed that the divine order of the universe is the source of the wise man's free speech.[27] This point Epictetus stresses in his highly Stoicized

---

[18] Dem., frg. 21; Dion. Hal. *Ant. Rom.* 7.31.2; Lib. *Or.* 15.57.

[19] Eur. *Phoen.* 390–92. See also Dion. Hal. *Ant. Rom.* 19.18.3–4.

[20] For this theme in Herodotus, see V. Ehrenberg, "Origins of Democracy," *Historia* 1 (1950) 526–27. See also Dem. *Or.* 7.1; Dion. Hal. *Ant. Rom.* 4.42.5; 4.46.4; Diod. Sic. 32.26.2; Plut. *Dion* 34.4; *Tim.* 37.3; *An virt. doc. poss.* 240B.

[21] See K. Joël, *Der echte und der xenophontische Sokrates* (2 vols.; Berlin: R. Gaertners Verlagsbuchhandlung, 1893–1901) 2.520–22, 1053–98; G. Giannantoni, *Socraticorum reliquiae* (4 vols.; Rome: Edizioni dell'Atheneo, 1983–85) 2.439–48; 3.405–11. Beyond the Diogenes tradition, see Teles, frg. III; Philo, *Prob.* 29–31; Epict. *Diss.* 3.22.49, 72–73.

[22] Eur. *Phoen.* 390–92.

[23] Plut. *De exil.* 606D. See also Mus. Ruf., frg. IX.

[24] Although Stoics and Cynics both advocated the notion of freedom as autonomy, their views are not identical. For the greater weight in Cynicism on action and alteration of life style in comparison with the Stoic emphasis on reason, see J. Rist, *Stoic Philosophy* (Cambridge: Cambridge University Press, 1969) 62–63.

[25] For vicious society and the virtuous Cynic sage, see Ps.-Crates, *Ep.* 7; Ps.-Diog. *Ep.* 28; Ps.-Heraclit. *Ep.* 2, 7, 9; Ps.-Hippocrates, *Ep.* 17.25–56; Dio Chrys. *Or.* 33.14–15. See G. A. Gerhard, *Phoinix von Kolophon: Texte und Untersuchungen* (Leipzig: Teubner, 1909) 67–68.

[26] A. J. Malherbe, "Self-Definition among Epicureans and Cynics," in *Self-Definition in the Greco-Roman World*, vol. 3 of *Jewish and Christian Self-Definition* (3 vols.; ed. B. F. Meyer and E. P. Sanders; Philadelphia: Fortress, 1982) 54.

[27] This is not simply a reaction against the voluntarism present in the Cynic view

description of the ideal Cynic. Unlike the false Cynic, who finds itinerancy convenient and the role of moral critic a pretext for self-assertion,[28] the true Cynic does not begin his mission without God.[29] Having God as his guide, the philosopher avoids the charge of arbitrarily setting off upon the course of improving others.[30] Dio Chrysostom also placed the philosopher's bold speech in the context of a divine commission.[31] He compares his mission to that of Socrates who acted in obedience to the command of God (τὸ τοῦ θεοῦ πρόσταγμα).[32]

So far we have examined the pattern of legitimation of free speech. We turn now to the issues of motives and benefits. Free speech was the cornerstone of Athenian democracy, the goad compelling citizens to do their duty, and the most effective means of preserving the city's freedom and safety.[33] To preserve and improve the city,[34] the orator must hide nothing,[35] open his mouth,[36] and proclaim the truth.[37] Demosthenes' concluding remark in *Or.* 4 points to the value of free speech:

> For my own part, I have never yet chosen to court your favor (πρὸς χάριν εἱλόμην λέγειν) by saying anything that I was not quite convinced would be to your advantage; and to-day, keeping nothing back (ὑποστειλάμενος), I have given free utterance (πεπαρρησίασμαι) to my plain sentiments.[38]

---

of philosophic mission but reflects the fundamental Stoic teaching that the freedom of the wise man depends on subordination to divine will. See K. Deissner, "Das Sendungsbewusstsein der Urchristenheit," *ZST* 7 (1930) 781–87.

[28] Epict. *Diss.* 3.22.9–12, 50; 4.8.34. For the condemnation of the use of bold speech for self-glorification, see Phld. *Lib.* frg. 72; col. IB; Ps.-Diog. *Ep.* 4; Dio Chrys. *Or.* 32.11; Philo, *Somn.* 2.83–89; Plut. *Pomp.* 60.4; *Dion* 8.1; Lucian, *Demon.* 48; *Icar.* 30–31; *Vit. Auct.* 10; *Pisc.* 31; *Peregr.* 18; Aristid. Rhetor, *Or.* 3.668; Chrys. *Pan. Bab.* 2 37, 45–48 (*PG* 50.543, 545–46).

[29] Epict. *Diss.* 3.22.2, 8, 52.

[30] Epict. *Diss.* 3.21.11–12. See also 3.22.95–97. This is the main point of Ps.-Socrates, *Ep.* 1.7–12. See M. Imhof, "Sokrates und Archelaos: Zum 1. Sokratesbrief," *MH* 41 (1984) 1–8.

[31] Dio Chrys. *Or.* 77/78.38.

[32] Dio Chrys. *Or.* 33.9.

[33] Dem. *Or.* 13.15; 60.25–26; Plut. *Phoc.* 2.3; Dio Chrys. *Or.* 32.27. For the Roman counterpart, see Plut. *Adulator* 60C.

[34] Plut. *Dem.* 12.3; 14.3; *Adulator* 60C; Lucian, *Deor. Conc.* 2–4, 14; Stob. *Flor.* 3.13.24.

[35] For ἀποκρύπτειν, see Xen. *Ages.* 11.5; Dem. *Or.* 6.31–32; Isoc. *Or.* 8.62; 15.43–44; Dion. Hal. *Ant. Rom.* 6.72.5; 10.13.6; Lib. *Prog.* 6.2.14. For ὑποστέλλειν, see Dem. *Or.* 19.237; Isoc. *Or.* 9.39; Aeschin. *Fals. Leg.* 70; Lib. *Decl.* 15.1.39. Cf. Acts 20:20, 27. Note the numerous synonyms in Lucian, *Deor. Conc.* 2.

[36] Isoc. *Or.* 12.96.

[37] For παρρησία making ἀλήθεια manifest, see Dem. *Or.* 6.31–32; 11.17; 23.204; 37.55; 60.26; Isoc. *Ep.* 4.6. In the philosophers, see Dio Chrys. *Or.* 32.7; Eus. Mynd., frg. 21.

[38] Dem. *Or.* 4.51. See also *Or.* 10.76. For other accounts of Demosthenes' παρρησία,

Isocrates, too, was adept at portraying the benefits of his παρρησία.[39] He contrasts himself with flattering orators who speak for the pleasure but not the benefit of their hearers.[40] Distinguishing his free speech from λοιδορία on the basis of the benefit intended,[41] he hides nothing and speaks painful words for the public's well-being.[42] The speaker's claim to benefit his audience became a standard rhetorical device to make vexing words less offensive.[43]

Philosophers also emphasized the benefits of free speech uttered in friendly concern. Demonax used free speech, but his goal was always to improve others and foster friendship.[44] Demonax also exemplifies the civic responsibility which characterized free speech in Athenian democracy.[45] He claims that his bold speech is motivated by philanthropy.[46] As Dio Chrysostom put it, the sage "does not hide his thoughts (οὐκ ἀποκρυπτόμενος) from others," especially his "fellow citizens and friends and kinsmen."[47] It is the duty of the philosopher to benefit (ὠφελεῖν) others, even if this requires a painful dose of παρρησία.[48] Dio claims that his own bold words of reproof are tolerable because they are beneficial and motivated by good will (εὔνοια).[49]

Bold speech was not limited to the improvement of public morals but was also an important feature of exhortation among friends.[50]

---

see Caecilius Calactinus, frg. 141; Plut. *Dem.* 9.1–2; 12.3; Aristid. Rhetor, *Or.* 2.186–87; Lib. *Decl.* 22.1.14; *Arg. D.* 7.4; Ps.-Lucian, *Dem. Enc.* 41–42.

[39] Isoc. *Or.* 8.5, 10.

[40] Isoc. *Or.* 8.3–5.

[41] Isoc. *Or.* 8.72–73. Cf. Isoc. *Or.* 4.130–31. For other instances of this distinction, see Phld. *Lib.* frg. 60; Caecilius Calactinus, frg. 139; Plut. *Adulator* 66A; 70E; Bas., *Ep.* 203.2; 204.4; Them. *Or.* 22.277A–C; Eus. Mynd., frg. 21.

[42] Isoc. *Or.* 8.38–41. Orators in later periods also saw the apologetic value of labeling their discourse παρρησία and pointing out its benefits. See Dio Chrys. *Or.* 38.4–5, 7; Aristid. Rhetor, *Or.* 23.4–5; Lucian, *Merc. Cond.* 4; Lib. *Or.* 15.12–13; 16.3,16; 30.30; 48.1; Gr. Naz. *Or.* 17.8 (*PG* 35.976); *Or.* 18.37 (*PG* 35.1036); *Or.* 33.1 (*PG* 36.216). In epistolary contexts, see Alciphr. *Ep.* 2.39.3; Bas., *Ep.* 58; 204.2; Gr. Naz. *Ep.* 17.2–3. For παρρησία as a figure of thought, see *Rhet. Her.* 4.36.48–37.50; cf. Quintilian's objections (*Inst.* 9.2.27; 9.3.99).

[43] Dem. *Or.* 3.3; 8.32; 9.3–4; Isoc. *Or.* 5.72; 8.72–73; Anaximenes (*Rh. Al.* 18.2) treats the speaker's claim of παρρησία as an instance of anticipation (προκατάληψις).

[44] Lucian, *Demon.* 7, 10.

[45] Lucian, *Demon.* 11. Cf. Philo, *Spec.* 1.319–23.

[46] Lucian, *Demon.* 11. Cf. Epict. *Diss.* 3.22.81–82, 96. For the importance of κηδεμονία in the administration of παρρησία, see Phld. *Lib.* frg. 26; Dio Chrys. *Or.* 32.11; 51.4; 77/78.39; Plut. *Adulator* 55B; 66D.

[47] Dio Chrys. *Or.* 77/78.42; cf. *Or.* 13.15.

[48] Epict. *Diss.* 3.1.10–11.

[49] Dio Chrys. *Or.* 32.5, 7, 11. Cf. Lucian, *Hermot.* 51.

[50] Plut. *Adulator* 55B–C; Max. Tyr. *Or.* 14.6C; 19.4C; Cic. *Amic.* 13.44; 18.65;

Isocrates mentions the bold speech of friends as a traditional means of moral development.[51] According to Plutarch, παρρησία is the language of friendship,[52] and only the friend can hurt another with salutary results.[53] Rather than simply the verbal expression of freedom,[54] bold speech for Plutarch is a "fine art (φιλοτεχνεῖν), inasmuch as it is the greatest and most potent medicine in friendship, always needing, however, all care to hit the right occasion (καιροῦ), and a tempering with moderation (μέτρον)."[55] To observe the καιρός meant to adapt words to the circumstances of the hearer.[56] To find the mean (μέτρον) in bold speech meant to steer between flattery and excessive severity.[57]

Friendship was a presupposition for the administration of παρρησία in Epicurean groups. Philodemus exhorted the older members to teach the duties of friendship to recent converts. The chief duty was to speak candidly about one another's faults.[58] The leader of the cell was to be regarded as the most eminent of friends from whom no secrets should or could be kept.[59] Furthermore, new members were to be reminded repeatedly about the moral improvement which resulted from παρρησία.[60] Philodemus thought that this instruction secured a positive reception of criticism given by the leader as well as

---

24.88–90; Sen. *Ep.* 25.1; Stob. *Flor.* 3.13.44; Ael. *VH* 8.12; Gr. Naz. *Ep.* 206.1. See G. Bohnenblust, *Beiträge zum Topos* ΠΕΡΙ ΦΙΛΙΑΣ (Berlin: Gustav Schade [Otto Francke], 1905) 35–36, 38–39; Scarpat, *Parrhesia*, 58–61. Most helpful are the following treatments: M. Gigante, "Philodème: Sur la liberté de parole," *Association Guillaume Budé: Actes du VIIIe Congrès* (Paris: Société d'Édition <Les Belles Lettres>, 1969) 196–98, 202–14, and I. Hadot, *Seneca und die griechisch-römische Tradition der Seelenleitung* (Quellen und Studien zur Geschichte der Philosophie 13; Berlin: Walter de Gruyter, 1969) 63–66.

[51] Isoc. *Or.* 2.3. Cf. Plut. *Adulator* 74C; *De prof. in virt.* 82A; *De cap. ex in. ut.* 89B.

[52] Plut. *Adulator* 51C. Cf. Philo, *Her.* 21.

[53] Plut. *Adulator* 55C; 59D.

[54] Plut. *Adulator* 59E.

[55] Plut. *Adulator* 74D. See also Sen. *Ep.* 29.1–3. For the administration of παρρησία as a τέχνη, see Gigante, "Philodème: Sur la liberté de parole," 202–11; Malherbe, "'In Season and Out of Season'," 236–40.

[56] Plut. *Adulator* 66B; 68D–70B. Cf. Phld. *Lib.* frg. 7.

[57] Plut. *Adulator* 66E. For τέχνη in the Epicurean search for the mean between constant severity and indulgence, see Phld. *Lib.* frg. 20; col. IIIB.

[58] Phld. *Lib.* frgs. 11, 15, 25. This duty was derived from the example of Epicurus himself. See Phld. *Lib.* frgs. 6, 20, 49 and W. Schmid, "*Contritio* und '*ultima linea rerum*' in neuen epikureischen Texten," *RhM* 100 (1957) 303–14. For a full discussion of Philodemus' treatment of παρρησία, see the essay by Clarence E. Glad in this volume (Chapter Two).

[59] Phld. *Lib.* frg. 41.

[60] Phld. *Lib.* frgs. 26, 28, 36, 39–41, 49–50.

by fellow students.[61] Experience taught that if a new convert forgot the benefits of bold speech he would react in confusion and anger.[62] Indeed, the main source of anger was the convert's belief that he was being treated insincerely.[63] If, however, the indoctrination was successful, he would be grateful for the candor and look upon the stinging words as an expression of friendship.[64]

Free Speech in the Pauline Epistles

Having reviewed the importance of legitimation and friendship in ancient discussions of παρρησία, we are now ready to investigate the term in the Pauline epistles. Paul makes a single but significant reference to his free speech in Phlm 8–9: "Although I have much free speech in Christ (πολλὴν ἐν Χριστῷ παρρησίαν) to command to you what is fitting, rather, on account of love, I exhort." The issue of legitimation is present in the phrase "in Christ." As we will see, Paul consistently locates his bold speech in Christ or in God. This has a formal parallel in the relationship between freedom and bold speech in the philosophers and especially the demand by Dio Chrysostom and Epictetus that the philosophic missionary seek divine approval. Obviously, the "in Christ" is a different legitimation than the Stoic view of providence and may even be understood as the apostle's attempt to distinguish the basis of his speech from philosophic legitimation.

We also find here the common association of παρρησία and friendship. Paul points out that on account of love he adapts his speech to Philemon. He exhorts (παρακαλεῖν) him as a friend rather than commanding (ἐπιτάσσειν) him as an inferior. This contrast is reminiscent of the debate between the harsh Cynics, whose παρρησία was often described in terms of tyranny,[65] and the mild Cynics and other philosophers who emphasized friendship and adaptability. At the heart

---

[61] Phld. *Lib*. frg. 12.
[62] Phld. *Lib*. col. XXIA.
[63] Phld. *Lib*. col. XVIB.
[64] Phld. *Lib*. frgs. 25 and 36; cols. VIIIB, XB, and XIVB. See N. De Witt, "Organization and Procedure in Epicurean Groups," *CP* 31 (1936) 207; A. T. Guerra, "Filodemo sulla gratitudine," *CErc* 7 (1977) 105–06.
[65] Dio Chrys. *Or*. 9.11–13; Ps.-Diog. *Ep*. 46; Ps.-Heraclit. *Ep*. 4.3; 7.4; Epict. *Diss*. 2.12.24; 4.8.26–29; Lucian, *Fug*. 12, 17.

of the debate was the philosopher's freedom.[66] Since παρρησία, the verbal expression of freedom, was the Cynic's highest value,[67] the issue was whether the philosopher could accommodate his words to the needs and circumstances of his hearers and still maintain his integrity.[68] Harsh Cynics, from whose perspective accommodation smacked of flattery and ruined freedom,[69] criticized Antisthenes and his characterization of Odysseus for weakness.[70] The significance of Phlm 8–9 is to be found in the context of this debate. Paul identifies himself with the position which found no contradiction between freedom and adaptability. He avoids causing shame to Philemon, and at the same time strategically maintains his παρρησία by appealing to the tradition which viewed free speech as a fine art best employed by a caring friend.

Another passage in which free speech plays an important role is 1 Thess 2:1–12. Abraham Malherbe has argued that here Paul portrays his ministry in commonplaces concerning the philosopher's demeanor and free speech.[71] I will make a few comments which support this position. Just as in Phlm 8–9, Paul claims the right to free speech but avoids the harsh Cynic connotations by stressing that his speech is hortatory, even comforting. Indeed, as Malherbe has pointed out, the capacity for weightiness to which Paul alludes in 2:7—only immediately to reject—evokes the stereotype of the harsh Cynic's παρρησία. Similarly, Paul's denial of seeking glory contrasts with the criticism made about Cynics whose free speech aimed at enhancing their own reputations for freedom.[72]

Remarkable also is the link between παρρησία and friendship in this passage. The hardships in Philippi and the phrase ἐν πολλῷ ἀγῶνι underscore the price Paul pays for his bold speech. The sage's endurance of hardships demonstrated his love of humanity, as we see from Antisthenes to Dio Chrysostom.[73] Furthermore, Paul's nurse-like quality, his desire to impart his very self, and his labor all demonstrate that his παρρησία is an expression of friendship.

---

[66] R. Hock, "Simon the Shoemaker as an Ideal Cynic," *GRBS* 17 (1976) 48–53.
[67] See Diog. Laert. 6.69.
[68] Dio Chrysostom has no doubt that he could (*Or.* 77/78.38).
[69] Ps.-Diog. *Ep.* 29.3, 5.
[70] Dio Chrys. *Or.* 8.2; Ps.-Crates, *Ep.* 19.
[71] "'Gentle as a Nurse,'" 208–17.
[72] See above note 28.
[73] See R. Höistad, *Cynic Hero and Cynic King: Studies in the Cynic Conception of Man* (Lund: Carl Blom, 1948) 97. Cf. Dio Chrys. *Or.* 32.8, 24; 33.15. For the dangers

The issue of the legitimation of free speech is also present in 1 Thess 2:1–12. Three times he calls attention to the divine origin of his speech: ἐπαρρησιασάμεθα ἐν τῷ θεῷ ἡμῶν (2:2); ἀλλὰ καθὼς δεδοκιμάσμεθα ὑπὸ τοῦ θεοῦ πιστευθῆναι τὸ εὐαγγέλιον (2:4); and θεῷ τῷ δοκιμάζοντι τὰς καρδίας ἡμῶν (2:4). The philosopher's consciousness of divine providence distinguished his παρρησία from self-assertion. In spite of this parallel, however, the theological legitimation of speech in Paul appears to have a different purpose. The characterization of God as one who tests hearts may help explain the force of linking his speech to God's approval. If the heart can be associated with the theme of friendship, then God's approval of Paul means approval of his use of παρρησία in the context of friendship. God sanctions Paul's adaptability in speech and his practice of taking into account the circumstances of his hearers.

We turn now to an examination of παρρησία in Paul's letter to the Philippians. The emphasis on the public character of the gospel in 1:12–20 is striking.[74] Paul refers to his own free speech in 1:20 (ἐν οὐδενὶ αἰσχυνθήσομαι ἀλλ' ἐν πάσῃ παρρησίᾳ ὡς πάντοτε καὶ νῦν μεγαλυνθήσεται Χριστὸς ἐν τῷ σώματί μου) after alluding in 1:14 to the bold speaking of the majority of the brothers (τολμᾶν ἀφόβως τὸν λόγον λαλεῖν). In both cases Paul insists that his imprisonment is not a cause for shame and silence.[75] Quite the opposite. The brothers in the Lord gain their confidence (πεποιθότας, 1:14), the psychological basis of bold speech,[76] from Paul's bonds (τοῖς δεσμοῖς μου, 1:14). What appears from a societal standpoint to inhibit free speech has actually contributed to making the gospel more public (εἰς προκοπὴν τοῦ εὐαγγελίου, 1:12). This paradox of the gospel entering and shaping the public realm through the suffering and shameful position of Christ, Paul, and the church will be developed further in the first two chapters of the letter.

Paul's manner of speech is the central topic of 2 Cor 1–7. In 3:12 and 7:4 he claims that he uses much free speech. Synonyms of

---

faced by bold speakers, see Lucian, *Pisc.* 20; *Peregr.* 32. See Malherbe, "'Gentle as a Nurse'," 209.

[74] Note the other terms denoting speech in the public realm: τὸν Χριστὸν κηρύσσουσιν (1:15); ἀπολογίαν τοῦ εὐαγγελίου (1:16); τὸν Χριστὸν καταγγέλλουσιν (1:17); Χριστὸς καταγγέλεται (1:18); μεγαλυνθήσεται Χριστός (1:20). On Philippians and Paul's use of friendship language in that letter, see the essays in Part Two of this volume by John Reumann, Ken L. Berry, Abraham J. Malherbe, and John T. Fitzgerald.

[75] For the connection between shame and silence, see below note 116.

[76] See below notes 103–106.

παρρησία occur throughout 2 Cor 1–7 at crucial points in the argument. This raises the question why so much of 2 Cor 1–7 is devoted to the topic of Paul's speech. In 2 Cor 10:9–10 we learn that the severity of the so-called "letter of tears" proved to Paul's critics in Corinth that he was capable of παρρησία. Yet, when they compared his letters with his mild and conciliatory manner in the presence of the church, they detected a major flaw in his character. He was bold through letters but an ironic deceiver in person. Paul's speech, they said, was attenuated (ὁ λόγος ἐξουθενημένος), a judgement couched in rhetorical terminology.[77] Rhetoric provided for the attenuation of speech, which consisted of orators intentionally resembling "untrained and unskillful speakers."[78] Attenuation was employed chiefly to achieve irony.[79] One reason, then, παρρησία figures so prominently in 2 Cor 1–7 is that Paul must answer the charge that he lacks bold speech in face to face situations. Paul responds to this charge in two ways: 1) brief affirmations of straightforward speech and denials of flattery and 2) a sustained defense of his ministry in 2 Cor 3.

We may begin with the affirmations and denials. In 1:12 Paul describes his behavior in terms of straightforward speech: ἐν ἁπλότητι and ἐν εἰλικρινείᾳ τοῦ θεοῦ. Chrysippus claimed that the wise man is always open (ἁπλοῦς), without disguise (ἄπλαστος) and never employs irony (τὸ εἰρωνεύεσθαι).[80] From the standpoint of rhetorical theory, speaking ἁπλῶς was the opposite of concealing one's thoughts under figures (σχηματίζειν).[81] Similarly, the notion of pure (καθαρός) speech, to which Paul refers in the phrase ἐν εἰλικρινείᾳ,[82] pointed to clear

---

[77] Julius Rufianus, *De figuris sententiarum et elocutionis* 6; J. C. G. Ernesti, *Lexicon technologiae Graecorum rhetoricae* (Leipzig: Fritsch, 1795) 114.

[78] Cic. *Orat.* 20.

[79] Hor. *Sat.* 1.10.11–15; Cic. *De Or.* 3.202; *Brut.* 292; Philostr. *VA* 1.17.

[80] *SVF* 3.161.3–6. Cf. Arist. *Eth. Eud.* 3.7.6. See L. Bergson, "Eiron und Eironeia," *Hermes* 99 (1971) 416. Later philosophers agreed that the person of solid character would be straightforward and conceal nothing. See R. Vischer, *Das einfache Leben: Wort- und motivgeschichtliche Untersuchungen zu einem Wertbegriff der antiken Literatur* (Studienhefte zur Altertumswissenshaft 11; Göttingen: Vandenhoeck & Ruprecht, 1965) 10–22. For deception versus straightforwardness, see Dio Chrys. *Or.* 51.1; 52:16; Epict. *Diss.* 2.22.35; Plut. *Dion* 8.3; *Adulator* 52B; 62C; Mar. Ant. *Med.* 11.15; Clem. Al. *Str.* 7.7.44.8; Julian, *Or.* 7.214A–C.

[81] Dion. Hal. *Rhet.* 8.3, 5. For the contrast between direct speaking and speech which relies upon cleverness and deception, see Antisth., frg. 51; Dio Chrys. *Or.* 35.1. See also Phld. *Lib.* frg. 10, for which the discussion provided by M. Gigante ("Philodème: Sur la liberté de parole," 208–09) is helpful.

[82] For unambiguous speech described as εἰλικρινής see Sext. Emp. *Pyr.* 1.134; 1.140; 1.207.

174 DAVID E. FREDRICKSON

language in contrast to the artificiality and concealment of figured speech.[83] Purity is the quality of unambiguous communication of the speaker's thought.[84] Paul reiterates this quality of his speech in 4:2 when he commends himself to the world by disclosing the truth (τῇ φανερώσει τῆς ἀληθείας),[85] a phrase synonymous with παρρησία.[86]

In 2:17 Paul denies that he is like one of the many selling (καπηλεύοντες) the word of God. Although καπηλεύειν has an important place in criticism of sophistic rhetoric,[87] there is no notion of "mixing" in Plato's original use of the term,[88] as there is in 2 Cor 2:17. Plato's criticism falls primarily on the sale of teachings.[89] Further investigation reveals that κάπηλος generally designated the innkeeper,[90] whose reputation for adulterating wine was widespread enough to generate a cliché about deception.[91] In 2:17 Paul's association of his speech with purity (ἐξ εἰλικρινείας) stands in antithesis to the κάπηλος metaphor and thus falls in line with the ancient cliché.

---

[83] Dion. Hal. Dem. 5, 7, 23; Thuc. 5, 8, 23, 41. See C. Smiley, "Latinitas and ΕΛΛΗΝΙΣΜΟΣ," Bulletin of the University of Wisconsin: Philology and Literature Series 3 (1906) 219–24.
[84] See J. F. Lockwood, "The Metaphorical Vocabulary of Dionysius of Halicarnassus," CQ 31 (1937) 199.
[85] Ancient exegetes thought that τῇ φανερώσει τῆς ἀληθείας referred to deeds conforming to preaching (e.g., Chrys. Hom. 7 in 2 Cor. 1 [PG 61.454]; cf. Hom. 23 in 2 Cor. 3 [PG 61.557]). Modern interpreters stress fidelity to the Gospel (e.g., Plummer, The Second Epistle of St. Paul to the Corinthians, 112; Furnish, II Corinthians, 246). Yet Barrett judiciously notes that "truth" here "has a much wider range of meaning than the Gospel" (The Second Epistle to the Corinthians [London: A. and C. Black, 1973] 129). Support for this view can be found in Basil (Reg. fus. 9 [PG 31.944]).
[86] See above notes 35 and 37.
[87] H. D. Betz, Lukian von Samosata und das Neue Testament (TU 76; Berlin: Akademie-Verlag, 1961) 114 n. 3; S. Hafemann, Suffering and the Spirit: An Exegetical Study of II Cor. 2:14–3:3 within the Context of the Corinthian Correspondence (WUNT 2.19; Tübingen: J. C. B. Mohr [Paul Siebeck], 1986) 103–26.
[88] Hafemann (Suffering and the Spirit, 106–09) is justified in his criticism of Windisch's view ("καπηλεύω," TDNT 3 [1966] 604–05) that we can arrive at the meaning "to adulterate" on the basis of the selling of doctrines by sophists and philosophers.
[89] The κάπηλος metaphor continued to be used against rhetors and philosophers who sold their services. In addition to the parallels cited by J. J. Wettstein (Novum Testamentum Graecum [1751; 2 vols.; repr. Gras, Austria: Akademische Druck-und Verlagsanstalt, 1962] 2.183), see SVF 3.172.28; Plut. Praec. ger. reip. 819E; Lucian, Nigr. 25; Aristid. Rhetor, Or. 3.664–69; Philostr. VA 1.13.
[90] T. Kleberg, Hôtels, restaurants et cabarets dans l'antiquité romaine: Études historique et philologique (Bibliotheca Ekmaniana Universitatis Regiae Upsaliensis 61; Uppsala: Almqvist & Wiksell, 1957) 1–6.
[91] Kleberg, Hôtels, restaurants et cabarets, 3–4, 111–13. For additional references, see Ar. Thesm. 347; Plut. De Is. et Os. 369C. Paul's straightforwardness (ἁπλότης) in 1:12 is thus reiterated in 2:17, since the adjectives καπηλικός and ἁπλοῦς were antonyms. See, for example, Strab. 11.4.4.1–2; 11.8.7.18.

Moreover, the explanation in the *Suda* of how καπηλικῶς came to be equivalent to πανουργικῶς demonstrates the connection between adulteration and trickiness,[92] a theme which Paul takes up again in 4:2. Against this background, then, Paul's denial in 2:17 should be understood as a refutation of the charge that he lacked παρρησία and used the tricks of rhetoric to deceive the church.[93]

In 4:2 the term πανουργία refers to Paul's alleged use of rhetorical figures.[94] Figures are devious, since they do not present the speaker's thought simply and openly.[95] Consequently, writers critical of sophistic rhetoric contrasted πανουργία with παρρησία.[96] The principal weapon of the flatterer (κόλαξ) and wily person (πολύτροπος) is πανουργία.[97]

In 4:3 a final charge has been formulated once again in terms taken from the field of rhetoric: εἰ δὲ καὶ ἔστιν κεκαλυμμένον τὸ εὐαγγέλιον ἡμῶν. The aspect of concealment suggests that the critics accused Paul of employing covert allusion (ὁ μετασχηματισμός).[98] Although distinguished from irony, covert allusion, by veiling thoughts

---

[92] *Suda* K 334 (ed. A. Adler, *Suidae lexicon* [4 vols.; *Lexicographi Graeci* 1.1–1.4; Leipzig: Teubner, 1928–35; repr. Stuttgart: Teubner, 1967–71] 3.28): ἐπεὶ οἱ κάπηλοι ὀνθυλεύουσι τὸν οἶνον, συμμιγνύντες αὐτῷ σαπρόν. See also Phryn. *PS* (I. Bekker, *Anecdota graeca* [3 vols.; Berlin: G. C. Nauckium, 1814–21] 1.49.9–11): κάπηλον φρόνημα: παλίμβολον καὶ οὐκ ὑγιές. ἡ μεταφορὰ ἀπὸ τῶν καπήλων μὴ πιπρασκόντων εἰλικρινῆ καὶ ἀκέραια τὰ ὤνια.

[93] For the contrast between παρρησία and adulterated speech which seeks to flatter and be pleasant, see Isoc. *Or.* 2.1–3; Lucian, *Hermot.* 51; Bas., *Reg. fus.* 25.2 (*PG* 31.985). Paul's denial in 4:2 of adulterating the word of God (μηδὲ δολοῦντες τὸν λόγον τοῦ θεοῦ) is a continuation of the same theme. See Windisch, "καπηλεύω," 604–05. A connection between καπηλεύειν and δολοῦν was recognized in ancient lexicography; see *Suda* K 337.

[94] P. Marshall (*Enmity in Corinth: Social Conventions in Paul's Relations with the Corinthians* [WUNT 2.23; Tübingen: J. C. B. Mohr (Paul Siebeck), 1987] 384) also maintains that Paul's denial of using πανουργία should be understood against the background of philosophic criticism of rhetoric. He suggests, however, that Paul attacks his opponents' tricks.

[95] Dion. Hal. *Lys.* 15; Plut. *Quomodo adol.* 27F–28A; "Longinus," *Subl.* 17.1–2.

[96] Plut. *Quaest. conv.* 715F–716B; *Praec. ger. reip.* 802F; Dio Chrys. *Or.* 1.26.

[97] κόλαξ: Lucian, *Pisc.* 18; *Dial. Mort.* 15.1–2; Plut. *Adulator* 51C; 60B; *De cap. ex in. ut.* 92D. πολύτροπος: Pl. *Hp. Mi.* 365E; Plut. *Quaest. nat.* 916C; Dio Chrys. *Or.* 1.61; cf. Plut., frg. 25.

[98] For the rhetorical figure σχηματίζειν, see Ernesti, *Lexicon*, 341–43. For veiled speech as a means of moral criticism, see F. Ahl, "The Art of Safe Criticism in Greece and Rome," *AJP* 105 (1984) 174–208. For Paul's familiarity with covert allusion, see B. Fiore, "'Covert Allusion' in 1 Corinthians 1–4," *CBQ* 47 (1985) 85–102, and John T. Fitzgerald, *Cracks in an Earthen Vessel: An Examination of the Catalogues of Hardships in the Corinthian Correspondence* (SBLDS 99; Atlanta: Scholars Press, 1988) 119–22.

under other meanings, closely resembled it.⁹⁹ Technical discussion of covert allusion in terms of hiding (κρύπτειν) one's thoughts goes back at least to Dionysius of Halicarnassus.¹⁰⁰ Hiding thoughts in figures was the opposite of παρρησία.¹⁰¹ A number of motives were given for veiled speech, including the desire not to cause offense when giving criticism with παρρησία.¹⁰²

Paul turns to the sustained defense of his ministry in 2:14–4:6. In 3:4 we discover that Paul's possession of confidence is the matter to be proved. The term πεποίθησις has the sense of confidence or boldness¹⁰³ and is synonymous with τόλμα¹⁰⁴ and θάρσος.¹⁰⁵ It is the condition of mind which serves as the basis of παρρησία.¹⁰⁶

In 3:5 Paul distinguishes his confidence from the legitimation granted by moral virtue in the philosophic tradition: οὐχ ὅτι ἀφ' ἑαυτῶν ἱκανοί ἐσμεν λογίσασθαί τι ὡς ἐξ ἑαυτῶν, ἀλλ' ἡ ἱκανότης ἡμῶν ἐκ τοῦ θεοῦ. The first half of this verse denies that his πεποίθησις rests on his own competence.¹⁰⁷ The second half of the verse argues that Paul does indeed have the competence, but this comes from God. By placing his boldness in the context of a divine source, Paul reflects the treatment of παρρησία in Epictetus and Dio Chrysostom, who established their philosophic mission upon the divine and thus distinguished

⁹⁹ Quint. *Inst.* 9.2.45–46, 65–66; Demetr. *Eloc.* 291.
¹⁰⁰ Dion. Hal. *Rhet.* 8.3, 8. Cf. Quint. *Inst.* 9.2.76. See also *Inst.* 9.2.65; Dio Cass. 37.58.1; Plut. *Adulator* 51D; *De prof. in virt.* 85C; Ps.-Lucian, *Am.* 3; Philostr. *VS* 542; Them. *Or.* 3.45D; Lib. *Or.* 18.19.
¹⁰¹ See Ahl, "The Art of Safe Criticism," 174–75. See also Dion. Hal. *Rhet.* 8.3; Caecilius Calactinus, frg. 157; Hermog. *Inv.* 13; Them. *Or.* 3.45D. Demetrius contrasts covert allusion with straight speaking (οὐκ ἐξ εὐθείας ἐροῦμεν) and Scythian speech (ἀπὸ Σκυθῶν), proverbial for παρρησία (*Eloc.* 292, 297).
¹⁰² For the motives ascribed to the use of figures, see D. M. Schenkeveld, *Studies on Demetrius on Style* (Amsterdam: Hakkert, 1964) 117–22; Fiore, "'Covert Allusion'," 91–93; Ahl, "The Art of Safe Criticism," 185–96, and Fitzgerald, *Cracks in an Earthen Vessel*, 120.
¹⁰³ Joseph. *AJ* 10.16.
¹⁰⁴ Joseph. *AJ* 1.73.
¹⁰⁵ Joseph. *AJ* 3.44–45.
¹⁰⁶ Phld. *Lib.* frg. 45; Joseph. *AJ* 19.317–18; *1 Clem.* 35.2; Eph 3:12. Synonyms also refer to the psychological basis of bold speech: Pl. *Leg.* 835C; Diod. Sic. 14.65.4; Dion. Hal. *Ant. Rom.* 9.32.7; Epict. *Diss.* 3.22.96; Philo, *Her.* 5–7, 19–21, 27–29; *Somn.* 2.83; *Ios.* 222; *Prob.* 150; Plut. *Adulator* 66A; Joseph. *AJ* 2.116; Mus. Ruf., frg. IX; Dio Chrys. *Or.* 3.13; 4.15; 11.27; 32.11; Lucian, *Demon.* 50; *Iupp. Trag.* 19; Aristid. Rhetor, *Or.* 28.147.
¹⁰⁷ Cf. Gal 6:3, for which Betz's citations of philosophic material are pertinent for 2 Cor 3:5 (*Galatians* [Hermeneia; Philadelphia: Fortress, 1979] 301). For ἱκανότης as a moral virtue, see *SVF* 3.68.3–4.

themselves from the insistence of the Cynics to make everything depend upon themselves.

I turn now to describe the way 3:7–18 supports Paul's claim of confidence in 3:4.[108] Proofs based on comparison (σύγκρισις) play an important role in forensic speeches,[109] demonstrating inferiority, equality, or superiority.[110] 3:7–12 is a σύγκρισις which demonstrates the superiority of the ministry of the Spirit, also called the ministry of righteousness, to the ministry of the letter. Whereas the ministry of the old covenant leads to death and condemnation, the ministry of the Spirit brings about righteousness. From this comparison, in 3:12 Paul draws the conclusion that based upon the expectation (ἔχοντες οὖν τοιαύτην ἐλπίδα) of the effects of the ministry of the Spirit in which he participates, he uses much free speech. Structurally, this argument is reminiscent of the connection between παρρησία and its benefits described above in the rhetorical and philosophical traditions. Confident use of free speech rested in knowledge of one's good intentions and the likelihood benefits would be bestowed on the hearers.

The second proof of Paul's confidence (3:13–18) consists of two examples, one negative (3:13–15) and the other positive (3:16–18). Apologies customarily employed both positive and negative examples as proofs.[111] The phrase οὐ καθάπερ regularly signals the beginning of a negative example.[112] The negative example using οὐ καθάπερ in a comparison is common.[113] In 3:13, the negative example contrasts Moses and Paul.[114] Moses' inability to stand up to the scrutiny of his

---

[108] If it is the case that 3:7–12 and 3:13–18 function as proofs supporting the same proposition (3:4), then Windisch's interpretation of 3:7–18 as a midrash treating the superiority of Christianity to Judaism is misguided (*Der zweite Korintherbrief*, 112).

[109] Cic. *Inv. Rhet.* 1.30.49; *Top.* 3.11; 4.23; 10.43; Quint. *Inst.* 5.10.86–94; *Rhet. Her.* 2.19.29; Theon, *Prog.* 1. See J. Martin, *Antike Rhetorik: Technik und Methode* (Handbuch der Altertumswissenschaft 2.3; Munich: Beck, 1974) 119–22.

[110] F. Focke, "Synkrisis," *Hermes* 58 (1923) 336–39; 347 n. 1; see also C. Forbes, "Comparison, Self-Praise and Irony: Paul's Boasting and the Conventions of Hellenistic Rhetoric," *NTS* 32 (1986) 2–8. See Cic. *Top.* 3.11; 4.23; Hermog. *Prog.* 8.

[111] Arist. *Rh.* 1.2.8–11; 2.20.1–2, 9; *Rhet. Her.* 4.45.59; 4.49.62.

[112] Dion. Hal. *Ant. Rom.* 4.40.1; Plut. *Alex.* 23.2; Dio Chrys. *Or.* 31.4; Lucian, *Rh. Pr.* 26; 1 Thess 4:13; John 6:58; 1 John 3:12.

[113] Plut. *Com. Thes. et Rom.* 4.1–2; *Com. Lys. et Sull.* 4.4; *Com. Dion et Brut.* 1.2.

[114] *Rhet. Her.* 4.46.59: "For a Comparison (*similitudo*) in the form of contrast is used when we deny that something else is like the thing we are asserting to be true." See also Anaximenes, *Rh. Al.* 8; Cic. *Top.* 11.47–49; Quint. *Inst.* 5.11.5–16, 30–31; Aps. *Rhet.* 8. See B. Fiore, *The Function of Personal Example in the Socratic and Pastoral Epistles* (AnBib 105; Rome: Biblical Institute Press, 1986) 26–32.

onlookers contrasts sharply with Paul's openness before the church, the world, and God in 1:12–13, 2:17b, and 4:1–2. This contrast suggests that Moses hides himself from a sense of shame,[115] since in ancient philosophy there was a frequent connection between shame and concealment.[116] Bad conscience requires hiding.[117] The veil indicates Moses' shame, a result of the old covenant (τὸ τέλος τοῦ καταργουμένου) whose ministry condemns even the one who is its minister.[118]

The second example (3:16–18) is positive. Moses' unveiled face signifies an end to his shame, and he comes to exemplify freedom (ἐλευθερία). The connection between unveiled face and freedom is made intelligible by the commonplace that freedom was dependent upon a good conscience.[119] The relevance of this proof for Paul's apology rests in the common association between παρρησία and ἐλευθερία. Bold speech finds its legitimate basis in the freedom granted by a good conscience.[120] Paul's likeness to Moses insofar as the latter

---

[115] Origen (*Hom. 5 in Jer.* 8–9 [*PG* 13.305–08]) recognized the connection between veil and shame in 3:13. Although van Unnik ("With Unveiled Face," 202) notes the association, he does not adequately explore the philosophic tradition. He gives extensive evidence of the connection in Jewish tradition in his "The Semitic Background of ΠΑΡΡΗΣΙΑ," 294–304.

[116] Xen. *Ages.* 9.1; Pl. *Phdr.* 243B; *SVF* 3.101.36–37; Philo, *Mut.* 198–99; Epict. *Diss.* 3.22.15–16; Plut. *Com. Lyc. et Num.* 3.2; *De prof. in virt.* 82B; *De sera* 565B; *Vit. X orat.* 845F; Ps.-Hippocrates, *Ep.* 17.48–50; Lucian, *Merc. Cond.* 2; *Pseudol.* 21; *Dial. Mort.* 20.11; Diog. Laert. 7.3; Mar. Ant. *Med.* 3.8; Petron. *Sat.* 7. Philo's polemic against Greek mystery rites (*Spec.* 1.321) offers a particularly instructive parallel to 2 Cor 3:7–18: "Let those who work mischief feel shame (αἰσχυνέσθωσαν) and seek holes and corners of the earth and profound darkness, there lie hid (ἐπικρυπτέσθωσαν) and keep the multitude of their iniquities veiled (ἐπισκιάζοντες) out of the sight of all. But let those whose actions serve the common weal use freedom of speech (παρρησία) and walk in daylight through the midst of the marketplace, ready to converse with crowded gatherings, to let the clear sunlight shine upon their own life." Here παρρησία is based upon the freedom of a good conscience and the benefits bestowed. Cf. Isoc. *Or.* 15.43–44.

[117] Isoc. *Or.* 1.16; Philo, *Ios.* 68; *Spec.* 3.54; 4.6; Plut., *De prof. in virt.* 85C; Lib. *Or.* 15.82–83; Sen. *Ep.* 43.3–5; 97.12–13; 105.7–8.

[118] Against some exegetes who view τὸ τέλος as cessation of glory (e.g., Plummer, *The Second Epistle of St. Paul to the Corinthians*, 97; Windisch, *Der zweite Korintherbrief*, 120; Furnish, *II Corinthians*, 207). Cf. Rom 6:21–22. I understand τοῦ καταργουμένου as a reference to the old covenant. In support I point to 3:11 where τὸ καταργούμενον and τὸ μένον refer to the two covenants. On this point, see Barrett, *The Second Epistle to the Corinthians*, 119.

[119] A saying attributed to Periander (Stob. *Flor.* 3.24.12) aptly puts the relationship: Περίανδρος ἐρωτηθεὶς τί ἐστιν ἐλευθερία, εἶπεν 'ἀγαθὴ συνείδησις'.

[120] Especially important are Epict. *Diss.* 3.22.18–19, 93–95; Dio Chrys. *Or.* 32.11; Philo, *Ebr.* 148–52; *Her.* 6–7; *Ios.* 67–68; *Spec.* 1.203; *Prob.* 99, 149–55. See J. F. Kindstrand, *Bion of Borysthenes* (Stockholm: Almqvist & Wiksell, 1976) 261–63.

experiences the removal of the veil is an example of the πεποίθησις before God which Paul claims for himself in 3:4.

After Paul's defense of his ministry in 2:17–4:6, there is decreasing emphasis on legitimation and greater attention given to friendship and reconciliation. Why is this so? We must return to the "letter of tears." In addition to proving to his critics that he was capable of bold speech, this letter had the effect of causing grief to its readers. This is implied in 2:4 and stated explicitly in 7:8. In order to heal this pain, Paul places his παρρησία in the Greco-Roman tradition of soul-care,[121] which emphasized friendship in the application of free speech. Paul's task in chapters 4–7 is to weave together παρρησία with φιλία in order to reconcile the church to himself.

Paul twice alludes to his bold speech in 6:6: ἐν ἀγάπη ἀνυποκρίτῳ[122] and ἐν λόγῳ ἀληθείας. Feigned friendship was routinely criticized,[123] particularly by those authors who praised the value of candid speech in friendship.[124] Often equated with flattery, feigned friendship was the opposite of παρρησία.[125] Feigned friendship is inappropriate in political leadership and moral exhortation where free speech must be balanced by kindness and good will but not hypocrisy.[126] Paul again refers to the place of bold speech in his ministry with the phrase ἐν λόγῳ ἀληθείας. That παρρησία is a matter of speaking the truth is a philosophic commonplace.[127] Reformation of the human condition requires truth and bold speech.[128]

Considering the frequent association of παρρησία and λύπη in the philosophic writings, it is not surprising that Paul surrounds his bold speech with claims concerning his purity (ἐν ἁγνότητι), self-knowledge

---

[121] For ancient psychagogy, in addition to the work of Hadot cited above in n. 50, see P. Rabbow, *Seelenführung: Methodik der Exerzitien in der Antike* (Munich: Kösel, 1954); B. L. Hijmans, *ΑΣΚΗΣΙΣ: Notes on Epictetus' Educational System* (Assen: Van Gorcum, 1959) 41–102; H. G. Ingenkamp, *Plutarchs Schriften über die Heilung der Seele* (Hypomnemata 34; Göttingen: Vandenhoeck & Ruprecht, 1971).

[122] This phrase appears also in Rom 12:9, where the topic is the proper method of moral exhortation. See also Jas 3:17 and 1 Pet 1:22.

[123] Joseph. *AJ* 16.211; *BJ* 1.318, 516; 2.587; Plut., frg. 48; Them. *Or.* 22.267B; 280A–282C; Olymp. *in Grg.* 36.2; Eus. Mynd., frg. 22.

[124] Cic. *Amic.* 18.65; 25.92.

[125] Ps.-Plut. *De lib. ed.* 13B; Philo, *Conf.* 48; *Prob.* 99; Cic. *Amic.* 25.92–94. See Bohnenblust, *Beiträge*, 16–21.

[126] Philo, *Ios.* 67.

[127] See Dem. *Or.* 6.31; 60.26; Isoc. *Or.* 15.43; Joseph. *AJ* 16.108; Lucian, *Cont.* 13; *Pisc.* 17; *Merc. Cond.* 4; *Pseudol.* 4; *Dial. Mort.* 21.4; Lib. *Or.* 30.30.

[128] Phld. *Lib.* col. XVB; Lucian, *Tim.* 36; *Vit. Auct.* 8.

(ἐν γνώσει),[129] patience (ἐν μακροθυμίᾳ),[130] kindness (ἐν χρηστότητι),[131] and the power of God (ἐν δύναμει θεοῦ).[132] With his emphasis on patience and kindness, Paul places his παρρησία in the Greco-Roman tradition of soul-care, according to which the combination of bold speech and gentleness does not reflect inconsistency, as his critics might assume, but is the practice both of caring teachers and of friends.

In 6:11 Paul refers to his friendly use of bold speech toward the church with the phrase "our mouth has remained open toward you (τὸ στόμα ἡμῶν ἀνέῳγεν πρὸς ὑμᾶς)."[133] Some ancient and modern exegetes correctly note the connection between an open mouth and παρρησία.[134] Two synonyms of παρρησία help explain this connection: ἐλευθεροστομεῖν and θρασυστομεῖν.[135] Friendship is implied in the notion of an expanded, joyful heart (ἡ καρδία ἡμῶν πεπλάτυνται).[136] The church is not restricted in his heart (οὐ στενοχωρεῖσθε ἐν ἡμῖν), even as he, as a friend, uses bold speech in moral admonition.[137]

---

[129] In Gal 6:1 Paul associates self-knowledge (σκοπῶν σεαυτόν) with gentleness in moral admonition.

[130] Patience was associated with the gentle treatment of sinners. See Ign. Pol. 6.2; 1 Clem. 13.1–4; 19.3; 49.5, 62.2; Bas. Ep. 22.1; 72. See Malherbe, "'Gentle as a Nurse'," 210–14.

[131] For χρηστότης as kindness, see C. Spicq, "Benignité, mansuetudé, douceur, clémence," RB 54 (1947) 321–24. For χρηστότης as doing good to others, see SVF 3.64.24, 41; 3.67.8; 3.71.31–37; Mus. Ruf., frg. XIV. According to the psychagogical tradition, frank moral admonition should aim to benefit rather than condemn. See Dio Chrys. Or. 32.5, 11, 24; 51.4–5; Plut. De aud. 46F–47A; Adulator 71D; 1 Clem. 56.2; Mar. Ant. Med. 11.13; Julian, Or. 7.213C; Them. Or. 22.277A–C; Bas. Reg. br. 113 (PG 31.1157).

[132] See above for discussion of the role of the divine.

[133] For the equivalence to παρρησιάζεθαι, see Isoc. Or. 12.96; Or. Enarr. in Job 3.1 (PG 17.68–69); Lib. Decl. 38.1.42; 47.1.30; Chrys. Incomprehens. 5.6 (PG 48.744); Bas. Ep. 29.

[134] Chrys. Hom. 13 in 2 Cor. 1 (PG 61.491); Barrett, The Second Epistle to the Corinthians, 191; Furnish, II Corinthians, 360, 368. Yet all understand the open mouth to be the personal warmth which they perceive in this section of 2 Cor. This sentimentalizes παρρησία and ignores its sense of pointed criticism.

[135] ἐλευθεροστομεῖν: Aesch. PV 180; Soph. Aj. 1258; Eur. Andr. 153; Dion. Hal. Ant. Rom. 6.72.5; Philo, Migr. 116; Her. 7; Prob. 99–100, 148–49; see also O. Hense, "Bion bei Philon," RhM 48 (1892) 231. θρασυστομεῖν: Aesch. Supp. 203; Th. 612; Ag. 1399; Soph. Phil. 380; Eur. Hec. 1286; Ion 672–75; Lib. Ep. 81.1. See also Joseph and Aseneth 12.6; Eph 6:19–20; Acts 8:32, 35; 10:24; 18:14; Acts Jo. 32–33. Influence of the LXX should not be ruled out. See the parallels adduced by Wettstein (Novum Testamentum Graecum, 2.193) and Windisch (Der zweite Korintherbrief, 210).

[136] So Chrysostom, Hom. 13 in 2 Cor. 1 (PG 61.491).

[137] The shrinking and expanding heart is a topos in Stoic psychology for grief and joy: SVF 1.51.19–25; 3.97.36–40; 3.98.30–32; 3.116.5–8; 3.119.30–31; Plut. De lib. et aegr. 1; Cic. Tusc. 4.31.66–67; Sen. Constant. 9.3. Plutarch's account of the pleasure

The topic of bold speech is indicated in 7:2–4 by the phrase πολλή μοι παρρησία πρὸς ὑμᾶς. Paul immediately refers to the salutary effect of his bold speech: πολλή μοι καύχησις ὑπὲρ ὑμῶν. Since Paul's pride and joy rest on the church's repentance (7:7, 9, 12, 15–16),[138] 7:4 suggests to the readers that his bold speech is justified on the basis of its good effect.

The theme of bold speech is developed antithetically in 7:2–4 in order to emphasize Paul's friendly motives and provide reasons why the church should make room for him in its heart. First, in a series of denials in 7:2, Paul dissociates himself from the stereotype of the self-aggrandizing enemy of social harmony and friendly relations: οὐδένα ἠδικήσαμεν, οὐδένα ἐφθείραμεν, οὐδένα ἐπλεονεκτήσαμεν.[139] In 7:3a, he denies that his speech aims to condemn his readers: πρὸς κατάκρισιν οὐ λέγω.[140] The uses of παρρησία for moral edification, on the one hand, and condemnation, on the other, were well known.[141] Harsh Cynics especially were noted for their unbridled use of free speech to condemn the ills of humankind.[142] They understood bold speech as punishment of human error.[143] In 7:3b he reminds the

---

friendly souls experience with one another may be compared with the Pauline imagery (De sera 564B–C).

[138] For the teacher's pride in the student's moral growth, see Sen. Ep. 10.3; 20.1; 34.1–2; Ps.-Diog. Ep. 9. Cf. 1 Thess 2:19. The expression of joy over the recipient's moral progress is a convention of the paraenetic letter. See Sen. Ep. 5.1; 19.1; 20.1; 34.1; 35.2–4; 59.1–4.

[139] His denials are reminiscent of the popular characterization of the harsh Cynic philosopher, who not only reviled his hearers but demanded money as well. See Epict. Diss. 3.22.10, 50; Dio Chrys. Or. 32.11; Lucian, Fug. 7, 13–20; Vit. Auct. 10–11; Aristid. Rhetor, Or. 3.666–671. A similar combination of denials prefaces Samuel's use of παρρησία in Joseph. AJ 6.86–88. See also Philo, Spec. 1.202–204; Acts 20:33–34; Gal 5:15. Note esp. Ps.-Heraclit. Ep. 7.3. The denials of 2 Cor 7:2 are similar to those in Paul's presentation of his παρρησία in 1 Thess 2:5–7. It is not the case that Paul here denies charges that have been made against him as claimed by Barrett (The Second Epistle to the Corinthians, 203) and Furnish (II Corinthians, 369).

[140] Paul reiterates the theme of punishment in 7:9: ἵνα ἐν μηδενὶ ζημιωθῆτε ἐξ ἡμῶν. Following Windisch (Der zweite Korintherbrief, 221–222), commentators regard 7:3a as Paul's attempt to mitigate the severity of the previous denials (7:2), which they misinterpret as his accusations against the church (e.g., Barrett, The Second Epistle to the Corinthians, 203; Furnish, II Corinthians, 369).

[141] Stob. Flor. 3.13.63; Isoc. Or. 4.130; 8.72; Phld. Lib. frgs. 37–38; col. IB; Lucian, Pseudol. 3; Deor. Conc. 2; Icar. 30; Ps.-Diog. Ep. 29.2–3; Mar. Ant. Med. 11.6.2. See Gerhard, Phoenix, 36.

[142] See above notes 25–26, 65. Democritus' laughter condemns (κατακρίνει) humanity for its inconsistency (Ps.-Hippocrates, Ep. 17.40). Cf. Ps.-Heraclit. Ep. 7.2; 9.8. See also Gnomol. Vat. 116, 487.

[143] For παρρησία as a whip (σκῦτος, μάστιξ), see Ps.-Diog. Ep. 29.1, 4; Ps.-Soc. Ep. 12; Plut. Vit. X orat. 842D. Cf. λοιδορία as a whip: Diog. Laert. 5.18; Philostr.

church of the friendship in which the bold words were written. Two *topoi* on friendship are present in this verse. The first (ἐν ταῖς καρδίαις ἡμῶν ἐστε) expresses Paul's mindfulness of the church.[144] The second (εἰς τὸ συναποθανεῖν καὶ συζῆν) indicates the depth of the friendship.[145]

Finally, in 7:8–12 Paul reviews for his readers the salutary effects of the rebuke conveyed in the letter of tears. These verses fully reflect the philosophic discussion of the use of free speech in friendship for the purpose of moral reformation. The progression in 7:9–10 from the grief the letter of tears caused (ἐλυπήθητε) to repentance (ἐλυπήθητε εἰς μετάνοιαν) and then to salvation (μετάνοιαν εἰς σωτηρίαν) places Paul's characterization of his treatment of the church in the letter of tears squarely in the psychagogical tradition.[146]

Conclusion

We may safely conclude from this study that Paul, his audiences, and his critics were well aware of the philosophic understandings of παρρησία. Paul's self-presentation as a bold speaker echoes the philosophic tradition's interest in the problem of legitimation and friendship. This is not to say, however, that Paul simply repeated traditional formulas. In fact, Paul's proximity to the philosophic tradition allows us to reflect on the sharp contrast with his intellectual environment and to gain insight into the theological character of his public ministry. This theology of public ministry, powerfully defended in 2 Cor 1–7, was in part Paul's response to his critics in Corinth, themselves most likely in sympathy with the harsh Cynic views on free speech, and who were no doubt irked by what they perceived to be Paul's inconsistency, lack of confidence, and adulteration of the word of God.

VS 487. The notion of the philosopher's rebuke of sin as the guilty verdict in a legal proceeding is found in Cynic self-description. See Ps.-Diog. *Ep.* 28.5. For the Cynic's task of punishing (κολάζειν) sinful humanity, see Ps.-Diog. *Ep.* 29.4; Ps.-Heraclit. *Ep.* 7.4; 9.3; Epict. *Diss.* 3.22.94, 97–98; Dio Chrys. *Or.* 9.8.

[144] The notion that friends are two bodies with one soul stands behind this formulation. See Bohnenblust, *Beiträge*, 39–40.

[145] For the *topos* that a friend is willing to die for a friend, see the texts cited at Furnish, *II Corinthians*, 367. For further examples, see Arist. *Eth. Nic.* 9.8.9; Diog. Laert. 10.120; Cic. *Amic.* 7.24; Sen. *Ep.* 9.10; Lucian, *Tox.* 6, 36–37. Cf. Rom 5:7; 2 Cor 5:14–15; Phil 2:30.

[146] See above for discussion of the role of frank criticism in psychagogy.

In opposition to the philosophic tradition, in which the issues of legitimation and friendship were conceptualized either separately or opposed to one another, Paul consistently and conspicuously brings them together. The Paul who uses much free speech (2 Cor 3:12 and 7:4) is the same Paul who places that speech in the context of extreme expressions of friendship (7:2–7). We have seen this union of freedom of speech and friendship in Phlm 8–9, 1 Thess 2:1–12, and especially in 2 Cor 3 where the Spirit both frees Paul from shame (cf. Phil 1:12–20) and empowers him to participate in the ministry of righteousness. Paul is simultaneously free to speak his mind and bound to speak for his hearers' good. This paradox lies at the heart of παρρησία in the Pauline epistles.

ΠΑΡΡΗΣΙΑ IN ACTS[1]

S. C. WINTER

"'Freedom of speech'," writes W. C. van Unnik, "has a prominent place in Acts. Everyone perusing its pages will see that the noun and the verb often recur in all parts of the book, so that it may be styled one of the 'keywords'."[2] This "prominent place" is just as much a function of where in the narrative παρρησία occurs as it is a function of the number of occurrences. Both the noun παρρησία and the verb παρρησιάζεσθαι are found, the noun in narratives taking place in Jerusalem and Rome, the verb in the intervening accounts of travel.[3] The noun παρρησία occurs four times in the account of Pentecost and its aftermath, first at Pentecost (2:29), second in connection with Peter and John's defense in Jerusalem (4:13), and twice immediately thereafter (4:29, 31). After this cluster of occurrences the noun does not occur again until the very end of the book in 28:31 (κηρύσσων τὴν βασιλείαν τοῦ θεοῦ καὶ διδάσκων τὰ περὶ τοῦ κυρίου Ἰησοῦ Χριστοῦ μετὰ πάσης παρρησίας ἀκωλύτως). The verb occurs seven times in Acts 9–26. All occurrences but the last are doublets. The verb is found twice in connection with Saul's conversion (9:27 and 9:28), twice in the account of Paul's first missionary journey (13:46 and 14:3), twice in Ephesus (18:26 and 19:8) and once in the account of Paul's interview before Agrippa (26:26).[4]

The word παρρησία has an extensive tradition in Greek philosophy. In the classical period "freedom of speech" meant the right of the male citizen to express himself in the assembly (ἐκκλησία) of the

[1] I am most grateful to Richard I. Pervo, Robin Scroggs, Michael White, John T. Fitzgerald (the editor of this volume), and my colleagues in the Hellenistic Moral Philosophy and Early Christianity Group for invaluable discussion and constructive critique of an earlier version of this paper.

[2] W. C. van Unnik, "The Christian's Freedom of Speech in the New Testament," *Sparsa Collecta: The Collected Essays of W. C. Van Unnik* (3 vols.; NovTSup 29–31; Leiden: Brill, 1973–83) 2.279.

[3] In general observations, παρρησία will stand for "παρρησία or παρρησιάζεσθαι." I translate these terms as "frank speech" and "speaking frankly," and, alternatively, as "bold speech" and "speaking boldly."

[4] There are four variant readings, not well attested, which may be ignored: 6:10; 9:20; 14:19; 16:4 (van Unnik, "The Christian's Freedom of Speech," 283).

πόλις. When παρρησία is employed in its classical sense, H. Schlier observes, three aspects of the term may be emphasized: (i) παρρησία is close to ἐξουσία when the *right* to speak is emphasized; (ii) παρρησία is associated with ἀλήθεια when accuracy of speech is emphasized (or claimed); and (iii) the boldness of παρρησία may be emphasized if obstacles to speech are at issue.[5]

In the Roman and Hellenistic period "frank speech" acquired the meaning of speech by the friend, who, unlike the flatterer, does not seek to please but to be honest.[6] In this period παρρησία is most often associated with the moral freedom (ἐλευθερία) to speak truth (ἀλήθεια). In this context παρρησία is a quality or virtue of an individual, not a right possessed by a group. The individual may be required to exercise παρρησία in the face of intimidation because the moral philosopher is obligated to speak the truth to a ruler.[7]

Van Unnik finds in Acts a connection between παρρησία and proclaiming Jesus to Jews in the presence of opposition and threats.[8] He writes that παρρησία in Acts "is closely connected with the proclamation of the gospel; it denotes the freedom with which it is proclaimed by him who himself is there [in Rome] on trial. It is, however, not the profession in the law-court, but the missionary activity that is carried out with all clearness and without outward hindrance."[9] Here van Unnik describes the usage of παρρησία in Acts to be that of public discourse and thus consistent with the classical meaning of the word. But van Unnik's observations require refinement in three regards. First, not all the references to παρρησία in Acts entail opposition. Apollos speaks in Ephesus without opposition (18:26) and Acts concludes with the statement that παρρησία in Rome is unhindered

---

[5] Heinrich Schlier, "παρρησία, κτλ.," *TDNT* 5.871–86, esp. 871–72.

[6] This usage is analyzed most thoroughly in the papers in Part One of this volume.

[7] David Konstan, "Friendship, Frankness and Flattery" (paper presented to the Hellenistic Moral Philosophy and Early Christianity Group at the annual meeting of the Society of Biblical Literature, San Francisco, CA, November, 1992) 18. A revised version of this paper appears as Chapter One of this volume. See also Chapter Two, where Troels Engberg-Pedersen discusses Plutarch's treatment of this point in his treatise *How To Tell a Flatterer from a Friend.*

[8] "In Acts it is typical that this παρρησία is always mentioned in connection with preaching in the synagogues and to the Jews" ("The Christian's Freedom of Speech," 280). "It is not so much the opposition which provokes the 'freedom of speech' on the side of the Christians," van Unnik contines, "but their παρρησία which provokes opposition and danger" (*ibid.*, 282).

[9] Ibid., 279.

(28:31). Second, the last two occurrences of παρρησία do not describe proclamation to Jews. In 26:26 Paul speaks to Agrippa, whose religious affiliation in the narrative is at least ambiguous.[10] In Acts 28:31, moreover, Paul is in Rome speaking to "all" who come to him. Third, in Acts bold speech is not exclusively public speech. The last two occurrences of παρρησία include a dimension of interpersonal interaction. Indeed, in 26:26 the interpersonal element overshadows the sense of public proclamation.

In this essay I analyze each of the twelve occurrences of παρρησία and παρρησιάζεσθαι in narrative sequence. The significance of παρρησία in Acts is expressed both in features that are common to all or most occurrences and in features unique to each occurrence or group of occurrences. Although my study is historical-critical, I explore each narrative segment that contains a reference to παρρησία from a literary critical perspective. Analysis of παρρησία in Acts requires a mixed method, so to speak, because the use of παρρησία in Acts is complex. The exceptions to van Unnik's characterization of παρρησία in Acts occur towards the end; παρρησία is a critical term for the author of Acts, the connotations of which, presented through literary critical allusions in the narrative, shift over the course of the narrative, corresponding to changes in the community of believers depicted. The end of the book gives—with Paul's interviews with Jewish leaders in Rome—a picture very different from that of Peter's encounters with Jerusalem authorities and the first believers. The two pictures differ because the author changes the literary allusions and allusive language with which the narrative is constructed. To bring out these differences I pay particular attention to the literary critical context of each occurrence and point out features of the language employed and in some instances suggest literary allusions.

Acts 2–4

The noun παρρησία occurs both first and most often in the account of Pentecost and the first believers (Acts 2–4). The occurrences are

---

[10] According to van Unnik, in Acts Agrippa is to be considered a Jew. He writes concerning 26:26 that "the 'freedom of speech' is directed to somebody who is considered a Jew" ("The Christian's Freedom of Speech," 281). The assertion in

arranged in two doublets. First, Peter claims "boldness" in his Pentecost speech (2:29). Subsequently it is stated (4:13) that the elders and scribes of Jerusalem, together with the high priest and his relatives, observe the bold speech of Peter and John. This second occurrence of παρρησία confirms the bold speech that Peter has claimed in 2:29. Indeed, Peter's claim is doubly confirmed because the narrator reports Peter and John's bold speech as an observation by authoritative bystanders.

The Pentecost narrative begins in "the house" (2:2). Perhaps already in 2:5, but certainly by 2:14,[11] the scene has shifted to public space.[12] Acts 2:14 describes Peter assuming the pose of a Greek orator speaking publicly.[13] Peter's speech is divided into three parts by three vocatives. Two of these—ἄνδρες Ἰουδαῖοι καὶ οἱ κατοικοῦντες Ἰερουσαλὴμ πάντες[14] in 2:14 and ἄνδρες Ἰσραηλῖται in 2:22—are typical of Greek oratory.

Here παρρησία is introduced in the third section of the speech when Peter claims it as a right (ἐξὸν εἰπεῖν μετὰ παρρησίας πρὸς ὑμᾶς, 2:29). It may be, as commentators maintain, that this section of Peter's speech mentions that David died to show, for Peter, that the Scripture citation cannot have been a prophecy about David.[15] Peter's reference to David's death, burial and tomb, however, is curiously emphatic. Mention of David's tomb need have no relevance to the assertion that David prophesied Jesus' resurrection.[16] After all, Jesus' tomb, because it was empty, evokes arguments that he was

---

26:3, however, that Agrippa is familiar with Jewish customs argues that the reader of Acts is to consider Agrippa non-Jewish. Ernst Haenchen apparently assumes so (*The Acts of the Apostles: A Commentary* [ET; Philadelphia: Westminster, 1971] 682). F. F. Bruce writes, "Agrippa evidently took his responsibilities as 'lay governor of the Jewish church' very seriously" (*The Acts of the Apostles* [3rd rev. ed; Grand Rapids, MI: Eerdmans, 1990] 497).

[11] Hans Conzelmann, *Acts of the Apostles* (ET; Hermeneia; Philadelphia: Fortress, 1987) 14.

[12] The Pentecost speech is situated in a unit comprising the replacement of Judas (1:15–26) and the Pentecost event. One summary precedes this larger unit (1:14) and a second summary concludes it (2:42–47). For a discussion of these summaries, see esp. H. J. Cadbury and Kirsopp Lake, *Additional Notes to the Commentary*, vol. 5 of *The Beginnings of Christianity* (ed. F. J. Foakes-Jackson and K. Lake; 5 vols.; London: Macmillan, 1920–33) 5.392–402.

[13] "σταθείς, to take up the stance of a (Greek) orator" (Haenchen, *Acts*, 178 n. 1).

[14] Ἄνδρες Ἰουδαῖοι is as ἄνδρες Ἀθηναῖοι (Acts 17:22). Similarly, Ἐφέσιοι καὶ οἱ κατοικοῦντες (*SIG* 352.4; 4th century BCE) refers to the citizens and residents.

[15] Haenchen, *Acts*, 182; Conzelmann, *Acts*, 21.

[16] Acts 2:27 is a citation of Ps 16:10. The NRSV's translation of Acts 2:27 ("you will not abandon my soul to Hades or let your Holy One experience corruption") is quite different, however, from its rendering of Ps 16:10 in the Book of Psalms.

raised. Peter's speech does not remark on whether the tomb is empty. The reference to David's death in Peter's speech is emphatic. The listeners' attention is drawn to David's tomb (καὶ ἐτελεύτησεν καὶ ἐτάφη, καὶ τὸ μνῆμα αὐτοῦ ἔστιν ἐν ἡμῖν ἄχρι τῆς ἡμέρας ταύτης, 2:29). Also in this same verse, unusually, David is called πατριάρχης. The word occurs rarely in the NT and the LXX, and in the NT only in reference to premonarchic figures.[17] In Peter's speech, David may be called "patriarch" to show he was head of a dynasty.[18] The strange emphasis on David's burial in a sentence that introduces παρρησία in its classical usage suggests an allusion to Pericles' funeral oration, a speech praising Athenian democracy, which had παρρησία as its salient feature.[19]

Pericles' funeral speech is found in Thucycides' *History of the Peloponnesian War* (2.34.1–46.2). A reference to this history is also likely in Acts 20:35, indeed, so likely that the 26th edition of Nestle-Aland's Greek NT cites Thucydides 2.97.4 in the margin. E. Plümacher has recently supported this identification by arguing that the correspondence extends for three verses, with Acts 20:33–35 alluding to 2.97.3f.[20] Plümacher observes that at the time when Acts was composed, Thucydides' history was considered a classic and worthy of imitation.[21]

In classical Athens the funeral oration was part of a public burial ceremony. Pericles' speech, from the winter of 431, includes standard elements but is unique in emphasizing Athens' present; it includes a praise of Athenian democracy.[22] There are some literary correspondences between the beginning of the oration and the third

---

[17] It occurs in the NT in Acts 7:8, 9 ("the twelve patriarchs") and Hebr 7:4 (of Abraham); in the LXX it occurs in 1 Chr 24:31; 27:22; 2 Chr 19:8; 23:20; 26:12; 4 Macc 7:19; 16:25.

[18] Bruce, *Acts*, 126.

[19] J. S. Rusten writes concerning 40.1–2 that "Plato has this passage in mind when he ridicules the 'democratic' man as unable to concentrate on a single life (*Resp.* 561D)" (*The Peloponnesian War, Book II* [Cambridge: Cambridge University Press, 1989] 153). Other features of democracy mentioned by Plato in the same passage (*Resp.* 557B.4–6) are also associated with παρρησία in Acts (see the conclusion below.)

[20] E. Plümacher, "Eine Thukydidesreminiszenz in der Apostelgeschichte (Act 20, 33–35–Thuk.II 97.3f.)," *ZNW* 83 (1992) 270–75.

[21] Ibid., 272–73.

[22] Rusten (*The Peloponnesian War*, 135–36) summarizes as follows: "[W]e may see the traditional themes of an ἐπιτάφιος: praise of the ancestors, praise of the fallen warriors, exhortation to citizens, and consolation to relatives.... The present oration acknowledges such a pattern, but departs strikingly from it by subordinating all these themes to the glorification of *contemporary* Athens itself (τὴν πόλιν ὕμνησα, 42.2)."

section of Peter's speech. Pericles' speech praises first the ancestors, the πρόγονοι, and asserts that "they transmitted freedom to our time."[23] Pericles speaks of honor to the ancestors.[24] Analogously, "patriarch" is a respectful title for David.

The setting of Peter and John's appearance before the High Council is also one of public discourse, suggesting immediately that παρρησία is also used here in its classical sense. Peter's ἡμεῖς . . . ἀνακρινόμεθα (4:9) indicates a legal proceeding,[25] and Peter and John affirm in the words of Socrates that they will not obey the Council (4:19–20).[26] And the statement that the Council saw that Peter and John were uneducated and simple serves not only to contrast them implicitly with their educated and refined interlocutors but also to evoke the memory of Socrates' ironic claim not to be wise.

Subsequently, παρρησία occurs a third and fourth time in the narrative describing Peter and John returning to their own (οἱ ἴδιοι, 4:23). The believers pray for boldness (4:29) and immediately wonders occur. There is an earthquake, the believers are filled with the Holy Spirit, and they speak the word of God μετὰ παρρησίας (πάσης) (4:29, 31). In the believers' prayer παρρησία carries its classical sense of bold speech in public assembly. Here opposition to παρρησία becomes explicit, with Acts emphasizing the threats of the authorities and asserting that the believers speak the truth in the face of these threats (4:27,29). The prayer (4:24–30) begins by citing scripture; the opening words are from Psalm 146:6, followed by Psalm 2:1–2. The prayer interprets the rulers who oppose the Lord's anointed in Psalm 2 to be Herod, Pilate, the Gentiles, and the peoples of Israel, and then asks for παρρησία in the face of "their" threats. The prayer emphasizes that the believers speak the truth. Speaking the truth in the face of threats characterizes παρρησία. "[O]bstacles may be posed by those to whom παρρησία applies. In the face of such obstacles παρρησία is the courage of openness, i.e., candour. This candour opposes all those who would limit the right to reveal the truth or

---

[23] Thuc. 2.36.1: μέχρι τοῦδε ἐλευθέραν . . . παρέδοσαν. For a translation of the speech, see Charles Forster Smith, *Thucydides, History of the Peloponnesian War* (LCL; 1st ed., 1919; rev. ed.; Cambridge, MA: Harvard University Press, 1928).

[24] Thuc. 2.36.1: τὴν τιμὴν ταύτην τῆς μνήμης δίδοσθαι.

[25] "In Attic Gk., this verb [ἀνακρίνομαι] is used of a preliminary inquiry; in Hellenistic Gk., of any legal questioning" (Bruce, *Acts*, 151).

[26] Pl. *Ap.* 29D. See Ernst Haenchen, "The Book of Acts as Source Material for the History of Early Christianity," *Studies in Luke-Acts* (ed. L. E. Keck and J. L. Martyn; Philadelphia: Fortress, 1980) 262.

hamper the unveiling of the truth."[27] The believers' prayer connects ἀλήθεια with παρρησία for the first time.[28]

The sequence of events described in 4:31 recapitulates the miracle of Pentecost—an earthquake, the giving of the Spirit, and bold speech. The noun παρρησία occurs as a doublet also here—first in direct discourse when the believers ask for παρρησία in prayer (4:29), then in a statement by the narrator that the believers spoke with boldness (4:31). Acts 4:31 attests to παρρησία requested in 4:29, just as παρρησία in 4:13 attested to Peter's initial claim to παρρησία in 2:29. But the narrative gives a significant new dimension to παρρησία in 4:31. Initially Peter claimed a right to bold speech in front of the people of Jerusalem, and presumably the basis for his claim was that he, too, was a Jerusalemite. The Pentecost-like wonders that accompany the giving of παρρησία to the believers in 4:31 serve to redefine παρρησία as a right of the believers.

In Acts 2–4 references to παρρησία are set within allusions to classical writings. Elsewhere Acts depicts events in Jerusalem in language that combines allusions to ancient Israel with allusions to classical Athens. For example, in 1:26 the believers throw lots (κλήρους) to determine Judas' replacement. "Matthias was enrolled with the eleven apostles (μετὰ τῶν ἕνδεκα ἀποστόλων)" is literally "was reckoned along with."[29] Throwing "lots" (κλῆρον βάλλειν) was a practice (for divining) in ancient Israel and is mentioned in Biblical narrative. The verb συγκαταψηφίζομαι, however, comes from ψῆφος and ψηφίζω, the "pebble" with which Athenian citizens voted and "voting with a pebble."[30] The language evokes a description of Jerusalem that is a conflation of ancient Israel and classical Athens.

Analysis of the first four occurrences of παρρησία shows that in these instances Acts intends the term in its classical sense of public speech. The literary context of each occurrence reinforces this sense of παρρησία through allusions to concepts associated with classical usage. They include allusions that associate παρρησία with authority (ἐξουσία), that associate παρρησία with speaking the truth, that imply that παρρησία is speech in the face of threats, and that associate παρρησία with the πόλις. These allusions cast Jerusalemites as an

---

[27] Schlier, "παρρησία," 873.
[28] Ibid., 872–73.
[29] LSJ, s.v. συγκαταψηφίζομαι (II).
[30] In Acts 26:10 Paul describes "casting his vote" to condemn followers of Jesus (ἀναιρουμένων τε αὐτῶν κατήνεγκα ψῆφον).

Athenian assembly. Jerusalem, like Athens, is a πόλις,[31] and in Acts 2–4 the temple serves as the place for public assembly. The "Judeans and inhabitants of Jerusalem" (2:14) before whom Peter speaks implicitly constitute an assembly, although not designated as such.

Acts 4:27 implies that truth resides with the believers, not the πόλις. The truth is *not* being spoken in the πόλις, but it *is* being spoken by the believers. The prayer of the believers at the end of Acts 4 introduces a shift. To the degree that παρρησία is understood as a right of the citizen of the πόλις, 4:31 sets the stage for narrating the establishment of an alternative "polis" among the believers. In 2:29 Peter claims ἐξουσία, and 4:13 informs the reader that the authorities recognized it. When the believers pray for παρρησία for themselves, they are asking for ἐξουσία, for power granted by an authority.[32] The believers ask for παρρησία from God (4:29), and God is the authority that grants it to them (4:31). In the next narrated event the believers will be called an assembly (ἐκκλησία, 5:11). In this way the narrative recognizes that they have separated from the Jerusalem πόλις and have constituted their own assembly under the authority of God. Classically παρρησία was a right of the δῆμος, so one might expect that Acts would proceed with the story of this new δῆμος. Analysis of the usage of παρρησία in the next chapters of Acts will make clear, however, that Acts avoids depicting the believers as a δῆμος, and indeed describes their development into something quite different.

ΠΑΡΡΗΣΙΑΖΕΣΘΑΙ and the Journeys

The first pair of occurrences of παρρησιάζεσθαι is in Acts 9:27 and 28. The subject of the participle is Paul, but in the first instance Barnabas, narrating within the story,[33] attests to Paul speaking boldly in the name of Christ (9:27). Paul's bold speech in the name of Jesus, following his vision of the Lord, is an indication of his new status as disciple, as Barnabas explains to the apostles (9:27). Barnabas' witness in direct discourse is immediately verified in 9:28 by the statement that Paul spoke boldly in Jerusalem in the name of the Lord.[34]

---

[31] The prayer of the believers refers to Jerusalem as "this πόλις" in 4:27 (ἐν τῇ πόλει ταύτῃ).

[32] Werner Foerster, "ἐξουσία," *TDNT* 2.562–3.

[33] An "intradiagetic" narrator.

[34] Παρρησιάζεσθαι occurs first as a finite verb (aorist middle, 3d pers. sing. in 9:27), then as a present participle (in the nom. sing. in 9:28).

The narrative recounting both occurrences in Acts 9:26–30 is situated in Jerusalem, though Barnabas' account (9:27) describes Paul's activity in Damascus. Significantly, what was characterized in 9:20 with κηρύσσειν (ἐν ταῖς συναγωγαῖς ἐκήρυσσεν τὸν Ἰησοῦν) is now described with παρρησιάζεσθαι.

Until this point the narrator had employed παρρησία and now παρρησιάζεσθαι only in connection with Jerusalem. With Saul, it is now used of both Damascus (9:27) and Jerusalem (9:28). The μὲν οὖν in 9:31, moreover, which occurs in the summary of 9:31–32 that follows the story of Saul's conversion in 9:1–30, indicates that a new phase of the ἐκκλησία is underway.[35] From here on, the narrative will employ παρρησία only in connection with speech outside Jerusalem.

The verb παρρησιάζεσθαι occurs, again in a doublet, in the account of Paul's first missionary journey. This first journey is a "model journey."[36] Here, as in Acts 9:27–28, the occurrences are paired, the first coming towards the end of the visit to Pisidian Antioch, the second only nine verses later in the brief account of Paul and Barnabas' activity in Iconium. As in 9:27–28, the narrator continues to associate Paul with Barnabas in this exercise of frank speech. The verb παρρησιάζεσθαι has the same form in 13:46 and 14:3, in both instances a nominative plural participle. In each case, Paul and Barnabas are both the subject of the participle.

Eventually Acts will focus on Paul alone. Pairing Paul with Barnabas serves to make the transition to an account of Paul's activity more gradual by providing an intermediate step. This pairing is a narrative device that contributes to constructing what J. C. Beker argues is a theme of continuity in transmission of the tradition.[37]

---

[35] "μὲν οὖν . . . A new period of the history is now beginning" (Haenchen, *Acts*, 333).

[36] Conzelmann, citing Menoud, writes, "Luke understands this as a 'model journey,' furnishing the pattern for subsequent missionary activity. It sets forth the problem, which is then solved in chapter 15. In actual fact it replaces the thirteen years of missionary work mentioned in Gal 1:21 and 2:1" (*Acts*, 98). The formulaic, impersonal use of παρρησιάζεσθαι in 13:46 and 14:3 is appropriate to a "model journey."

[37] J. Christiaan Beker, "Luke's Paul as the Legacy of Paul," *Society of Biblical Literature 1993 Seminar Papers* (ed. E. H. Lovering, Jr.; SBLSP; Atlanta: Scholars, 1993) 511–19. Beker argues that three subthemes shape Luke's picture of Paul, including "(1) the theme of the unity of the church. . . . (3) The theme of the theological legitimacy of the church, which stresses the continuity between the church and Israel" (514–15.) This narrative device might also be understood as a device that serves to legitimate Paul; see, for example, Robert L. Brawley, "Paul in Acts: Lucan Apology and Conciliation," *Luke-Acts: New Perspectives from the Society of Biblical Literature Seminar* (ed. C. H. Talbert; New York: Crossroad, 1984) 129–47. See also Jacob Jervell, *Luke and the People of God* (Minneapolis: Augsburg, 1972).

Ephesus

The narrative centered around Ephesus provides the last pair of occurrences of παρρησιάζεσθαι.[38] Here the verb occurs in different forms, an infinitive in 18:26, then an imperfect in 19:8, and it occurs with different subjects, Apollos in 18:26 and Paul in 19:8. The two occurrences are separated by a fair amount of narrative. Nevertheless, παρρησιάζεσθαι in 18:26 and 19:8 do constitute a doublet. Both refer to bold speech at Ephesus, and the narrative sets up a correspondence between Apollos, who knows only the baptism of John, and Paul, who baptizes "about twelve" disciples who know only the baptism of John.[39]

The correspondence that Acts sets up between Apollos and Paul is to some degree a negative one. In direct contradiction to 1 Cor 16:12, Acts keeps Paul and Apollos apart.[40] Acts does have Paul travel to Corinth first (agreeing with 1 Cor 3:6, "I planted, Apollos watered"), but describes Paul at Corinth, then Apollos in Ephesus. While Apollos is in Corinth, the narrative has Paul return to Ephesus.[41] Acts 18:25 states that Apollos knew only the baptism of John, and subsequently Acts has Paul baptize disciples who knew only the baptism of John (19:1-7).

Both of these occurrences of παρρησιάζεσθαι are unusual. The first is unusual because opposition to Apollos' bold speech is absent, and because the verb occurs as an infinitive after ἤρξατο. The second is unusual because the narrative, though describing a standard pattern of events—Paul preaching in the synagogue, encountering problems, then departing—does not in this instance describe the conflict. Acts 19:9 simply notes that some "stubbornly refused to believe and spoke evil of the Way" (NRSV) but does not elaborate.

---

[38] The usage of παρρησία in this section is unusual. Richard I. Pervo comments on the unusual narratives that Acts locates in Ephesus; see his *Profit with Delight* (Philadelphia: Fortress, 1987) 9–10. Ephesus and Antioch play very different roles in Acts. Paul's missionary journeys begin and end in Antioch. "The course of the first journey as a whole is determined by the reference to Antioch as the starting point and the goal. This city appears as the *historical* center for the expansion of Christianity into Gentile territory" (Conzelmann, *Acts*, 98).

[39] Michael Wolter, "Apollos und die ephesinischen Johannesjünger (Act 18:24–19:7)," *ZNW* 78 (1987) 49–73.

[40] Ibid., 59.

[41] "Our author also severs all ties between Paul and Apollos. While the latter was active in Ephesus and Corinth, Paul was absent—on a pilgrimage to Jerusalem" (Pervo, *Profit*, 9–10).

Michael Wolter offers a thorough analysis of the redaction and significance of 18:24–19:7. Wolter argues that the two incidents are linked by the theme of Apollos and Paul.[42] He argues further that the account of Paul baptizing (19:1–7) contrasts with Apollos, whose teaching is corrected (in Paul's absence) but who is not baptized as the "about twelve" are.[43] This negative correspondence shows Acts to be taking Paul's part in the conflict with Apollos and depicting Paul as the one who accurately transmits the apostolic tradition.[44]

In this connection Acts' use of ἄρχεσθαι in 18:26 is noteworthy. Some consider ἄρχεσθαι in Acts to be simply a neutral auxiliary verb.[45] The correspondence between Paul and Apollos argues, however, that some sense of beginning should be present in 18:26, as Bruce suggests for ἄρχεσθαι in 1:1.[46] The phrase may be translated "Apollos initiated speaking boldly" or "Apollos began." Then παρρησιάζεσθαι in 19:8 gives another dimension to Wolter's argument. The two occurrences of παρρησιάζεσθαι show Paul as Apollos' successor in Ephesus.[47]

---

[42] Wolter, "Apollos," 52. Wolter argues (49–51) against the positions formulated by Käsemann (that the two stories in Acts 18:24–19:7 are connected by Luke's theological concern to depict Apollos and baptist communities integrated into one, holy, apostolic church as "embryonic" Christians) and Schweizer (that the two stories are to show continuity in sacred history). See E. Käsemann, "Die Johannesjünger in Ephesus," ΖΤΚ 49 (1952) 144–54 (ET in his *Essays on New Testament Themes* [SBT 1.41; London: SCM, 1964] 136–48), and E. Schweizer, "Die Bekehrung des Apollos, Apg 18:24–26," *EvT* 15 (1955) 247–54.

[43] Wolter, "Apollos," 73.

[44] Ibid. Using Beker's argument, we may understand the narrative treatment of Apollos and Paul to serve both the subtheme of "unity of the church" and the subtheme of Paul as a link that establishes continuity ("Luke's Paul," 514–15).

[45] For example, Haenchen (*Acts*, 137), who observes that it corresponds to how the LXX renders Hebrew ה נ ע and is a "periphrasis for the finite verb," and also notes that popular Latin employed *coepi* for tenses of finite verbs.

[46] Bruce writes regarding ἤρξατο in 1:1, "As the Gospel records what Jesus *began* to do and teach (cf. Lk. 3:23, ἀρχόμενος), so Acts records what he *continued* to do and teach, by his Spirit in the apostles...." (*Acts*, 98), and he comments on 18:26 that Apollos "began to speak freely in the synagogue" (403). But on ἤρξαντο in 2:4 he writes that it is "possibly an example of the redundant auxiliary, used (like Aram. *šārē'*) to form a periphrastic variant of the simple verb" (114).

[47] Acts 18:26 depicts Apollos initiating bold speech that is later carried on by others. Paul's preaching in 19:8, however, does not really complete what Apollos initiated because it is interrupted. It is possible to view Paul's activity in Rome as the intended continuation. Acts 28:31 describes Paul in Rome in Markan language, "preaching the kingdom of God and teaching...." Viewing 19:8 in this way suggests that Acts 19:8 differs from the usual pattern and describes no conflict in the synagogue, because it only foreshadows Paul's discussion with Jewish leaders in Rome in 28:17–28.

The pair of occurrences of παρρησιάζεσθαι in 18:26 and 19:8, like the other pairs, serves to add to Paul's authority. In 19:8 Paul implicitly receives authority from Apollos by continuing what Apollos began. The structure of the narrative hides the conflict that Paul's letters indicate took place between Apollos and Paul. The double occurrence of παρρησιάζεσθαι here helps render Paul as Apollos' successor, not his competitor.

Acts 26:26

Paul alone is the subject of παρρησιάζεσθαι in 26:26. Paul speaks before Festus and King Aggripa and Berenice (26:2–29) in Caesarea before his departure for Rome. Before this interview, Acts has Paul exercising his παρρησία in the synagogue. Paul's *apologia* before Agrippa (26:2–29) is the fifth public explanation following his arrest, and with 28 verses it is the longest. It follows Paul's explanation to the tribune (21:37–40), his *apologia* in the courtyard of the temple (22:1–21), his speech before the high priest and the Sanhedrin (23:1–6), and the *apologia* at his trial before the procurator Felix (24:10–21). Festus brings Paul before Agrippa and Berenice in an audience hall (25:23), so the scene is set as public discourse. But the interview proceeds as a dialogue between Paul and Festus and between Paul and Agrippa.

Abraham Malherbe has argued that particularly in this incident, as well as in Paul's visit to Athens and in his farewell speech at Miletus, Acts portrays him as a moral philosopher.[48] Malherbe observes that Paul's assertion in 26:26 that he has conducted his work "not in a corner" fits within an ancient dispute about the proper sphere of philosophical activity. It reflects the conviction that the moral philosopher should not withdraw from society but rather participate in public life.[49] Also, Acts depicts Paul speaking before Agrippa partly in order to refute the criticism that Christians were uneducated.

Although the interview with Agrippa is set as public discourse, the literary context of 26:26, that of debates among moral philosophers

---

[48] Abraham J. Malherbe, "'Not in a Corner': Early Christian Apologetic in Acts 26:26," in his *Paul and the Popular Philosophers* (Minneapolis: Fortress, 1989) 147–70.

[49] "[T]herefore, 'to speak in a corner' was used pejoratively, especially by orators or philosophers of rhetorical bent, of people, particularly philosophers, who did not engage in public life" ("Not in a Corner," 156).

concerning the value of public life, indicates that παρρησιάζεσθαι here is used with the sense it acquired in Hellenistic moral philosophy. Paul's παρρησία here is a moral virtue. Acts has Paul exhibiting courage because he dares speak the truth before people in power.[50]

ΠΑΡΡΗΣΙΑ in Acts 28:31

The noun παρρησία occurs for the fifth and last time in Acts 28:30–31. This two-verse conclusion describes Paul preaching the kingdom of God and teaching about Christ μετὰ πάσης παρρησίας ἀκωλύτως. The narrative (28:17–28) that leads up to the concluding verses recounts Paul's arrival and his conversations with Jewish leaders in Rome. Like the accounts of Paul in Pisidian Antioch (13:46) and Corinth (18:6), Paul's discussions with Jewish leaders in Rome conclude with a statement concerning salvation going to the Gentiles (28:28). It has been argued that Acts has events in Rome repeat a pattern seen in the missionary journeys (Paul preaches in the synagogue, meets hostility, then leaves the synagogue) in order to show that Jewish refusal to accept Jesus as the Messiah in Rome definitively compels the Gentile mission.[51] Analysis of παρρησία, however, highlights ways in which Acts depicts Paul's encounter with Jews at Rome differently and suggests a more complex motivation than previously has been proposed for Acts' negative picture of Judaism.

Acts' account of Paul's encounters with the Jews in Rome differs in significant respects from the accounts of his encounters in Corinth and Pisidian Antioch. Although Paul's address (ἄνδρες ἀδελφοί, 28:17) at the first interview and the formal arrangements made for the second

---

[50] In his 1992 SBL paper on "Friendship, Frankness and Flattery," 19, David Konstan observes, "In the latter portion of the treatise, which forms a separate section devoted to the idea of παρρησία, Plutarch draws most of his examples from the sphere of kings and courtiers."

[51] Haenchen writes, "These three scenes, representative of all corresponding incidents, make visible the fundamental experience of Paul and the Christian mission generally. Against the will of the Christian missionaries their proclamation, through its rejection by the Jews, is forcibly directed to the Gentiles, among whom Luke will also have included Paul's visitors (v. 30)" (*Acts*, 729). Conzelmann writes, "the final example of Paul's schematized preaching first to Jews at the synagogue. . . . The scene has been constructed with the express purpose of conveying the impression that the situation with the Jews was hopeless. . . . Luke does not look beyond the present hardening to a future conversion of Israel. Rather, the time of the Gentile church has now broken in" (*Acts*, 227).

(28:23) convey a sense of public discourse, it is important to note that Paul has invited the leaders (28:17) to his lodgings (28:23). The locale is πρὸς αὐτόν, thus κατ' οἶκον.[52]

Both interviews in Rome are framed in legal language. In marked contrast to Peter and John's appearance before the Council in Jerusalem in Acts 4, the Roman interviews are described not in terms of Attic democracy, but in terms drawn from Roman civic life and law. The πρῶτοι in Rome are equivalent to the *primi*, the Latin term for the "eminent," "distinguished" people (28:17).[53] The words ἐναντίον ποιήσας τῷ λαῷ (28:17) literally translate the Latin *contra facere*, meaning "violate, transgress."[54] In 28:23 ταξάμενοι ἡμέραν is a Latin expression (*constituo diem*, "arrange, assign a day, especially for judicial proceedings");[55] Greek would have them arranging the hour (ὥρα) rather than the day. Finally, the duration of the interview, ἀπὸ πρωΐ ἕως ἑσπέρας in 28:23, also agrees with Roman law, in that the case was to be started before noon, and if both parties were present might continue until sunset.[56]

Acts presents Paul's interviews in Rome in a tone quite different from that of Paul preaching in the synagogue. Acts portrays the Jews in Rome as philosophers. In Rome no synagogue is mentioned. The Roman interviews resemble Paul's encounter with the philosophers in Athens. Like the Athenian philosophers, the Roman Jews are curious. They say that they welcome a chance to hear what Paul has to say (28:21–22). In both instances there are two discussion sessions—an initial encounter followed by an assignation. The statement in 28:24 that some were persuaded and others not recalls the ambivalent outcome of Paul's discussion with the Athenian philosophers (17:32). Paul's discussions with the Roman Jews conclude without conflict. There is no angry mob and no need for Paul to call upon Roman authorities. As observed above, the language with which Acts describes the events implies that the interviews proceed according to Roman law. The meetings take place in Paul's own lodgings, so at

---

[52] This may be of necessity, as Haenchen notes (*Acts*, 729). The passage does, however, emphasize Paul's agency. Paul invites his visitors; they agree together on a time to meet.

[53] LS, s.v., *primus* (II B).

[54] LS, s.v., *contra* (I B.8): "Of violation of law, contracts, etc.: contra facere or contra committere, *to violate, transgress a law*, etc."

[55] See LS, s.v., *constituo* (II. D.1); *dies* (I. B.1). The expression is also found in Acts 12:21 (τακτῇ δὲ ἡμέρᾳ).

[56] The Twelve Tables I, 6–9.

the conclusion of the discussions Paul does not leave in distress or get thrown out. Paul's interlocutors are his guests and they leave politely.[57] Even Paul's remark about salvation going to the Gentiles appears less conflict-laden than the corresponding ones in 13:46 and 18:6, because in 28:28 Paul says only that salvation goes to the Gentiles, not that he will go to the Gentiles; and he adds αὐτοὶ καὶ ἀκούσονται, which may be translated, "they *also* will listen."

The concluding observations that follow elaborate on how the author of Acts depicts the Jews in Rome less negatively than Paul's co-religionists in the East.

Concluding Observations

The word παρρησία was used in one sense in the classical period and in a very different sense in the Hellenistic period. In Acts a neutral succession of events provides a framework for the narrative, but at important junctures a speaker will shape the events into a past and present, or even past, present, and future. Peter's statement in 15:7, for example, in which he describes his early activity with ἀφ' ἡμερῶν ἀρχαίων, treats the early period clearly as "antiquity." Less explicit, perhaps, is Acts' depiction of the early community holding property in common, suggesting a primitive ideal.[58] And Paul's farewell speech at Miletus shapes his own activity into a past, present, and future, beginning with ἀπὸ πρώτης ἡμέρας in 20:18. This is the part of the narrative in which the sense of παρρησία shifts to the frank speech of the moral philosopher. The classical sense of παρρησία is relegated to "antiquity."

The usage of παρρησία in Acts brings out some of the ways in which the narrative establishes Paul's reliability in the tradition, whether to legitimate him or to reinforce continuity in the tradition. Paul's exercise of the Christian παρρησία is first verified because Barnabas observes it (Acts 9:27), then reinforced because the narrative pairs Paul with Barnabas and doubles its description of the two of them exercising their παρρησία (Acts 13–14). Finally, through a negative correspondence Paul receives the legacy of Apollos (19:8) to exercise παρρησία.

---

[57] The theme is found even more emphatically in 28:29, which describes the guests debating among themselves as they depart.

[58] Conzelmann, *Acts*, 24.

A shift in the locations where παρρησία is exercised accompanies the shift in παρρησία from its classical to Hellenistic sense. Classically, παρρησία was exercised in public assembly. As a virtue of friendship, it was exercised interpersonally.[59] Acts depicts the ἐκκλησία as an association that functions on the intimate level of friendship as well as publicly. The two statements about the believers sharing all things in common—εἶχον ἅπαντα κοινά (2:44) and ἦν αὐτοῖς ἅπαντα κοινά (4:32)—describe the early community as an ideal philosophical community.[60] Sharing of property characterizes the early community as a group of "friends," though the word φίλοι is lacking.[61] According to 5:42, moreover, they teach ἐν τῷ ἱερῷ καὶ κατ' οἶκον. Thus, at first the activity of the believers alternates between public and private space.

It may be proposed that Acts treats as extreme both the purely public assembly (the Jews in Jerusalem) and the overly private one because both eventually disappear from view. In the primitive ideal community παρρησία is never mentioned, and when it is exercised publicly conflict ensues. In 26:26 παρρησία is exercised appropriately, by Paul the moral philosopher. There he asserts that he is not the philosopher who withdraws from public life and speaks only "in a corner." In his farewell speech in Miletus Paul asserts that he has spoken both δημοσίᾳ and κατ' οἶκον (20:20).

In Rome the discussions take place in an intermediate space, in locations that are at the same time both private and public. Paul's interactions with the Jewish leaders occur in Paul's lodgings, but are described in legal language. Such an intermediate domain in "private residence" that was regulated by law existed in Roman social organization in the form of the Roman household. This extended household was both private and subject to regulation by law. It encompassed individuals who did not reside in the household (clients and freedpersons). It supported, for example, the household-client system, a set of social institutions based around the household but

---

[59] See the essays by Clarence Glad and Troels Engberg-Pedersen in this volume (Chapters Two and Three).

[60] A. Malherbe writes, "so he [Luke], too, sketches a picture of the Jerusalem church in which it realizes the philosophical ideal of a communal sharing of resources, and does so in language that would have made his intention clear to a cultivated reader (Acts 2:44–45; 4:32)" ("Not in a Corner," 150).

[61] Alan C. Mitchell, "The Social Function of Friendship in Acts 2:44–47 and 4:32–37," *JBL* 111 (1992) 255–72; Conzelmann, *Acts*, 24.

involving public affairs and regulated by law.[62] The narrative depicts Paul's lodgings as a Roman household in that they are both a public and a private domain.

Classically, παρρησία is a right belonging to the δῆμος, and the enemy of the δῆμος, the enemy of παρρησία, is the τύραννος.[63] Peter claims παρρησία in 2:29, presumably on the basis of being a Judean Jew, and by implication a member of the δῆμος. Acts 4 depicts the Jewish leaders as τύραννοι, those who threaten truth in speech.[64] In analyzing παρρησία in Acts 2–4, I have argued that this section of the history concludes with the believers beginning to establish their own assembly (ἐκκλησία) to replace the assembly at the temple in Jerusalem. We would expect Acts to describe subsequently the formation of a new people, a new δῆμος. But Acts never depicts the believers as a δῆμος. Indeed the word δῆμος has negative connotations in Acts. It occurs only to describe an angry irrational mob— the Tyrians and Sidonians in 12:22, who think Herod is a god, the Thessalonian Jews in 17:5, who "riot" (θορυβέω), and the Ephesian mob in 19:30, 33.

An unwillingness to depict the believers forming a δῆμος is consistent with a Roman suspicion of democracy that may lie behind Acts' negative portrayal of what could be termed the "Judean democracy." As observed in the first part of this paper, the words with which Plato characterizes democracy in the *Republic*—ἐλευθερία, παρρησία, and ἐξουσία—either appear or are alluded to in connection with παρρησία in Acts 2–4.[65] But Plato did not cite these features in praise of democracy. He argues that greed for freedom leads to democracy's downfall, mob rule. The portrait of "Judean democracy" and its branches in the Diaspora in Paul's missionary cities is unfavorable. The veiled implication that Judean love of freedom (democracy) leads

---

[62] The households were the domain of the wealthy and, needless to say, were for the most part politically conservative.

[63] Schlier, "παρρησία," 873.

[64] Cf. the Western text of Acts 5:39 (esp. Codex Bezae = D), where Gamaliel advises against Jewish attempts to suppress the believers' bold speech, arguing that "neither you nor kings nor tyrants (οὔτε ὑμεῖς οὔτε βασιλεῖς οὔτε τύραννοι)" can successfully overthrow the disciples if God is on their side.

[65] Pl., *Resp.* 557B.4–6: Οὐκοῦν πρῶτον μὲν δὴ ἐλεύθεροι, καὶ ἐλευθερίας ἡ πόλις μεστὴ καὶ παρρησίας γίγνεται, καὶ ἐξουσία ἐν αὐτῇ ποιεῖν ὅ τί τις βούλεται; "In the first place, are they [the poor who have established the democracy] not free; and is not the city full of freedom and frankness—a man may say and do what he likes?" The translation is that of Benjamin Jowett, *The Portable Plato* (ed. Scott Buchanan; New York: Viking, 1976) 605.

to mob rule would be consistent with the perception in Rome after the Jewish War, the likely time of composition of Acts, that Judean excessive love of freedom led to excessive violence.[66]

Analysis of παρρησία in Acts shows some ways in which Acts depicts Jews in Jerusalem and the Eastern Diaspora negatively. It shows also that παρρησία occurs at the end of Acts alongside a more favorable depiction of Jews in Rome. Acts depicts the Jews in Rome as distinct, even isolated from their co-religionists. They behave like philosophers, not like an angry mob, and carry on debates politely in a Roman "household." With the Jews of Rome Paul has courteous, law-abiding dialogue, but ultimately no religious affiliation. Perhaps intentionally, even the word order describing Paul's frank speech in Rome is changed. In 4:29 the believers are described as speaking μετὰ παρρησίας πάσης. This construction with the adjective following its noun corresponds to the Hebrew and is the style of the LXX. Acts 28:31 employs classical Greek word order, the adjective between the preposition and the noun, to describe frank speech that is unhindered in Rome, μετὰ πάσης παρρησίας ἀκωλύτως.

---

[66] Fergus Millar writes, "The details of the siege of Jerusalem need not concern us. What is significant is that it took this very substantial force, representing roughly one-seventh of the whole Imperial army, five months, from April to September of AD 70, to complete the capture of the city" (*The Roman Near East* [Cambridge, MA: Harvard University Press, 1993] 76). When this paper was in page proofs a colleague drew my attention to an article by David L. Balch, "Paul in Acts: '... You teach all the Jews ... to forsake Moses, telling them not to ... observe the customs' (Act. 21, 21)," *Panchaia: Festschrift für Klaus Thraede* (ed. M. Wacht; JAC Ergänzungsband 22; Münster: Aschendorff, 1995) 11–23. Balch argues several points pertinent to this essay, for instance that "[o]fficial Roman policy promoted each nation preserving its own, ancient customs and allowing other people to practice theirs" (23). He discusses Acts 28:31 in this light.

HOLDING ON TO CONFIDENCE: ΠΑΡΡΗΣΙΑ IN HEBREWS

Alan C. Mitchell, S.J.

According to Stanley Marrow, the NT's use of παρρησία is quite
different from that usually found in the ancient Mediterranean world,
where it was typically employed to express freedom of speech, frankness in friendship, and boldness.[1] Marrow's assessment may seem to
call into question the appropriateness of a study of the word in Hebrews for a volume entitled *Friendship, Flattery, and Frankness of Speech.*
Perhaps it is the very peculiarity of the NT usage, and the importance of παρρησία in Hebrews, that merits this chapter a place among
essays which delineate the richness of this word in antiquity.

Introduction

The problem of the characteristic use of παρρησία in Hebrews is
readily seen in the attempts commentators make to reconcile the
meaning assigned the word by the letter's author with the history of
its usage in the Greek language. This history includes the NT itself,
which witnesses to its own appropriation of παρρησία in ways that
are both like and unlike what one finds in non-Christian sources.
That this approach has yielded uneven results can be seen in W. C.
van Unnik's criticism of H. Schlier's treatment of παρρησία in the
TWNT. According to van Unnik, Schlier "leaves aside the question
whether there was a special reason for certain NT authors to use
this word."[2] In his own attempt, van Unnik does a better job at
explaining the various shades of meaning and contexts which accompany παρρησία in the NT. Whether he has brought us any closer
to knowing the special reasons why NT authors adopted the word is
another question. Perhaps van Unnik came to understand why Schlier
could not have been more etiological in his survey of the meanings
of παρρησία in the NT.

---

[1] S. Marrow, *"Parrhēsia* and the New Testament," *CBQ* 44 (1982) 431–46.
[2] W. C. van Unnik, "The Christian's Freedom of Speech in the New Testament," in *Sparsa Collecta: The Collected Essays of W. C. van Unnik* (NovTSup 29–31;
Leiden: E. J. Brill, 1973–83) 2.272.

The problem is difficult, given the use of the term in Greek literature as mainly a political concept describing the right to free speech enjoyed by citizens in Greek cities.[3] Saying exactly how its meaning evolved by the time it made its way into the NT and was transformed by a Christian theological perspective challenges an easy interpretation. The question of where one should begin is only part of the problem. Should one look to hellenistic Judaism in seeking a solution, or does one do better by examining the hellenistic moralists? Can the hellenistic-Jewish usage already have been influenced by the Greek philosophical tradition by the time the term is adopted by NT authors?[4] Do NT authors direct the meaning of παρρησία away from the secular Greek and hellenistic-Jewish trajectory? An interest in locating the meanings assigned this word by the NT within the semantic range of the word's history has led many recent commentators to see the hellenistic-Jewish background as the main filter for παρρησία's entrance into NT discourse. In light of the influence of the hellenistic moral tradition on hellenistic-Judaism, this constitutes a fully reasonable way of proceeding. Still, this approach is not without its problems.

Fortunately, the task at hand for this writer is not to explain the use of the word παρρησία in the entire NT, but only in the Letter to the Hebrews. Whereas several commentators have given adequate descriptions of just how peculiar the use of παρρησία in Hebrews is, they have said little about the author's motivation for adopting the term. This chapter will return to van Unnik's concern about previous studies of παρρησία in the NT and will ask whether the author of Hebrews had a special reason for choosing it. It will argue that the peculiarity of the use of παρρησία in Hebrews stems from the situation of the readers it addresses. The recipients are Jewish Christians who no longer enjoy the παρρησία they received in their con-

---

[3] See H. Balz, "παρρησία, ας, ἡ; παρρησιάζομαι," *EWNT*, 3.106–11; H.-C. Hahn, "Openness, Frankness, Boldness," *The New International Dictionary of New Testament Theology* (ed. C. Brown; Exeter: Paternoster, 1971) 734–37; E. Peterson, "Zur Bedeutungsgeschichte von Παρρησία," *R. Seeberg Festschrift* (ed. W. Koepp; 2 vols.; Leipzig: D. W. Scholl, 1929) 1.283–97; H. Schlier, "παρρησία, κτλ.," *TWNT* 5.869–84; R. Schnackenburg, "Parrhesia," *LTK* 8.110–11.

[4] See A. J. Malherbe, "Hellenistic Moralists and the New Testament," *ANRW* 2.26.1 (1992) 332; J. Goldstein, "Jewish Acceptance and Rejection of Hellenism," *Aspects of Judaism in the Greco-Roman Period*, vol. 2 of *Jewish and Christian Self-Definition* (ed. E. P. Sanders, A. I. Baumgarten, and A. Mendelson; 3 vols.; London: SCM, 1980–82) 64–87; H. D. Betz, "Hellenismus," *TRE* 15, 20–21; C. Andresen, "Antike und Christentum," *TRE* 3, 52–55; Peterson, "Zur Bedeutungsgeschichte," 289.

version to Christianity. Disillusioned with Christianity and nostalgic for the synagogue from which they came, they now contemplate a return there. The author of Hebrews must reaffirm their παρρησία and help them to regain the security of their faith in the efficacy of the sacrificial death of Christ for the forgiveness of sin and the purification of their consciences.[5] Thus the author's aim is a pastoral one, which encourages the readers to hold on to παρρησία and not throw it away.

The Meaning of ΠΑΡΡΗΣΙΑ in Hebrews: A Brief Forschungsbericht

A survey of the literature on the use of παρρησία in Hebrews 3:6, 4:16, 10:19, and 10:35 shows a remarkable compatibility among interpretations. Most studies agree on the definition of the term and, while one finds attempts at refinements, there is little substantive variation among the interpretations. Of particular interest is the background of παρρησία, which features prominently in these studies as does the question of whether its use in Hebrews constitutes a special case within the NT.[6] In addition to the basic agreement on what the word means, there is also a consistency in the kinds of questions posed about its history and usage.

One of the earliest studies of παρρησία is Erik Peterson's, which appeared in a *Festschrift* for Reinhold Seeberg. Although Peterson gives little attention to the NT and says hardly anything at all about Hebrews, the essay is seminal and provides much helpful information about the history of the word in Greek literature, politics, and philosophy. Peterson's analysis has often served as the basis for what others would later claim, and the repeated reference to his essay in scholarly footnotes indicates how well it has been received. For this reason it is possible to make only brief remarks on the significance of Peterson's work for the understanding of παρρησία in Hebrews.

Perhaps what ought to presage most the problem of παρρησία's meaning in the NT is the fact that, after situating the concept in

---

[5] This thesis rests on B. Lindars's description of the community situation and modifies it by considering the pivotal role παρρησία plays in the author's dealing with it, something not attended to by Lindars ("The Rhetorical Structure of Hebrews," *NTS* 35 [1989] 382–406).

[6] Van Unnik clearly believes this to be the case: "In the Epistle to the Hebrews we have quite a different situation" ("The Christian's Freedom of Speech," 285).

Greek antiquity, Peterson devotes little space to the NT. He simply claims that the NT usage stems from both hellenistic-Greek and hellenistic-Jewish sources, without specifying what role these sources play in particular NT authors. So, while one finds in Peterson's essay a great interest in the historical development of παρρησία, there is little or no interest in questions which NT scholars normally raise. In an almost apologetic footnote he says, "Ich behandle nur einige Stellen."[7] Regarding Hebrews, he takes 4:16 and 10:19 together and posits as the background of these statements a "throne scene" before which one has the courage to approach God. The background here is forensic, and with help from his interpretation of Eph 3:12, Peterson posits also for Hebrews the situation where one has the right of access to God as well as the right to say everything in God's presence. Curiously, he does not say how the word should be translated.[8]

Ernst Käsemann deserves credit for contributing one of the most influential interpretations of παρρησία in Hebrews, despite the fact that he prefaced his comments with the following words of caution: "So wenig hier ausfürlich die Wortgeschichte des letzteren Begriffes [παρρησία] dargelegt werden kann, so umstritten ist seine Verwendung in unserem Briefe."[9] In agreement with B. Weiss and O. Michel that παρρησία connotes a subjective state, which they identified as "Freudigkeit,"[10] Käsemann pushed the notion further. Thus he claimed that παρρησία contains not only a subjective but also an objective dimension, and that it connotes both an attitude and a pretext. This idea originated in the relationship he saw between παρρησία and πίστις. Noticing that in Heb 11:1 πίστις is connected with ἔλεγχος and ὑπόστασις, he suggested that ἐλπίς, also a part of faith there, should feature in the author's understanding of "conviction." The connection between παρρησία and ἐλπίς already exists in Heb 3:6 where it is linked to καύχημα τῆς ἐλπίδος.[11] Since καύχημα is somewhat objective here, one should understand παρρησία not only as a

---

[7] Peterson, "Zur Bedeutungsgeschichte," 292 n. 2.

[8] Ibid., 292.

[9] E. Käsemann, *Das wandernde Gottesvolk: Eine Untersuchung zum Hebräerbrief* (Göttingen: Vandenhoeck & Ruprecht, 1957) 23 [ET: *The Wandering People of God* (Minneapolis: Augsburg, 1984) 42–43].

[10] B. Weiss, *Hebräerbrief* (MeyerK 13; Göttingen: Vandenhoeck & Ruprecht, 1897⁶) 262 n. 1; O. Michel, *Der Brief an die Hebräer*, (MeyerK 13; Göttingen: Vandenhoeck & Ruprecht, 1936⁷) 43–44.

[11] James Moffatt makes a similar claim that the confidence stems from hope (*Epistle to the Hebrews* [ICC; Edinburgh: T. & T. Clark, 1952] 46).

subjective attitude, but also find in it the objective basis for the subjective state. Παρρησία in this sense is grounded in the promises made by God, and so it is more than simply a subjective trust. It is also the joyful defense of something already guaranteed by God. That objective something is the hopeful conviction Christians have about the future fulfillment of these promises. This interpretation moved the understanding of παρρησία in Hebrews more towards a theological and away from a political/philosophical understanding of the term, making the ground of Christian confidence eschatological. Thus Käsemann understood παρρησία as something akin to faith in the firm promises of God for the future. Later this bipolar understanding of παρρησία features prominently in many interpretations of its use in Hebrews.[12]

One clear instance of Käsemann's influence is found in the *TWNT* article on παρρησία authored by H. Schlier. When he discusses Hebrews, Schlier is quite dependent on Käsemann, even though he quotes him almost anonymously.[13] Building on the ideas of Käsemann, Schlier waxes eloquent on the meaning of παρρησία as "die *Freiheit* des Zuganges zu Gott, die *Macht*, in das Heiligtum einzutreten, die *Offenheit* für den neuen, lebendigen Weg, den Jesus uns erneuert hat (10, 19)." Apart from the inspiration drawn from Käsemann, Schlier's analysis is little more than a paraphrase of Hebrews that attempts to unify the four instances of the word in the letter. Despite his dependence on Käsemann, Schlier has not heeded his warning that the less one says specifically about παρρησία in Hebrews, the more disputed will its understanding be. While Schlier is right to connect παρρησία with the author's understanding of the sacrificial work of Jesus, which grounds the hope of believers, the lack of precise exegesis of the relevant passages leaves the reader to wonder how these things fit together.

In light of this W. C. van Unnik simply says Schlier "leaves aside the question of whether there was a special reason for certain NT

---

[12] Käsemann, *Das wandernde Gottesvolk*, 23. On the danger of overstressing the subjective/objective dimensions to the point of dichotomy, see O. Glombitza, "Erwägungen zum kunstvollen Ansatz der Paraenese im Brief an die Hebräer–X 19–25," *NovT* 9 (1967) 132–50.

[13] "παρρησία hat, wie man mit Recht gesagt hat, 'einen eigenartig gegenständlichen Charakter'" (Schlier, *TWNT* 5.882). See C. Maurer: "παρρησία ist mehr als nur subjektive Freimütigkeit, es ist das objektiv gegebene Recht zu dieser" (*TWNT* 6.768 n. 2).

authors to use this word."[14] Drawing more on the hellenistic-Jewish background of παρρησία as found in Philo and Josephus, van Unnik stresses the remarkable use of the word in the NT, in particular where it is applied to one's relationship with God.[15] The origin of this development away from the secular Greek usage must be located in the Jewish synagogue and can not be said to have originated in Christianity. Curiously, though, van Unnik claims that the LXX plays no direct role in influencing the NT usage of παρρησία.[16]

Turning to Hebrews, van Unnik claims that the usage there constitutes quite a different situation from what one finds in the rest of the NT. Παρρησία, occurring in the context of admonition, "is addressed to Christians who are in danger of apostasy, because their faith is flagging and the outward oppression is heavy."[17] In Hebrews παρρησία describes "the content of the Christian attitude in the world, the security of God's salvation and the open confession amidst opposition."[18] In the end he gives it two meanings that combine in a unified concept, "the free right to approach God, given in the sacrifice of Christ, and the open confession of this faith, which is an unshakable hope."[19] In this sense van Unnik finds παρρησία to be both a gift and a task.

Erich Grässer followed up on Käsemann's idea of παρρησία as both objective and subjective and wished to strengthen the view that the word in Hebrews is eschatologically referred. Grässer claimed all four instances of παρρησία in Hebrews are eschatologically directed, giving the content of the term a double meaning.[20] On the one hand,

---

[14] Van Unnik, "The Christian's Freedom of Speech," 272.

[15] Interesting here is the contrast between the secular Greek use of παρρησία in relation to the gods and what one finds in the LXX and Hellenistic Judaism. Isocrates, *Busiris* 40, considers παρρησία before the gods to be blasphemy, which indicates ἀσέβεια, whereas Prov 13:5 sees the ἀσεβής precisely as someone who does not have παρρησία before God. On this point, see W. Klassen, "ΠΑΡΡΗΣΙΑ in the Johannine Writings" (paper presented to the Hellenistic Moral Philosophy and Early Christianity Group at the annual meeting of the Society of Biblical Literature, San Francisco, CA, November, 1992) 9–10. A revised version of this paper appears as Chapter Eleven of this volume (see p. 235). See also Peterson, "Zur Bedeutungsgeschichte," 4.

[16] Van Unnik, "The Christian's Freedom of Speech," 274; idem, "The Semitic Background of ΠΑΡΡΗΣΙΑ in the New Testament," *Sparsa Collecta: The Collected Essays of W. C. van Unnik* (NovTSup 29–31; Leiden: E. J. Brill, 1973–83) 2.289–306.

[17] "The Christian's Freedom of Speech," 285–86.

[18] Ibid., 286–87.

[19] Ibid., 287.

[20] E. Grässer, *Der Glaube im Hebräerbrief* (MThSt 2; Marburg: N. G. Elwert, 1965) 16–17, 36, 109. See also idem, "Mose und Jesus: Zur Auslegung von Hebr 3, 1–6,"

it is the freedom of access to God (4:16), which empowers one to enter the sanctuary (10:19). Here the objective dimension is based on the promises of the past and the way opened up through the high priesthood of Jesus. On the other hand, it is an attitude, "das Offenhalten der εἴσοδος durch unwandelbares Stehen bei der Sache," and this constitutes the subjective element. By taking παρρησία as synonymous with ἐλπίς (6:11, 18; 7:19; 10:23), ὑπόστασις (3:14; 11:1), ὑπομονή (10:36; 12:1) μακροθυμία (6:12, 15) and πληροφορία (6:11; 10:22), Grässer is led to agree with Michel that the eschatological dimension of the subjective side of παρρησία is located in an expectation for the future. Adding the notion of πίστις to the mix helps one to grasp the process of coming to faith required by eschatological existence and described by all of those synonyms. The relationship between πίστις and παρρησία is so close in Grässer's estimation that one could replace πίστις with παρρησία in Heb 4:3; 11:1, 6, 7; 6:12; 10:22; and 10:39.[21]

Grässer's distinctive contribution to the discussion παρρησία in Hebrews comes in his discussion of the term as thoroughly hellenistic. He cites texts from the LXX, Josephus and Philo in order to present what he sees as a needed dimension of the comparative background of the term in Hebrews. Unfortunately, he does not take the time to show precisely what the value of this material is. So, for example, Grässer admits that there are no direct parallels in the hellenistic material to the use of παρρησία in Heb 3:6, where the readers are exhorted to hold fast to their confidence. He finds, however, enough comparable hellenistic material on firm faith and hope to claim that the author of Hebrews understood it to be a Christian virtue, which characterizes a stance before God that the recipients have won and must maintain.[22]

Especially interesting in this regard is his treatment of παρρησία as a religious virtue, illustrated by the person of Moses. Here Grässer is dependent on Philo, whom he understands to draw on the hellenistic

---

in *Der Alte Bund im Neuen: Exegetische Studien zum Israelfrage im Neuen Testament* (WUNT 35; Tübingen: Mohr-Siebeck, 1985) 307.

[21] Grässer, *Der Glaube*, 17. See also idem, "Zur Christologie des Hebräerbriefs. Eine Auseinandersetzung mit H. Braun," *Neues Testament und christliche Existenz* (H. Braun Festschrift; ed. H. D. Betz and L. Schottroff; Tübingen: Mohr-Siebeck, 1973) 151–52, 203–204; idem, "Die Heilsbedeutung des Todes Jesu in Hebr 2, 14–18," *Theologica crucis—signum crucis* (E. Dinkler Festschrift; ed. C. Andresen and G. Klein; Tübingen: Mohr-Siebeck, 1979) 179.

[22] Grässer, *Der Glaube*, 99.

friendship tradition in his description of the relationship between Moses and God. The application of the term "friend of God" to Moses can mean that the same is possible for humans, when they, too, have won such a relationship. Such friendship results from a free and confident stance before God, which empowers a person to free and open speech and the ability to approach God with a clear conscience. This background applies to Hebrews in two ways. First, Grässer sees a connection between the Philonic tradition of Moses as a friend of God and Heb 3:1–6, which draws upon Num 12:7 to describe Moses as a faithful servant in God's house. Philo refers to the same tradition in his presentation of Moses as a friend of God.[23] Second, Grässer finds the friendship tradition modified in Hebrews where instead of φίλος θεοῦ one finds μέτοχος τοῦ Χριστοῦ (3:14).[24]

Diverging from the consensus formed over the previous 25 years, W. S. Vorster tried a different methodological approach to the problem of παρρησία in Hebrews. Critical of NT word studies based on the *TWNT*, Vorster called into question the work done on παρρησία in the NT.[25] Using Michel as a foil, he reexamined the studies of Peterson, Schlier, and van Unnik and challenged them on methodological grounds. Criticizing them for paying insufficient attention to the context of παρρησία in particular sentences, Vorster argued that not enough work had been done on what the letter's author intended by using παρρησία. Unfortunately, his criticism of earlier studies is not always on the mark, and the results of his new methodological approach are not all that different from what preceded it.

Vorster employed a modern linguistics componential analysis in his reexamination of the meaning of παρρησία in Hebrews. He found that in the NT, in general, one can distinguish between two seman-

---

[23] Ibid., 97–98; Philo, *Leg.* 3.204. Again, a lack of precision in saying just what is the relationship between παρρησία in Heb 3:1–6 and the friendship tradition in Philo's description of Moses is evident. Curiously, παρρησία is not predicated of Moses' relationship with God in this text, just as it is absent from the Philonic citation Grässer appeals to (*Leg.* 3.204). To find Philo's discussion of παρρησία in relation to Moses, one must look to *Her.* 21. Grässer is not alone in this. In the introduction to his commentary on Hebrews, C. Spicq (*L'Épître aux Hébreux* [Ebib; 2 vols.; Paris: Gabalda, 1952–53] 47) claims that Heb 3:1–6 is directly dependent on Philo, *Cher.* 106. For a refutation of this claim, see R. Williamson, *Philo and the Epistle to the Hebrews* (ALGHJ 4; Leiden: E. J. Brill, 1970) 109–14.

[24] Unfortunately, Grässer does not show exactly how this shift occurs and merely asserts it to be true (*Der Glaube*, 98).

[25] W. S. Vorster, "The Meaning of ΠΑΡΡΗΣΙΑ in the Epistle to the Hebrews," *Neot* 5 (1971) 51–59.

tic markers for the term. It either denotes an action, a way of doing something, or a quality or characteristic feature.[26] Under the first stand three possible meanings: to act 1) with frankness of speech, 2) without limitation or hindrance, and 3) openly. Under the second, another three: the quality of 1) frankness, boldness, fearlessness, courage, 2) freedom, and 3) conviction.[27] He concluded that the use of παρρησία in Hebrews correlates with the wider NT usage. So in Heb 3:6 παρρησία means "conviction," in 4:16 it refers to "boldness" or "frankness" in approaching God, in 10:19 this boldness connotes "freedom" to enter the sanctuary and appear before the throne of God[28] in and through the death of Christ,[29] and in 10:35 the readers are exhorted not to throw away their παρρησία, which here as in 3:6 means "conviction." According to Vorster, ἀποβάλλειν παρρησίαν should be seen as the opposite of κατέχειν παρρησίαν in 3:6.[30]

The differences between Vorster and those he criticizes seem to be more semantic than anything else. He says, for example, that in 4:14–16 the recipients "are being commanded to approach the throne of God with *frankness* because their High Priest enables them to do so."[31] Is this really any different from those who say the access to God, of which the recipients can be quite confident, is grounded on or was won for them by the blood of Jesus Christ? Regarding 10:19, Vorster says, "The believer has the *freedom* to enter the sanctuary and appear before the throne of God in and through the death of Christ."[32] Vorster's new methodology, by and large, confirmed the findings of previous scholars.

---

[26] Cf. Schlier, *TWNT*, 5.870–71.

[27] Vorster, "The Meaning of ΠΑΡΡΗΣΙΑ," 54. Unfortunately, Vorster presents only the results of his componential analysis of the noun παρρησία in the NT, and his categories are not clearly enough defined. So it is difficult to tell why "conviction" in Phil 1:20 is different from "courage," which fits the context better. Also under "freedom" Vorster lists only Eph 3:12. Both Schlier (*TWNT*, 5.881) and Peterson ("Zur Bedeutungsgeschichte," 292) interpreted παρρησία there as "freedom of access to God." Is that really different from Vorster's simple freedom?

[28] Vorster, "The Meaning of ΠΑΡΡΗΣΙΑ," 57; cf. Peterson, "Zur Bedeutungsgeschichte," 292.

[29] See Schlier, *TWNT*, 5.882–83; van Unnik, "The Christian's Freedom of Speech," 287; O. Michel, *Der Brief an die Hebräer* (MeyerK 13; Göttingen: Vandenhoeck & Ruprecht, 1966[12]) 180.

[30] Vorster, "The Meaning of ΠΑΡΡΗΣΙΑ," 57; cf. Michel, *Hebräer*[12], 360.

[31] Vorster, "The Meaning of ΠΑΡΡΗΣΙΑ," 55.

[32] Ibid., 56. This is no different from what van Unnik claimed for 10:19, that because of Jesus' sacrifice Christians have the free right to enter the sanctuary ("The Christian's Freedom of Speech," 286).

Stanley Marrow's article on the meaning of παρρησία in the NT was heralded as something that was long overdue, since so little on the term existed in English. Marrow's study is more thorough than previous ones because it examines not only the secular Greek usage of the term but also treats the LXX and hellenistic-Jewish usage in great detail, thus filling a lacuna left by earlier work. So, for example, after his analysis of the LXX citations he says, "In the boldness of the righteous before God in prayer we have the most relevant use of *parrhēsia* in the New Testament, and that particularly in Hebrews and 1 John."[33] Marrow also posits a more specific point of reception for παρρησία in the religious sphere: hellenistic Judaism. Curiously, he wants to expand van Unnik's appreciation of the Jewish background as he clearly values the LXX material more.[34] Still, he shares something of van Unnik's reservation about assigning too great a role to the LXX in exerting influence on NT authors.

> The use of *parrhēsia* in the Gentile Hellenistic world remained within the sphere of human relations. In the evidence we possess, its crossing into the religious sphere must have taken place in the Hellenistic-Jewish circle of the LXX translators, and in the works of Philo and Josephus. It is curious—and perhaps not much more than this—that the NT use of *parrhēsia* and its verb reflects none of the meanings current in the Gentile world, though, of course the term itself does maintain the basic meaning of saying everything freely and openly. The expected influence of the LXX, on the other hand, should not be exaggerated.[35]

Two texts from Josephus (*AJ* 2.4.4§52; 5.1.13§38) help Marrow to solidify his claim for the uniquely hellenistic-Jewish usage of παρρησία in relation to God (πρὸς τὸν θεόν), where it passes out of the sphere of human relations into the religious arena.[36]

Specifically on Hebrews, Marrow advances the discussion of 10:19–25 where he finds "an altogether new element" in our understanding of παρρησία. The newness derives from his notice of the parallelism between "a true heart in full assurance of faith" in v. 22 and "the confession of our hope without wavering" in v. 23, which he com-

---

[33] Marrow, "*Parrhēsia*," 438.

[34] Van Unnik had observed, "But is it correct to say with Russell Scott that the application in the N.T. stands quite apart and that it is 'a new ingredient put into the religious consciousness by Christianity'? The witness of Philo and Josephus makes this an unwarranted statement" ("The Christian's Freedom of Speech," 274).

[35] Marrow, "*Parrhēsia*," 439–40.

[36] Ibid. See also Schlier, *TWNT*, 5.883.

bines with the eschatological foundation of the saving event itself in v. 25 ("as you see the day drawing near").[37]

According to Marrow, the distinctive NT use of παρρησία lies in the understanding that it is a "gift granted to the Christian for direct access to God in prayer and for the untrammeled freedom to proclaim, 'in season and out of season,' the gospel of his Son."[38] So, too, his claim that in the NT "openness towards God distinguishes it [παρρησία] from mere freedom of speech, from frankness and openness of amity and friendship, and from the cynic boldness of unbridled discourse and mindless criticism."[39]

Otto Michel defines παρρησία in Hebrews as an element of faith characterized by confidence and joy for a community whose faith is at risk. He gives it an interpersonal dimension when he says, "Sie äußert sich sowohl im Verhältnis zu Gott wie auch zu den Menschen."[40] Now following Käsemann, Michel agrees that παρρησία has subjective and objective dimensions, encompassing both an inner gift and the external expression of it.[41] This applies especially to the use of the word in Heb 3:6 and 4:16. Distinctive in Michel's interpretation of παρρησία is his disagreement with Peterson's claim that in the NT the term should be understood to derive as much from hellenism as from hellenistic Judaism.[42] Rather, says Michel, "Es geht im Hebr um Kultrecht und Gewißheit der eschatologischen Gemeinde, nicht um das Vorrecht einzelner Frommer oder Philosophen."[43] Michel is thus quite willing to regard the background of hellenistic Judaism, especially in the context of the synagogue, as more influential on the NT appreciation of παρρησία than is the secular Greek usage.[44] Especially in Hebrews is παρρησία shaped by the saving deed of Jesus

---

[37] Ibid., 440–41. For a similar assessment, see D. Peterson, *Hebrews and Perfection: An Examination of the Concept of Perfection in the 'Epistle to the Hebrews'* (SNTSMS 47; Cambridge: Cambridge University Press, 1982) 79–81.

[38] Marrow, "*Parrhēsia*," 446.

[39] Ibid., 444. Marrow sides with Michel (*Hebräer*[12], 181) in questioning Peterson's view that the NT background of παρρησία is as much hellenistic as hellenistic-Jewish ("Zur Bedeutungsgeschichte," 192). For independent confirmation of the differences between the Cynic understanding of παρρησία and its use in Q and John, see Klassen, "ΠΑΡΡΗΣΙΑ in the Johannine Writings," 25 (in this volume, pp. 233, 243–44, 251–54).

[40] O. Michel, *Der Brief an die Hebräer* (MeyerK 13; Göttingen: Vandenhoeck & Ruprecht, 1984[14]) 77.

[41] Ibid., 179.

[42] See Peterson, "Zur Bedeutungsgeschichte," 292.

[43] Michel, *Hebräer*[14], 181.

[44] Ibid., 180.

Christ, which makes possible the community's approach to God and its reception of grace (4:16). If there is any secular hellenistic background to this understanding of παρρησία in Hebrews, it may derive more from oriental royal law than from philosophy.[45]

Michel revisits the question of subjective/objective dimensions of παρρησία when he comments on Heb 10:19 and 10:35. His discussion helps us to see how difficult it is to grasp these dimensions and their relation to one another. In 10:19 the objective element is quite present since the instrument of surety for entrance into the sanctuary is clearly expressed: the blood of Christ. When one turns, however, to 10:35, where the community is exhorted not to throw away its παρρησία, one sees the author tilting more towards the subjective. Michel, however, concludes that the objective element may include the subjective, but the subjective does not include the objective.[46]

Commenting on Heb 3:1–6, Harold Attridge echoes, too, the idea that παρρησία has both subjective and objective aspects. To the secular Greek understanding of free speech he joins the confidence in approaching God, especially in prayer, which derives from hellenistic Judaism and the NT. That sense, he says, is characteristic of the use of the word in Hebrews, with the addition that "it also refers to a public demonstration of Christian commitment."[47] The subjective aspect is captured by the sense of confidence with which the Christian may stand before and approach God, while the objective aspect derives from the fact that such free access was made possible through the sacrifice of Christ. Commenting on παρρησία in Heb 10:19, Attridge claims that it is the forgiveness resulting from the shedding of Christ's blood that grounds the Christian's confidence and makes possible entry into the divine presence.[48] Both aspects, subjective and

---

[45] Ibid., 181; see also H. Jaeger, "Παρρησία and fiducia," *SP* 1 (TU 63; ed. K. Aland and F. L. Cross; Berlin: Akademie, 1957) 225; H. Montefiore, *Commentary on the Epistle to the Hebrews*, (London: Adam & Charles Black, 1964), 92; Moffatt, *Hebrews*, 60.

[46] Michel, *Hebraer*[14], 344; Grässer, *Der Glaube*, 109; N. A. Dahl, "A New Way of Living: The Approach to God According to Hebrews 10:19–25," *Int* 5 (1951) 100–12. For the opposite view, see C. Spicq, *L'Épitre aux Hébreux*, 2.315.

[47] H. Attridge, *The Epistle to the Hebrews* (Hermeneia; Philadelphia: Fortress, 1989) 111–12. See also Montefiore, *Hebrews*, 73. This brings the use of the word closer to its use in John and constitutes, too, a distinctive NT meaning for παρρησία, since, as Klassen points out, "the use of παρρησία as synonymous with public (vs. private) is practically unknown in Hellenistic Greek although it approaches the way Philo uses it once" ("ΠΑΡΡΗΣΙΑ in the Johannine Writings," 23; in this volume, p. 243).

[48] Ibid., 284–85.

objective, are found again at Heb 10:35, where the warning against apostasy, Μὴ ἀποβάλητε οὖν τὴν παρρησίαν ὑμῶν, attempts to inculcate an attitude of boldness that is related also to faith and hope. Of this Attridge says, "Yet this public boldness is rooted in the assurance of access to God through the sacrifice of Christ."[49]

Several things emerge as distinctive in Attridge's treatment. Like Marrow, he shows a greater willingness than previous commentators to grant to the LXX and hellenistic Judaism a more influential role in defining the background of the NT's use of παρρησία. So he draws on texts such as Wis 5:1 and Philo, *Her.* 5 and 21, to set the background of confidence in prayer.[50] He stresses the public dimension of παρρησία in Hebrews, which remains implicit in only a few previous interpretations.[51] Attridge disagrees with Grässer's view of παρρησία as a synonym for πίστις and ὑπομονή. He grants, however, that taken together these concepts contribute to the attitude Hebrews is trying to inculcate in its recipients.[52]

In his massive commentary on Hebrews, Hans-Friedrich Weiss gives a clear summary of his understanding of παρρησία, which is then consistently articulated in the individual comments on the four places where the word occurs.[53] Weiss' understanding of Hebrews as a "Trost- und Mahnrede" directed to Christians who need strengthening in their faith, hangs to a large extent on the role he assigns to παρρησία.[54] Critical to his appreciation of Hebrews as consolation and warning are 4:14–16 and 10:19–39, two controlling paraenetic sections of the letter where παρρησία plays a key role.[55] As consolation and warning, Hebrews has a pastoral aim which seeks to win the conscience

---

[49] Ibid., 300.

[50] Ibid., 111. On the LXX background linking παρρησία to prayer, see W. Stählin, "Parousia und Parrhesia," *Wahrheit und Verkündigung: M. Schmaus Festschrift* (ed. L. Scheffczyk, W. Dettloff, and R. Heinzmann; München, Paderborn; Wien: F. Schöningh, 1967) 233, and Klassen, "ΠΑΡΡΗΣΙΑ in the Johannine Writings," 9–10; see pp. 234–35 of this volume.

[51] Perhaps this is what van Unnik means by its being "the open confession amidst opposition" ("The Christian's Freedom of Speech," 286), and what Vorster means by the freedom that the individual has before God and other humans ("The Meaning of ΠΑΡΡΗΣΙΑ," 57).

[52] Attridge, *Hebrews,* 300; see van Unnik, "The Christian's Freedom of Speech," 286.

[53] H.-F. Weiss, *Der Brief an die Hebräer* (MeyerK 13; Göttingen: Vandenhoeck & Ruprecht, 1991¹⁵) 251–53.

[54] Ibid., 48.

[55] Weiss calls these two sections "entscheidende Schaltstellen" (decisive control centers) for the letter's composition (ibid., 52).

of the recipients. This purpose is especially clear in the use of the word παρρησία, which is a key concept meaning "confidence" and "surety."

About παρρησία Weiss makes three main observations. First, παρρησία is always related in context to ὁμολογία, the confession of the community. To that extent it means "confidence" as a quality of faith and can be exchanged with πίστις and μακροθυμία. Second, it has both a subjective and an objective meaning. The confidence is subjective, but the empowerment to confidence is objective because it is grounded in the salvific work of Christ. Agreeing with Käsemann, Weiss sees this as the "acquisition of a pretext." Third, παρρησία has an eschatological character, especially in 10:19, where it is linked to the confession of hope. Thus παρρησία and ἐλπίς belong together in Hebrews.[56]

In my opinion, Weiss pays more attention to function than previous interpreters and grants παρρησία a greater role in Hebrews as a whole. This extends, too, to the definition of its genre as "Trost-und Mahnrede," since Weiss sees παρρησία as integral to the form and function of Hebrews. In part, he comes to this view through an attempt to synthesize the results of previous studies. Evidence for this synthesis presents itself in the way Weiss uses Käsemann's subjective/objective distinction, Grässer's concern for the place of παρρησία in the faith thematic of Hebrews, and Marrow's interest in the eschatological character of the word. By integrating these previous interpretations and assigning παρρησία a greater role in the overall purpose of Hebrews, Weiss makes it more important not only for the explanation of the genre of Hebrews but for its theology as well.

One may question whether Weiss has too easily combined the work of previous commentators with his own distinctive view of the function of παρρησία in Hebrews. Given the problems which stem from determining precisely the background, meaning, and function of the word in Hebrews, has he oversimplified?

This review of literature on παρρησία in Hebrews has revealed an amazing agreement among interpreters over a long period of time. There are some disagreements and attempts to modify previous positions, but a clear consensus exists on at least three points: (1) that the word has the basic meaning of "confidence", with both a subjective and objective moment to it; (2) that the objective aspect is

---

[56] Ibid., 53, 252–53.

grounded in the work of Jesus as high priest and the guarantee of the promises made of old; and (3) that its look to the future gives it eschatological character. The repetition and refinement of these ideas testify to a development that builds on the works of previous authors. Most of the substantive disagreements have to do with background issues, especially the question whether the secular Greek background plays a greater role than the LXX and hellenistic Judaism or vice versa. Weiss follows in suit but also takes the discussion one step further by synthesizing the work of past scholars. By integrating the views of Käsemann, Grässer, and Marrow and placing them within a wider context, he shows the durability of the collective wisdom on the use of παρρησία in Hebrews.

The Need for ΠΑΡΡΗΣΙΑ in Hebrews

There is little need to rethink the definition of παρρησία in Hebrews, given the consensus of past scholarship on the basic meanings of "confidence" and "openness" before God. It may be worthwhile, however, to return to the question posed by van Unnik about the special reasons why NT authors used this word, and to examine further the function of παρρησία in Hebrews.

Whatever can be said about the situation of the Hebrews community that occasioned this letter must be related to the dialectic created by the alternation of theological exposition with paraenesis within the letter. As Attridge has noted, Hebrews is structured around two polarities. On the one hand, we have the letter's christology, which is developed mainly through the exposition of scripture. On the other hand, there is the exhortation to faithfulness. Attridge sees the latter advanced through two types of paraenesis, one static and the other dynamic. These two are summarized respectively in the expressions "let us hold fast" (Heb 3:6, 14; 4:14 and 10:22) and "let us approach" (4:16, 10:22).[57]

Interesting for our study is the way παρρησία plays an integral role in both types of paraenesis. Three out of the four instances of its use in the letter are found among these places which articulate the main impulses of the letter's paraenesis. That is no mere coincidence, but underscores the fact that the appropriation of παρρησία

---

[57] Attridge, *Hebrews*, 21–23.

in Hebrews has a deliberate purpose. As the attitude the author wishes to instill in the readers, it accompanies the main hortatory directives, thus qualifying precisely how one should hold fast and in what way one should approach, boldly and with confidence. Why that is especially necessary for the readers to do has not been clearly enough articulated in the past. Some commentators have suggested that this was necessary because of apostasy, wavering faith, or a situation of persecution within the community. Unfortunately, the actual situation which requires such a dramatic reassurance is often only vaguely described. What is meant by apostasy, wavering faith, or persecution is left to the imagination of the readers.

Barnabas Lindars, on the other hand, has proposed a quite specific community problem which the letter addresses, one that can shed light on why the author exhorts the readers to παρρησία.[58] It is unfortunate, however, that whereas Lindars describes well a situation where a restoration of confidence in the salvific work of Christ is badly needed, he never mentions the role of παρρησία in this. As a modest contribution to the discussion of the place of παρρησία in Hebrews, I would like to suggest that Lindars' description of the community problem gives convincing reasons for the author's special use of παρρησία. In my opinion, παρρησία plays a distinctive role in the self-definition of the Hebrews community.

The situation Lindars describes is one that calls for a persuasive argument that will capture the imaginations of the readers and provide them with the reason for the restoration of their confidence in Christ. For this reason, Lindars emphasizes that Hebrews is a piece of deliberative rhetoric, aimed at winning over community members who have serious doubts and reservations of conscience about the efficacy of Christ's death for atonement and the forgiveness of sin.[59]

These Christians were once hellenistic Jews. Shortly after their conversion they were no longer sure that the sacrificial death of Christ was effective for the atonement of sins. This crisis of conscience drove them back to their Jewish roots. Whether they were actually offering sacrifices for sins, Lindars can not say with certainty. He stresses, however, the emotional connection between these community members and their Jewish heritage, which takes a form of solidarity with the old tradition. This, he says, subjected them to the emotional

---

[58] B. Lindars, "Rhetorical Structure," 382–406.
[59] Ibid., 383.

attraction of the Judaism they had left behind. Therefore, all they needed to do was to resume practices that expressed this solidarity, and if this involved resumption of contact with Judaism, a "return to the local synagogue where they could obtain the benefit of purification of sins," that could have been enough to force a break with Christianity.[60]

The task, then, for the author is to persuade them that they need not return to this solidarity with their past. While Lindars agrees with many commentators that the center of the argument is located in 7:1–10:18, he disagrees with them that this is also where the climax of the argument is to be found. Rather, he locates that in 10:19–12:29.[61] Interesting here is the way the central christological exposition works together with the final great exhortation that follows.

In the christological exposition it is necessary to provide the ground of renewed confidence, so that these community members will not feel the need to return to the synagogue rituals in order to obtain atonement for sins. The author relies solely on the requirements for atonement found in the Pentateuch and does not supplement them with the actual practice of the Jerusalem Temple. This is an important signal for Lindars that the author here is really only interested in the standards for sacrifice, atonement, and purification as established in the law. If the author can show how the death of Jesus meets the requirements for atonement set forth by the law, then the main objective will have been achieved. Thus the lost or threatened confidence of the diffident community members will be restored. For this reason, the author chooses those requirements of the law which the readers can agree on as central to the Jewish understanding of atonement, and he applies them to the death of Christ.[62] The stress on the ability of Christ's death to purify their consciences (9:14) shows the author's interest. So, according to Lindars, the writer needs only to describe the effects of Christ's death and does not have to explain how his sacrifice works to bring about atonement.[63]

---

[60] Ibid., 384–90; 402–04.

[61] Ibid., 384.

[62] Lindars singles out the following: "Atonement requires the ministry of the High Priest: Jesus is a high priest. Atonement requires the sprinkling of blood: Jesus' blood was shed. Atonement requires the entry of the high priest through the veil into the holy of holies: Jesus passed through the veil of his flesh to enter into the presence of God in heaven" ("Rhetorical Structure," 403).

[63] Ibid., 399.

As I have argued elsewhere, how the sacrificial death of Jesus brings about effective atonement is addressed by this author.[64] As an essential part of the author's attempt at persuasion, he makes the propriety of Jesus' death a necessary element of the letter's christological argument; he does so in order to demonstrate the superiority of Christ's sacrifice. If this propriety were not established, then—apart from the permanence of the sacrifice (9:12)—there would only be parity between the effects of the sacrifices required by the law and the effects of Christ's sacrificial death. In the interest of persuasion, the author must demonstrate how the high priestly work of Jesus is more efficacious and exceeds the mere requirements of the Jewish law for sacrifice, atonement, and purification.

On this ground, too, rests the cause for παρρησία in Hebrews. If the addressees have lost the παρρησία they once had, or are on the verge of losing it, then the author not only must exhort them to renew it but must also provide the ground for this renewal in the main christological argument of the letter. Therefore, where παρρησία occurs in Hebrews, one also finds the basis for why such confidence "to hold fast" and "to approach" is not in vain. That fact is confirmed in the discussion of the subjective/objective quality of παρρησία in Hebrews.

Thus the author provides a rationale for confidence. In 3:6 the exhortation to παρρησία rests on the superiority of Christ to Moses. In 4:16 and 10:19 the παρρησία that enables the approach to the throne of grace and the entrance into the sanctuary rests on the superiority of Christ's high priesthood. In 10:35 the exhortation not to throw away their παρρησία recalls what confidence the believers had when they first left Judaism and came to Christianity. This entailed suffering, exposure to public abuse and sympathy with those abused. All this was happily endured because of their belief that they indeed had a better and a more permanent possession (10:32–34).

The contrast motif in this paraenesis is striking. Reminding the readers of what they already know or had previously experienced is, of course, quite typical of epistolary paraenesis.[65] Given Lindars' description of the community situation, the contrast of what they once knew with what they now know is all the more interesting. So one wonders what the move from the synagogue to Christianity was

---

[64] A. C. Mitchell, "The Use of πρέπειν and Rhetorical Propriety in Hebrews 2:10," *CBQ* 54 (1992) 681–701.

[65] See Malherbe, "Hellenistic Moralists," 280–82.

like and what role παρρησία may have played in helping Christians make a transition from one to the other. As has already been noted, many recent authors are willing to regard the synagogue setting as the most likely origin of the word's reception into Christianity. Is it possible that παρρησία functioned in a similar way in both contexts and became a point of self-definition for Christians, particularly for the Hebrews' community? Can that be why the author stresses the objective ground of confidence for the readers? A look at what van Unnik saw as particular to the use of παρρησία in Acts is instructive here.

Van Unnik found that in Acts παρρησία is used in relation to "the preaching in the synagogues and to the Jews."[66] Often in these contexts is παρρησία characteristic of the bold defense Christian preachers must make in order to maintain their beliefs in the face of opposition in the synagogue or before the authorities (Acts 4:13, 29, 31; 9:27 [see 9:22]; 13:46; 14:3; 18:26; 19:8; 26:26). It seems, then, that in Luke's view the synagogue setting afforded one the right to proclaim boldly one's belief before God and fellow humans. This right appears to have been extended to people with differing views, i.e. those who may espouse different beliefs, regardless of the consequences of their free speech. Prescinding from the question of the historicity of these accounts, one can say, at the very least, that Luke understood the context of free speech in the synagogue to have created opportunities for Christian preachers to apply παρρησία in their work. Perhaps this Lucan view offers further evidence for the claim that Jewish Christians, accustomed to the right to παρρησία in the synagogue, had indeed mediated its use to Christian communities.

That παρρησία played an important role in the synagogue setting can also be inferred from Philo's discussion of what happens to proselytes in the conversion process. He speaks of their need to appropriate certain virtues. Conversion means basically passing from an unvirtuous state to a virtuous one. Thus he lists passing from ignorance to knowledge, from senselessness to good sense, from incontinence to continence, from injustice to justice, and from timidity to boldness.[67] The word he uses to connote boldness is θαρραλεότης,

---

[66] Van Unnik, "The Christian's Freedom of Speech," 280. For a new assessment of Acts' use of παρρησία, see the treatment by Sara C. Winter in Chapter Nine of this volume.

[67] Philo, Virt. 180.

which along with other forms of the verb θαρρεῖν is a substitute for
παρρησία elsewhere in his writings.[68]

Philo speaks, too, of the conditions of conversion and what kind
of special care is necessary for the neophytes. His remarks may attest
to the practice of hellenistic psychagogy within the context of the
synagogue.[69] He tells of how Moses welcomed the proselytes and
exhorted others to do likewise, and how they needed to be afforded
special friendship because they have left "their country, their kinsfolk
and their friends for the sake of virtue and religion."[70] This is especially interesting in light of what he says about his own confidence
before God:

> Am I not a wanderer from my country, an outcast from my kinsfolk,
> an alien from my father's house? Do not all men call me excommuni-
> cate, exile, desolate, disenfranchised? But Thou, Master, art my coun-
> try, my kinsfolk, my paternal hearth, my franchise, my free speech
> (παρρησία), my great and glorious and inalienable wealth.[71]

This text is found within a discussion of confidence before God, where
one has the courage to say what one feels. The contrast motif here,
too, is quite striking, and the designation of God as a replacement
for all that is lost or inaccessible, including παρρησία, provides the
objective ground for confidence and free speech. Do we find here
evidence of a process role that seeks to bring one to παρρησία from
the time of conversion, through the various stages of nurturing, to
mature religious faith, the point where an advanced individual, such
as Philo, has total confidence before God?

---

[68] Philo, *Her.* 19–30; *Ios.* 222. Josephus also uses the words synonymously in *AJ*
2.4.4.§52; 2.6.7§131–33. See also Epict. *Diss.* 3.22.93–96, where one finds θαρρήσῃ
παρρησιάζεσθαι; Lucian, *Demonax* 50; and Klassen, "ΠΑΡΡΗΣΙΑ in the Johannine Writings," 7 n. 2. The substitution of θαρρεῖν for παρρησιάζεσθαι is also found at Hebrews 13:6 (see P. Joüon, "Divers sens de παρρησία dans le Nouveau Testament,"
RSR 30 [1940] 241 n. 3). Peterson noticed the phenomenon in Plutarch and noted
that in Christian literature the two concepts belong together ("Zur Bedeutungsgeschichte," 291 n. 6).

[69] On hellenistic psychagogy, see Malherbe, "Hellenistic Moralists," 301–04; idem,
Moral Exhortation: A Greco-Roman Sourcebook (LEC 4; Philadelphia: Westminster, 1986)
48–67; E. Asmis, "Philodemus' Epicureanism," *ANRW* 2.36.4 (1990) 2393–95; and
C. Glad, "Frank Speech, Flattery, and Friendship in Philodemus" (paper presented
to the Hellenistic Moral Philosophy and Early Christianity Group at the annual
meeting of the Society of Biblical Literature, San Francisco, CA, November, 1992).
A revised version of this paper appears as Chapter Two of this volume.

[70] Philo, *Spec.* 1.51–52; see also 4.178.

[71] Philo, *Her.* 26–27; the translation is that of F. H. Colson in the LCL.

Against this background, παρρησία in Hebrews is especially interesting. If the wavering believers are relatively new converts, as Lindars has suggested, and are now under pressure to return to the local synagogue, it might be good to consider the function of exhorting to firm παρρησία as psychagogic.[72] Whether the pressure they suffer is from the outside or is self-imposed, they are living in a situation of uncertainty and stand in need of spiritual guidance.[73] Tension between the community and the local synagogue seems, then, to be part of the community's history.[74] Perhaps they are not unlike the proselytes Philo describes, who have left family, home and friends.

So Lindars is right to think that Heb 10:19–39 addresses not so much a situation of apostasy or faith-at-risk as it does the intended return to the synagogue by community members who have lost confidence in the efficacy of the death of Christ for atonement and purification of conscience. Had Lindars noticed the presence and function of παρρησία in this section, he could have strengthened his argument.

In an attempt to offer the troubled believers consolation, the author's exhortation not to throw away their παρρησία plays a vital role on two fronts. The first front is structural, as it forms an *inclusio* in 10:35 with 10:19. Lindars observed that the structural symmetry often noticed by commentators rests on the rhetorical device of inclusion and on the letter's balanced proportions. The inclusion is designed to help the audience grasp the argument or a particular part of it.[75] Here the inclusion is doubly important. On the one hand, it reinforces the paraenesis of 10:19–35, and, on the other, it forms a wider inclusion with 4:14–16. The repeated mention of παρρησία through the technique of inclusion helps to accomplish the mnemonic function that is

---

[72] H.-F. Weiss has stressed the pastoral purpose of the letter as a whole and how the exhortation to παρρησία forms an integral part of this "pastoral-seelsorgerliches Grundanliegen" (*Hebräer*, 51–53.).

[73] Lindars calls it a pressure of conscience but does not identify the source. That there would be external pressure is not implausible, since Lindars presupposes that the community had earlier made a break with Judaism (Lindars, "Rhetorical Structure," 389).

[74] On the tensions leading to the separation of Christian communities from the synagogue, see B. Wander, *Trennungs-prozesse zwischen Frühem Christentum und Judentum im 1.Jahrhundert n. Chr.* (TANZ 16; Tübingen and Basel: A. Francke, 1994); D. Flusser, *Bermerkungen eines Judes zur christlichen Theologie* (Abhandlung zum christlich-jüdischen Dialog 16; München: Kaiser, 1984) 94–102; G. Theissen, "Zur Entstehung des Christentums aus dem Judentum," *Kirche und Israel* 3 (1988) 179–89.

[75] Lindars, "Rhetorical Structure," 384.

so important in paraenesis. In addition to that, as several commentators have observed, this wider inclusion is especially important because it frames the letter's main theological argument.[76]

The second front is paraenetic. The ability to enter the sanctuary and to draw near with true hearts and clear consciences and to hold fast to the ὁμολογία rests on the firm conviction that comes from παρρησία. Only those who have true hearts and clear consciences can so conduct themselves before God and fellow humans with παρρησία.[77]

Fascinating here in the appeal not to throw away this παρρησία is the implication that such a rejection will occur when they return to the synagogue. They, of course, could have argued that a return to the synagogue would restore the παρρησία they once had, which was then based on the efficacy of synagogue rituals to purify their consciences.[78] One must wonder if such claims and counter-claims were made. We have seen that it is likely that bringing the proselyte to confidence was part of the psychagogic traditions of hellenistic Judaism. Hebrews witnesses to a similar phenomenon within a Christian community, where psychagogy is employed to sustain one's confidence

---

[76] Peterson sees these two paraenetic sections, 4:14–16 and 10:19–35, as pivotal in the letter's structure (*Hebrews and Perfection*, 75). H.-F. Weiss agrees, too, on the importance of these sections in delineating the genre and purpose of Hebrews (*Hebräer*, 52). Attridge recognizes the *inclusio* formed by the mention of παρρησία in 10:19 and 10:35 and the close parallel "in its internal structure and phraseology" between 4:14–16 and 10:19–25 (*Hebrews*, 283–84). See also, F. J. Schierse, *Verheißung und Heilsvollendung: Zur theologischen Grundfrage des Hebräerbriefes* (MüThSt 9; München: K. Zink, 1955) 199–203; W. Nauck, "Zum Aufbau des Hebräerbriefes," *Judentum, Urchristentum, Kirche* (J. Jeremias Festschrift; ed. W. Eltester; BZNW 26; Berlin: A. Töpelmann, 1960) 203–04.

[77] On the relationship of conscience and heart in Hebrews, see Peterson, *Hebrews and Perfection*, 133–36. Marrow sees the link between conscience and the ability to speak openly with God as uniquely hellenistic-Jewish ("*Parrhēsia*," 438–39), and for the author of Hebrews it is likely that this is the origin of the idea (see Philo, *Her.* 5–7; *Spec.* 1.203; Josephus, *AJ* 2.4.4§52; Peterson "Zur Bedeutungsgeschichte," 298). Yet one has to reckon with Epict. *Diss.* 3.22.93–96, where the Cynic as a friend and servant of the gods can speak confidently with παρρησία because of purity of conscience. See also A. J. Malherbe, *Paul and the Popular Philosophers* (Minneapolis: Fortress, 1989) 13 n. 10; 102, 157. On the relationship between conscience and cult in hellenistic Judaism and the transformation of it in Hebrews, see J. Stelzenberger, *Syneidesis im Neuen Testament* (Abhandlungen zur Moraltheologie 1; Paderborn: F. Schöningh, 1961) 56–65.

[78] Without positing a return to Judaism as the cause, but rather "sluggishness" in faith, D. Peterson understands 10:32–39 to "indicate a certain *regression* from a former state of boldness and faith in confrontation with public hostility" (*Hebrews and Perfection*, 178).

as well. Is this, then, part of what Christians learned in the synagogue setting and brought over to Christianity? Can it be that this
is one way that παρρησία made its way into the NT? It is likely that
in Hebrews the word was taken over from hellenistic Judaism and
adapted to a Christian psychagogic purpose, where it was redefined
with respect to its objective ground, the sacrificial death of Jesus.[79]
Thus the author appears to distinguish between the παρρησία one
finds in the synagogue and that found within the community addressed in the letter. These certainly seem to be the implications in
Hebrews for the exhortations to hold on to παρρησία and not to
throw it away.

Therefore, the use of παρρησία in Hebrews is indeed striking. It
connotes a boldness to stand before God and fellow humans and to
be confident in what one believes. To this extent it is used in a
way similar to what we find in other NT writings where such
confidence plays a role in the relationship of the Christian community to Judaism, such as in Acts and John.[80] In Hebrews the use of
παρρησία is quite specifically tailored to a situation where there is
some tension between both groups. The author's stress on maintaining παρρησία helps to clarify what is at stake in the interface between the two.

If the community members, who want to return to the synagogue,
believe that they will recover there the παρρησία they once enjoyed
and now miss, the author of Hebrews strongly disagrees. Rather,
in this author's estimation, a return to the synagogue will bring
about a loss of παρρησία. Whereas the troubled believers may have
argued that they can only receive the purity of conscience they
seek by participating in synagogue rituals of atonement, the author of Hebrews is certain that it can come only from the high
priestly work of Jesus, whose sacrificial death is the solid basis for
παρρησία.

---

[79] According to Klassen ("ΠΑΡΡΗΣΙΑ in the Johannine Writings," 22–23 [see pp.
240–43 of this volume]), παρρησία in John means speaking plainly or openly in a
situation of conflict (John 10:24; 18:19–23). On other aspects of synagogue life taken
over and transformed by Christians, see P. Borgen, *Philo, John, and Paul: New Perspectives on Judaism and Early Christianity* (BJS 131; Atlanta: Scholars, 1987) 207–32.

[80] Van Unnik ("The Christian's Freedom of Speech," 279–83) has certainly stressed
this in his discussion of the word in Acts, and, although Klassen does not emphasize
this side of the word's use in John, he has noted the frequency of it ("ΠΑΡΡΗΣΙΑ in
the Johannine Writings," 22–23, 36).

Conclusion

This study has tried to show that the meaning of παρρησία in Hebrews is best grasped when it is understood against the background of the community situation addressed by the letter. Thus the stress has been on the paraenetic function of παρρησία in Hebrews, where an appreciation of the pastoral problem, which the author faces, can highlight the importance of παρρησία in the letter. The author's psychagogic approach is directed to the support of believers who need their confidence renewed. The main tactic is to be quite positive in encouraging the readers to renew their παρρησία. This task is facilitated by the author's own understanding of παρρησία, which we delineated in the review of literature on its meaning in Hebrews. It is a subjective feeling based on the objective reality of the Christ event. It flows from a pure conscience and a true heart. It is required for faith and hope, but is not synonymous with them. It is the virtue that empowers the proclamation of the Christian ὁμολογία and facilitates the approach to the throne of grace and entrance into the heavenly sanctuary. In this regard it is needed very much in the present, but it enables the believers to look to the eschatological future, which is the reward that accompanies it. But the author knows, too, that for all the strength it connotes, it is fragile and can slip from one's grasp as easily as it can be thrown away. So we understand the meaning and function of the author's exhortation to "hold on to confidence."

ΠΑΡΡΗΣΙΑ IN THE JOHANNINE CORPUS

William Klassen

Introduction

Slightly over a decade ago Stanley Marrow observed that although the occurrence of παρρησία in the NT was not infrequent and its significance not unimportant, there was only one English article on it in the vast amount of literature on word studies in the NT.[1] That observation no longer holds about the word itself; nevertheless, it still remains the case that no one has analysed the usage of the word in the Johannine corpus. No special study of the use of παρρησία in John exists, and even in the many studies of the word in the NT which are now published,[2] little attention is paid to the Johannine corpus. This paper examines whether the evidence justifies such a lack of attention to Johannine usage. Our purpose then is: (1) to review the results of the research into the place of παρρησία in Stoic-Cynic thought;[3] (2) to review the results of the research into

---

[1] Stanley B. Marrow, "*Parrhēsia* and the NT," *CBQ* 44 (1982) 431–46, esp. 431. Marrow mentions W. C. van Unnik, "The Christian's Freedom of Speech in the New Testament," *BJRL* 44 (1962) 466–88, now reprinted in *Sparsa Collecta: The Collected Essays of W. C. van Unnik* (3 vols.; NovTSup 29–31; Leiden: Brill, 1973–83) 2.269–89. Van Unnik refers to the articles on "Boldness" in *ERE* 2 (1909) 785–86 by D. Russell Scott and in *DAC* 1 (1915) 156–57 by T. Nicol. In his article on "Boldness" in *DB* 1 (1898) 309–10, James Hastings describes τολμηρός as "reckless" and by way of contrast refers to παρρησία as a "nobler boldness" which "reaches a higher manifestation under the Gospel, which is its very foundation." He has only two passing references to texts in John. E. Peterson, "Zur Bedeutungsgeschichte von παρρησία," *Reinhold Seeberg Festschrift* (ed. Wilhelm Koepp; 2 vols.; Leipzig: D. W. Scholl, 1929) 1.283–97, is a fine beginning for any study. He deals with John on pages 292–93.

[2] For example, Marrow, "*Parrhēsia* and the NT," 40–41; Peterson, "Zur Bedeutungsgeschichte," 292–93; H. Jaeger, "Παρρησία et fiducia," *SP* 1 (1957) 221–39, esp. 226; G. J. M. Bartelink, "Quelques observations sur παρρησία dans la littérature paléo-chrétienne," *Graecitas et latinitas christianorum primaeva*, Supplementa 3 (Nijmegen: Dekker & Van de Vegt, 1970) 7–57, esp. 33. The best treatment of παρρησία in the Johannine writings is by Schlier, "παρρησία, παρρησιάζομαι," *TWNT* 5 (1954) 869–84, esp. 877–80.

[3] See the essays in Part One of this volume by David Konstan, Clarence E. Glad, and Troels Engberg-Pedersen. In addition to these treatments, Jan Kindstrand, *Bion of Borysthenes* (Acta Universitatis Upsaliensis: Studia Graeca Upsaliensis

the meanings of the term in Hellenistic Judaism, especially in
the LXX and the Pseudepigrapha;[4] and (3) with the above as
backdrop, to ascertain the place this word or concept has in the
Johannine literature. The third of these three is the major goal of
this paper.

ΠΑΡΡΗΣΙΑ in Cynic-Stoic Sources

In order to understand the distinctiveness of Johannine usage it is
essential to study παρρησία among the Cynics of this time. It was a
self-defining term for them. Cynicism was either being revived or in
the ascendancy at the time John was writing.[5]

Clarence Glad in his analysis of frank speech, flattery and friendship in Philodemus concludes that παρρησία means "frank criticism"
or "frank speech" and that it is a "type of ὁμιλία and a *sine qua non*
of friendship." It may also be a behaviour or a way of life but always is a characteristic of friendship.[6]

One superb illustration of what we may call this friendly view of
παρρησία is Musonius Rufus.[7] Standing as he does between the Cynics
and the Stoics and living in the latter half of the first century CE,
his views on παρρησία are of particular interest. In one speech he
enumerates a number of things which are not evils and can be overcome even in exile, such as being cut off from friends, being unable
to cultivate the virtues, lacking the necessities of life, and being of ill-
repute. In this regard, he addresses the issue of whether exiles lose,
as Euripides seems to suggest, their personal liberty when deprived
of παρρησία. Musonius quotes Euripides' portrayal of Jocasta asking
Polyneices, her son, what misfortunes an exile has to bear. Polyneices

---

11; Stockholm: Almqvist & Wiksell, 1976), Margarethe Billerbeck, *Epiktet, Vom Kynismus*
(Philosophia Antiqua 34; Leiden: Brill, 1978) and *Der Kyniker Demetrius* (Philosophia
Antiqua 36; Leiden: Brill, 1979), and A. J. Malherbe, *Paul and Popular Philosophers*
(Minneapolis: Fortress, 1989) have made valued contributions to my work.

[4] Lack of space prevents an examination of the term in Philo and Josephus.

[5] Ronald F. Hock, "Cynics," *ABD* 1 (1992) 1221–26.

[6] Clarence E. Glad, "Frank Speech, Flattery, and Friendship in Philodemus" (paper
presented to the Hellenistic Moral Philosophy and Early Christianity Group at the
annual meeting of the Society of Biblical Literature, San Francisco, CA, November,
1992). A revised version of this paper appears as Chapter Two of this volume.

[7] On παρρησία, see Frg. IX, "That Exile is not an evil." All citations are from
Cora Lutz, "Musonius Rufus, 'The Roman Socrates,'" *YCS* 10 (1947) 3–147. Her
translations have occasionally been slightly modified.

answers: ἓν μὲν μέγιστον, οὐκ ἔχει παρρησίαν, "The greatest one of all, no longer having freedom of speech."[8] She replies: "You name the plight of slaves, not to be able to say what one thinks."[9] Musonius then goes on to describe the importance of παρρησία (freedom of speech):

> You are right, Euripides, when you say that it is the condition of a slave not to say what one thinks when one ought to speak, for it is not always, nor everywhere, nor before everyone that we should say what we think. But that one point, it seems to me, is not well-taken, that exiles do not have freedom of speech (παρρησία), if to you freedom of speech means not suppressing whatever one chances to think. For it is not as exiles that people fear to say what they think, but as people afraid lest from speaking pain or death or punishment or some other thing shall befall them. Fear is the cause of this, not exile (Frg. IX, Lutz 73–75).

In a quite incidental way Musonius thus declares his own view on παρρησία: always, everywhere, before everyone to say what we think.

Musonius cites Diogenes as the supreme model of freedom of speech (Frg. IX, Lutz 75). But he comes closer home and draws on his own experience. Though exiled, he has παρρησία and practices his freedom to speak:

> Have you or anyone else ever seen me cringing before anyone just because I am an exile.... No, I'll wager that you would say that you have never seen me complaining or disheartened because of my

---

[8] Lutz, "Musonius," 73. The passage quoted by Musonius is Eur. *Phoen.* 391. Demosthenes (frg. 21) also described παρρησία as the greatest value of citizenship in Athenian democracy and to lose it, its greatest conceivable loss (οὐδὲν ἂν εἴη τοῖς ἐλευθέροις μεῖζον ἀτύχημα τοῦ στέρεσθαι τῆς παρρησίας). Teles, in enumerating what people say about the plight of exiles, says that "they do not rule, cannot be trusted, and do not have παρρησία" (Frg. III, 23,4–5 Hense). For the text with a translation, see Edward O'Neil, *Teles [The Cynic Teacher]* (SBLTT 11; Missoula: Scholars Press, 1977) 23.

[9] Lutz, "Musonius," 73, quoting Eur. *Phoen.* 392. This aspect of the "plight of slaves" no doubt varied considerably. Athens especially sought to extend παρρησία to slaves. Menander (frg. 359) suggests that as long as you let slaves remain slaves they will become much better if you give them παρρησία, freedom to speak their minds. Demosthenes (*Or.* 9.3) asserts that in Athens slaves possess more παρρησία than do citizens elsewhere. Plutarch's comparison between the παρρησία of the Roman slaves who had been ordered to answer only questions directly put to them and the Athenian slaves, who were much freer to tell their masters whatever they cared to, also carries with it a recommendation that the latter course be followed (*De garr.* 511E). See L. Schmidt, *Die Ethik der alten Griechen* (2 vols.; Berlin: W. Hertz, 1882) 2.211.

banishment, for if I have been deprived of my country, I have not been deprived of my ability to endure exile (Frg. IX, Lutz 75).[10]

It is considered to Musonius' credit that he was able to affirm παρρησία and yet avoid the errors of the Cynics in the abuse of this gift. So Cora Lutz considers it laudable that "although he was aware of the morbid condition of both the individual and of the state, he neither fell into passive pessimism and despair nor thundered forth in invective." According to Lutz, he taught instead a "positive" program for creating a healthy and rational society and he did so with "fine courage and healing optimism."[11]

He consistently involved himself in correcting the ills of his society and paid the price for it without complaining. There is no doubt that Musonius had the boldness to address social issues of his time, whether that was blind faith in violence,[12] the role of women[13] or the basic issue of *philanthropia*.[14] He did it all from a fundamental ethical stance which assumed that good persons could have within themselves goodness as a "living law" and therefore each could be a royal personage.[15]

Musonius' student, Dio of Prusa, also considers παρρησία essential to a philosopher. For Dio, it is an integral part of independence to rise above the foolish talk of the crowd, paying no heed to it but rather "mocking their loquacity."[16] He cites Heracles as an example and concludes: "Unless you bring yourself to look with scorn (καταφρονῆσαι) upon all others, you will never end your state of wretchedness; instead you will always lead ... a hare's life," fearing the dogs, nets and eagles; "you will go about cowering and quaking before what people say" (*Or.* 66.24).

---

[10] See Max Pohlenz, *Die Stoa* (2 vols.; 2d ed.; Göttingen: Vandenhoeck & Ruprecht, 1959) 1.303.

[11] Lutz, "Musonius," 29 n. 128.

[12] See W. Klassen, "A 'Child of Peace' (Luke 10.6) in First Century Context," *NTS* 27 (1981) 488–506.

[13] See W. Klassen, "Musonius Rufus, Jesus, and Paul: Three First-Century Feminists," *From Jesus to Paul: Studies in Honour of Francis Wright Beare* (ed. P. Richardson and J. C. Hurd; Waterloo: Wilfrid Laurier Press, 1984) 185–206.

[14] See W. Klassen, "Humanitas as seen by Epictetus and Musonius Rufus," *Studi storico-religiosi* 1 (1977) 63–82.

[15] See W. Klassen, "The King as 'living law' with particular reference to Musonius Rufus," *SR* 14 (1985) 63–71.

[16] Dio Chrys. *Or.* 66.23: ἀδολεσχίας καταγελᾷ, jeers their prating/garrulity. Translations of Dio Chrysostom's orations are those of H. L. Crosby in the LCL, though sometimes slightly modified.

People, he says, are of two kinds, and of these, "the [better] one is reasonable and gentle and truly mild, disposed to accept παρρησία and not caring to be pampered in everything . . . grateful to those who admonish and instruct, these are the people whom I regard as partaking of the divine and royal nature . . ." (*Or.* 32.27). The gentleness which accepts παρρησία also gives it in like manner. A standard comparison in this period is the contrast between the harshness of certain types of παρρησία "with gentle speech such as that of a nurse who knows her charges."[17]

It is today fashionable to see lines of influence from Cynicism to Jesus; indeed, a popular book on Jesus by John Dominic Crossan promotes the view that he was "a peasant Jewish Cynic."[18] Burton Mack concludes that "the earliest layers of the Gospel tradition depict a Jesus whose themes and style of teaching as well as his social role of critic are closest to those of the Cynics."[19] And Leif Vaage has done considerable work on the relation of Jesus to the Cynics, including their common interest in the significance of simple clothing.[20] In light of such claims one may ask, "What connection, if any, exists between the Cynics and Jesus in regard to παρρησία?"

Most instructive for our question is the work of John Moles[21] on the way in which the Cynic viewed social corruption. Moles highlights the role of the Cynic as reconciler in both the private and public sphere and documents Cynicism as a movement with a strong sense of mission expressed to some extent in the following terms as role definitions:

παιδαγωγός—guide, attendant	νουθετητής—monitor, warner
εὐεργέτης—benefactor	σωφρονιστής—one who chastises
κατάσκοπος—scout, spy	ἰατρός—healer

---

[17] For a good treatment of this point in Dio, see A. Malherbe, "'Gentle as a Nurse': The Cynic Background to I Thess ii," *NovT* 12 (1970) 208–10. The quotation is taken from the reprinted version of the essay in *Paul and the Popular Philosophers*, 43. How important a term this is can be seen from the frequency of reference to παρρησία in Malherbe's work.

[18] J. D. Crossan, *The Historical Jesus: The Life of a Mediterranean Jewish Peasant* (San Francisco: Harper, 1991) 421.

[19] Hock, "Cynics," 1225, citing Burton Mack, *A Myth of Innocence* (Philadelphia: Fortress, 1988) 67–74, 179–92. In regard to Mack's claim, one must ask: Closer in comparison with whom? the Pharisees? the Essenes? the Zealots?

[20] Leif Vaage, "Like Dogs Barking: Cynic παρρησία and Shameless Asceticism," *Semeia* 57 (1992) 25–40.

[21] John Moles, "'Honestius quam ambitiosius'? An Exploration of the Cynic's Attitude to Moral Corruption in his Fellow Men," *JHS* 103 (1983) 103–23.

διδάσκαλος—teacher
ἀγαθὸς δαίμων—good daimon

All of these terms are respectful of the human predicament and envision a role which will bring betterment. In each παρρησία plays a distinct role. The Cynic's main role is to "help"[22] and Heracles is depicted as Saviour of the earth and of the human race (σωτήρ τῆς γῆς καὶ τῶν ἀνθρώπων).[23]

The way in which that role will be carried out, the main agenda of the Cynics, "the principal focus of Cynic teachings," was "its unrelenting attack on the dominant aristocratic ethos of the Greco-Roman society, an ethos that . . . valued good birth, reputation, and wealth."[24] It is especially wealth that became the focus of their attacks.

> Concern for the well-being of one's fellow human is basic to Cynicism in all its forms, though this concern could be articulated in contrasting ways—harshly and aggressively, à la Diogenes, or humanely and benignly, à la Crates. . . . To Peregrinus' accusation that Demonax is not a true Cynic because of the humanity and jocularity he deploys in his relations with his fellow human beings (οὐ κυνᾷς), Demonax replies that Peregrinus has taken his Cynicism to such extremes that he can no longer be counted a member of the human race. . . . [Epictetus' Cynic] feels φιλανθρωπία towards all . . . the notion of the philosopher as 'the reconciler' is very Cynic. . . . The description of Alexander as 'reconciler of the whole world' may therefore reflect a Cynic concept of the unity of mankind.[25]

For all its crudity, Cynicism held progressive views on issues of social justice we today consider important (e.g., the equality of the sexes, the breaking down of social barriers, the claims of internationalism over nationalism). This is one of the many apparent paradoxes of Cynicism. How these progressive views relate to that crudity is not evident, but, then as now, you do not need to be clever and sophisticated to hold enlightened views.

In any case, among the Cynics παρρησία was considered a hallmark of their identity. Lucian writes: "But Demonax, who was passing by, begged him to pardon the man for making bold to speak his

---

[22] Crates, frg. 1.5 Diels; Bion, frg. 75 Kindstrand; Ps.-Diogenes, *Ep.* 29.4; Lucian, *Peregr.* 33; Julian, *Or.* 6.201C. What the Cynic knows best is to be "a liberator of people and a physician to their ills, in short I desire to be a prophet (προφήτης) of truth and of παρρησία" (Lucian, *Vit. Auct.* 8).

[23] Dio Chrys. *Or.* 1.84.

[24] Hock, "Cynics," 1224.

[25] Moles, "Honestius," 113–15.

mind in the traditional Cynic way."²⁶ Diogenes, when asked what was the most beautiful thing in the world (ἐν ἀνθρώποις), reportedly replied: "Παρρησία."²⁷ There is also the often repeated anecdote about his meeting Philip at his camp: "And did Diogenes lack freedom of speech when he appeared at the camp of Philip? Accused of being a spy he replied, 'I have indeed come to spy on Philip's insatiable greed and folly in coming to stake on the cast of the dice in a few decisive moments both his empire and his person.'"²⁸ Plutarch repeats the story that Demetrius once dreaded Crates' approach "anticipating some cynical frankness (παρρησίαν κυνικὴν) and harsh language," but the encounter turned out well. It is rather a good example of rebuke without reviling.²⁹

In a Cynic epistle of the first century "Socrates" invokes the myths of Bellerophon, who lived shamefully because he "had lost his foundation, which is not speaking as we are accustomed to, but is that boldness of speech (παρρησία) upon which each person's life is set upright."³⁰ A high place indeed for confident speaking!

If Cynics were deeply committed to social criticism, the question arises whether such a commitment is discernible in John the Baptist, Jesus and among early Christians, specifically in the Johannine literature. Before we answer that question we must review the use of the term in other sources.

In concluding this topic we venture the suggestion that the similarities between Jesus and the Cynics have been exaggerated and the differences not allowed to come sufficiently to the surface. As far as Gospel traditions about Jesus are concerned, at least, verbally abusing others is not a mandate of Jesus, and 1 Peter urges that abuse be repaid with a blessing (3:9).³¹ Was Jesus perhaps telling his disciples *not* to be like the Cynics in their exercise of free speech? Further conclusions must await a review of the term in other literature.

---

²⁶ Lucian, *Demonax* 50, κατά τινα πάτριον τοῖς Κυνικοῖς παρρησίαν θρασυνομένῳ. The translation is that of A. M. Harmon in the LCL. The participle θρασυνομένῳ is from θρασύνω, "embolden" and is related to θαρσέω, bold in bearing (see LSJ).

²⁷ Diog. Laert. 6.69.

²⁸ Plut. *De exil.* 606C; see also *Adulator* 70C–D. The translation is a modified version of F. C. Babbitt's in the LCL.

²⁹ Plut. *Adulator* 69C–D (trans. by Babbitt in the LCL).

³⁰ Ps.-Socrates, *Ep.* 1. The translation is that of A. J. Malherbe (ed.), *The Cynic Epistles: A Study Edition* (SBLSBS 12; Missoula: Scholars Press, 1977) 227.

³¹ For a sober reminder that the primary context of Jesus must be Judaism and not Cynicism, see E. P. Sanders, "Jesus in Historical Context," *TToday* 50 (1993) 429–48, and also *The Historical Figure of Jesus* (London: Penguin, 1993).

The Usage in the LXX and Pseudepigrapha

One might expect that W. C. van Unnik's essay dealing with the Semitic background of παρρησία in the NT, first published in Dutch in 1962, would touch on the LXX, but he dismisses the LXX occurrences as "but seldom" and concludes that παρρησία did not receive a "specifically Jewish imprint."[32] Peterson refers only once in passing to Job 27:10 but finds the concept in Philo and Josephus and asserts that "all the connections shown to exist in classical Greek literature are also found in Jewish-hellenistic literature."[33]

The verb and noun are used about twenty-one times in the LXX. The only occurrence in the Pentateuch describes the way in which the people have become confident because of their deliverance from Egypt. Yahweh, who released them from slavery, says, "I broke the bars of your yoke and enabled you to walk upright" (Lev 26:13).[34] The context is the dwelling of God among the people, and Jews of the Greco-Roman world did not hesitate to attribute their παρρησία to God's deliverance from Egypt. Παρρησία connotes more than merely the freedom to speak; it refers to a general bearing towards life which involves assertiveness and the confidence that one lives under a covenant with a fundamentally gracious and benevolent God. This confidence is considered a gift given by that god.

In the book of Job the word appears predominantly in the context of prayer and Job asks if the godless man will be able to experience that παρρησία before God in prayer (27:10 LXX). In Eliphaz's speech Job is admonished to come to terms with God and promised that he will prosper if he returns to God in true sincerity (22:23–27 LXX). Then he will boldly in the immediate presence of God look joyfully upward: εἶτα παρρησιασθήσῃ ἔναντι κυρίου ἀναβλέψας εἰς τὸν οὐρανὸν ἱλαρῶς (22:26 LXX). Here, too, the presupposition of παρρησία is justice or righteousness, but the gift of being able to be hilariously (ἱλαρῶς = עָנַג) confident before God and to stand erect looking up towards heaven bespeaks a piety far removed from any grovelling in

---

[32] "The Semitic Background of ΠΑΡΡΗΣΙΑ in the NT," *Sparsa Collecta: The Collected Essays of W. C. van Unnik* (3 vols.; NovTSup 29–31; Leiden: Brill, 1973–83) 2.290–306, esp. 2.290.

[33] Peterson, "Zur Bedeutungsgeschichte," 289.

[34] LXX: συνέτριψα τὸν δεσμὸν τοῦ ζυγοῦ ὑμῶν καὶ ἤγαγον ὑμᾶς μετὰ παρρησίας. The LXX translates וָאוֹלֵךְ אֶתְכֶם קוֹמְמִיּוּת ("with head held high") with παρρησία.

the dirt; it is the reward for doing justice. But more than that, when such openness to God exists, "You will pray to him, and he will hear you" (22:27 LXX). It seems that the Greek democratic right or privilege is transferred to the heavenly court, especially into the context of judgement. Far from such an attitude being designated as blasphemy,[35] this is considered part of the people's relationship to God.

It appears in a different connection in Esth 8:12s where it seems to be equivalent to freedom of religion: ἐκθέντες ἐν παντὶ τόπῳ μετὰ παρρησίας ἐᾶν τοὺς Ιουδαίους χρῆσθαι τοῖς ἑαυτῶν νομίμοις. . . . The usage here is ill-defined for the text reads: "Put up copies of this letter everywhere, allow the Jews to observe their own customs freely (μετὰ παρρησίας), and come to their help against anyone who attacks them. . . ." (Esth 8:12s).[36]

In Prov 1:20 the word appears to be the equivalent of "public." Here Wisdom cries aloud in the open air, "in the streets she increases confidence (ἐν δὲ πλατείαις παρρησίαν ἄγει)."[37]

The most striking usage as "frank criticism" occurs in Prov 10:10: ὁ δὲ ἐλέγχων μετὰ παρρησίας εἰρηνοποιεῖ. Here two fundamental terms from Greek moral teaching are brought together: to rebuke and to do so courageously. The process of doing this is described as "making peace," a more Jewish formula. How should the word be translated here? Frankly? Boldly? Courageously? If we take it to mean "openly" rather than privately, then we are in conflict with all Jewish teaching about rebuke, for that was to be done in private and never in public.[38] Had the authors of the LXX meant "in public," they would in any case have translated the Hebrew with ἐν παρρησίᾳ or perhaps παρρησίᾳ, using the dative case. This usage is close to the Cynic use of the term for confrontation and rebuke.

Prov 13:5 is also an unusual occurrence. The text reads: "The just man hates an unjust word (λόγον ἄδικον μισεῖ δίκαιος), but the impious one is put to shame and will have no confidence" (ἀσεβὴς δὲ αἰσχύνεται καὶ οὐχ ἕξει παρρησίαν). The contrast between shame and

---

[35] Isoc. Or. 11.40: παρρησία εἰς τοὺς θεούς he considers βλασφημία and a sign of ἀσέβεια.

[36] Cf. JB: "allow the Jews freedom to observe their own customs."

[37] For a similar construction (ἦγον παρρησίαν), see Josephus, AJ 2.131; 16.219; 19.318.

[38] James Kugel, In Potiphar's House: The Interpretive Life of Biblical Texts (San Francisco: Harper, 1990) 214–43, offers a rich collection of texts on this subject.

confidence is unique and παρρησία is seen as an admirable trait missing in the profligate.

A special concern was the question whether women could possess παρρησία. So Sir 25:25 applies the word to female behavior. The text reads as follows:

> Do not leave a leaky cistern to drip
> or allow a bad wife freedom of speech.[39]
> If she does not accept your control,
> Divorce her and send her away.

This author's concern is apparently with "control" over a wife and he considers a bad wife like a chafing yoke, "controlling her is like clutching a scorpion" (Sir 26:7). Of course, he is also convinced that "woman is the origin of sin and through her we all die" (25:24).[40] Did admonitions like this make it easier for Herod to execute his first wife, Mariamne? According to Josephus, the reason he killed her was her "excessive παρρησία" (AJ 15.238).

Another woman who has a problem with παρρησία is Aseneth, who has had a heavenly visitor, and after he leaves she says: "What a foolish and bold (τολμῆρα) woman I am because I have spoken with frankness (παρρησία) and said that a man came into my chamber from heaven. . . . And she said in herself, 'Be gracious, Lord, to your slave, and spare your maidservant, because I have spoken boldly (παρρησία) before you all my words in ignorance'" (JoAsen. 17:9).[41] Here it is assumed that it is inappropriate for a maiden to speak so openly with a heavenly visitor.

It appears elsewhere in the Greek Bible in a variety of meanings. In 1 Macc 4:18 it means "plunder freely." In 3 Macc 4:1, the public/private contrast appears. Here the hatred that Gentiles feel in their hearts towards the Jews is given open expression, so that it is now public instead of private. In 3 Macc 7 the meaning is not clear, but it could simply mean "boldly." Here King Ptolemy Philopator

---

[39] LXX: μὴ δῷς . . . μηδὲ γυναικὶ πονηρᾷ παρρησίαν. NEB: "Do not . . . allow a bad wife to say what she likes"; NRSV: "allow . . . no boldness of speech to an evil wife."

[40] Modern writers point out that the author has nothing against women per se; he was simply not able to transcend the male chauvinism of his time. K. E. Bailey, "Women in Ben Sirach and the New Testament," For Me to Live: Essays in Honor of James Kelso (ed. R. A. Coughenour; Cleveland: Dillon\Liederback Books, 1972) 56–73; H. McKeating, "Jesus ben Sira's Attitude towards Women," ExpT 85 (1973–74) 85–87; W. C. Trenchard, Ben Sira's View of Women: A Literary Analysis (BJS 38; Chico, CA: Scholars Press, 1982).

[41] The translation (with parentheses removed) is that of C. Burchard in the OTP.

receives a request from Jews to punish their fellow Jews who have transgressed the law. In response, "the king acknowledged the truth of what they said, and praising them, he granted them full indemnity, without let or hindrance (μετὰ παρρησίας) or any royal license or investigation,[42] to destroy anywhere in the Kingdom those who had transgressed the law of God" (3 Macc 7:12).

In later Christian literature the term is often applied to the behaviour of martyrs, and it appears already in that sense in 4 Maccabees. "They were angered at the bold speech of the (third son to be martyred)" (4 Macc 10:5).

In one psalm where God is addressed as Lord of vengeance, ὁ θεὸς ἐκδικήσεων ἐπαρρησιάσατο, the appearance of the verbal form of παρρησία is totally unexpected and inexplicable unless the translator seeks to promote a God eager to avenge (Ps 93:1 LXX).

Prov 20:9 represents an intriguing usage in which the question of the integrity of a person is brought into the discussion. The king works at being impartial by winnowing all evil from his eyes. And the author asks: "Who can boast, I have a clean heart? Or who is so bold (παρρησιάσεται) as to claim to be pure from sin?" In both cases the LXX translators supply the verbal form when strictly speaking it is not called for.

It also appears in connection with servants in one text. The author is describing how fair weather friends behave; they sit at table when you are prosperous and will be like a second self and "speak boldly to your servants" (Sir 6:11, καὶ ἐν τοῖς ἀγαθοῖς σου ἔσται ὡς σὺ καὶ ἐπὶ τοὺς οἰκέτας σου παρρησιάσεται).[43]

The verb παρρησίαζομαι also appears in connection with the way servants have παρρησία. For example, 3 Baruch 9:8 reads, "Listen: Just as servants are unable to speak freely (παρρησία) before kings, so also before the sun, the moon and the stars are unable to shine" (ἄκουσον ὥσπερ ἐνώπιον βασιλέως οὐ δύναται οἰκέται παρρησιασθῆναι οὕτως οὐδὲ ἐνώπιον τοῦ ἡλίου δύναται).[44]

---

[42] NRSV: "a general license so that freely, and without royal authority or supervision."

[43] The NEB reads "make free with your servants," and the NRSV has "and lord it over your servants." While the Hebrew literally means "in your misfortune leave you," the JB has "ordering your servants about." Obviously, these translations are not rendering παρρησία, although they are based on the Greek text.

[44] The translation is that of H. E. Gaylord in the OTP. The date of 3 Baruch, although uncertain, can perhaps be set at the first part of second century. See Gaylord's discussion in OTP 1.654–60.

In the Jewish extra-biblical literature the term appears as well. For example, in *T.Reu.* 4:2 one finds: ὡς κἀγώ, ἄχρι τελευτῆς τοῦ πατρὸς ἡμῶν οὐκ εἶχον παρρησίαν . . . ἀτενίσαι εἰς πρόσωπον Ἰακὼβ ἢ λαλῆσαι τινι. . . .[45]

> For until my father's death I never had the courage to look him in the face or speak to any of my brothers because of my disgraceful act. Even until now my conscience harasses me because of my impious act.

Here the term is used in connection with a bad conscience and its effect, the inability to look someone in the face.

Speaking boldly is also related to the cheerful face as in the description of Levi speaking to Pharaoh's son; he does so "with frankness (παρρησία), his face cheerful (ἱλάρω[46] προσώπῳ), and anger was not in him (καὶ ὀργὴ οὐκ ἦν ἐν αὐτῷ), but in meekness of heart he spoke to him" (*JoAsen.* 23:10). The gentle rebuke is here seen as a sign of friendship which can lead to peace.

In a similar category the king is considered fortunate to have "frank advice (παρρησία) given him by his friends" (*Ep. Arist.* 125:3; trans. by R. J. H. Shutt in the *OTP*).

Another text looks forward to the time when the righteous dead shall behold the face of the great judge, the Lord of all: "The seventh order, which is greater than all that have been mentioned, because they shall rejoice with boldness, and shall be confident without confusion, and shall be glad without fear, for they hasten to behold the face of him whom they served in life and from whom they are to receive their reward when glorified."[47]

Moreover, other usages project such confidence into the next world and the appearance before the judgement throne. In Wis 5:1, the just person is described as full of assurance (τότε στήσεται ἐν παρρησίᾳ πολλῇ ὁ δίκαιος) in the presence of those who revile and seek to destroy the righteous one. Dieter Georgi translates it "sovereign freedom" (*souveräne Freiheit*) and concludes: "The sovereign freedom which

---

[45] The text cited is that of Albert-Marie Denis, *Concordance grecque des pseudépigraphes d'Ancien Testament* (Louvain-la-Neuve: Université Cathol. de Louvain Inst. orientaliste, 1987). Translations of the *Testaments of the 12 Patriarchs* are those of H. C. Kee in the *OTP*.

[46] The combination of cheerfulness with παρρησία occurs in Esth 5:1b as well as in the text cited above from Job (22:26 LXX).

[47] 4 Ezra 7:98. The translation is that of B. M. Metzger in the *OTP*. The work is dated about 100 CE, originally written in Hebrew or Aramaic. Note the striking similarity with 1 Cor 4:5.

the just man has is not any more, as it was originally in the Greek concept, the democratic freedom of the citizen, but the freedom of the one exalted to the heavenly world, the freedom of the children of God, namely that of the angels."[48]

Obviously, a term which had its origin in and therefore still carried connotations of democracy and political participation remains in the social realm when it is used for slaves and women, but it becomes theological when applied to God's activity among the people, including an ultimate encounter with God.

New Testament Usage: Frequency

The noun παρρησία appears in the NT a total of 31 times, the verb, παρρησιάζομαι, an additional nine times as follows:

	NOUN	VERB
Paul:	(8x) 2 Cor 3:12; 7:4; Eph 3:12; 6:19; Phil 1:20; Col 2:15; 1 Tim 3:13; Phlm 8	(2x) Eph 6:20; 1 Thess 2:2
Mark:	(1x) 8:32	
John:	(9x) 7:4, 13, 26; 10:24; 11:14, 54; 16:25, 29; 18:20.	
1 John:	(4x) 2:28; 3:21; 4:17; 5:14	
Heb:	(4x) 3:6; 4:16; 10:19, 35	
Acts:	(5x) 2:29; 4:13, 29, 31; 28:31	(7x) 9:27, 28; 13:46; 14:3; 18:26; 19:8; 26:26

Accordingly, of the forty appearances of the word, about a third occur in the Johannine corpus. Even though that corpus takes up only 12% of the NT, it has about three times as many of the occurrences as one might proportionately expect. The fact that the word does not appear in the gospels except once in Mark may lead us to conclude that John is dependent here upon the Marcan tradition; in any event he uses the word far more than the others and this may shed light on its function in the Fourth Gospel.[49] At least it clearly

---

[48] Dieter Georgi, *Weisheit Salomos* (JSHRZ 3.4; Gütersloh: Gerd Mohn, 1980) 416. His way of translating it contradicts its usage throughout OT sources. The NRSV translates it "with great confidence"; the NEB with "full of assurance," and the JB as "stands up boldly."

[49] The possibility that John was dependent upon Mark for the Gospel literary form is now once again open for discussion. Especially his possible indebtedness to

merits an investigation. That investigation may well be fuelled by the question whether the community in which the Fourth Gospel and the epistles were written had a special interest in παρρησία.⁵⁰ Since the word was a seminal term for Cynics, it could of course be anywhere in the Empire for M.-Odile Goulet-Cazé has documented how very widespread Cynicism was in the Roman Empire.⁵¹

ΠΑΡΡΗΣΙΑ in the Fourth Gospel

An analysis of the contexts in which the Fourth Gospel uses the word indicates that it has the following meanings:

1. Παρρησία has the usual mundane sense of the opposite of "secret, hidden, or esoteric." Jesus was not a sectarian building his community in the desert, and his was not a secret society. Thus it appears for the first time as a statement of his brothers who are urging Jesus to go to the feast in Jerusalem, for "surely no one can hope to be 'in the public eye (ἐν παρρησίᾳ)' if he works in seclusion. If you really are doing such things as these, show yourself to the world" (7:4 NEB). Raymond Brown suggests that this is a Johannine description of a temptation paralleling the third temptation of Luke 4.⁵² What is remarkable is that this usage is set in the context of the unbelief of his brothers and that Jesus is described as having a temptation placed in his way by his next of kin.

Although he rejected the suggestion of his brothers as not being timely, after they had gone to the feast, Jesus too decided to go, but he did not go publicly but secretly (οὐ φανερῶς ἀλλὰ ὡς ἐν κρυπτῷ, 7:4); and when the feast was half over, he decided to go and teach in the Temple. There was murmuring and dissension among the

---

Mark for the passion narrative opens up the possibility that παρρησία with its connotations of a public epiphany came to John from Mark. On the general subject see the excellent article by D. Moody Smith, "John and the Synoptics and the Question of Gospel Genre," *Studia Neotestamentica: Collected Essays* (ed. M. Sabbe; BETL 98; Leuven: Leuven University Press, 1991) 1783–97, esp. 1784, 1794–95.

⁵⁰ Virtually anywhere in the Roman Empire the use of the term παρρησία would have assisted the church in its growth for it brought a very strong aspect of her inner identity to expression with a term much in vogue. Changes, adaptations or revisions made by them in its use would especially attract attention.

⁵¹ "Le cynisme à l'époque impériale," *ANRW* 2.36.4 (1990) 2720–2833.

⁵² R. E. Brown, *The Gospel according to John* (2 vols.; AB 29–29A; Garden City, NY: Doubleday, 1966–70) 1.308.

Jews about him, but no one talked about him publicly (οὐδεὶς μέντοι παρρησίᾳ ἐλάλει περὶ αὐτοῦ) on account of their fear of the Judeans (διὰ τὸν φόβον τῶν Ἰουδαίων, 7:13). Here one could translate the word simply "in public." At the same time it is necessary to add the word "favourably" to the word παρρησία here. The sense is that no one had the courage to speak on his behalf for fear of those seeking to take him in.

The same is true of the third occurrence in this chapter, 7:26. The "crowd"[53] of Jerusalem accuses Jesus of "being possessed" (δαιμόνιον ἔχεις) because he defends his action of healing a man on the sabbath (7:19). And they ask: "is not this the man they want to put to death? And here he is speaking openly and they have nothing to say to him" (7:26). If in the Greek city state the freedom to speak was provided for all citizens, Jesus here practices that freedom, but according to some of the Jerusalem residents, those seeking to kill him did not (yet) confront him publicly. For Jesus had gone into hiding (cf. 8:59, where Jesus is "not seen" and 11:54, 57; 12:36).

2. Παρρησία sometimes means "speaking plainly." For instance, an occurrence in chapter 11 supports this usage. It describes Jesus as changing his enigmatic references to the sleep of Lazarus to "plain talk," so that he now forthrightly says: "Lazarus is dead" (11:14).

After the decision had been made to put Jesus to death and the plotting began, John reports that Jesus left Judea and went to the country bordering on the desert, to a town called Ephraim, where he stayed with his disciples (11:54). For John this is perhaps the clearest text showing that παρρησία meant "publicly." But it also stands alone in stating that Jesus actually withdrew from Jerusalem as the conflict was heating up.[54] At his capture and trial (Matt 26:55 = Mark 14:49 = Luke 22:53 = John 18:20) all gospels stress that he taught in the Temple and that whatever he did was done publicly for the world to see. Moreover, in the Fourth Gospel the high priest asks Jesus

---

[53] In the synoptic Gospels the crowds follow Jesus in Galilee and hear him teach and preach. In John Jesus is in heated discussion with the "crowds" and they figure primarily in Jerusalem. The usage of the term ὄχλος is as follows: Mark: 38×; Matt: 49×; Luke: 41×; and John: 20×, of which 14 occur in chapters 7 (8×) and 12 (6×).

[54] J. H. Charlesworth translates John 11:54: "Therefore Jesus no longer went about openly among leaders in Judea, but he went from there (Judaea) into a region near the wilderness, into a city called Ephraim. He remained there with his disciples" (*Explorations* 7 [1993] 3).

concerning his disciples and his teaching. Jesus answers: ἐγὼ παρρησίᾳ λελάληκα τῷ κόσμῳ (John 18:20), and he elaborates that he taught wherever all the Jews gather together, including the temple and the synagogue, and he further stresses, "I never taught in secret" (ἐν κρυπτῷ). The whole pericope (John 18:19–23) seeks to demonstrate that all that Jesus did was open and above board. That John devotes so much more time to this matter than do the synoptics is an indication of its importance for him. There is no messianic secret in John. The slogan of Jesus' teaching for John could very well be coloured along Cynic lines, ἐγὼ παρρησίᾳ λελάληκα τῷ κόσμῳ.[55]

Another occurrence in the context of conflict appears in the challenge of the Jews in 10:24. "How long must you keep us in suspense? If you are the Messiah, say so plainly" (εἶπε ἡμῖν παρρησίᾳ).[56] Here the opposite of παρρησία is lack of clarity or mystery. But again the call for παρρησία comes from the enemies of Jesus, or as John puts it, from the "unbelievers."

There are, furthermore, two occurrences in 16:25 and 16:29 in which Jesus, while conversing with his disciples, tells them that he has previously spoken to them in riddles (παροιμίαι), but the time is coming when he will do so no longer but rather speak to them "in plain words" (παρρησίᾳ) about the Father.[57] Indeed, the disciples are delighted that "this is plain speaking; this is no figure of speech. We are certain now that you know everything and do not need to be questioned; because of this we believe that you have come from God" (16:25–31). To be sure, Jesus challenges their confidence by predicting that before long they will all leave him alone. So that even this evidence that belief comes from παρρησία is short-lived. At the same time the inference is clear: παρρησία can bring about faith in Jesus as coming from God.

In summary, παρρησία appears in the Fourth Gospel in three distinct meanings:

---

[55] Note the remarkable similarity with Mark: καὶ παρρησίᾳ τὸν λόγον ἐλάλει (8:32), which neither Luke nor Matthew picked up.

[56] Reading εἰπέ with Nestle-Aland[27] rather than the εἶπον of the 25th edition. The harder reading, however, is clearly εἶπον; see BDF 43.

[57] Apparently this is not a contrast which is at home in either the LXX, where the word παροιμία appears only seven times, or in classical Greek, where it is a standard term for a byword and stands with γνῶμαι (Arist. *Rh.* 2.21 [1395a17]). See F. Hauck, "παροιμία," *TWNT* 5.852–55.

1. Public versus private (John 7:4, 13, 26; 11:54).
2. Plain against obscure (10:24; 11:14; 16:25, 29).
3. Bold or courageous against timid (7:26; 18:20, related to meaning number 1 as well).

To use παρρησία as synonymous with public (vs. private) is practically unknown in Hellenistic Greek, although it approaches the way in which Philo uses it once.[58] Elsewhere it never appears with that connotation in Josephus or in Philo.

Rudolf Bultmann has suggested that παρρησία means "visibility to the public" (*Öffentlichkeit*), to be sure not in the sense of the world, as a demonstrative obtrusiveness, but rather publicly in the sense of "undemonstrative ordinariness" (18:20).[59] He takes παρρησία "naturally as meaning here publicly." He recognizes that this is not what it meant originally in Greek, where it meant "the right or even the courage to be in public, freedom of speech, or openness." He states that later on it often meant "publicly" but cites no evidence. In this sense the word went over into Rabbinic writings as a loanword.[60]

Did the word enter into the Johannine corpus through Mark? The statement in Mark is an editorial comment about Jesus' affirmation about the need of the son of man to suffer and reads: καὶ παρρησίᾳ τὸν λόγον ἐλάλει (8:32).[61]

Given the widespread usage of the word in the first century and especially its central place in Cynic values, is it possible that its occurrence in Mark and its frequency in John may be one of the

---

[58] Philo, *Flacc.* 4; cf. *Spec.* 1.321.
[59] *Das Evangelium des Johannes* (Göttingen: Vandenhoeck and Ruprecht, 1957) 219.
[60] See Str-B 2.485 and A. Schlatter, *Der Evangelist Johannes* (3d ed.; Stuttgart: Calwer, 1960) 186–87.
[61] H. B. Swete, *The Gospel according to St. Mark* (London: Macmillan, 1898) 169, translates "without reserve," but also notes that in John it contrasts with "in secret" and "in riddles." E. P. Gould, *A Critical and Exegetical Commentary on the Gospel according to St. Mark* (ICC; New York: Charles Scribner's Sons, 1912) 154, renders it "without any reserve." Ernst Lohmeyer, *Das Evangelium des Markus* (MeyerK 1.2; Göttingen: Vandenhoeck & Ruprecht, 1959) 167, concludes that "the sentence is hardly intelligible." He finds the solution in the African text which places the proclamation of the word after the resurrection. There is a distinct difference between Johannine usage and that of Mark. For discussion, see Jonathan Bishop, "Parabole and Parrhesia in Mark," *Int* 40 (1986) 39–52; H. Räisänen, *The Messianic Secret in Mark* (Edinburgh: T. & T. Clark, 1990) 103–04; and J. M. Robinson, "Gnosticism and the New Testament," *Gnosis: Hans Jonas Festschrift* (Göttingen: Vandenhoeck & Ruprecht, 1978) 125–43, esp. 140–43.

strongest support bases for a relation between Jesus and the Cynics? John Dominic Crossan, who has concluded that "the historical Jesus was, then, a peasant Jewish Cynic" and that Jesus is to be interpreted against "a philosophical praxis of what might be termed, if adjective and noun are given equal weight, a Jewish Cynicism,"[62] does not touch upon this evidence. At the same time Leif Vaage has argued extensively that "if, as is often assumed, the formative stratum of Q is essentially coincident with the historical Jesus, then Jesus was for all intents and purposes likewise a Cynic."[63] The circle is closed in the suggestion of Burton Mack that the word παρρησία describes the verve which is found both in Jesus and the Cynics. "Verve was therefore the Cynic virtue. It was generated by a sense of self-reliance, but involved the capacity for taking a lively interest in any and every encounter with another human being. Verve could also be used as a standard to diagnose human well-being, rank human achievement, and assess the merits of social systems and their cultural symbols."[64]

Mack concludes: "The forthrightness with which social critique was registered in Q was exactly like that of the Cynics' attitude called parresia, or bold outspoken manner."[65] The gifts and graces of the Cynics

> ranged from the endurance of a life of renunciation in full public view, through the courage to offer social critique in high places (called parresia, or 'boldness of speech'), to the learning and sophistication required for the espousal of Cynic views at the highest level of literary composition.[66]

Is it not pushing it a bit too far to describe the social critique of Q as "exactly" like that of the Cynics? Or to conclude that "the formative stratum of Q is essentially coincident with the historical Jesus"? Finally, can we be so sure that παρρησία equals the "courage to offer social critique in high places"? It clearly is not used that way

---

[62] Crossan, *The Historical Jesus*, 421.

[63] "Q: The Ethos and Ethics of an Itinerant Intelligence" (Ph.D. Diss., Claremont Graduate School, 1987) 495, cited from Hans Dieter Betz, "Jesus and the Cynics: Survey and Analysis of an Hypothesis," *JR* (1994) 11. See now Vaage's *Galilean Upstarts: Jesus' First Followers* (Valley Forge, PA: Trinity Press International, 1994).

[64] Burton L. Mack, *The Lost Gospel: The Book of Q and Christian Origins* (San Francisco: Harper, 1993) 119.

[65] Ibid., 46.

[66] Ibid., 115.

in the gospel tradition and Jesus spends remarkably little time rendering social critique in high places.

On the other hand, the frequency of this word in John must surely have something to do with its popularity among the Cynics. What were the reasons behind it?

The question cannot be answered here. It could, however, be pointed out that παρρησία as used in the Fourth Gospel has a totally different connotation than it does in any of the Cynic sources. Is this perhaps one more instance in which the early Christian writers radically turned a term around? Before we answer that question we must look at the way in which the term is used in the First Epistle of John.

ΠΑΡΡΗΣΙΑ in 1 John[67]

George B. Caird concluded that 1 John

> defies precise analysis, because its thought moves, not forward in a logical progression, but spirally, with the same few ideas constantly recurring for new consideration and new development.[68]

The fullest study of this pattern in the epistle was provided in the classic work by Robert Law.[69]

The word παρρησία appears four times in 1 John (2:28; 3:21; 4:17; 5:14). The broader context of each usage will be reviewed.

1. 1 John 2:28: καὶ νῦν, τεκνία, μένετε ἐν αὐτῷ, ἵνα ἐὰν φανερωθῇ σχῶμεν παρρησίαν καὶ μὴ αἰσχυνθῶμεν ἀπ᾽ αὐτοῦ ἐν τῇ παρουσίᾳ αὐτοῦ. "And now children, remain in him in order that when he is

---

[67] For background materials on 1 John, see R. Kysar, "John, Epistles of," *ABD* 3 (1992) 900–12, and Raymond Brown, *The Community of the Beloved Disciple* (New York: Paulist, 1979) 93–144.

[68] G. B. Caird, "John, Letters of," *IDB* 2 (1962) 946–52, here 948.

[69] See R. Law, *The Tests of Life* (Edinburgh: T. & T. Clark, 1909) esp. 280, 285–90, 303. One of the finest studies of the structure of 1 John is by Theodor Häring, "Gedankengang und Grundgedanke des ersten Johannesbriefes," *Theologische Abhandlungen: Carl Weizsäcker zu seinem siebzigsten Geburtstage* (Freiburg: J. C. B. Mohr, 1892) 173–200. Häring saw two main ideas developed three times in the book. They are ethical, without love there can be no fellowship with God, and christological, the importance of affirming that Jesus is the Christ. See also Wolfgang Nauck, *Die Tradition und der Charakter des ersten Johannesbriefes* (Tübingen: Mohr, 1957), who analyses Bultmann's source hypothesis and rejects it.

made manifest, we will have confidence (παρρησία) and not be ashamed of him in his presence (παρουσία)."[70]

Several features of this usage of παρρησία are noteworthy. There is first the stress on inviting them to remain—indeed that is the central imperative. The shift from the third person plural to the second person is significant. If they do not remain, then "we" will not have confidence and "we" will be ashamed.

It has been demonstrated that Johannine usage of "remaining" did not come from the LXX or from Greek literature, that it is unique in the NT, and that the usage in 1 John connected with ἐν is distinctive. Of the 24 usages in 1 John, 21 are combined with ἐν.[71] The writer is greatly concerned about the constancy of his readers and one of his major concerns is to stanch the flow of people out of the church.[72] But, most important, he is convinced that anyone who does not remain in Christ forfeits that new reality which has come in Jesus. For Jesus has invited his disciples to "remain in me" (John 15:4) and to "remain in his love" meant to remain a new being. Those who remain in his love and in him, hear his words and keep his commandments and "are secure in the house of love for God remains in them."[73]

The ἵνα-clause in 1 John 2:28, the term παρουσία, and the possibility of "shame" on his appearance indicate that the author is thinking in terms of an eschatological event. The word παρουσία is not found elsewhere in the Johannine literature and so we may either translate it along the lines of other NT writers as "coming" or as "presence," a meaning more closely aligned with Johannine emphasis on the presence of Christ.

Finally, the ἵνα-clause also invites consideration as a literary technique, for the ἵνα purpose clause when used to designate purpose of writing is largely confined to the Johannine literature. In the total corpus Paulinum, ἵνα-clauses in relation to purpose in writing appear only three times. In John they deal with the basic outlines of

---

[70] R. Brown, *The Epistles of John* (AB 30; Garden City, NY: Doubleday, 1982) 380–81. R. Schnackenburg, *Die Johannesbriefe* (2d ed.; Freiburg: Herder, 1963) 162–66; R. Bultmann, *Die kirchliche Redaktion des ersten Johannesbriefes* (Stuttgart: Evangelisches Verlagswerk, 1951) 195–97.

[71] The best overall study of the subject is J. Heise, *Bleiben, Menein in den johanneischen Schriften* (Tübingen: Mohr, 1967).

[72] Ibid., 28.

[73] Ibid., 171.

Christian instruction and the desired reaction of the reader. They enforce the desire of the writer to strengthen the readers' allegiance to Christ.[74]

The appeal is related to the danger of being ashamed in the presence of Christ. Shame is often related to παρρησία in the literature, but, if I mistake not, it is only in Jewish literature dealing with the hereafter that it appears analogously to this usage. There is a similar saying preserved in Mark 8:38 and Luke 9:26 to the effect that if anyone is ashamed of Jesus and his own in this wicked age, "the Son of Man will be ashamed of him, when he comes in the glory of his father and of the holy angels." Although reference is made to "coming," the word παρουσία is not used. Nevertheless, many would agree with C. H. Dodd that "we can hardly miss a reminiscence of sayings attributed to Jesus in the Gospels."[75] The sanction of "shame" is present in both texts.[76]

Our next text illustrates that it is not only the hereafter that calls for παρρησία in one's encounters with God.

2. 1 John 3:21: Ἀγαπητοί, ἐὰν ἡ καρδία μὴ καταγινώσκῃ, παρρησίαν ἔχομεν πρὸς τὸν θεόν. "Beloved, if the heart[77] does not condemn, we have confidence or boldness in God's presence."

---

[74] Noted by Harald Riesenfeld, "Zu den johanneischen ἵνα Sätzen," *ST* 19 (1965) 213–20.

[75] C. H. Dodd, *The Johannine Epistles* (MNTC; New York: Harper & Row, 1946) 64.

[76] Shame and παρρησία are placed as opposites also by Paul in Phil 1:20. And in 2 Cor 10:8 he says "I will not be put to shame." The peculiar expression "to be ashamed before someone" has Septuagintal precedence (ἐπί, Isa 1:29; ἀπό, Jer 12:13; cf. Sir 41:17–42:8, which has a series of things to be ashamed of and things not to be ashamed of, always using the preposition ἀπό). The phrase ἀπ᾽ αὐτοῦ in the sense used here is only found in Jer 12:13 and as *v.l.* in Isa 1:29 (contrary to BAGD 25). The construction appears also with the verb καταισχύνειν; see Psalm 119:116, καὶ μὴ καταισχύνῃς με ἀπὸ τῆς προσδοκίας μου; Jer 2:36; 31:13. As noted above, Prov 13:5 provides an example of the juxtaposition of shame and παρρησία. The text reads: "the impious one is put to shame and will have no confidence" (ἀσεβὴς δὲ αἰσχύνεται καὶ οὐχ ἕξει παρρησίαν).

[77] The heart as condemning or being open to persuasion is relatively unknown in classical Greek sources of the period nor does it appear in Josephus. The LXX seems to prefer the expression "the heart smote him," as in 1 Kgdms 24:6; 2 Kgdms 24:10. The "condemning heart" is found, as far as I can tell, only in Sir 14:2, but even there the Greek is ψυχὴ· μακάριος οὗ οὐ κατέγνω ἡ ψυχὴ αὐτοῦ. The verb καταγινώσκω appears in connection with καρδία also in *T.Gad* 5:3, where the just person is described as ashamed to commit an injustice, "not because someone else will pass judgement on him but out of his own heart, because the Lord considers his inner deliberations."

This statement deals with the bad and good conscience, and the bad conscience is described as one that detects unacceptable behaviour, condemning or judging the heart in a downward direction. When the conscience or heart does not condemn then we have παρρησία— an openness and freedom towards God. *T.Gad* 5:3 has an almost identical usage: "Not by another are we being condemned but by our own hearts."

Epictetus also lays side by side the bold confidence and the good conscience. He is concerned about intemperate Cynics who "revile tactlessly" (λοιδορεῖσθαι ἀκαίρως, *Diss.* 3.22.50). The true Cynic is a servant and friend of Zeus, sharing in the government of Zeus; "why should he not have the courage to speak freely (θαρρήσῃ παρρησιάζεσθαι) to his own brothers, to his children, in a word, to his kinsmen?"[78]

It is, of course, well known that John's basis for παρρησία, that God is greater than our hearts and knows all things, has been interpreted to mean that God's condemnation will be even more severe than our own. Thus the variant reading: "that even if our own heart [conscience] condemns us, still more will God who is greater than our conscience."[79] Schnackenburg correctly observes that the statement "that 'God is greater than our hearts' is one of the great theological affirmations of 1 John, the good news that God is grace and love." Any attempt to read into this text God's attributes of greatness which brings fear or judicial strictness introduces a foreign element. Thus the Christian who is being condemned by conscience is protected not only by the works of love tangibly seen, but above all is cast onto the sea of Divine eternal goodness, understanding and mercy.[80] The text is, as Schnackenburg wryly notes, not an especially strong support for Lutheran belief which stresses that sinfulness and presumably guilt are multiplied even as deeds of love are. It finds its closest parallel in Paul's affirmation in 1 Cor 4:1–6 that even though one's conscience may be clear, one's case rests ultimately not on the evaluation of one's peers or oneself but only on the character of the judge who confronts us. Paul joins with 1 John in a ringing affirmation that when all secrets are laid bare, "then will be the time for each to receive from God ἔπαινος."[81] That is not the customary way

---

[78] Epict. *Diss.* 3.22.96. The translation is that of W. A. Oldfather in the LCL.
[79] So the NEB.
[80] Schnackenburg, *Die Johannesbriefe*, 201–04.
[81] It is truly amazing that the NEB can translate, "Then will be the time for each to receive from God such praise as he deserves." Cf. the JB: "whatever praise he

judgement is described, although as noted above there are Jewish precedents.

Leon Morris, although he cites 1 Cor 4:3–5, overlooks the fact that what he refers to as "the Lord's perfect judgment" actually consists of handing out praise. He never gets around to the punch-line in 1 Cor 4 although he saw it in 1 John.[82] What is perhaps equally surprising is that scholars who have worked on conscience in the NT overlook this text from 1 John, for they are looking only for the technical word "conscience."[83]

The nature of the last judgment or encounter with God at death was discussed very widely in Judaism. On the one hand, Baruch proclaims that the just can look forward to the end for they have a good hope. They can leave this world without fear, for they are confident of the world which God has promised them with an expectation full of joy (Bar 14:12–14). Others express fear and trembling at the prospect and concentrate on the gap that exists between them and the just patriarchs. In the final analysis, the NT writers John and Paul remain true to that part of their Jewish heritage which affirms that God will judge the people of the covenant, quickly and mercifully, "standing up" rather than sitting down, for it won't take long.

The mercy of God will triumph over justice, and therefore one of the main themes struck by many Jewish writers of our period was totally consistent with what both Paul and 1 John say about judgement and the παρρησία with which one can face it.[84]

3. 1 John 4:17: Ἐν τούτῳ τετελείωται ἡ ἀγάπη μεθ' ἡμῶν, ἵνα παρρησίαν ἔχωμεν ἐν τῇ ἡμέρᾳ τῆς κρίσεως. "In this is love perfected among us, that we have παρρησία in the day of judgement."

---

deserves." The NRSV translates "each one will receive commendation from God." Much better is the NIV: "each will receive his praise." C. H. Dodd also sees a parallel here between Paul and 1 John; see *The Johannine Epistles*, 90.

[82] See his very perceptive section on the place of παρρησία in 1 John in *The Biblical Doctrine of Judgment* (Grand Rapids: Eerdmanns, 1960) 55–56; on παρρησία, 72.

[83] So C. A. Pierce, *Conscience in the NT* (SBT 15; London: SCM, 1955); J. Stelzenberger, *Syneidesis im Neuen Testament* (Abhandlungen zur Moraltheologie 1; Paderborn: Schoningh, 1961). Robert Wall does not treat this text in "Conscience," *ABD* 1 (1992) 1128–30. The *ABD* has no entry on "Heart," "Confidence" or "Boldness." On Paul's view of conscience, the work by Hans-Joachim Eckstein, *Der Begriff Syneidesis bei Paulus* (Tübingen: Mohr, 1983) was inaccessible to me.

[84] Paul Volz, *Die Eschatologie der jüdischen Gemeinde im neutestamentlichen Zeitalter* (2d ed.; Tübingen: Mohr, 1934) 106–17, 293–96. In spite of some very negative statements about the law, Volz elaborates this point with impressive documentation.

These verses deal with the way in which love becomes mature or complete and how it relates to fear, but, as Bultmann has noted, above all they celebrate the possibilities given in παρρησία.[85] Conscious that God is near, the writer speaks of a certain elevation; prayers are being heard and παρρησία brings confidence to meet God as judge, "so now before the Father we have the consciousness of artless and perfect simplicity and freedom."[86]

The strongest contribution παρρησία makes to the argument here is that perfect love does not exist beside fear. Judged by the evidence from the Hebrew Bible, the contrast between fear and love was not present in the Jewish approach to God. Rather, the writers treated fear and love as synonymous. Furthermore, "in a large preponderance of cases, it can be clearly seen that fear and love of Jahweh refer to a kind of conduct or action rather than to a mental or emotional state."[87] The base text often cited was Deut 10:12, which calls for fear of God, love for God, service and keeping the commandments. So the relation of fear and love was likely more avidly discussed among Jewish religious thinkers than among Greeks and has a natural place in 1 John.

John states that the basis for παρρησία is love. His contemporaries found friendship as the state in which παρρησία blossomed. John says hardly anything about friendship, for he follows other early Christians (perhaps Jesus himself) in stressing family terms like "brother" and "sister" which displace the warm appreciation for friendship expressed by their contemporaries. To Epicurus is attributed the saying: "Without confidence (παρρησία) there is no friendship."[88] For John it might well be the other way around: Without love there is no confidence. Caird concluded:

> The Christian then, because love has become the dominant principle of his life, constantly has free access to God. His conscience, it is true, may sometimes trouble him, but these occurrences should never be allowed to interrupt his normal state of calm assurance, based as it is,

---

[85] R. Bultmann, *Die drei Johannesbriefe* (MeyerK 7; Göttingen: Vandenhoeck & Ruprecht, 1967) 78 n. 4.

[86] E. Haupt, *The First Epistle of St. John* (Edinburgh: T. & T. Clark, 1879) 229.

[87] B. J. Bamberger, "Fear and Love of God in the OT," *HUCA* 6 (1929) 39–52, here 50. The best treatment of this topic is still R. Sander, *Furcht und Liebe im palästinischen Judentum* (Stuttgart: Kohlhammer, 1935) 125–26, who deals with a large number of texts.

[88] Diog. Laert. 10.11. For commentary, see W. Klassen, "Friend, Friendship in the NT," *IDBSup* 348.

not on his own achievement, but on God's knowledge of him. This state can also be described as keeping Christ's commandments, abiding in him, or having the gift of the Spirit.[89]

In the Fourth Gospel the category of "friend" is still present, but in 1 John it is already gone and replaced by more familial terms like "beloved," "little children," and "brother."[90]

In the larger context the author raises one of the fundamental questions dealing with παρρησία: the role of fear. Already Xenophon had argued that fear is essential for the correction of slaves: "For confidence breeds carelessness, slackness, disobedience: fear makes people more attentive, more obedient, more amenable to discipline."[91] Fear has been removed by παρρησία and in its place is a trust which can speak the truth in love. Love may be feeble and poor, yet it has reached fulfillment in believers so that they may have boldness in the day of judgement.[92]

4. 1 John 5:14: καὶ αὕτη ἐστὶν ἡ παρρησία ἣν ἔχομεν πρὸς αὐτόν, ὅτι ἐάν τι αἰτώμεθα κατὰ τὸ θέλημα αὐτοῦ ἀκούει ἡμῶν. καὶ ἐὰν οἴδαμεν ὅτι ἀκούει ἡμῶν ὃ ἐὰν αἰτώμεθα, οἴδαμεν ὅτι ἔχομεν τὰ αἰτήματα ἃ ᾐτήκαμεν ἀπ' αὐτοῦ. "And this is the παρρησία which we have in his presence, that if we ask anything according to his will, he hears us and provides us with what we ask. We even know that we will receive from him what we ask for."

Whatever one may think about Cynic influences upon Christianity, words like this cause us to think twice before drawing too close a connection. The affirmation of what the Christian has now is daring and presumptive. Although John has previously spoken in the subjunctive mood (1 John 2:28–29; 4:17) and conditionally (3:21), here (5:14) he affirms a present state. Following Job 22:27, he links it with the promise that when you pray to God you will be heard.

This philosophy of prayer is a polar opposite to that of the Cynics.[93] In John's view, prayer itself is an expression of the eternal life in the believer. Consequently, joyful confidence in prayer comes from

---

[89] Caird, "John, letters of," 949.
[90] Friend as a Christian self-designation appears only in 3 John 15.
[91] Xen. *Mem.* 3.5.5. The translation is that of E. C. Marchant in the LCL.
[92] Law, *The Tests of Life*, 288.
[93] See Kindstrand's note on prayer, *Bion*, 231–33. Diogenes is said to have rebuked men in general about their prayers (Diog. Laert. 6.42), although it would seem that he is criticizing them for what they were asking (αἰτέω) for, not for the act of prayer itself. Joachim Jeremias has tried to show that Judaism had a unique view

knowing that we have eternal life (5:13).[94] In the Greco-Roman world of the time, prayer was often lampooned and certainly no one affirmed that you get what you ask for. For this writer, however, "prayer is asking (αἰτεῖν); not devout meditation, but definite petition; not to wish only, but to will. The peculiar characteristic of Christian prayer is confidence (παρρησία)."[95]

In the later history of the church there was much discussion about the boldness implicit in addressing God as Father. Such confidence was expressed even in the posture of the pray-er, for Christians followed Jewish practice, followed by Jesus himself, of praying while standing upright and lifting the face towards heaven and often raising the arms aloft. That body language conveys something quite different from lying prostrate on the ground or from piously folding one's hands, as many religious people do.[96]

Timon is also cited as an aggressive and cheeky pray-er by Lucian (*Timon* 11). Hermes states that shouting loudly, being annoying and impudent is useful to petitioners to Heaven. Timon, now wretchedly poor, will become rich in an instant, for Zeus has turned to him "because he prayed vociferously and outspokenly and drew the attention of Zeus" because of his boldness at prayer (βοήσας καὶ παρρησιασάμενος ἐν τῇ εὐχῇ).[97]

Likewise for John, prayer is not the mere abject cry that pain, helplessness, or blank despair sends up to an unknown God on the chance that he may hear and help. Christian prayer is essentially an active identification of the human will with the Divine Will; and confidence, which is its distinctive privilege, consists in two things—first, the persuasion that our will is in harmony with God's; and, second, the certainty that God's will shall be done.[98] The former is contingent upon our heart not condemning us and our keeping

---

of prayer among the peoples of its time and that Jesus also broke with the traditions of his time (*The Prayers of Jesus* [SBT 2.6; London: SCM, 1967]).

[94] Law, *Tests of Life*, 301 n. 2.

[95] Ibid., 303.

[96] On prayer in Judaism see J. Charlesworth, "Prayer," *ABD* 5 (1992) 449–50. See also C. W. F. Smith, "Prayer," *IDB* 3 (1962) 857–67, whose treatment of posture in prayer is important for our discussion. He concludes: "It is God who says: 'son of man, stand upon your feet'" (867). Early Christian tradition has Jesus looking up towards heaven when he prays (Mark 6:41; 7:34; Matt 14:19; Luke 9:16).

[97] The theme of reversal of fortunes shared by Job and Timon separates in that Timon becomes rich through prayer, whereas Job is promised answers to prayers if he makes God his treasure of gold and silver.

[98] Law, *The Tests of Life*, 303.

his commandments; the latter is the absolute assurance that when we ask, God answers.

Conclusion

The frequency of usage of the term παρρησία in 1 John suggests that as the Johannine community spread farther in Asia Minor it had to come to terms with the way in which παρρησία dominated the concerns of those people who were either Cynics or attracted to them. To such, this community seems to say that it, too, has confidence, but it has redefined it by taking as its starting point the Jewish eschatological hope of παρρησία at the time of the final judgment. Above all, each usage of the term has for 1 John a reference point towards God. None has anything to say about what one does in the presence of a fellow human being or in society or in church. Certainly if Mack is right in identifying παρρησία as "verve" to criticize a corrupt social order, no hint of such a critique is found in 1 John. The agenda of that book revolves around building a strong κοινωνία, and although the author has no doubt that he and his addressees have παρρησία, he also is aware that it could slip from them. The author may therefore have been aware of Cynics and their love for the term, but he shows no interest in their agenda or what they made of the term.[99]

John does not pick up the motif of the importance of speech found so much in popular ethics of the first century and indeed in the rest of the NT. Missing is a call to instruction and admonition, the invitation to "speak in the name of the Lord Jesus" (Col 3:17), the warning that every thoughtless word will have to be judged and that "out of your own mouth you will be acquitted, out of your own mouth you will be condemned" (Matt 12:37). The detailed crusade against the tongue found in James (esp. 3:1–12) is far from the world of 1 John.

---

[99] J. A. T. Robinson, "The Destination and Purpose of the Johannine Epistles," *NTS* 7 (1960) 56–61 claims that C. H. Dodd depicts I John as having "more rather than less of a Jewish ring" (60). Dodd, however, says that "the Epistle is not only less Hebraic and Jewish; it is also more free in its adoption of Hellenistic modes of thought and expression." (*The Johannine Epistles*, liii). Finally, for an example of a non-Christian author using a famous Cynic term (σύντομος) in a non-Cynic way, see Ps.-Cebes, *Tabula* 33.4 and the comments of J. T. Fitzgerald and L. M. White, *The Tabula of Cebes* (SBLTT 24; Chico, CA: Scholars Press, 1983) 163.

Even the admonition to avoid certain kinds of humour found in Eph 5:4 finds no resonance in our literature.[100]

Instead, John is theologically directed and seems to see παρρησία almost exclusively in terms of the divine-human encounter (How does one speak to God?) both here and now and in the future. This is true of the Fourth Gospel where the term is used only in connection with the mission of Jesus, and thus it has theological overtones. But there it deals not with the way Jesus relates to God the father but only with the way Jesus carries out his mission and the way he relates to his disciples and the world of Judaism. If this author is aware of the Cynics and the importance of the concept for them, he does not acknowledge it, or, if so, only obliquely.

This conclusion is not unimportant in our discussion of the relation of Cynics to early Christians. Certainly it should sharpen our awareness of the possibility that early Christians forged a normative group identity and had the confidence to use terms which were widespread, recasting them along their own lines. If at the heart of the Cynic movement was the ability to remint the coinage,[101] the early Christians showed no less courage and strength to recast familiar words like εὐαγγέλιον and παρρησία and to have language serve their ends and purposes by blending Jewish and Greek usages. Given the strength of both movements, perhaps we can conclude that both addressed certain fundamental human needs.

The mystery which surrounds any divine-human encounter and the ability to overcome fears of meeting the other were both addressed by Cynics and Christians. Beyond the use of the same word, this study of the Johannine body of literature alerts us to the possibility that although the same word was used, both groups went their separate ways in the content they poured into the word, or the meaning they found in it.

---

[100] P. W. van der Horst, "Is Wittiness Unchristian? A Note on εὐτραπελία in Eph 5:4," *Miscellanea Neotestamentica* (ed. T. Baarda, A. F. J. Klijn, and W. C. van Unnik; 2 vols.; NovTSup 47–48; Leiden: Brill, 1978) 2.163–77.

[101] νόμισμα παραχαράττων, which clearly does not mean "adulterating currency." See Heinrich Niehues-Pröbsting, *Der Kynismus des Diogenes und der Begriff des Kynismus* (München: Fink, 1979) 43–86. He also reminds us that we possess nothing, not one writing, not one saying, not even one act about Diogenes that is definitely authentic. He is therefore a truly mythical figure (21–22).

INDEX OF ANCIENT AUTHORS AND TEXTS

The abbreviations used for the citation of primary texts follow, in general, the guidelines of the Society of Biblical Literature as published in the *Journal of Biblical Literature* 107 (1988) 579–96. Where no abbreviation has been recommended by the SBL, preference in the citation of ancient authors and texts is given to the abbreviations employed by N. G. L. Hammond and H. H. Scullard (eds.) in *The Oxford Classical Dictionary* (2d ed.; Oxford: Clarendon, 1970). Other abbreviations are either self-evident or are derived from one or more of the following works: P. G. W. Glare (ed.), *Oxford Latin Dictionary* (Oxford: Clarendon, 1982); G. W. H. Lampe (ed.), *A Patristic Greek Lexicon* (Oxford: Clarendon, 1961); C. T. Lewis and C. Short, *A New Latin Dictionary* (New York: American, 1907); H. G. Liddell and R. Scott, *A Greek-English Lexicon* (rev. H. S. Jones and R. McKenzie; 9th ed.; Oxford: Clarendon, 1940); A. Souter, *A Glossary of Later Latin to 600 A.D.* (Oxford: Clarendon, 1949); and *The Studia Philonica Annual* 5 (1993) 250–56.

NOTE: n = footnote(s). If the same page of this volume contains a reference in both the text and the footnotes to the same passage or author, only the reference in the text is indicated in the following index. Pseudonymous works are listed, in general, under the supposed author.

1. HEBREW BIBLE (OLD TESTAMENT)

Exod		**Jer**	
33:11 LXX	15n	2:36 LXX	247n
		12:13 LXX	247n
Num		31:13 LXX	247n
12:7	210		
		Ps	
Lev		2	190
26:13 LXX	234	2:1–2	190
		16:10	188n
Deut		93:1 LXX	237
10:12	250	119:116 LXX	247n
		146:6	190
1 Kgdms			
24:6	247n	**Prov**	
		1:20 LXX	235
2 Kgdms		10:10 LXX	235
24:10	247n	13:5 LXX	208n, 235, 247n
		18:24	104
Isa		20:9 LXX	237
1:29	247n		
41:8 Vg	15n	**Job**	
53	91	22:23–27 LXX	234

2. APOCRYPHA AND PSEUDEPIGRAPHA

3. JOSEPHUS AND PHILO

5. Non-Canonical Christian Literature

6. Other Ancient Texts and Authors

INDEX OF MODERN SCHOLARS

SUPPLEMENTS TO NOVUM TESTAMENTUM

ISSN 0167-9732

2. STROBEL, A. *Untersuchungen zum eschatologischen Verzögerungsproblem auf Grund der spätjüdische-urchristlichen Geschichte von Habakuk 2,2 ff.* 1961. ISBN 90 04 01582 5

6. *Neotestamentica et Patristica.* Eine Freundesgabe Herrn Professor Dr. Oscar Cullmann zu seinem 60. Geburtstag überreicht. 1962. ISBN 90 04 01586 8

8. DE MARCO, A.A. *The Tomb of Saint Peter.* A Representative and Annotated Bibliography of the Excavations. 1964. ISBN 90 04 01588 4

10. BORGEN, P. *Bread from Heaven.* An Exegetical Study of the Concept of Manna in the Gospel of John and the Writings of Philo. Photomech. Reprint of the first (1965) edition. 1981. ISBN 90 04 06419 2

13. MOORE, A.L. *The Parousia in the New Testament.* 1966. ISBN 90 04 01593 0

15. QUISPEL, G. *Makarius, das Thomasevangelium und das Lied von der Perle.* 1967. ISBN 90 04 01595 7

16. PFITZNER, V.C. *Paul and the Agon Motif.* 1967. ISBN 90 04 01596 5

17. BELLINZONI, A. *The Sayings of Jesus in the Writings of Justin Martyr.* 1967. ISBN 90 04 01597 3

18. GUNDRY, R.H. *The Use of the Old Testament in St. Matthew's Gospel.* With Special Reference to the Messianistic Hope. Reprint of the first (1967) edition. 1975. ISBN 90 04 04278 4

19. SEVENSTER, J.N. *Do You Know Greek?* How Much Greek Could the first Jewish Christians Have Known? 1968. ISBN 90 04 03090 5

20. BUCHANAN, G.W. *The Consequences of the Covenant.* 1970. ISBN 90 04 01600 7

21. KLIJN, A.F.J. *A Survey of the Researches into the Western Text of the Gospels and Acts.* Part 2: 1949-1969. 1969. ISBN 90 04 01601 5

22. GABOURY, A. *La Stucture des Évangiles synoptiques.* La structure-type à l'origine des synoptiques. 1970. ISBN 90 04 01602 3

23. GASTON, L. *No Stone on Another.* Studies in the Significance of the Fall of Jerusalem in the Synoptic Gospels. 1970. ISBN 90 04 01603 1

24. *Studies in John.* Presented to Professor Dr. J.N. Sevenster on the Occasion of His Seventieth Birthday. 1970. ISBN 90 04 03091 3

25. STORY, C.I.K. *The Nature of Truth in the 'Gospel of Truth', and in the Writings of Justin Martyr.* A Study of the Pattern of Orthodoxy in the Middle of the Second Christian Century. 1970. ISBN 90 04 01605 8

26. GIBBS, J.G. *Creation and Redemption.* A Study in Pauline Theology. 1971. ISBN 90 04 01606 6

27. MUSSIES, G. *The Morphology of Koine Greek As Used in the Apocalypse of St. John.* A Study in Bilingualism. 1971. ISBN 90 04 02656 8

28. AUNE, D.E. *The Cultic Setting of Realized Eschatology in Early Christianity.* 1972. ISBN 90 04 03341 6

29. UNNIK, W.C. VAN. *Sparsa Collecta.* The Collected Essays of W.C. van Unnik Part 1. Evangelia, Paulina, Acta. 1973. ISBN 90 04 03660 1

30. UNNIK, W.C. VAN. *Sparsa Collecta.* The Collected Essays of W.C. van Unnik Part 2. I Peter, Canon, Corpus Hellenisticum, Generalia. 1980. ISBN 90 04 06261 0

31. UNNIK, W.C. VAN. *Sparsa Collecta.* The Collected Essays of W.C. van Unnik Part 3. Patristica, Gnostica, Liturgica. 1983. ISBN 90 04 06262 9

33. AUNE D.E. (ed.) *Studies in New Testament and Early Christian Literature.* Essays in Honor of Allen P. Wikgren. 1972. ISBN 90 04 03504 4

34. HAGNER, D.A. *The Use of the Old and New Testaments in Clement of Rome.* 1973. ISBN 90 04 03636 9

35. GUNTHER, J.J. *St. Paul's Opponents and Their Background.* A Study of Apocalyptic and Jewish Sectarian Teachings. 1973. ISBN 90 04 03738 1

36. KLIJN, A.F.J. & G.J. REININK (eds.) *Patristic Evidence for Jewish-Christian Sects.* 1973. ISBN 90 04 03763 2

37. REILING, J. *Hermas and Christian Prophecy.* A Study of The Eleventh Mandate. 1973. ISBN 90 04 03771 3

38. DONFRIED, K.P. *The Setting of Second Clement in Early Christianity.* 1974. ISBN 90 04 03895 7

39. ROON, A. VAN. *The Authenticity of Ephesians.* 1974. ISBN 90 04 03971 6

40. KEMMLER, D.W. *Faith and Human Reason.* A Study of Paul's Method of Preaching as Illustrated by 1-2 Thessalonians and Acts 17, 2-4. 1975. ISBN 90 04 04209 1

42. PANCARO, S. *The Law in the Fourth Gospel.* The Torah and the Gospel, Moses and Jesus, Judaism and Christianity According to John. 1975. ISBN 90 04 04309 8

43. CLAVIER, H. *Les variétés de la pensée biblique et le problème de son unité.* Esquisse d'une théologie de la Bible sur les textes originaux et dans leur contexte historique. 1976. ISBN 90 04 04465 5

44. ELLIOTT, J.K.E. (ed.) *Studies in New Testament Language and Text.* Essays in Honour of George D. Kilpatrick on the Occasion of His Sixty-fifth Birthday. 1976. ISBN 90 04 04386 1

45. PANAGOPOULOS, J. (ed.) *Prophetic Vocation in the New Testament and Today.* 1977. ISBN 90 04 04923 1

46. KLIJN, A.F.J. *Seth in Jewish, Christian and Gnostic Literature.* 1977. ISBN 90 04 05245 3

47. BAARDA, T., A.F.J. KLIJN & W.C. VAN UNNIK (eds.) *Miscellanea Neotestamentica.* I. Studia ad Novum Testamentum Praesertim Pertinentia a Sociis Sodalicii Batavi c.n. Studiosorum Novi Testamenti Conventus Anno MCMLXXVI Quintum Lustrum Feliciter Complentis Suscepta. 1978. ISBN 90 04 05685 8

48. BAARDA, T. A.F.J. KLIJN & W.C. VAN UNNIK (eds.) *Miscellanea Neotestamentica.* II. 1978. ISBN 90 04 05686 6

49. O'BRIEN, P.T. *Introductory Thanksgivings in the Letters of Paul.* 1977. ISBN 90 04 05265 8

50. BOUSSET, D.W. *Religionsgeschichtliche Studien.* Aufsätze zur Religionsgeschichte des hellenistischen Zeitalters. Hrsg. von A.F. Verheule. 1979. ISBN 90 04 05845 1

51. COOK, M.J. *Mark's Treatment of the Jewish Leaders.* 1978. ISBN 90 04 05785 4

52. GARLAND, D.E. *The Intention of Matthew 23.* 1979. ISBN 90 04 05912 1

53. MOXNES, H. *Theology in Conflict.* Studies in Paul's Understanding of God in Romans. 1980. ISBN 90 04 06140 1

55. MENKEN, M.J.J. *Numerical Literary Techniques in John.* The Fourth Evangelist's Use of Numbers of Words and Syllables. 1985. ISBN 90 04 07427 9

56. SKARSAUNE, O. *The Proof From Prophecy.* A Study in Justin Martyr's Proof-Text Tradition: Text-type, Provenance, Theological Profile. 1987. ISBN 90 04 07468 6

59. WILKINS, M.J. *The Concept of Disciple in Matthew's Gospel, as Reflected in the Use of the Term 'Mathetes'.* 1988. ISBN 90 04 08689 7

60. MILLER, E.L. *Salvation-History in the Prologue of John.* The Significance of John 1: 3-4. 1989. ISBN 90 04 08692 7

61. THIELMAN, F. *From Plight to Solution.* A Jewish Framework for Understanding Paul's View of the Law in Galatians and Romans. 1989. ISBN 90 04 09176 9

64. STERLING, G.E. *Historiography and Self-Definition.* Josephos, Luke-Acts and Apologetic Historiography. 1992. ISBN 90 04 09501 2

65. BOTHA, J.E. *Jesus and the Samaritan Woman.* A Speech Act Reading of John 4:1-42. 1991. ISBN 90 04 09505 5

66. KUCK, D.W. *Judgment and Community Conflict.* Paul's Use of Apologetic Judgment Language in 1 Corinthians 3:5-4:5. 1992. ISBN 90 04 09510 1

67. SCHNEIDER, G. *Jesusüberlieferung und Christologie.* Neutestamentliche Aufsätze 1970-1990. 1992. ISBN 90 04 09555 1

68. SEIFRID, M.A. *Justification by Faith.* The Origin and Development of a Central Pauline Theme. 1992. ISBN 90 04 09521 7

69. NEWMAN, C.C. *Paul's Glory-Christology.* Tradition and Rhetoric. 1992. ISBN 90 04 09463 6

70. IRELAND, D.J. *Stewardship and the Kingdom of God.* An Historical, Exegetical, and Contextual Study of the Parable of the Unjust Steward in Luke 16: 1-13. 1992. ISBN 90 04 09600 0

71. ELLIOTT, J.K. *The Language and Style of the Gospel of Mark.* An Edition of C.H. Turner's "Notes on Marcan Usage" together with other comparable studies. 1993. ISBN 90 04 09767 8

72. CHILTON, B. *A Feast of Meanings.* Eucharistic Theologies from Jesus through Johannine Circles. 1994. ISBN 90 04 09949 2

73. GUTHRIE, G.H. *The Structure of Hebrews.* A Text-Linguistic Analysis. 1994. ISBN 90 04 09866 6

74. BORMANN, L., K. DEL TREDICI & A. STANDHARTINGER (eds.) *Religious Propaganda and Missionary Competition in the New Testament World.* Essays Honoring Dieter Georgi. 1994. ISBN 90 04 10049 0

75. PIPER, R.A. (ed.) *The Gospel Behind the Gospels.* Current Studies on Q. 1995. ISBN 90 04 09737 6

76. PEDERSEN, S. (ed.) *New Directions in Biblical Theology.* Papers of the Aarhus Conference, 16-19 September 1992. 1994. ISBN 90 04 10120 9

77. JEFFORD, C.N. (ed.) *The* Didache *in Context.* Essays on Its Text, History and Transmission. 1995. ISBN 90 04 10045 8

78. BORMANN, L. *Philippi – Stadt und Christengemeinde zur Zeit des Paulus.* 1995. ISBN 90 04 10232 9

79. PETERLIN, D. *Paul's Letter to the Philippians in the Light of Disunity in the Church.* 1995. ISBN 90 04 10305 8

80. JONES, I.H. *The Matthean Parables.* A Literary and Historical Commentary. 1995 ISBN 90 04 10181 0

81. GLAD, C.E. *Paul and Philodemus.* Adaptability in Epicurean and Early Christian Psychagogy. 1995 ISBN 90 04 10067 9

82. FITZGERALD, J.T. (ed.) *Friendship, Flattery, and Frankness of Speech.* Studies on Friendship in the New Testament World. 1996. ISBN 90 04 10454 2